WBI DEVELOPMENT STUDIES

Resolution of Financial Distress

An International Perspective on the Design of Bankruptcy Laws

Edited by
Stijn Claessens
Simeon Djankov
and
Ashoka Mody

The World Bank
Washington, D.C.

The World Bank Institute was established by the World Bank in 1955 to train officials concerned with development planning, policymaking, investment analysis, and project implementation in member developing countries. At present the substance of WBI's work emphasizes macroeconomic and sectoral policy analysis. Through a variety of courses, seminars, workshops, and other learning activities, most of which are given overseas in cooperation with local institutions, WBI seeks to sharpen analytical skills used in policy analysis and to broaden understanding of the experience of individual countries with economic and social development. Although WBI's publications are designed to support its training activities, many are of interest to a much broader audience.

The finding, interpretations, and conclusions in this book are entirely those of the authors and should not be attributed in any manner to the World Bank, to its affiliated organizations, or to members of its Board of Executive Directors or the countries they represent. The World Bank does not guarantee the accuracy of the data included in this publication and accepts no responsibility for any consequence of their use. The boundaries, colors, denominations, and other information shown on any map in this volume do not imply on the part of the World Bank Group any judgement on the legal status of any territory or the endorsement or acceptance of such boundaries.

The material in this publication is copyrighted. The World Bank encourages dissemination of its work and will normally grant permission to reproduce portions of the work promptly.

Permission to photocopy items for internal or personal use, for the internal or personal use of specific clients, or for educational classroom use, is granted by the World Bank, provided that the appropriate fee is paid directly to the Copyright Clearance Center, Inc., 222 Rosewood Drive, Danvers, MA 01923, U.S.A., telephone 978-750-8400, fax 978-750-4470. Please contact the Copyright Clearance Center before photocopying items.

For permission to reprint individual articles or chapters, please fax your request with complete information to the Republication Department, Copyright Clearance Center, fax 978-750-4470.

All other queries on rights and licenses should be addressed to the Office of the Publisher, World Bank, at the address above or faxed to 202-522-2422.

The backlist of publications by the World Bank is shown in the annual Index of Publications, which is available from the Office of the Publisher.

Library of Congress Cataloging-in-Publication Data

Resolution of financial distress: an international perspective on the design of bankruptcy laws/edited by Constantijn Claessens, Simeon Djankov, Ashoka Mody.
     p.cm. -- (WBI development studies)
     Includes bibliographical references.
     ISBN 0-8213-4906-6
     1. Bankruptcy. 2. Debtor and creditor. I. Claessens, Constantijn. II. Djankov, Simeon. III. Mody, Ashoka. IV. Series.

K1370.R47 2001
346.07'8--dc21

00-065484

Contents

Foreword

In late 1997 and through most of 1998, the world experienced a financial crisis that threatened the integrity of the global financial system. Though these global concerns were foremost in the minds of policymakers, there was also widespread recognition of the microeconomic nature of the crises: enterprises and financial institutions through much of East Asia, and also in other parts of the developing world, were facing severe financial distress. Emerging from the crises, therefore, required not only measures to improve global liquidity and win back consumer and investor confidence, but also a significant restructuring of the distressed corporate and financial sectors.

However, little research existed on mechanisms to engineer corporate and financial restructuring, particularly when the distress is widespread. In an effort to assess the magnitude of the problem and to help identify practical solutions, the World Bank invited leading international scholars and practitioners to a workshop in Washington D.C. in June 1999. The papers presented at this workshop were subsequently revised in light of the discussions, and edited to reflect the most recent World Bank research and analysis.

Although many questions remain to be answered, this book contributes to the literature by providing an analytical and practical approach to the design of bankruptcy systems. It discusses a range of topics including voluntary mechanisms for facilitating agreements between creditors and debtors, the role of international mergers and acquisitions, and the specific issues and concerns that arise in the course of restructuring financial institutions. While the book was motivated by events that took place after the crisis in East Asia, it also draws on experiences from other regions as well as on historical insights.

I believe *Resolution of Financial Distress: An International Perspective on the Design of Bankruptcy Laws* is a valuable addition to the World Bank

Institute's Development Studies series. The book will be of particular interest to policymakers involved with financial and corporate sector reform, as well as business school professors and students, law students, and practitioners of bankruptcy law.

Vinod Thomas
Vice President
The World Bank Institute

Contributors

Arthur Alexander is a director of the Japan Economic Institute in Washington, D.C. He was previously with the research department of the Rand Corporation. His research interests include macroeconomic and financial policy in Japan and comparative economic growth in Japan and the United States. His research has been published in *The Quarterly Journal of Economics* and *The Review of Economics and Statistics*.

Stijn Claessens is a professor of finance at the University of Amsterdam and a consultant to the World Bank. Before joining the finance faculty, he was a lead economist at the World Bank. He received his Ph.D. in finance from the University of Pennsylvania. Professor Claessens has published widely in the areas of corporate finance, transition economics, and international finance. He has published articles in *The Journal of Finance*, *The Journal of Financial Economics*, *The Quarterly Journal of Economics*, and *The European Economic Review*.

Simeon Djankov received his Ph.D. from the University of Michigan, Ann Arbor. Currently, he is a senior financial economist with the Financial Sector Policy Group at the World Bank. His work has been published in *The Journal of Financial Economics*, *The European Economic Review*, *The Canadian Journal of Economics*, and *The Journal of Comparative Economics*. He is currently on the team developing the World Bank's *World Development Report 2001—Institutions for Markets*. His research has also been cited in a number of national news and business periodicals, including *The Financial Times*, *Forbes*, and *The Economist*.

Perry Fagan is a researcher at the Harvard Business School. His interests include corporate control and organizational change, bankruptcy reform, and financial distress issues. His previous work, co-authored with Michael Jensen, covered corporate governance issues.

C. Fritz Foley is a Ph.D. candidate at the Harvard Business School. His research interests focus on bankruptcy law reform in East Asia and resolution of financial distress in out-of-court settlements. His earlier work included studies on the growth of U.S. multinational affiliates, and the legal protection of creditors.

Stuart C. Gilson has been a member of the Harvard Business School faculty since 1991. He has a Ph.D. in finance from the University of Rochester. Professor Gilson has done extensive research in the area of corporate bankruptcy. His publications have appeared in *The Journal of Finance, The Journal of Financial Economics, The Financial Analysts Journal*, and *The Journal of Applied Corporate Finance*. His research has also been cited in a number of national news and business periodicals, including *The Wall Street Journal, The New York Times, Business Week, The Economist*, and *U.S. News and World Report*.

Stephan Haggard is an interim dean and professor of pacific international affairs at the University of California, San Diego. Professor Haggard's research interests center on the political economy of development in East Asia and Latin America. His most recent books include *The Political Economy of the Asian Financial Crisis* and *From Silicon Valley to Singapore: Location and Competitive Advantage in the Hard Disk Drive Industry* co-authored with David McKendrick and Richard Doner. He is currently conducting research on the restructuring of Korean corporations, fiscal federalism in Latin America, and the politics of social welfare in middle-income countries.

Donald B. Hausch is a professor of managerial economics in the School of Business at the University of Wisconsin, Madison. He has a Ph.D. from Northwestern University and masters and bachelor of science degrees from the University of British Columbia. Hausch's research interests include the economic design of organizations, contracting, competitive bidding, procurement, bankruptcy reorganization, and financial restructuring. He has co-authored two books and an edited volume and written articles that have been published in *The American Economic Review, Management Science, The Journal of Business, The Review of Financial Studies, The International Economic Review, The Journal of Applied Corporate Finance, Economic Theory*, and *The RAND Journal of Economics*.

Daniela Klingebiel is a senior financial economist in the Financial Sector Policy Group of the World Bank. She has written widely on financial distress, producing papers that measure the magnitude of the burden of financial crises, the resolution of financial distress, and stock market development. Currently she is leading a World Bank project on electronic finance.

Rafael La Porta is an associate professor in the Department of Economics at Harvard University. He received a Ph.D. in economics from Harvard in 1994. His research interests include corporate finance and asset pricing. He has published articles in *The Journal of Finance*; *The Journal of Financial Economics*; *The Quarterly Journal of Economics*; *The European Economic Review*; *The Journal of Political Economy*; and *The Journal of Law, Economics, and Organization*.

Florencio Lopez-de-Silanes is an associate professor of public policy at Harvard University. His research covers corporate governance, financial economics, and industrial organization and privatization as applied to the analysis of privatization and legal reform. He is currently an economic adviser to the Egyptian, Mexican, and Peruvian governments. His publications deal mainly with privatization, deregulation, legal reform, finance, and trade and industrial policy. He graduated from the Instituto Tecnológico Autónomo de Mexico and received a Ph.D. in economics from Harvard University in 1993.

Joseph Mason is an assistant professor of finance at Drexel University. He received his Ph.D. in finance from the University of Illinois in 1995. His research interests include bankruptcy reform and the determinants and effects of the Reconstruction Finance Corporation's assistance to banks during the great depression. His research has been published in *The American Economic Review*.

Ashoka Mody is a lead specialist in international finance in the World Bank's Economic Policy and Prospects Group. He was recently the principal author of the World Bank's *Global Development Finance 2001*. He has been a visiting professor at the Wharton School and has also worked for AT&T's Bell Laboratories. His recent research included analysis of the microstructure of international financial markets.

Alberto Mulás is undersecretary of the Social Development Secretariat in Mexico. He graduated in chemical engineering from the Iberoamerican

University and obtained his masters in business administration from the University of Pennsylvania Wharton School. Since 1997, he has served on the board of directors of several companies, including Synkro, Serfin Financial Group, Salinas and Rocha, Cintra, Camino Real Hotels, and the SIDEK Group. He was also managing director of the Mexico office of Donaldson, Lufkin, and Jenrette Securities Corporation; restructuring coordinator of the coordinating unit for the Enterprise Banking Agreement; representative and director of Lehman Brothers, Inc. of Mexico; and vice president of JP Morgan's local representation office in Mexico.

Shoko Negishi is an economist in the Economic Policy and Prospects Group at the World Bank. Since joining the World Bank in 1997, she has been one of the authors of the Global Development Finance reports. Her recent publications focus on determinants and developmental impacts of foreign direct investment and the implications of corporate and financial restructuring in East Asia. Before joining the World Bank, she worked as an economist at the Research Institute of Infrastructure and Investment at the Development Bank of Japan.

S. Ramachandran is a senior economist at the World Bank. He received his masters degree from the London School of Economics and Political Science and a Ph.D. from the University of Chicago. He was an assistant professor at the University of Wisconsin, Madison. Ramachandran left academia to join the research department of the International Monetary Fund, and later joined the World Bank where he has worked extensively with transition economies and other countries undertaking major reforms in their banking systems. Ramachandran and his colleague Donald B. Hausch designed the auction-based bankruptcy process, which is described in their contribution to this volume.

Joseph E. Stiglitz is a professor of economics at Stanford University. He received his Ph.D. from the Massachusetts Institute of Technology in 1967. From 1997 to 2000 he served as the World Bank's senior vice president of development economics and as chief economist. From 1993 to 1997, Dr. Stiglitz served as a member and then as the chairman of the U.S. Council of Economic Advisers. Before his appointment at Stanford University, he was a professor at Princeton University, Yale University, and All Souls College, Oxford. Dr. Stiglitz helped create a branch of economics—The Economics of Information—that has been widely applied throughout the economics discipline. In 1979, the American Economics Association awarded Dr. Stiglitz its biennial John Bates Clark Award.

Jay Westbrook is a professor of law at the University of Texas at Austin. A distinguished scholar in the field of bankruptcy and a pioneer in empirical studies in this area, Professor Westbrook teaches and writes about commercial law and international business transactions. He is co-author of *The Law of Debtors and Creditors* (1996), *As We Forgive Our Debtors: Bankruptcy and Consumer Credit in America* (1989), and *The Fragile Middle Class* (2000). He has been a visiting professor at Harvard Law School and the University of London and is a member of the American Law Institute, the National Bankruptcy Conference, and the American College of Bankruptcy. He is also co-head of the U.S. delegation to the United Nation's conference on international insolvency.

Michelle J. White received her Ph.D. from Princeton University and has served on the faculties of the University of Pennsylvania, New York University, and the University of Michigan at Ann Arbor. She has been a board member of the American Economics Association's Committee on the Status of Women in the Economics Profession, a member of the advisory panel to the law and social sciences program at the National Science Foundation, and first vice president of the Midwest Economics Association. She is currently an editorial board member of *The Journal of Urban Economics* and *The American Law and Economics Review* and a board member and treasurer of the Social Science Research Council.

Resolution of Financial Distress: An Overview

Stijn Claessens, Simeon Djankov, and Ashoka Mody, The World Bank

Recent financial crises involving the corporate and financial sectors in emerging markets, especially in East Asia in 1997–98, have raised important questions about the proper role of governments in preventing and alleviating financial distress. Government actions to assist specific companies and financial institutions raise equity issues, as governments will need to tax these companies and institutions in the future to service the additional public debt. Government interventions also raise the concern that private sector entities will come to expect such assistance in the future and may behave in imprudent ways, leading to future crises.

However, if governments take no action, significant sections of the economy may remain distressed for a long period of time, resulting in large, socially unacceptable losses in output and employment. This dilemma has led to the search for arrangements that would automatically trigger orderly processes to resolve systemic financial distress. In this book, the search is presented in parallel with a global review of the frameworks that currently exist for resolving financial distress at the level of individual corporations. In many countries, these frameworks are undergoing changes as governments revise bankruptcy and related laws.

In a systemic crisis, the government's first role is to define rules that lead to efficient private restructuring efforts. In the event that these private initiatives prove insufficient for acceptably resolving distress, the government's second role lies in providing direct assistance. Neither role is obvious, however. For instance, analysts have intensely debated the degree to which excessively debtor-friendly or creditor-friendly regimes aggravate financial crises. An equally disputed area is whether direct support helps to resolve a financial crisis or merely accelerates the coming of the next one.

Another dimension of government involvement in financial crisis resolution is the opportunity it presents to introduce reforms that political interest groups would otherwise stymie. Thus, while resuscitating ailing companies and banks is of paramount importance to policymakers in times of financial distress, such periods can also provide a window of opportunity to pass legal and judicial reforms that enhance the long-term growth path of the economy. Examples of such reforms are the passage of improved bankruptcy laws in the Republic of Korea, Malaysia, and Thailand in the wake of the financial crisis and the formation of specialized bankruptcy courts in Indonesia and Thailand.

This book deals with the principles of and practical approaches to addressing the difficult public policy trade-off involved in systemic corporate and financial sector crises and the lessons gained from the changes taking place in bankruptcy frameworks around the world. It brings together research on recent public policy initiatives for distress resolution or market-based restructuring. The book also includes papers that discuss the direct role governments should play when these contractual and market-based methods are not sufficient. Finally, the scope of opportunity for revision of existing laws is assessed.

This overview chapter summarizes the main findings of the thirteen papers in the volume and the findings of some other recent studies of insolvency reform. In recent years, considerable new research on insolvency has been conducted independently of the crises in emerging markets. This literature provides important guidelines for the long-term development of bankruptcy rules and procedures. However, while bankruptcy processes are a critical complement to other initiatives, they have played a limited role in the emerging market crises. This is because the problem is so extensive, as is the time required for bankruptcy rules and institutions to become effective in economies where they have only recently been introduced.

In the second set of papers, we consider approaches to dealing with systemic financial distress. In particular, some papers address the government's role in facilitating resolution of financial claims through out-of-court arrangements that substitute for effective bankruptcy procedures. Other papers consider market-based restructuring by facilitating mergers and acquisitions and permitting a greater role for foreign investors. Finally, where neither bankruptcy procedures—including those specially directed toward dealing with systemic distress—nor market-based restructuring through takeovers of distressed firms are adequate, the government will often step in by assuming the financial losses of distressed firms and banks. In that context, the role of asset management companies and other forms of government support are discussed.

Insolvency Regimes: Current Interest and Principles

Insolvency regimes represent the balancing of several objectives, which includes on the one hand protecting the rights of creditors, essential to the mobilization of capital for investment and working capital, and on the other hand obviating the premature liquidation of viable enterprises. In most countries the framework for dealing with insolvency has evolved over time as the balance of political power between various interests has changed and the economy's structure has been transformed. As a consequence, bankruptcy regimes differ considerably, even among developed countries. Thus, even in countries with close sociocultural affinities and economic ties, such as the United Kingdom and the United States, significant differences exist in the basic treatment of the debtor.[1] Insolvency provisions, therefore, appear tailored to the circumstances in which the country finds itself, especially in times of systemic financial distress.

In spite of the differences among regimes, a working insolvency regime is clearly an essential part of a market economy. The absence of adequate insolvency regimes in the East Asian crisis economies, which surprised many observers, considerably complicated and slowed down the process of corporate restructuring. For years, these economies had grown rapidly, and institutional reforms to deal with corporate distress had not been high on the list of policymakers' priorities, although bankruptcy codes were better developed in Korea and Malaysia than in Indonesia and Thailand. Attempts to institute and refine bankruptcy mechanisms following the crisis led to a broader reevaluation of the goals of the insolvency mechanism in a market economy (most forcefully expressed in chapter 1 in this volume).

---

1. The U.S. Bankruptcy Act of 1800 was largely a copy of the English Statute of Anne. Today, the British system favors the creditor and results in relatively more liquidations. Chapter 11 of the U.S. bankruptcy code is more debtor-friendly and leads to more reorganization under the control of incumbent management. Recent changes in the British bankruptcy law have, however, moved it closer to the U.S. law. For details, see chapter 3 in this volume.

The East Asian financial crisis triggered much work in international forums on developing guidelines for bankruptcy regimes (see, for example, World Bank 2000a). In chapter 1, the author turns the discourse away from the fairness of bankruptcy codes to the important question of the behavioral incentives these codes create. What matters most to creditors is the level of clarity concerning what happens when debtors default. As long as insolvency rules are predictable, lenders will charge an interest rate commensurate with the risk involved. In turn, debtors end up with access to capital while paying the fair cost.

When the legal rights of creditors are well protected, firms' access to credit expands substantially, as does the breadth and depth of debt markets (chapter 4). This is because the laws protect creditors from expropriation by the managers and controlling shareholders of firms. A simple way to reward creditors in insolvency is to respect the absolute priority of claims in bankruptcy or restructuring, that is, senior creditors are paid first, followed by junior creditors, and followed finally by shareholders if any residual remains. At the same time, some analysts have pointed out that if shareholders receive nothing during bankruptcy, managers acting on behalf of shareholders will attempt to delay or avoid bankruptcy, including undertaking high risk projects when the corporation runs into financial distress. For this reason, Hart (2000) makes a case for preserving some portion of firm value during bankruptcy for shareholders, even when absolute priority would not leave any residual value for the owner.

Insolvency procedures can be compared on many levels and the author of chapter 1 provides a useful taxonomy of these dimensions. An important consideration is whether the law provides for an automatic trigger when a company needs to file for bankruptcy. The purpose of automatic triggers is to alleviate the loss of value associated with managers or major shareholders delaying the bankruptcy decision.

Such a trigger was introduced in Hungary in 1992 with the effect that more than 5,000 companies entered bankruptcy proceedings in a single year (Gray, Schlorke, and Szanyi 1996). While in the long run it spurred institutional building in the courts and the trustee profession, the adoption of the trigger mechanism clogged the courts for a number of months and made separating viable from nonviable firms difficult. The trigger was subsequently removed in the 1997 bankruptcy reform.

A trigger mechanism of a different type was introduced in the revision of the Thai bankruptcy law of 1999 (Foley 2000). If the debtor owed a group of plaintiff creditors more than baht 1 million, the main creditor had to petition for bankruptcy. While the trigger itself was well defined, the next step in the bankruptcy procedure—the determination of insolvency—was not. In particular, nine presumptions of insolvency were set forth in Section 8 of Bankruptcy Act 2483. These proved to be difficult to fill, which resulted in few bankruptcy cases being initiated even after the revised law came into force. The Thai example points to the necessity for complementarity of various laws and procedures that underlie the insolvency regime.

Another important issue in the adoption of bankruptcy laws is deciding who can file for reorganization or liquidation. Related concerns are the attention paid to the debtors' and the creditors' roles, roles of the company's management and other stakeholders in preparing reorganization proposals, the ability of management to stay during the reorganization, and whether an automatic stay of assets exists. In chapter 4, the authors show that each of these features significantly affect access to credit across countries. An example of the effect these features can have is evident in the fact that the ability of managers to hold onto their positions adversely affects creditor rights and is associated with less access to external finance.

How different countries combine these features to deal with financially distressed firms depends to a large extent on the values of all stakeholders. Other factors that influence the way countries deal with financial distress include general contract law; securities laws; criminal laws; the availability of extrajudicial options; the institutional development of country, for example, courts, creditors, banks, and government; the diversity of claims; and the degree of informational asymmetries. International dimensions can be important, as in the case of Indonesia where corporate sector debt was largely owed to foreign investors (Claessens, Djankov, and Lang 2000a). The general quality of information on firm value and the development of the financial markets to absorb distressed assets are other important factors.

While an optimal insolvency regime does not exist, badly written codes make everybody worse off. Several principles apply in the construction of a good insolvency regime. First, the regime should deliver an ex post efficient outcome, in the sense that the distressed firm obtains the highest total value. Specifically, the firm should be closed down, liquidated piecemeal, sold as a going concern, or reorganized based on whichever of option generates the most value to creditors, the debtor, and other shareholders such as workers. Second, a good insolvency regime should be ex ante efficient in that it prevents managers and shareholders from taking imprudent loans and lenders from giving loans with a high probability of default. Policymakers can use reductions in claims or job losses of the respective parties to discourage imprudent behavior.

How different countries deal with financially distressed firms also varies over time, as the structure of economic production and values of all stakeholders change. In chapter 3, the author reports a general trend toward moving from more creditor-friendly regimes to more debtor-friendly regimes. Recently bankruptcy procedures around the world have predominantly moved toward adopting U.S. Chapter 11-type procedures; Argentina, Australia, Indonesia, Thailand, and the United Kingdom have all undergone legal reforms (chapter 1).

The exception to this trend is the insolvency reform that took place in Mexico in 1998 that introduced an automatic trigger for entering bankruptcy. The greater focus on intangibles in the operation of firms appears to be motivating the move toward more debtor-friendly regimes, which makes preserving the ongoing value of a firm in a financial restructuring more important. An excessively creditor-friendly approach can result in too many liquidations.

Bankruptcy or other legal resolution techniques are not the only methods for dealing with financial distress. Economists have been proposing alternative procedures for some time. These center on versions of asset sales or cash auctions. Cash auctions are easy to administer and do not rely on the judicial system (chapter 5; Hart and others 1997). While attractive from a theoretical perspective, these proposals have not had recent followers, except for the Mexican reformers in 1998. This is because asset sales are empirically shown to fetch low prices, although this empirical evidence is mostly anecdotal (Pulvino 1998). A further downside of the auction mechanism is its reliance on liquid secondary markets.

At the same time, structured bargaining mechanisms, for example Chapter 11 reorganization, depend on strong judicial systems. In countries where the judiciary is relatively weak, as in many developing countries, one might consider a menu of options to deal with insolvency from which debtors can choose whether to use structured bargaining or cash auctions. In the short run, debtors may prefer structured bargaining, even though they pay for it with higher interest rates, because creditors will adjust for the uncertain outcomes of the restructuring process (Hart 2000). In the long run, as old debts expire, debtors are likely to switch to the cash auction procedure, as this lowers the cost of obtaining capital. Most importantly, however, offering a menu of options is likely to introduce an element of competition among alternative procedures. As a result, the less efficient procedures are likely to be eliminated over time.

Importantly, for firms facing financial distress, legal insolvency is but one restructuring option. In East Asia after the 1997–98 crisis a number of firms chose to sell equity and control to foreign investors (chapter 12; Freund and Djankov 2000), or renegotiated most of their debts out of court (chapter 6). In countries with better creditor rights and more efficient legal systems, the likelihood that financial distressed firms would file for insolvency was higher, although firms affiliated with business groups were less likely to file (Claessens, Djankov, and Klapper 1999). Even when bankruptcy procedures are not used in restructuring, however, they determine to a large extent the speed and process of restructuring.

Two of the papers in this volume look at the impact of changes in bankruptcy regimes on the resolution of financial distress. In chapter 10, the authors studied data from Indonesia, the Republic of Korea, Malaysia, and Thailand and found that a small share of distressed assets, less than 6 percent on average, was resolved through formal bankruptcy. Much more prevalent was the use of out-of-court settlements. The slow pace of the judicial process in part explains this. On average, it took more than two years for a bankruptcy case to reach a judicial decision in Thailand. Not surprisingly, the two countries with the most court delays, Indonesia and Thailand, instituted specialized bankruptcy courts. While the efficiency of in-court resolution improved significantly following these changes in the structure of the judiciary, few cases still reached the bankruptcy courts. As the authors show in chapter 10, in the Alphatec case in Thailand most bargaining took place outside the courts.

Related to the lack of willingness to use formal bankruptcy procedures is the effect of wealth distribution on changes in bankruptcy regimes. In the wake of the East Asian financial crisis, all affected countries passed new bankruptcy legislation. However, Indonesia and Thailand also introduced specialized bankruptcy courts. Foley (2000) further investigates the effect of legal reform on the value of both creditors and debtors. The key question is whether such legal changes merely redistribute pending claims, or whether the value of claims of both debtors and creditors increases. Foley shows that values for all parties increased in reaction to anticipated events in the Thai bankruptcy process. Following positive news, the increase was large; equity values increased more than 25 percent in total. The equity values of companies or banks associated with financially healthy business groups were not greatly affected. The latter finding supports Claessens, Djankov, and Klapper's (1999) results concerning business groups acting as an alternative source of capital in East Asian countries.

Bankruptcy codes can also have general, more long-term effects. Not only does the strength of creditor rights determine the prevalent interest rates, but the balance between creditor and debtor rights can also determine the level of entrepreneurial activity (chapter 2). The more liability potential entrepreneurs face in case of default, the less likely they are to start new businesses. In chapter 2, the author provides empirical evidence on the number of start-up companies in the United States and explains the variations among states based in part on the different procedures for personal insolvency.

Systemic Distress and Corporate Restructuring

Corporate restructuring is an ongoing process that separates those firms that survive and prosper from those that are overwhelmed by new challenges and flounder. Governments have only a limited role to play in such restructuring, except to ensure an economic environment in which resources can be redeployed at minimal cost. However, when distress is widespread the danger is that it may be self-reinforcing. Several types of coordination issues arise. Firms may have few incentives to restructure because other distressed firms, and by implication consumers, have low demand for their products. In addition, distressed firms are unable to repay debts, which maintains the pressure on financial institutions, which in turn restricts the new lending that may be required to revive sectors where effective demand exists. Financial institutions may become insolvent, thus reducing the incentive of borrowers to repay loans. Finally, the judicial system will be overwhelmed with cases and have no prioritization mechanism.

Three approaches can be used to break out of the vicious cycle of self-reinforcing financial distress. The first strategy is to depend on economic recovery to release the constraint on demand and improve cash flows and firms' ability to repay their debts. Increased government spending can be used to encourage such recovery, but fiscal constraints may limit this option, particularly in times of systemic distress. Recovery may also occur if the demand for exports is buoyant, as was the case in Mexico after the 1994–95 crisis. Exports were also buoyant in the cases of Korea and Malaysia after the recent Asian crisis; both countries benefited from rapid growth in the trade of electronic products. However, relying on an economic upturn may be naive, as continued stagnation of the corporate sector in Japan over the last decade shows (chapter 9).

Economic recovery by itself has proven to be insufficient in countries like Indonesia and Thailand, where more than half of the corporate sector at some point experienced distress. Many firms were in distress not just because of an economy-wide crisis, but because business leaders had in the past made imprudent investment decisions. The evidence shows that the distress of such firms and financial institutions persists for long periods of time, rendering the economy vulnerable to renewed financial pressures.

For this reason, the next set of alternatives for breaking out of the vicious cycle of financial distress comprises a variety of market-based measures that may not require any fiscal layouts. In this approach the government sets the rules under which creditors and debtors work out their claims in a decentralized manner. These rules include rules governing normal restructuring and bankruptcy; enhanced measures for resolving financial claims through special rules or moral suasion that supplement existing bankruptcy procedures; reduction of barriers to transfer of ownership and redeployment of resources, including more liberal foreign direct investment, mergers and acquisitions, and greater mobility in labor markets; and super bankruptcy processes that, once again, change the incentives for restructuring claims.

The common feature of these decentralized approaches, whether normal creditor-led workouts or enhanced market-based or super bankruptcy approaches, is their reliance on incentives and penalties for restructuring rather than on either government fiscal stimuli (as in the case of an engineered recovery) or on government assumption of financial liabilities of bankrupt firms and financial institutions. In some cases, however, where economic recovery and enhanced incentives for restructuring are insufficient, governments may need to assume financial liabilities or provide other forms of government support to shore up the financial or corporate sectors. A related issue is the degree to which governments should exercise regulatory forbearance on financial institutions in distress. Where governments do expend fiscal resources and assume nonperforming loans, they also seek to recover some part of those resources through centralized asset management companies (AMCs).

Economic Recovery

In practice, the dependence on economic recovery, sharper incentives and tougher penalties, and the assumption of financial liabilities go together. Evidence from several countries demonstrates that this is the case. Isolating the effects and benefits of pursuing an approach that focuses solely on economic recovery is therefore difficult. While all East Asian countries engaged, after an initial contraction, in fiscal stimulus programs, Japan has relied the most on demand-led recovery, with fiscal stimulus being an important part of the approach. In chapter 9, the author describes the ongoing Japanese reforms, which so far have had mixed success, and analyzes complimentary structural reform efforts. Besides the fine-tuning of bankruptcy codes, policymakers have undertaken initiatives to increase labor mobility and facilitate mergers and acquisitions. Primarily, these initiatives involve the elimination of a number of restrictive rules, for example, the type of majority required within a distressed firm's board of directors to permit its takeover or merger with another firm.

Both the reported levels of bankruptcies and domestic and international mergers and acquisitions of Japanese firms are on the rise, although they are rising from a low base level. In the short run, these events are painful to the employees of affected firms and to the broader economy, as they serve to depress consumer confidence. However, such restructuring offers the best hope for the revival and long-term efficiency of the corporate and financial sectors in Japan. The fiscal stimulus approach has only raised public Japanese debt to high levels, while having few long lasting benefits. More generally, the capacity of economic recovery alone to overcome a systemic crisis is limited.

Market-Based Approaches

In any circumstance, the government sets the rules for distress situations that encourage the settlement of claims and facilitate the transfer of ownership and the redeployment of resources. The government's role in a situation of systemic distress may differ from its normal functions in the degree and speed with which it acts and the extent to which it temporarily creates tighter rules to encourage restructuring. In addition, certain significant reforms, for example, those related to corporate governance, liberalization of foreign direct investment, and easier mergers and acquisitions, may be undertaken during periods of systemic distress. These correct deficiencies that lead to the problems, but are likely to have permanent benefits as the systemic crisis recedes. This political economy of reform is not uncommon, of course, and a crisis is often the best way to get difficult structural reform accepted.[2]

While various ways in which governments can enhance the restructuring process exist, in designing the rules for restructuring the main responsibility has to be with the debtor and creditors themselves. The usual way of resolving financial distress is an out-of-court creditor-led voluntary

---

2. Domowitz and Tamer (1997) show that the pace of legal activity in the United States from 1790 to 1994 supports the proposition that legislative initiatives with respect to bankruptcy are countercyclical in nature, that is, bankruptcy legislation is usually passed after a deep downturn in the economy. Berglof and Rosenthal (2000) find additional evidence for the countercyclical nature of bankruptcy reform in the United Kingdom and the United States.

workout. These voluntary workouts will differ by the type of debtor, for example, small versus large firms, the structure of creditors, for example, the amount of secured versus unsecured creditors, and according to many other criteria. In all cases, however, the formal insolvency regime serves as the background. Debtors could always pull out of negotiations if they thought they could fare better in the formal procedure. As a result, voluntary workouts have had limited success in countries where formal bankruptcy was cumbersome, for example, in Indonesia, because of deficiencies in the framework or a weak judicial system (chapter 10).

A lack of equity capital and barriers to the mobility of resources may also stymie private sector restructuring. Where past owners are unable to deal with the problems, transfer of ownership to new owners may offer the best solution to maintaining some of the value of the resources employed. Also, financial distress can signal that resources may also be better used in other sectors of the economy. The crisis in East Asia and the poor Japanese growth performance have revealed the rigidities of resource mobility in these economies. As part of reforms in this region following the financial crisis, governments have undertaken several steps to facilitate capital mobility. Some governments now allow transfer of assets to settle claims, and in some economies, reforms have longer-run implications for increased efficiency of operation. In particular, foreign investment regimes have been liberalized and mergers and acquisitions made easier (chapter 12; World Bank 2000b).

In chapter 12, the authors show that in the crisis countries of East Asia, mergers and acquisitions have occurred mostly in the nontradable sectors, where distress has been most pronounced. These include the wholesale and retail trade, transportation, real estate, and financial sectors. Observers have expressed concerns that acquisitions by foreigners may represent fire sales, resulting in a net transfer of wealth from the crisis economies (Krugman 1998). Though the evidence is not conclusive, the jump in mergers and acquisitions in the East Asian economies may represent a shift from a relatively autarkic policy stance—prior to the crisis, few East Asian countries allowed entry into their financial sectors, for example—to a more open one. Mergers and acquisitions are likely to further the integration of these economies into the global economy. The high rate of mergers and acquisitions in Korea, for example, which had the lowest incidence of corporate distress among the crisis countries, demonstrates the importance of this long-term shift relative to the incidence of fire sales. However, in chapter 12, the authors also conclude that the problems of distressed firms lies deep in past investment and financial structure decisions and hence the influence of the wave of mergers and acquisitions may only be discerned over time.

Normal bankruptcy and restructuring frameworks might not be sufficient given coordination problems and weaknesses in institutional frameworks. First used in the Mexican crisis (chapter 7) and expanded in the context of the East Asian crisis, bankruptcy rules can be supplemented with so-called London rules[3] involving enhanced mechanisms to get creditors and debtor to agree on restructuring (chapters 10 and 11). Enhancements have involved encouraging most financial institutions to sign these out-of-court accords under regular contract or commercial law. In the case where this has taken place, agreements reached among the majority of creditors can be applied to other creditors without going through formal judicial procedures. Also, formal arbitration with specific deadlines has sometimes been made part of the accord. With such arbitration, an out-of-court system does not have to rely as much on the formal judicial process to resolve disputes and its associated costs and delays. In addition, some of the approaches have involved specific penalties that can be imposed for failure to meet deadlines. The degree to which countries have adopted these enhancements has varied among East Asian countries; the framework in Thailand, followed by those in Korea and Malaysia, is the most conducive to out-of-court restructuring, and the framework in Indonesia is the least. These differences explain in part the variations in the speed of restructuring in these countries.

The most far-reaching proposal to enhance restructuring is that of super bankruptcy, a temporary tool to be used when a country faces systemic bankruptcy brought on by huge macroeconomic disturbances (chapter 1). The basic presumptions of super bankruptcy are that management automatically stays in place and a forced debt-to-equity conversion takes place. The existence of such a bankruptcy code is likely to result in higher interest rates in normal times, especially for short-term foreign lenders, and raise the moral hazard of worse management and higher risk-taking. However, in a systemic crisis super bankruptcy can preserve the going concern value of firms by preventing too many liquidations and keeping existing managers, who most often know how best to run the firms, in

---

3. The London rules are principles for corporate reorganization that were first enunciated in the United Kingdom in the early 1990s. Since the London rules were not designed for systematic corporate distress, countries have tried to tighten them in various ways.

place. An important design issue is when to call for super Chapter 11, that is, when is the crisis of a systemic nature, and who has the authority to call for such a suspension of payments? Political economy factors should be taken into account here as wealth is often concentrated in emerging markets, and some debtors would stand to gain disproportionately from a suspension of payments (Claessens, Djankov, and Lang 2000b).

The evidence from East Asia suggests that adopting a temporary super Chapter 11 is unnecessary. Corporations and banks moved slowly to restructure outstanding debt, in the hope that economic recovery would obviate the need for write-offs (for banks) or the surrender of equity control (for large shareholders). However, few firms were prematurely liquidated, in part because a working bankruptcy regime was often not in place. When economic recovery indeed came about in 1999, few firms were liquidated or had gone through bankruptcy procedures, and no significant loss of value seems to have occurred as a result of not adopting super bankruptcy rules. If anything, observers have argued that too many firms were allowed to continue to operate for too long, as in the case of several business-group affiliated firms in Korea, and that equity holders bore too little of the costs of restructuring.

Direct Support by the Government

Injection of new government funds is the most difficult aspect of restructuring. In principle, governments should not be in the business of paying for the mistakes of private companies and financial institutions. However, the need to revive the economy may force the government's hand, and government support should then be part of the most efficient or most necessary approach to resolving a systemic crisis.

In particular, governments often have contractual obligations, for example, insuring depositors or issuing general guarantees to stabilize the financial system and restore confidence. In such situations, a key issue that governments face concerns the speed of their actions. They may choose to acknowledge their liabilities, but delay the injection of funds by exercising regulatory forbearance (that is, not enforcing prudent capital requirements) on financial institutions. In another scenario, they may choose to take the fiscal losses that result from restructuring the banks up front and start with a clean slate. The experience is that forbearance, though fiscally attractive in the short-run, can lead to mounting costs overall. The lesson here is that by accepting early losses governments can help stop continued distress. For such a course of action to be successful, strong restructuring initiatives and complementary structural reforms, along the lines suggested earlier in the chapter, should accompany it to prevent the recurrence of financial distress.

A variety of approaches exist with respect to government assumption of financial losses in the banking system. These include direct injection of capital or subordinated debt, provision of loss-sharing arrangements on some pool of assets, grants of government loans, or placement of deposits (chapter 13). Each has advantages and disadvantages.

Recently countries have increasingly used publicly owned AMCs. Unfortunately, the efficacy of AMCs in resolving a systemic bank crisis is questionable, as their track records have been mixed at best. In chapter 13, the author distinguishes between two main types of AMCs. The first type is set up to help and expedite corporate restructuring, whereas the second type is established to dispose of assets acquired or transferred to the government during the crisis. The latter are known as rapid asset disposition vehicles.

The author discusses seven cases for which data are publicly available. The governments of Finland, Ghana, and Sweden set up restructuring vehicles. Two corporate restructuring AMCs (the exception is Sweden) did not achieve their narrow goals of expediting corporate restructuring, which suggests that AMCs are rarely good tools to accelerate corporate restructuring. Only the Swedish AMC successfully managed its portfolio, acting in some instances as lead agent in the restructuring process. In Mexico, the Philippines, Spain, and the United States, governments set up rapid asset disposition agencies. Rapid asset disposition vehicles fared somewhat better with two out of the four agencies, the Spanish and U.S. agencies, achieving their objectives.

However, achieving these objectives even with an AMC required many ingredients. These include professional management, political independence, a skilled resource base, appropriate funding, adequate bankruptcy and foreclosure laws, good information and management systems, and transparency in operations and processes. Arguably the most important ingredient is the political will of the government to address the issues. Success is also more likely if the assets acquired are mostly real estate related assets, because these are easier to restructure than corporations. In addition, success is more likely if the amount of assets transferred is small relative to the banking system, making it easier for the AMC to maintain its independence and not to succumb to political pressure. As always, explicitly considering political economy elements when adopting this model is important (chapter 11).

An example of a different form of government support is the U.S. Reconstruction Finance Corporation (RFC) (chapter 8). The RFC, which lasted from 1932 to 1957, provided loans for or invested more than US$40 billion in 5,685 banks, 40 percent of all insured banks in the United States. These banks were initially thought to be illiquid, but by 1933 many banks were found to be insolvent and needed to be closed or get additional capital, so a preferred stock program was established. RTC officials' discretion to support banks was limited, and to be eligible for this program banks had to agree to limit dividends and devote earnings to retiring the stock of the bank, or essentially buying out the government's position. The RFC, whose stock was senior to all others, could also only hold a maximum of 49 percent of the equity in a bank, which meant private funds were needed. While difficult to evaluate its success, the intervention appears to have contributed to a recovery of confidence and output, until monetary tightening reversed both trends in 1937. However, the government recovered its initial capital and did not leave nonviable banks in business.

The Fondo Bancario de Protección al Ahorro (FOBAPROA) agency in Mexico (chapter 7), with the objective of both restructuring banks and recovering nonperforming loans, had a mixed record. During 1996, the year following Mexico's 1995 financial crisis, the government started the recapitalization of the banking system that enabled banks to sell bad loans, on a 2-to-1 ratio based on every dollar of new equity invested by shareholders, to the FOBAPROA trust. Such sales were generally executed on a risk-shared basis, with the selling bank retaining 25 percent of the risk, and were implemented not as actual asset, or loan, sales, but as purchases of loans' cash flows. The program led to the transfer of underlying cash flows valued at approximately US$18 billion in loans to FOBAPROA, which resulted in deterioration of loan administration procedures and dislocation in the asset-client relationship. Concurrent with the loan sales, several banks with severely depleted capital, whose shareholders would not commit fresh equity to capitalize them, were sold to foreign financial institutions. In these instances, FOBAPROA purchased the banks' bad loan portfolios, further reducing the incentives for other banks to write off bad loans.

In the end, countries often choose a mixture of these various approaches when dealing with a systemic crisis. Of the four East Asian crisis countries, Indonesia, the Republic of Korea, Malaysia, and Thailand, three employed AMCs; all have employed some form of out-of-court-system; and most have used, after an initial period of a year or so, fiscal stimulus and monetary policy to foster economic growth (chapter 10). In addition, all have enhanced their basic frameworks for private sector operations, including more effective provisions for bankruptcy, corporate governance, liberalization of entry, and other matters. Similarly, Mexico's government used both an AMC and a more decentralized approach to resolve financial distress in 1995. In the end, export led-growth started the Mexican recovery, although it did not resolve the banking problems.

As the case studies show, the weights of these various policy options vary by country. Solutions to financial crises have to be country-specific. Systemic crises differ in many dimensions; one is the size of the problem, specifically, the number of nonperforming loans and the degree of corporate distress. Another dimension is the type of distress, for instance, is real estate or are corporations involved? Other aspects of systemic crises are the amount of foreign and domestic debt, both public and private, which limits the scope for taking on new liabilities or the difficulty in restructuring; the quality of the initial institutional framework and human resource capacity; the macroeconomic policies being pursued; the existing ownership structures; and the political economy structure of the country. Given these differing dimensions, governments have to tailor their approach to each specific circumstance.

Conclusions

Insolvency regimes are an essential part of a market economy, in cases of both nonsystemic and systemic financial distress. The ability to resolve normal insolvencies efficiently allows an economy to operate more effectively. Based on the basic requirements for a well-functioning insolvency regime that have been documented, best practices are continually reviewed. As a result, global regimes are tending toward less liquidation and more rigorous processes and depending less on the use of market-based resolution techniques.

Some lessons concerning systemic restructuring have become clear. The government's role must be limited to establish an enabling environment for the private sector to do the necessary restructuring. In addition, adjusting the approach according to the type of assets that are causing the distress is clearly important.

To the extent that governments directly intervene in systemic restructurings, they should be careful how they deal with banks suffering from financial distress. They should not close these banks without alternative financial intermediation mechanisms and a comprehensive program of bank restructuring. They should not recapitalize banks too quickly, and should instead try to link recapitalization with bank privatization where possible.

Instead of focusing on companies experiencing financial crisis, governments should try to support businesses that can effectively weather financial distress by providing tax relief or other support to healthy corporations. In addition, governments should help small and medium sized firms that are often the victims of the credit crunch that tends to follow a financial crisis. This can take the form of automatic reschedulings, or tax and regulatory relief.

Finally, to resolve the debt overhang that hinders recovery, governments need to have loss-absorption mechanisms. In many cases, this requires the injection of public funds. Designing the proper incentive structures for these mechanisms then becomes critical. If, for example, recapitalization is necessary to restore the banking system, linking the recapitalization of an individual bank to the degree of progress it makes in restructuring its nonperforming loans becomes an important issue. Because banks should not be expected to undergo corporate restructuring, inviting participation from other investors early and providing them with loss-absorption mechanisms will also be crucial. This may often result in mixed public-private restructuring funds, where private, sometimes foreign, management runs a government-owned distress fund.

References

Berglof, Erik, and Howard Rosenthal. 2000. "The Political Economy of American Bankruptcy: the Evidence from Roll Call Voting, 1800-1978." Department of Economics, Princeton University, Princeton, New Jersey. Processed.

Claessens, Stijn, Simeon Djankov, and Leora Klapper. 1999. "Resolution of Corporate Distress: Evidence from East Asia's Financial Crisis." Policy Research Working paper no. 2133. World Bank, Washington D.C.

Claessens, Stijn, Simeon Djankov, and Larry Lang. 2000a. "East Asian Corporations: Growth, Financing, and Risks." *Emerging Markets Quarterly* 4(1): 37–56.

_____. 2000b. "The Separation of Ownership and Control in East Asian Corporations." *Journal of Financial Economics* 58(1): 81–112.

Domowitz, Ian, and Elie Tamer. 1997. "Two Hundred Years of Bankruptcy: A Tale of Legislation and Economic Fluctuations." Department of Economics, Northwestern University, Evanston, Illinois. Processed.

Foley, Fritz. 2000. "Going Bust in Bangkok: Lessons from Bankruptcy Law Reform in Thailand." Harvard Business School. Processed.

Freund, Caroline, and Simeon Djankov. 2000. "What Do Foreigners Buy? Evidence from Korea." Policy Research Working paper no. 2450. World Bank, Washington D.C.

Gray, Cheryl, Sabine Schlorke, and Miklos Szanyi. 1996. "Hungary's Bankruptcy Experience, 1992-1993." *World Bank Economic Review* 10(3): 425–50.

Hart, Oliver. 2000. "Different Approaches to Bankruptcy." Working paper no. 7921. National Bureau of Economic Research, Cambridge, Massachusetts.

Hart, Oliver, Rafael La Porta, Florencio Lopez-de-Silanes, and John Moore. 1997. "A New Bankruptcy Procedure with Multiple Auctions." *European Economic Review* 41(3-5): 461–73.

Krugman, Paul. 1998. "Fire-sale FDI." Available at http://web.mit.edu/krugman/www/FIRESALE.htm.

Pulvino, Todd. 1998. "Do Asset Fire Sales Exist? An Empirical Investigation of Commercial Aircraft Transactions." *Journal of Finance* 53(3): 939–78.

World Bank. 2000a. "Effective Insolvency Regimes: Principles and Guidelines." Part of the Global Insolvency Laws project. Available at http://www.worldbank.org/legal.

World Bank. 2000b. *Global Economic Prospects*. Washington, D.C.

1

Bankruptcy Laws: Basic Economic Principles

Joseph E. Stiglitz, Stanford University

Financial experts agree that complete recovery from the 1997 East Asian crises necessitates widespread corporate reorganization of the affected countries, particularly resolution of the massive bankruptcies. Thus far such reorganization falls far short of that required for successful recovery. By some accounts 65 percent of Indonesia's firms, 41 percent of the Republic of Korea's firms, and 23 percent of Thai firms were technically insolvent in September 1998.[1] Indeed, without addressing the bankruptcy issue, East Asian economies will experience difficulties in fully resolving weaknesses in the financial sector, which is so essential for the restoration of the flow of credit that underpins a healthy economy. If firms remain in bankruptcy, the incidence of nonperforming loans will also remain high, and it will

---

1. Given the focus of this paper on fundamental economic principles, the term *bankruptcy* is used somewhat loosely and interchangeably with *insolvency* and *default*. Also, some distinctions of significance for purposes of legal or empirical analysis, for example, between *technical insolvency* and *illiquidity* (when debt service obligations exceed earnings) are not dwelt upon. Thus, the figures quoted above correspond to an average insolvency of 31 percent for the five affected East Asian countries, but the proportion of illiquid firms was more than double that figure— 63 percent. The issue is more than academic because the latter figure relates to understanding the implications of high interest rates and the importance of restoring credit flows (see Claessens, Djankov, and Ferri 1999).

even be difficult to ascertain the full magnitude of capital infusions necessary to restore viability to the banking institutions within these countries.

More broadly, inadequacies in bankruptcy law and the capacity to implement these laws effectively have often been cited as some of the underlying institutional weaknesses in Asian and other emerging markets, including the transition economies. Until the most recent global financial crisis, originating in Asia, much of the attention on bankruptcy regimes focused on Eastern Europe, where bankruptcy (the existence of old firms) and its twin, entrepreneurship (the creation of new ones), were seen as necessary ingredients for economic revitalization and development of postsocialist market economies. Yet a decade of transition, including advice from sophisticated bankruptcy experts, has yielded meager results; the institution of bankruptcy, seen as a vital ingredient for hardening the budget constraint for enterprises, has failed to take root.

As policymakers of emerging market economies approach the task of designing or redesigning bankruptcy laws, they need to think carefully about some of the basic underlying principles, which all too often have been ignored, set forth both in the popular press and by the visiting "firemen" from the industrial countries proffering their advice and counsel. Policymakers will also need to understand why bankruptcy has failed to work in so many countries. This chapter principally aims to identify the reasons for the failure of bankruptcy procedures in some of these countries. Its second major objective focuses on a critical issue for dealing with economic crises, namely, the big difference between dealing with isolated cases of financial distress and with widespread bankruptcies due to systemic financial or currency crises. We propose a major reform in the design of bankruptcy law that, if widely adopted, promises to reduce the severity of the kinds of crises recently experienced in East Asia (associated with private debt)—reforms that will, in effect, entail an automatic bailing in of the private sector, which should reduce the need for external bailouts, and will mitigate some of the moral hazard problems—the profligate lending without due diligence—that have played such a central role in recent events.

Key Principles

Bankruptcy contains three key principles. First, the central role of bankruptcy in modern capitalist economies is to encourage reorganization. Modern capitalism could not have developed without limited liability corporations. Almost by definition, the notion of limited liability requires the concept of bankruptcy. In most industrial economies, the concept of bankruptcy has evolved far from its etymological roots in medieval Italian custom (*banca rupta*, meaning "broken bench"), in which it signified social opprobrium or punishment for an individual or entity of an economic state whose assets were less than the individual's or entity's debts. Today, in many countries, most notably the United States since 1978, bankruptcy cannot be equated with liquidation or a simple transfer of ownership from debtor to creditor. Not surprisingly, creditors view these forms of bankruptcy as letting borrowers off the hook, or allowing debtors to unilaterally abrogate contracts. These views on bankruptcy, however, are as misguided as those that viewed debtor prisons as the natural and just punishment for those who failed to meet their financial obligations. Indeed, a well-functioning bankruptcy regime is critical for an efficient market economy, and for creditors there must be a clear understanding of the consequences when debtors cannot meet their obligations. Bankruptcy law has such importance for modern capitalism that firms are typically not allowed to write contracts that override the provisions of the bankruptcy code, provisions such as the procedures for dispute resolution and other rules.[2]

Second, there is no single universal bankruptcy code. Any bankruptcy regime balances several objectives, including protecting the rights of creditors (which is essential to the functioning of capital markets and the mobilization of capital for investment) on the one hand, and obviating the premature liquidation of viable enterprises on the other hand. Most countries' bankruptcy laws have evolved over time with a change in the balance of political power between various interests, along with the structural transformation of the economy and historical development of the society at large. Thus, even in countries with close sociocultural affinities and economic ties such as the United States and the United Kingdom, significant differences exist in the basic treatment of debtors.[3] Bankruptcy provisions, therefore, need to be tailored to the individual country and the circumstances in which it finds itself, although countries should recognize the great advantage of adhering to widely accepted standards.

There is no single bankruptcy code that is unambiguously best for everyone in society. Some individuals may do better under one code than

---

2. This is unlike most other commercial law in the United States, where most items can be altered by mutual agreement among the contracting parties (see, for instance, Schwartz 1997).

3. The British system favors the creditor and results in relatively more liquidations, while Chapter 11 of the U.S. bankruptcy code is more debtor-friendly and leads to more reorganizations under the control of incumbent management.

under another. Hence, historically, bankruptcy codes have been the subject of intense political debate, as seen by the recent furor over revisions in the U.S. bankruptcy code. To be sure, some of this debate is misguided: debtors, for instance, may fail to take into account the effect of greater debtor protections on interest rates. This has strong implications: bankruptcy codes cannot be imposed from the outside, and one should be suspicious of bankruptcy codes designed by one party, for example, lenders, or those representing primarily their own interests.

But the observation that there is no single Pareto dominant efficient code should not lead one into the opposing fallacy—that the design of a code is simply a matter of politics. Badly written codes may actually make debtors, creditors, and others worse off. In other words, some codes are Pareto inferior dominated by others. In the United States and a few other countries, bankruptcy focuses mainly on debtors and creditors. Bankruptcy affects not only lenders and borrowers, but other stakeholders as well, most importantly, workers. There is thus an important externality: the resolution of bankruptcy disputes between lenders and borrowers affects innocent bystanders. Workers being affected is only one issue; workers may also have rights that need to be recognized in bargaining between lenders and borrowers.[4] There is typically an implicit commitment between workers and the firm. If workers continue to work effectively, the firm will continue not only to employ them, but also to pay wages commensurate with their abilities and effort. Of course, this commitment has limitations: if the firm's sales decline precipitously, the worker, as well as the firm's shareholders, bear some of the risk. The commitment is usually not explicit simply because it is impossible to write down all the relevant conditions. Anglo-American common law recognizes these implicit commitments. In bankruptcy proceedings, a payment due to workers for work already performed has seniority even over other senior creditors. There are broader, and typically unresolved, issues concerning other "obligations" toward workers (those embedded in the implicit contract) and other creditors. The nature of the implicit commitment (the social contract) may differ from country to country, which is another reason why bankruptcy laws need to be adapted to the circumstances of each country.

---

4. As I shall argue later in the chapter, what is critical is the clarity of those rights; presumably, the terms of the contract can be adjusted to reflect those rights, for example, if severance pay does not have "senior" status, and workers know it, they can insist on higher wages to offset the risks incurred. Different bankruptcy rules do impose different information burdens and imply different allocations of risk bearing, and some of these arrangements may actually be inefficient.

Other examples of stakeholder interest pertain to utilities or other monopolies (natural or otherwise) in which the liquidation or even a significant hobbling of a firm can have major adverse impacts on consumers or cause severe economic dislocation.[5] Modern bankruptcy bases itself on the theory of incomplete contracts. A complete contract would specify what actions should be taken in every state of nature. A complete contract would thus specify clearly what should be done in the event that the borrower could not meet his obligations. It would detail not only the priorities of claimants, but also the resolution of residual claims and control. Contracts are not complete for several reasons. One is simply the difficulty of doing so; the transaction costs of fully specifying a contract would be prohibitive. However, this explanation is incomplete, for if this were the sole reason, bankruptcy law would not override provisions of contracts, which it usually does. This issue relates to, but is somewhat different from, the argument for standard contracts. That deviation from norms provides a signal causes concern. On the one hand, there may be a concern that such signals may result in a "signaling" equilibrium, and the social costs of such signaling can be quite high.[6] There may be efficiency gains from "pooling," more than offsetting the losses from the reduced information flow (Stiglitz 1975). Standard bankruptcy law can be conceived of as restricting the range of admissible signals. More generally, there is a concern that asymmetries of information will lead one side of the market to take advantage of the other, so that when a contract dispute does occur (which is not uncommon), any deviation from the standard contract will be interpreted against the party writing the nonstandard provision. This in itself discourages contract innovation, but does not explain why governments would not allow contracts to be written with alternative provisions for bankruptcy. Other reasons pertain to the fact that a firm typically has more than one creditor who may differ in preferences but also contract asynchronously. This is important because, as noted earlier, virtually any contract provision affects other parties—both those with formal contracts and those with informally defined rights. Standard bankruptcy contracts reduce the information burden imposed on these

---

5. One of the more notorious U.S. bankruptcy cases related to users of a company's products, namely, asbestos.

6. A fundamental proposition in the signaling literature is that for an action (a contract) to convey information, it must be costly, but it must be less costly to the party trying to send the positive signal than to other parties. Not only are signals costly, but, in general, market signaling equilibria are not (constrained) Pareto efficient (see Greenwald and Stiglitz 1986).

parties: they can assess the impact of loans in a far more straightforward way than they otherwise could.[7]

While it fills the incomplete gaps in contracts, bankruptcy law is itself incomplete: it typically does not provide a simple formula that can automatically be invoked. Judges in the United States specializing in the intricacies of such matters are called upon to make rulings interpreting the bankruptcy law in different circumstances. Ambiguity often exists in the priorities of different creditors, and sometimes the interests of other stakeholders are taken into account. While all residual value is turned over to the creditors when a firm cannot meet its obligations in simple models of bankruptcy, in practice the original equity owners generally retain a significant share. (There is often a disagreement about the "equity" value of the firm and, therefore, the adequacy of compensation of the creditors, with the original owners claiming the market has simply temporarily undervalued their shares. Thus, while equity owners may believe that the creditors have received more than the value of their claims, creditors may believe that they are inadequately compensated. Of course, if markets worked perfectly, such disparities would not exist—but neither would there be liquidity problems, which are often at the root of bankruptcies.) Indeed, one of the cornerstones of corporate finance textbook treatment of bankruptcy, namely, the "absolute priority rule," is honored more in its breach in corporate reorganizations (see, for example, Altman and Eberhart 1994; Eberhart, Moore, and Roenfeldt 1990). In addition to equity owners retaining some share, especially if they include managers, deviations also include junior classes of debtors receiving some compensation even when more claims have not (necessarily) been fully satisfied.

These ambiguities have one further implication: because bankruptcy law affects the likely outcome if a dispute has to be resolved by the courts, bankruptcy law affects the outcome of the bargaining process designed to avoid the uncertainty and delay of relying on court-mandated resolutions. Thus bankruptcy law provides the backdrop—the default or "threat point"— against which bargaining occurs. Not surprisingly, laws that give creditors or debtors more or less rights affect the outcome of the bargaining process in ways that retroactively affect creditors and debtors differentially.

---

7. Indeed, provisions imposed by different contracts could even be mutually contradictory, presenting a legal nightmare. Moreover, these uncertainties compound other uncertainties, leading to higher risk premiums and/or more extensive debt covenants, which restrict debtor flexibility.

Economic analyses of bankruptcy law presents such difficulty because bankruptcy does occur, and bankruptcy law is important precisely because standard neoclassical theory fails. Given that so much of standard economic analysis is rooted in that paradigm, analysts find it difficult comprehending the central issues. It has already been noted that incomplete contracts underlie bankruptcy law; they fail to specify clearly what happens when debtors cannot fulfill their obligations. The problems run deeper, however. Under standard neoclassical theory, there would be unanimity concerning the actions a firm should take. The manager who maximizes the firm's stock market value would manage the firm, and maximization of stock market value would result in Pareto efficiency. Indeed, each of these propositions is not generally true when an incomplete set of markets exists; generally, there is not unanimity about what the firm should do, so control does matter (see, for example, Grossman and Stiglitz 1977 and the references cited there). The owners do not necessarily seek to maximize the firm's stock market value, and the takeover mechanism works imperfectly at best (see, for example, Grossman and Hart 1980). Finally, stock market value maximization is not necessarily Pareto efficient (see, for instance, Stiglitz 1972). If firms always chose the manager who maximized their stockholder value, and if there were always unanimity about what action that entailed, there would be no need to resort to bankruptcy courts. With the backdrop of bankruptcy, at least under the absolute priority system, it would be clear what actions should be taken and who should manage the firm. The value maximizing strategy would Pareto dominate all other strategies.

Of course, many disagree about what policies will maximize market value in the relevant horizon and whether that is the appropriate policy; for example, whether to focus myopically on today's market value or to have longer term objectives. There is a widespread belief that firms should have long-term objectives; but once one entertains that prospect, one is on treacherous ground, for it suggests that the market may exhibit either irrational exuberance or pessimism. Precisely these disputes about valuation ("fundamental value" as opposed to today's market value) underlie so many disputes that make their way to bankruptcy court.

Efficiency and Incentive Issues

In defining bankruptcy laws, efficiency concerns, including the efficiency with which markets share risks, are paramount. In a sense, equity or fairness is not an issue, provided the rules are perfectly clear and unambiguous, which is never the case. As long as the rules are clear, lenders will receive an interest rate that compensates them for the risks they face. To be sure, given differential abilities of different lenders in screening, and rents that different lenders may receive because of particular niches they occupy, different bankruptcy rules may affect those rents. For instance, lenders who make a living by lending to those who normally do not repay loans on their own and, therefore, obtain returns from their differential ability to collect debts, may find the value of those skills diminished under a regime that gives debtors more rights; hence the resulting adjustment in interest rates is likely to decrease the demand for loans among such deadbeats and, thus, the total demand for "loan collectors" will diminish.

Debt contracts contain a number of key efficiency issues related to the following:

- Ex ante screening. Such screening serves two functions: one is to ensure that capital is allocated to high-return uses.[8] The second related objective is to ensure that borrowers pay interest rates commensurate with the risks. In the absence of such screening, markets will treat those with different risks the same; significant inefficiencies can result from the consequent ignorance. Likewise, if interest rates do not respond to risks, individuals will not have an incentive to avoid risks: the "selection problem" thus leads to an "incentive" or moral hazard problem.

- Ex post monitoring. After the loan has been made, banks perform an important social role in monitoring the use of funds. Their sole incentive, of course, is to ensure that they get repaid—banks do not care about the surplus in excess of that amount. Elsewhere (Stiglitz 1982), I have discussed the free rider problems associated with monitoring on the part of shareholders, unless there is a single large shareholder. Bank monitoring typically has an externality on equity owners: they at least prevent the worst abuses.

By making the lender bear more of the risk, the lender has greater incentives both to engage in ex ante screening and ex post monitoring, with benefits accruing to others.

- Borrower actions prior to bankruptcy. Borrower actions are never perfectly monitored, and it has long been recognized that the borrowing

---

8. However, the lenders do not seek to maximize expected returns per dollar invested, but only the expected returns they themselves capture.

firm's interests often differ markedly from those of other stakeholders, including lenders. This is seen most vividly after bankruptcy, if they receive no equity interest. Then, they may have a strong incentive to engage in asset stripping (sometimes tamed slightly by reputational concerns); only strong trustee oversight usually suffices to prevent such abuses. And the inadequacies of court oversight are usually such that it behooves debtors and creditors to give the bankrupt management some equity stake in the firm (as evidenced in the recent long-term capital management bailout in the United States).

As the firm approaches bankruptcy, there often arises a concern that the managers will "gamble on resurrection." Limited liability makes the firm payoff function convex, inducing risk-taking behavior, even among managers who in more normal times would be averse to risk (see Stiglitz and Weiss 1981). So strong is this incentive for risk-taking that firms will undertake low expected return projects with high variance—one can think of the high variance as having more "option value." Creditors—and the economy generally—pay a price for such risk-taking behavior.

Such risky behavior resembles an attempt to shift more of the (expected) income from bankruptcy states (when the owner captures nothing) to the nonbankruptcy state. Given that at the margin the owner captures all of the latter return, and none of the former, the scope for distortionary behavior seems clear.

Moreover, managers, recognizing that the determinants of what they receive after bankruptcy depends on the outcome of a bargaining game, take actions that affect the outcome of that bargaining, attempting to make themselves more indispensable. In a slightly different context (that of staving off takeovers), Morck, Shleifer, and Vishny (1988) and Edlin and Stiglitz (1995) have analyzed the potential for such managerial entrenchment.[9]

In short, borrowers under financial distress have incentives to (a) take actions that shift income from bankruptcy states of nature, in which they are disenfranchised, to prebankruptcy states, in which they receive all the returns, and (b) take actions that increase their postbankruptcy income.

Much of the earlier bankruptcy literature aimed at a very different incentive issue: the avoidance of bankruptcy in the first place. By penalizing

---

9. Was it an accident that the creditors in the long-term capital management bailout felt that the only way the positions of long-term capital management could be unwound was to retain existing management?

management (equity owners) strongly in the event of bankruptcy (reducing the amount they will have in the postbankruptcy situation), the other two distortionary forms of incentives are increased. Earlier discussions have focused on a second issue: ensuring that resources are efficiently deployed after bankruptcy. Several, sometimes conflicting, factors enter here: (a) slow resolution of bankruptcy ties up assets, deprives the firm of future opportunities, and can lead to asset stripping; (b) the quickest and smoothest resolutions entail leaving existing management in charge—the same management that produced the problem in the first place; and (c) existing management is also most likely to be sensitive to the concerns of noncreditor stakeholders.

Interestingly, if confidence existed in standard market processes ("Coasian bargaining"), then no matter how control issues were settled in bankruptcy, resources would be efficiently deployed. As long as there is clarity of property rights, the "owner" will deploy assets in such a manner as to maximize value. Transaction costs are significant and, hence, the initial assignment of property rights after bankruptcy does indeed make a difference.

Risk Sharing

The resource deployment issues—from who gets loans to how they are employed—are critical. Risk-sharing issues represent another area receiving little attention. The bankruptcy provisions entail implicit forms of risk sharing. In a pure equity contract, the amount the supplier of funds receives is proportional to the profit of the company (the return net of interest payments). By contrast, in a pure debt contract with no bankruptcy, in which the amount that the supply of funds receives is independent of the firm's performance, a contract with bankruptcy (ignoring any incentive effects) is a mixture—effectively a debt credit in the nonbankruptcy states and an equity contract in the bankruptcy states. With limited liability, every debt contract (with indebtedness over some critical threshold) is actually of this mixed form. The terms of the contract (bankruptcy provisions) can affect the degree of risk sharing. For instance, compare a contract that entails the creditor retaining a 20 percent equity interest following bankruptcy, with one in which the debtor receives nothing. Ignoring for the moment any incentive effects, in order for the lender to receive the same expected return (assuming risk neutrality), the lender must receive a higher interest rate before bankruptcy. The loan that lets the borrower off the hook by allowing the retention of a larger equity share, even when the borrower fails to fulfill the obligation to the lender, is more effective in risk sharing; it "transfers" income from the borrower to the lender in the "good states" (the nondefault states) for greater income of the borrower in the "bad states," the states when the debtor is likely to especially value income.

The natural question arises: Why do markets in general not provide better risk sharing, that is, rely more on equity and equity-like contracts? Previous literature, such as Myers and Majluf (1984) and Greenwald, Stiglitz, and Weiss (1984), provides explanations based on asymmetries of information: both moral-hazard and adverse-incentive effects are associated with raising capital through equity contracts. Accordingly, the issuance of new equity finances a relatively small proportion of new investment. Loan contracts, even with some equity-like features (as a result of bankruptcy), do not suffer from the adverse selection or moral-hazard effects, at least not anywhere near the extent that full equity contracts suffer.

Asymmetries of Information and Differences in Beliefs

Another important element missing in earlier discussions arises from the existence of differences in beliefs and knowledge about the occurrence of different events that affect the profitability of the firm.[10] Typically, the entrepreneur may be more optimistic than the creditors about the firm's prospects.[11] The result is that the debtor believes that the expected payment to the creditor is greater than the creditor believes he is receiving. The debtor, for instance, might believe that the probability of default is zero, and so the expected payment is close to the promised interest rate, while the creditor may think that the probability of default is significant. In a sense, a deadweight loss results, as if in the process of transferring money from the debtor to the creditor, some of it disappears. The bankruptcy code affects how much of it disappears. For instance, consider a two-state model in which the firm goes bankrupt in one state (the bad state). Then, providing the

---

10. See Stiglitz (1972) for an early presentation of such a model. Note that if there were a complete set of Arrow-Debreu securities, differences in beliefs would not matter for the efficiency of the market economy.

11. Knight (1933) stressed the importance of this entrepreneurial confidence in the workings of the capitalist economy. He was concerned with the discrepancy between the seeming expectations of returns and the ex post facto returns; the irrational exuberance served to offset the information spillovers that, by themselves, would have implied that the market would have invested too little in innovative activity.

debtor with increased income in the bankruptcy state (not entirely wiping him out), compensated for by an increased interest rate in the nonbankruptcy state sufficient to leave creditors just as well off, makes debtors better off provided

$$Y^b_B / 1 - p^b_B > Y^c_B / 1 - p^c_B$$

where Y^b_B is the expected income (from the borrower's perspective) in the bankruptcy state, Y^c_B is the expected income from the creditor's perspective in the bankruptcy state, p^b_B is the probability of bankruptcy from the borrower's perspective, and p^c_B is the probability of bankruptcy from the lender's perspective.

Asymmetries of information have other implications for the impact of bankruptcy codes. They affect the extent to which self-selection (or adverse selection) occurs in the process of applying for loans. One of the arguments made for debtor prisons was that they discouraged from applying for loans those who did not intend to repay them, or who knew they were unlikely to be able to repay them. Today, however, the issue does not center on sending to prison those who do not fully repay their loans, but on how much they should be allowed to keep in the bankruptcy state. In general, the effect is ambiguous. Again consider the two-state model described above, and consider the effect of increasing the share of the income the debtor can retain in the bankruptcy state, offset by an increase in the interest rate paid in the good state. A borrower with a low probability assessment on bankruptcy does not value the increase in share in the bankruptcy state much, but values highly the increase in the payment in the good state. By contrast, a borrower who believes that income in the bankruptcy state is high (that is, if the firm cannot meet its obligations, it misses the mark by a small amount) highly values the increase in the share of the income that is retained. To the extent that information is imperfect, and self-selection mechanisms have ambiguous effects, greater reliance needs to be placed on creditor screening; in that case, the incentives associated with stronger debtor rights become more important.

Absolute Priority

Many financial authorities presume that in bankruptcy codes creditors should be fully satisfied before debtors receive anything. In practice, this does not often occur. Many of the controversies about valuation of assets, in effect, amount to discussions over whether creditor claims are fully satisfied. The discussion so far has argued that, from the perspective of economic efficiency, bankruptcy codes that give the debtor something, even when creditors are not fully satisfied, may be preferable because they (a) improve risk sharing, (b) may reduce the "ignorance wedge," (c) may improve the effectiveness of self-selection, (d) typically improve the efficiency of resource allocations after bankruptcy, if the debtor-manager has some advantage in managing the resources, and (e) reduce the prebankruptcy diversion of income from bankruptcy states to nonbankruptcy states.

Seller Beware

A quite different line of reasoning from that above emphasizes debtor rights, one based on somewhat paternalistic notions: sellers often try to exploit unaware consumers, and consumers need some protection from such exploitation. The United States and other countries have enacted truth in lending laws, intended to ensure that borrowers are at least informed concerning true interest rates. There are many instances of lenders preying on consumer weaknesses, attempting to induce them to buy on credit more than they can afford, and then repossessing the goods and keeping the amounts paid when the borrowers cannot pay what is owed. Much of the debate concerning personal bankruptcy centers on these issues. Making the creditor bear more of the risk of default discourages this kind of opportunism and encourages lenders to do due diligence.

The criticism of this approach is that poor but honest borrowers will be forced to pay higher interest rates. This argument assumes that creditors cannot, or do not, adequately screen; if the market differentiates among borrowers, then good borrowers will not have to pay a higher interest rate. (To be sure, debtor-friendly bankruptcy laws may exacerbate the self-selection problem, so that with any given "quality" of screening, the mix of borrowers is poorer.)

Implications for Policy

Analysis of the design of bankruptcy laws presents an important issue in identifying the central distortion present in the market. In some countries, a key problem concerns development of a credit culture. Part of the credit culture results from the sanctions that others impose on those who go into bankruptcy; for instance, social sanctions or lack of access to future credit. If such sanctions are strong or, more broadly, if the credit culture is strong, the marginal benefits derived from imposing further penalties through bankruptcy law are limited, and the forward-looking incentive benefits and improved risk distribution from greater debtor rights suggest that bankruptcy law should be tilted in debtors' favor. By contrast, in an economy where these sanctions are not present, no moral aversion attaches to bankruptcy and, consequently, many "rational calculators" arise, calculating the maximum amount that can be extracted out of the system in excess of individuals' income.[12]

By contrast, if a central problem seems to be a failure in lending practices—so that lenders do not perform due diligence—bankruptcy codes that impose higher costs on lenders seem appropriate. Several reasons—beyond sheer incompetence—explain why lending practices may be at fault. For instance, there can be (and are) important agency problems within lending institutions. Often, lending officers are rewarded on the basis of the amount of loans that they extend, or on returns—not appropriately risk adjusted. In the aftermath of the last major regional economic crisis, in Latin America, many lending officers were, or at least believed they were, rewarded on the basis of relative performance (Nalebuff and Stiglitz 1983). If officers had not lent to Latin America—and there had not been a crisis—their lending portfolios would have been smaller and yielded lower returns. In the event of a crisis, each lending officer would claim as much prudence as the other; clearly, if the entire class fails the exam, the students cannot be blamed. And such was the case in the Latin American crisis. While I have not seen a detailed analysis of what happened to those who were responsible for the lending (or, more broadly, for the banking institutions at the time the lending occurred), my impression is that many continued to rise in the organization, and few were made to bear the costs of their bad lending decisions.

An alternative explanation for excessive borrowing lies in weak bank regulation in creditor countries, where banks with negative or low net worth "gamble on resurrection" (Kane 1990).[13] In either of these cases, lenders may be willing to lend at interest rates below actuarial fair values, inducing borrowers to engage in excessive borrowing. Such cases do not

---

12. One colleague calculated that given the sanctions and practices prevalent in the United States, he should have three personal bankruptcies during his life. These calculations were conducted in the late 1960s, when I first began working on bankruptcy. I have not checked to see how the optimal number of bankruptcies has changed since then.

13. Note that strict enforcement of capital adequacy standards can actually exacerbate these problems, especially in the absence of accounting regulations requiring marking to market. See Hellman, Murdock, and Stiglitz (2000).

make apparent that the borrower should be blamed for the consequences: the borrowers' actions were perfectly rational responses to attractive lending offers. To the extent that bankruptcies are related to these creditor failures, bankruptcy laws that weigh the interests of debtors more heavily improve both incentives and risk distribution.

The recent global financial crisis has highlighted the downside risks of unstable short-term capital. More important, large externalities become associated with such capital flows. Innocent bystanders, such as workers and small businesses in the affected countries, suffered greatly from the resulting recessions and the associated domestic credit contractions and usurious interest rates. Bankruptcy laws that enhanced debtor rights might well result in higher interest rates, and higher interest rates might result in a diminution of short-term capital flows. However, all of this may be for the better—at least partially improving the major discrepancy between the private and social costs associated with these capital flows.

In some countries, creditors who prey on uninformed consumers represent a major problem. They induce consumers to borrow beyond their means, often to purchase overpriced goods, and charge usurious interest rates. More debtor-friendly bankruptcy laws discourage such practices.

The design of bankruptcy law has a key trade-off between simplicity and adapting to the current situation. Simplicity—well defined rules that serve as backstops for the bargaining process—encourage quick resolution. By contrast, such rules provide less fine-tuned incentives. If, for instance, the prevalent problem in society is that creditors fail to undertake due diligence. A legal framework that provides debtor-friendly rules may, on average, make sense; but it leaves open an opportunity for scurrilous borrowers to take advantage of the provisions. However, a law that tailors its provisions to the situation opens the way for costly litigation. Part of the answer as to how these considerations should be balanced depends on the nature of the legal system. There should be less discretion in a corrupt legal system that is open to influence. Some countries that have bankruptcy laws that, on paper, seem quite reasonable have flaws in the implementation of the law, not just by judicial delay, but by the ability of one party or the other to exercise influence over the judicial process.[14] All too often the assumption exists that a judiciary is capable of making the fine distinctions

---

14. Addressing judicial malfeasance is, of course, a complex issue beyond the scope of this chapter. Suffice it to say that institutions promoting media freedom and judicial accountability, tempering arbitrary exercise of judicial powers, are likely ingredients.

required by sophisticated bankruptcy laws, and that the judiciary is immune from incentives. In some countries, incentives delay resolutions. While the firm remains under trusteeship, the trustees benefit from the fees as long as the bankruptcy remains unresolved.

The Theory of Systemic Bankruptcy

Arguably one of the high-priority issues of economic policy in the world today concerns hastening and broadening the incipient recovery in economies affected by the economic crises of 1997–98 and ensuring sustainability of the recovery. As indicated earlier, not only have the countries of East Asia faced systemic bankruptcies due to the sharp devaluations and steep increases in interest rates, but many economies in transition face similar problems, although the systemic roots are quite different and varied. In the Czech Republic most of the large industrial conglomerates are insolvent, while the problems in Russia's enterprises are too complex to easily characterize. However, bankruptcy codes designed to deal with isolated bankruptcies are not well suited for addressing the special problems that arise in these cases of systemic bankruptcy. Some of the obvious reasons for this are the following:

- When a single firm goes bankrupt, a reasonable inference can be made that the firm itself did something wrong. There is a strong presumption that management made a mistake. With systemic bankruptcy that presumption is reversed. The situation is analogous to a single student who has not understood an exam question; the student is probably to blame—he or she did not pay attention or study hard enough. If, however, 70 percent of the students fail to understand a question, the teacher probably failed to communicate the point effectively. If interest rates soared to 40 percent or higher, many seemingly well-managed firms in most countries of the Organisation for Economic Co-operation and Development would go bankrupt too. A firm's managers demonstrate flawed business policy by assuming there exists a high probability of interest rates soaring to those levels next year, or counting on the economy contracting by 15 percent—unless, of course, such forecasts are commonplace at the time the debt is undertaken. By contrast, the management of a firm that did not purchase appropriate insurance against important risks, such as fire or currency devaluation, should be questioned. Even if legitimate questions exist, one must be careful—is overall management deficient, or is a new corporate finance officer required?

- When a single firm goes bankrupt, there is typically a large supply of alternative managerial teams. When half of the firms in the economy go bankrupt, it becomes impossible to replace all the managers. This again reinforces the presumption for the retention of existing management. While in some cases there may be advantages to importing some managerial skills from abroad, outside managers will probably not fully understand the situation within the country. The challenge will be to combine international experience with local knowledge. Blending the two has constituted one of the true sources of economic strength of East Asian economies over the past decades. The remarkable performance of these economies during an extended period suggests enormous managerial talent. In today's complex international financial world, there may be a greater need to import this specific type of expertise. There is no convincing case that selling corporations to foreign owners will generally enhance the level of productivity or the pace of growth.
- When there is systemic financial distress, ascertaining the net worth of a firm, or indeed valuing many of the financial claims, becomes difficult. This is because many of the assets of a corporation may be claims on other firms that are themselves bankrupt. Furthermore, transfer of assets to settle claims is typically problematic, as the creditors are themselves preoccupied with their own financial distress and reorganization and may have restrictions on their activity, such as in the case of banks in which regulatory authorities may have intervened.
- Usually, large legal and specialist resources are deployed to resolve individual bankruptcies. Indeed, many authorities criticize current practices in the United States, where even the direct pecuniary legal and administrative costs of individual transactions appear to be staggering. The affordability or feasibility of the traditional approach, with its high concentration of specialists and advisers (accountants, lawyers, turnaround specialists, financial engineers, restructuring experts), is a matter of serious doubt in situations in which half or more of the firms have to deal with insolvency. Not enough bankruptcy lawyers and other trained personnel are available.
- Most important, even in the most experienced and fine-tuned regimes, bankruptcy proceedings are often protracted. For example, despite the improvements made possible by the 1978 reforms in the United States, the time period for a typical Chapter 11 reorganization is approximately two years. Such delays impose significant private costs of which the direct (legal and administrative) costs are

usually the smaller part. The indirect costs of bankruptcy, or more precisely, financial distress in general are even more significant. An important part of these, namely, agency costs, were dealt with earlier in the discussion of efficiency and incentive issues. Another major part of the indirect costs relates to the impaired ability to do business. Suppliers become less responsive, demand early payment, and so forth, while customers faced with greater delivery risk reduced or canceled orders. Not only are such private costs likely to escalate over time, but the associated social costs may significantly exceed the private costs under systemic bankruptcy.

- In particular, when a single firm goes bankrupt, there is normally little concern about macroeconomic consequences (occasionally, however, a firm is so large that the too big to fail doctrine is invoked). With systemic bankruptcy, macroeconomic concerns become paramount. Delay in resolving an isolated bankruptcy may lead not only to loss in output during the intervening period, but, worse, to asset decay, or even asset stripping. When a large number of firms are left in limbo, unemployment increases, financial institutions experience large repercussions, and a vicious cycle ensues. As suppliers and customers are left in limbo, firms cannot meet their own commitments, even if they do everything right. To protect themselves, firms must cut back on production, using up inventories and freezing hiring, thus contributing to the overall economic downturn.

A simple solution to this conundrum involves a new super Chapter 11 to be imbedded in every country's bankruptcy code. In the U.S. bankruptcy code, Chapter 11 is distinguished from Chapter 7 in that under Chapter 11 management proposes a continuation of its own control of the firm; existing management/controlling shareholders typically receive more than is their due—that is, existing shareholders are not totally wiped out financially, even if creditor obligations are not fully satisfied, simply because doing so erodes the management structure and, hence, the efficiency of the firm. This was brought home forcefully by the reorganization of long term capital management, the U.S. hedge fund that had an exposure of more than US$1 trillion, and thus presented (at least in the view of some participants in the private bailout) a systemic risk to the global financial system. Even as lenders were bailing out the firm, the principal equity owners, who under "straight" bankruptcy proceedings should have received nothing, retained a 10-percent equity share.

Chapter 11 is designed for a quick resolution of bankruptcy disputes, but even under this rule, proceedings typically take almost two years. To protect against wastage or mismanagement of assets in the interim, courts typically take a strong trusteeship role. With systemic bankruptcy, not only is the cost of delay greater—as unemployment mounts and financial institutions weaken—but the effectiveness of interim monitoring is reduced. There simply is not an adequate supply of bankruptcy trustees. Even the United States, with its wealth of experience in sophisticated bankruptcy law, could not meet the challenge.

A super Chapter 11 is required to address the exigencies a country faces with systemic bankruptcy, especially if such bankruptcy results from huge macroeconomic disturbances—for example, major economic contractions, huge increases in interest rates, and massive devaluation. There would be a presumption that existing management would remain and that there would be a debt-to-equity conversion. There would be three major differences from a standard Chapter 11 bankruptcy: (a) given the importance of speed of resolution, the time within which the courts would have to rule would be shortened considerably, and there would be a heavier burden placed on those attempting to delay; (b) there would be a stronger presumption in favor of the management remaining in place and on management proposals that, in the reorganization, give management/old shareholders enough of an equity industry to have adequate incentives. In other words, the burden of proof would be placed on creditors to demonstrate that the management proposal was "grossly inequitable"; and (3) to facilitate quick resolution, a wider set of default/guideline provisions would be specified. These "default options" would provide the backdrop for a speedy resolution of the debtor-creditor bargaining problem and would aim at ensuring fairness in protecting other claimants (such as workers) and in balancing the claims of creditors with claims denominated in foreign currency, and those in domestic currency, in an environment of rapidly changing exchange rates.

Such a super Chapter 11 might be an effective way out of the impasse, which is costing so much for everyone in the countries facing systemic distress. Such a bankruptcy code might, however, lead to somewhat higher interest rates, especially by short-term foreign lenders. It may, however, be beneficial for lenders to focus more clearly on the risks inherent in such lending—risks that extend well beyond the parties to the transaction, parties that have been repeatedly hurt under the current financial regime. Such a bankruptcy regime would be fairer than the current one, especially if it were known in advance. Adjustments in interest rates charged would compensate lenders for any changes in risk assumed. Even under the current circumstances, one could argue that a movement to this new code would be fair, because so much of the burden of the delay is being borne by third parties, and the current regime gives too much power to the creditors, who frequently have already been well compensated for the risks they bore in terms of the high interest rates received.

Even ignoring the systemic benefits, the quick resolution provided by such a provision would have distinct efficiency advantages: it would eliminate asset stripping. Such a provision is even advantageous in terms of incentives prior to bankruptcy; considerable evidence now exists that firms facing a high probability of imminent bankruptcy may engage in value-decreasing, risk-taking behavior, which enhances equity values in the event the disaster does not occur, but decreases asset values in the event it does occur. At the time loans are made, the macroeconomic prospect of a firm may look good. In the world of rapid financial movements and changes in investment sentiment, these prospects can change dramatically, providing considerable scope for these perverse incentives. A super Chapter 11 provision would reduce such perverse incentives.

A change in bankruptcy code along these lines would also reduce the need for public funds in the corporate reorganization process. Once the economy has begun working again, capital markets would once again be willing to provide funds to those firms that have good projects with high returns. Remember that corporate reorganizations are simply a rearrangement of claims on the assets of the firm. Indeed, such rearrangements, if not done or done badly, have strong implications for the performance of firms. The reorganization process itself does not require funds, except in the event of costly and litigious bankruptcy proceedings, and the super Chapter 11 would, by design, reduce the incentives for such litigation. In the past there have often been proposals for an injection of funds from public agencies as a carrot to induce faster reorganization. If taken seriously, such discussions are counterproductive, for they provide an incentive for a delay in reorganization in the hopes that such delay will reap some part of the public largesse. Far better ways to spend scarce public funds are available—focusing on high-multiplier, job-creation programs with benefits targeted especially to the poor. Incentives for faster bankruptcy resolution may be needed, but these should take the form of sticks rather than carrots. Fears that such sticks will dry up a future supply of capital, especially from abroad, are almost surely unfounded. Lenders are forward looking; they look at future prospects, not only past results. A clearly defined bankruptcy regime, a well-functioning economy with high employment, a lack of the kind of social and political unrest that inevitably accompanies extended periods of unemployment—all of these are of prime importance, and all of these would be enhanced by the new bankruptcy code. Given these enhanced opportunities and increased certainties, creditors would be able to better ascertain the interest rates to be charged to adequately compensate themselves for their risks. The historical experience has confirmed these theoretical propositions: lenders returned relatively quickly even after the massive defaults that have periodically plagued Latin America. The situation indicates that the experience will be replicated in East Asia.

Such a systemic bankruptcy code produces other advantages. It can be thought of as a decentralized alternative to the widely discussed bail-in proposals (at least in cases like East Asia, where the debt obligations were private). Private creditors would be "forced" to participate, through the automatic workings of the bankruptcy law. Indeed, when combined with truly flexible exchange rates, the need for public bailout funds would be greatly reduced, if not eliminated. And such a provision might even serve to stabilize the economy. Elsewhere, I have analyzed a model in which multiple equilibriums arise (Stiglitz 1999). As the exchange rate falls, the developing country with foreign-denominated debt becomes increasingly poorer, reinforcing the falling exchange rate. There is a good equilibrium at a high-exchange rate and a bad equilibrium at a low exchange. The super Chapter 11 bankruptcy provision limits the extent of wealth transfer to the creditor country, and may thereby eliminate the bad equilibria. Interestingly, once the possibility of the bad equilibrium has been eliminated, the economy remains within the good equilibrium, so that the provisions of the super Chapter 11 do not actually have to be invoked.

The foregoing proposal for dealing with systemic bankruptcy is clearly one of several possible approaches that may be considered, including those involving concerted government action. The experience of Chile in the early 1980s and Mexico more recently provide both positive and negative lessons to draw upon. Whichever avenue is pursued, many details would need to be fleshed out and several complicated issues addressed, especially those relating to moral hazard as well as demands on implementation capacity.

Conclusion

Bankruptcy laws are essential for a well-functioning economy. Well-designed bankruptcy laws facilitate better risk sharing and provide better incentives, not only to avoid bankruptcy, but also to avoid other distortions.

They can provide incentives for lenders to engage in better selection and more effective monitoring, and they can help ensure that assets are better managed after bankruptcy. Bankruptcy, and how bankruptcy is resolved, affect not only debtors and creditors, but workers and other stakeholders in the firms as well. In addition, the effects are felt both at the time bankruptcy occurs and before bankruptcy, for instance, in the terms at which capital is provided.

The design of bankruptcy requires a delicate balance: excessive protection of debtors can result in a complete stifling of credit markets. If borrowers know that creditors have no recourse, then borrowers will have no incentive to repay, and creditors will then have no incentive to lend. The legal system must provide some protection to creditors (see chapter 4 in this volume). However, excessive deference to creditors attenuates their incentives to engage in due diligence, worsens the sharing of risk between creditor and debtors, encourages predatory behavior by creditors, and weakens creditors' incentives to engage in monitoring. Striking the proper balance defies an easy solution. Clearly, the means used to strike that balance will differ from country to country. Most important, a major reform in bankruptcy law is required to address the kinds of systemic bankruptcies that now plague so many countries worldwide.

References

Altman, Edward I., and Allan C. Eberhart. 1994. "Do Priority Provisions Protect a Bondholder's Investment?" *Journal of Portfolio Management* 20(4): 65–75.

Claessens, Stijn, Simeon Djankov, and Giovanni Ferri. 1999. "Corporate Distress in East Asia: Assessing the Impact of Interest and Exchange Rate Shocks." *Emerging Markets Quarterly* 3(2): 8–14.

Greenwald, Bruce C., and Joseph E. Stiglitz. 1986. "Externalities in Economies with Imperfect Information and Incomplete Markets." *Quarterly Journal of Economics* 101(2): 229–64.

Greenwald, Bruce C., Joseph E. Stiglitz, and Andrew Weiss. 1984. "Informational Imperfections in the Capital Market and Macroeconomic Fluctuations." *American Economic Review* 74(2): 194–99.

Grossman, Sanford, and Oliver Hart. 1980. "Disclosure Laws and Takeover Bids." *Journal of Finance* 35(2): 323–34.

Grossman, Sanford, and Joseph E. Stiglitz. 1977. "On Value Maximization and Alternative Objectives of the Firm." *Journal of Finance* 32(2): 389–402.

Eberhart, Allan C., William T. Moore, and Rodney L. Roenfeldt. 1990. "Security Pricing and Deviations from the Absolute Priority Rule in Bankruptcy Proceedings." *Journal of Finance* 45(5): 1457–69.

Edlin, Aaron C., and Joseph E. Stiglitz. 1995. "Discouraging Rivals: Managerial Rent-Seeking and Economic Inefficiencies." *American Economic Review* 85(5): 1301–12.

Hellman, Thomas F., Kevin C. Murdock, and Joseph E. Stiglitz. 2000. "Liberalization, Moral Hazard in Banking, and Prudential Regulation: Are Capital Requirements Enough?" *American Economic Review* 90(1): 147–65.

Kane, Edward J. 1990. "Principal-Agent Problems in S&L Salvage." *Journal of Finance* 45(3): 755–64.

Knight, Frank. 1933. *Risk, Uncertainty, and Profit*. London: London School of Economics and Political Science.

Morck, Randall, Andrei Shleifer, and Robert Vishny. 1988. "Management Ownership and Market Valuation: An Empirical Analysis." *Journal of Financial Economics* 20(1): 293–315.

Myers, Stewart C., and Nicholas S. Majluf. 1984. "Corporate Financing and Investment Decisions When Firms Have Information that Investors Do Not Have." *Journal of Financial Economics* 13(2): 187–221.

Nalebuff, Barry J., and Joseph E. Stiglitz. 1983. "Information, Competition, and Markets." *American Economic Review* 73(2): 278–83.

Schwartz, Alan. 1997. "Contracting about Bankruptcy." *Journal of Law, Economics, and Organization* 13(1): 127–46.

Stiglitz, Joseph E. 1972. "Optimality of Stock Market Allocation." *Quarterly Journal of Economics* 86(1): 25–60.

_____. 1975. "Incentives, Risk, and Information: Notes towards a Theory of Hierarchy." *Bell Journal of Economics* 6(2): 552–79.

_____. 1982. "The Inefficiency of the Stock Market Equilibrium." *Review of Economic Studies* 49(2): 241–61.

_____. 1999. "Interest Rates, Risk, and Imperfect Markets: Puzzles and Policies." *Oxford Review of Economic Policy* 15(2): 59–76.

Stiglitz, Joseph E., and Andrew Weiss. 1981. "Credit Rationing in Markets with Imperfect Information." *American Economic Review* 71(3): 393–410.

2

Bankruptcy Procedures in Countries Undergoing Financial Crises

Michelle J. White, University of Michigan

This chapter considers the role of bankruptcy procedures in countries undergoing financial crises. Divided into two sections, the chapter's first section deals with the basic economic issues and tradeoffs involving corporate bankruptcy, and the second section addresses the effect of bankruptcy law on the incentives of potential entrepreneurs to set up and run small firms. Both sections consider how bankruptcy issues differ among Asian and European countries and the United States.

Economic Issues in Corporate Bankruptcy

Corporate bankruptcy procedures maximize the value of assets of firms that are already in financial distress or may be in financial distress in the future. Maximizing value involves considerations at several different time periods: (a) after firms file for bankruptcy, (b) when firms are in financial distress but not in bankruptcy, and (c) before firms are in financial distress. After firms have filed for bankruptcy, an important aspect of an efficient bankruptcy policy entails determining which firms will be reorganized and which firms will be liquidated. When firms are in financial distress but not in bankruptcy, common property problems become important because firms' ownership is unclear. Bankruptcy aims to mitigate both creditors' and managers' incentives to protect their individual interests in ways that reduce the overall value of the firm. Before a firm enters financial distress, creditors lend money to the firm based on agreements of how much the firm is obliged to repay and what happens if the firm defaults. The treatment of creditors' claims when the firm defaults affects creditors' overall return and, therefore, their incentive to lend. An ideal bankruptcy procedure maximizes the value of failing firms' assets at all three time periods. However, in actuality, bankruptcy procedures involve tradeoffs, so that changes that increase efficiency at one time period may reduce efficiency at other time periods. Perhaps, as a result, bankruptcy procedures are quite variable internationally, and there is no widely used universal pattern.

Common Property Problems when Firms Are in Financial Distress but Not in Bankruptcy

When firms are in financial distress, the value of their assets is insufficient to repay all of their creditors' claims. Therefore, ownership of the firm becomes uncertain, because equity will be worthless if the firm is forced to repay creditors' claims in full. Creditors have an incentive to be first to collect on their claims, because some creditors will be forced to take losses, and those that collect earliest will receive the most. Managers have an incentive to gamble with failing firms' assets, because a gamble that pays off will save the firm and a gamble that fails will leave managers and equity no worse off than they would have been anyway.

When creditors perceive that a firm may be insolvent, they have an incentive to race to be first to collect on their claims. For example, suppose a firm has two creditors, each of whom are owed US$100. One or both of the creditors perceive that the liquidated value of the firm's assets is less than US$200, meaning neither creditor can be repaid in full. Therefore, as in a bank run, both creditors have an incentive to seek quick repayment by taking legal action against the firm. Although both loans may have due dates in the future, loan agreements generally involve many covenants. If the firm violates any of the covenants, the creditor has the right to declare the loan in default and demand full repayment immediately. Firms in financial difficulties are likely to be in violation of many of their covenants. The first creditor to succeed in their legal action seizes the firm's assets that are easily liquidated and, therefore, receives full payment as long as the firm has assets whose liquidated value is US$100 or more. The second creditor seizes the remaining assets and sells them. Assuming that the liquidated value of the remaining assets is less than US$100, the second creditor receives only partial repayment.

When creditors race to be first to collect, two types of inefficiencies may occur. First, because assets are liquidated piecemeal, they are worth less than if all of the firm's assets were sold together. Second, piecemeal liquidation of assets causes firms to shut down. Some of these firms may be worth more if they continued in operation and were subsequently sold as going concerns, even though they are in financial distress. Because few firms are liquid enough to repay all their creditors at once, the perception that a firm is insolvent may be a self-fulfilling prophecy, leading to firms' shutting down because creditors remove essential assets. Thus, even profitable firms may be shut down if creditors race to be first to collect.

To go back to the example, suppose the firm's assets consist of three machines. If the machines were sold individually, each would be worth US$50. If the two creditors race to be first to collect from the firm, the first creditor to succeed would liquidate two machines and would receive full payment of US$100. The second creditor would liquidate the remaining machine and receive US$50, making the total value of the firm's assets US$150 if creditors race to be first to collect. If the three machines were sold together, suppose they would be worth US$170, because a new manager could easily take over and restart the firm's operations. Finally, if the firm were sold as a going concern under its old managers, suppose it would be worth US$180. Thus, in the example, the cost of the race to be first is either US$20 or US$30, depending on the quality of the current manager relative to a new manager.

A bankruptcy procedure increases efficiency by substituting collective liquidation of failing firms' assets for partial private liquidation by creditors. Suppose an individual creditor attempts to collect on an unpaid debt by seizing particular assets and the firm's managers file for bankruptcy, then creditors' attempts to collect from the firm are stayed, and they must collect through the bankruptcy process. In bankruptcy, the bankruptcy court judge appoints a trustee. The trustee sells all of the firm's assets and uses the proceeds to settle all creditors' claims. In the example, suppose the trustee either sells the firm's three machines for US$170 or sells the firm as a going concern for US$180, depending on whether the firm shut down before entering bankruptcy. If the two creditors have equal priority in bankruptcy, each will then receive either US$85 or US$90. When there is a collective bankruptcy procedure, individual creditors anticipate that racing to be the first to collect is not worthwhile, because managers will file for bankruptcy and, in bankruptcy, individual creditors will receive the same amount regardless of whether they race to be first or not.[1] Given the mandatory bankruptcy procedure, the outcome is both more efficient and fair.

The role of bankruptcy law in preventing creditors from racing to be first to collect relates closely to the reason why bankruptcy procedures in most countries are mandatory rather than discretionary. Many aspects of corporation and contract law are default rules, meaning that parties can either adopt them (by doing nothing) or adopt some alternative (by specifying it in a contract or in the firm's corporate charter). Most countries mandate bankruptcy procedures to prevent managers from making an enforceable promise to creditors that they will never file for bankruptcy.[2] The United Kingdom serves as the primary example of a country without a mandatory bankruptcy procedure. Most U.K. firms have a single creditor, called a floating charge creditor, who retains the right to liquidate certain assets of the firm, particularly inventory and accounts receivable, if it defaults on its contract with the creditor. The proceeds of the partial liquidation repay the floating charge creditor. Managers cannot file for bankruptcy unless the floating charge creditor consents. Because the floating charge creditor partially liquidates the firm's assets, the assets cannot be sold together, and the firm cannot be sold as a going concern, lowering the payoff to the other creditors and reducing efficiency.[3] Other industrial countries mandate bankruptcy procedures.

In the Asian countries, the race by creditors to be the first to collect probably presents less of a problem than in the industrialized countries, because creditors generally have weaker legal rights against firms that default. Even if creditors perceive that a firm is in financial distress, they have

---

1. In the case of two creditors, they may have equal priority in bankruptcy (as assumed in the text) or one creditor may have higher priority than the other where priority is based on creditors' original loan agreements with the firm. If the two creditors have unequal priority, the creditor with lower priority has a stronger incentive to race to be first, because the gain from being paid in full is greater when the creditor's payoff in bankruptcy is lower. Even a low-priority creditor's incentive to race to be first becomes muted if managers respond by filing for bankruptcy (see Jackson 1986 and White 1989 for general discussion). See LoPucki (1983) for examples showing that U.S. firms often file for bankruptcy just ahead of creditors who would seize assets.

2. See Schwartz (1997) for a discussion of whether creditors would adopt bankruptcy procedures and what their characteristics would be if bankruptcy were not mandatory.

3. See Webb (1987, 1991) for a discussion of U.K. bankruptcy law and an analysis of the race by creditors to be first to collect as a prisoner's dilemma game.

little incentive to race to be the first to collect because managers can prevent them from seizing the firm's assets.

The other side of the common property problem when firms are in financial distress involves managers with an incentive to use the firm's assets inefficiently. Because their firms may shut down, managers anticipate they may lose their jobs. And because the value of the firm's equity amounts to zero in liquidation, managers no longer have an incentive to behave in equity holders' interest. One possible outcome is that managers strip firms of their most valuable assets, perhaps by transferring these assets at a low price to new firms that managers control. Another possibility entails managers who use the firm's capital to make risky investments with a low probability of a high payoff. If the investments succeed, the firm will be saved. If the investments fail, the firm will shut down, but managers and equity will be no worse off than they would have been without the risky investments. Because of equity's limited liability, creditors bear the loss of the risky investments because their payoff in bankruptcy falls. Clearly, managers have an incentive to undertake risky investments even if the investments have a negative expected payoff, such as trips to the gambling tables (see Jensen and Meckling 1976; Stiglitz 1975).

The industrial countries have developed various practices that mitigate the common property problems of firms in financial distress. The secured loan represents one particularly important practice. Secured creditors lend to the firm on condition that they receive a security interest in a particular asset, such as a building, a vehicle, a piece of equipment, inventory, or some of the firm's accounts receivable. If the firm defaults, secured creditors are allowed to seize their lien assets quickly and, in most cases, without going to court. Secured creditors also assume the right to be repaid first from the proceeds of selling the assets subject to the security interest, provided the security interest is publicly registered. (This applies regardless of whether the firm has filed for bankruptcy.) A lien on a particular asset reduces secured creditors' need to monitor the firm's financial condition because secured creditors either get repaid in full or get their lien assets back. Their return, therefore, does not depend on being first. Secured creditors need only monitor firms' use of their lien assets to prevent abuse.[4]

---

4. If the value of the collateral is less than the secured creditor's claim, the remainder becomes an unsecured claim that gives the creditor an interest in racing to be first to collect.

Secured loans also reduce mangers' ability to gamble with the firm's assets. In the United States, secured interests are registered with the government of the state where the firm is located, and a public record of liens is maintained. New lenders to firms routinely check the public record before lending to ensure managers have not offered new lenders security interests in assets already subject to prior creditors' liens (unless the new creditor agrees that its lien will be subordinate to the earlier creditor's lien). Most firms in financial distress have few assets not already subject to liens. Therefore, managers of firms in financial distress are unlikely to be able to borrow new funds to finance risky investments. Moreover, transferring an asset to a new company becomes less attractive if the asset is subject to a lien, for the lien survives the transfer, necessitating that the creditor be repaid if the new firm is to retain the asset.[5]

One of several drawbacks of secured loans, however, is that the more strongly secured creditors are protected, the less inclination lenders have to lend on an unsecured basis. Furthermore, secured loans make it more difficult for firms to reorganize in bankruptcy.

Managers usually have a choice between filing for bankruptcy earlier or later. Their choice of when to file relates to their choice of whether to gamble with or steal the firm's assets. If filing for bankruptcy means that the firm shuts down immediately and managers lose their jobs, then managers have an incentive to delay bankruptcy as long as possible and use the extra time to gamble with or steal the firm's assets. However, if filing for bankruptcy means that managers remain in control while the firm is reorganized, they possess less incentive to delay bankruptcy. European countries' bankruptcy laws require managers to file for bankruptcy within a few days after their firms first become insolvent. Sanctions, including jail terms, may be used against managers who delay filing. European countries' bankruptcy laws also encourage creditors and other interested parties to initiate involuntary bankruptcy filings. The U.S. bankruptcy code, however, takes the opposite approach and relies on rewards rather than sanctions to encourage managers to file early for bankruptcy. Rewards include the option for managers to file for bankruptcy reorganization rather than bankruptcy liquidation as well as retaining control of the firm, at least during the initial stages of the reorganization process (see White 1996 for discussion and references).

---

5. When there is no public record of liens (as in Germany), secured creditors have an incentive to race to be first to reclaim their lien assets because another creditor may have a lien on the same asset.

In most Asian countries, managers generally avoid bankruptcy, both because bankruptcy procedures are undeveloped and because creditors cannot force firms to shut down by seizing assets. This gives managers too much control and exacerbates the common property problem. Either increasing creditors' rights outside of bankruptcy or instituting a bankruptcy reorganization procedure would reduce managers' incentive to steal or gamble with firms' assets, consequently improving efficiency.

The Decision to Liquidate versus Reorganize Firms in Bankruptcy

While firms that file for bankruptcy are always in financial distress, they may be either economically inefficient or economically efficient. For a firm in financial distress, being economically efficient means that no alternative use of the firm's assets with higher value exists. Being economically inefficient means that some alternative use of the firm's assets has higher value. In the previous example, the firm was economically efficient despite being in financial distress because when it was sold as a going concern under the old manager (US$180), the value of its assets exceeded the liquidated value of its assets sold piecemeal (US$150), or exceeded the liquidated value of its assets when it was sold as a whole under the operation of a new manager (US$170). If the firm were economically inefficient and sold as a going concern under the old manager, the value of its assets would be less than their liquidated value.

Firms that are economically efficient despite being financially distressed often have specialized assets that have no better alternative use. Therefore, to at least temporarily continue operating the firm seems worthwhile, because its revenues exceed its variable costs, even though revenues are less than fixed plus variable costs. It may not be worthwhile to replace the firm's capital when it wears out. A railroad whose tracks would be worth little as scrap steel if they were dismantled presents an example. Economically inefficient firms that should be liquidated include those in industries that have excess capacity, those that use less efficient technology than their competitors, and those that use unspecialized assets (because the assets are valuable in alternative uses).

Bankruptcy procedures aim to liquidate economically inefficient distressed firms and save or reorganize economically efficient distressed firms. Saving rather than shutting down efficient distressed firms preserves their value as a going concern. Saving rather than shutting down inefficient distressed firms prolongs the movement of their assets from less efficient to more efficient.

Classifying financially distressed firms into efficient or inefficient categories, however, proves extremely difficult. This is because classifying firms as efficient or inefficient requires determining how much their assets would be worth if they were employed in their best alternative use—information that cannot be found on firms' balance sheets. Managers cannot adequately judge whether their firms are efficient or inefficient, because they are only familiar with the existing use of the firm's assets. Thus, bankruptcy decides which firms should be liquidated and which should be saved or reorganized. Different countries do this in a number of different ways and additional ways have been proposed.

As soon as a firm files for bankruptcy in a European country, an appointed official either assumes management of the firm or oversees its managers. Generally, the official (or the bankruptcy judge, based on the official's recommendation) decides whether the firm will be reorganized or liquidated. Thus, a neutral expert with specialized training determines whether to liquidate or reorganize firms in bankruptcy. In the United Kingdom, the official—called an insolvency practitioner—is an accountant with specialized training in evaluating failing firms. However, the official's decision does not always depend exclusively on which alternative maximizes the value of the firm's assets. In France the official seeks primarily to save the firm rather than repay creditors. In the United Kingdom, appointment of the official usually follows the partial liquidation of the firm's assets by the floating charge creditor, resulting in little or no possibility of saving the firm.

Another possibility entails routine auction of bankrupt firms. Two advantages come from auctioning bankrupt firms. First, it preserves a firm's value as a going concern in case continuing to operate turns out to be the best use of its assets. Second, it passes the decision of whether to turn bankrupt firms over to the winners of the auction, who because they have their own money at stake are better decisionmakers than either the old managers or bankruptcy professionals.

However, no country practices routine auctioning of bankrupt firms because bankruptcy auctions tend to result in low values and, therefore, low payoffs to creditors. Whether routine use of auctions in bankruptcy causes additional competition in the market for bankrupt firms to develop and values to increase remains unclear. Because of the low valuations, bankruptcy judges tend to prefer bankruptcy reorganizations over bankruptcy liquidations, because reorganizations set artificially high valuations on sustainable firms only because no arm's length sales occur. Furthermore, routine use of auctions may discourage managers from filing for early bankruptcy as they anticipate that the new owner will install a new manager.

Because of the political reluctance to transfer bankrupt firms' assets at low prices to either foreigners or rich insiders, Asian countries would probably reject routine auctioning of firms in bankruptcy.[6]

Separate bankruptcy procedures for liquidation (Chapter 7) and reorganization (Chapter 11) exist in the United States. Managers are allowed to make the initial decision whether to liquidate or reorganize by choosing whether to file under Chapter 7 or Chapter 11. If managers file under Chapter 11, they retain control of the firm under the loose supervision of the bankruptcy court. Eventually, either a reorganization plan must be adopted by a vote of creditors and equity holders or the firm's bankruptcy filing shifts to Chapter 7, resulting in liquidation. Sometimes two years or more elapse before this occurs. Managers prefer reorganization over liquidation of their firms because they retain their jobs during at least the initial stages of the reorganization (see Gilson 1989, 1990; Gilson and Vetsuypens 1993; Hotchkiss 1995) for data on turnover of managers and directors during Chapter 11 reorganizations). Thus, the U.S. procedure for determining the liquidation or reorganization of bankrupt firms makes no pretense of basing the decision on efficiency considerations. Because managers almost always prefer reorganization over liquidation, the U.S. procedure allows too many financially distressed firms to reorganize (see White 1994 for a model). Allowing managers to remain in control while their firms reorganize also encourages managers to file for bankruptcy early, which preserves distressed firms' value as a going concern.

In Japan, Indonesia, and perhaps other Asian countries, governments have bailed out firms in financial distress (see chapter 10 in this volume). This amounts to an inefficient and wasteful policy for several reasons. First, suppose government policy permits bailout of only those firms in the worst financial condition. This gives managers an incentive to worsen their firms'

---

6. See Baird (1986) for a discussion of the possibility of auctioning all firms in Chapter 11. Much of the discussion in the literature concerns the issue of how to accurately value firms that are reorganized, because under Chapter 11 no arm's length transaction occurs. Creditors have an incentive to place a low value on the firm so that equity is eliminated, while equityholders have an incentive to place a high value on the firm so that equity claims remain intact. Roe (1983) proposed selling publicly 10 percent of the shares of firms in Chapter 11 as a means of accurately valuing the remaining shares. Aghion, Hart, and Moore (1992) and Bebchuk (1988) discuss a method of using options to accurately value the firm. In their model, junior creditors have an option to buy the firm by repaying senior creditors' claims in full.

financial condition so that they are more likely to qualify for a bailout. Managers can achieve this by stealing or gambling with the firm's assets, or using the firm's assets to lobby politicians for a bailout.[7] Second, suppose the firm has shut down because new lenders will not lend for working capital until managers and creditors agree on a plan to reorganize existing creditors' claims. Because the firm may receive a government bailout, the existing creditors have an incentive to delay agreeing to a plan, as managers will be willing to pay them more after a bailout. Creditors have an incentive to delay even with a small probability of the firm being bailed out. Thus, the prospect of a bailout delays firms' recovery. Third, bailing out failing firms is expensive because much of the bailout money goes to creditors and does not directly benefit the firm or its workers.

Asian countries must adopt bankruptcy laws and follow them routinely, because such laws constitute a commitment by the government to refrain from intervening in bankruptcy proceedings and from bailing out firms in financial distress. A bankruptcy law that is routinely followed sends a strong signal from the government that creditors and equity holders of firms in financial distress must bear the firms' losses, because the government will not bail them out. If creditors routinely expect that bankruptcies will follow the country's bankruptcy law, the costs just discussed would be avoided.[8]

The recent financial crisis in the Asian countries caused many firms (in some countries most firms) to become insolvent at the same time. The crises had no counterpart in any of the industrial countries, where only a small fraction of firms are insolvent at any one time. During a financial crisis, an unusually high proportion of financially distressed firms is likely to be economically efficient. This is true because in the event that distressed firms' assets are offered for sale, they are unlikely to find new buyers, because not enough potential buyers exist for every distressed firm for sale, and potential buyers cannot obtain bank loans to finance their bids. Moreover, while reductions in demand indicate a temporary excess capacity in many industries, demand is likely to recover quickly, and excess capacity will disappear once the financial crisis passes. These considerations suggest that a higher

---

7. See Aghion, Bolton, and Fries (1999) for a model in the context of bank bailouts.

8. The U.S. government bailout of the Chrysler Corporation is frequently cited as an example of the fact that the U.S. government bails out distressed firms, but this is the only occasion in which a private U.S. firm received a public bailout.

proportion of firms should be reorganized rather than liquidated in bankruptcy during a financial crisis as opposed to normal times. Bankruptcy procedures should, therefore, contain a crisis provision that saves more distressed firms during financial crises.

The legal process of bankruptcy reorganization in the United States and other industrial countries developed a number of features intended to prevent failing firms' assets from being dispersed and to preserve their going-concern value. At least some of these may be relevant for Asian countries that adopt reorganization procedures. As already discussed, once a firm files for bankruptcy, the automatic stay freezes creditors' legal actions against the firm and forces them to collect from the firm through the bankruptcy procedure. In the United States, the automatic stay also includes secured creditors, preventing them from seizing assets essential to firms' operations during the reorganization procedure. Interest payments on unsecured loans are suspended during the reorganization process, thereby increasing a firm's working capital and making it more feasible for the firm to continue operating. However, firms in reorganization must continue to make interest payments to secured creditors. Firms in reorganization possess the right to reject unprofitable contracts while retaining profitable contracts. This allows distressed firms to improve their profitability.[9] In the United States, for at least six months after the bankruptcy filing, the manager holds the exclusive right to offer a reorganization plan, and bankruptcy judges often extend the exclusivity period. Creditors must vote on the manager's plan before they are allowed to offer plans of their own. The right to make a take-it-or-leave-it offer to creditors increases managers' bargaining power, because creditors will accept lower repayment if the alternative is to wait a prolonged period until they are allowed to offer plans of their own. To obtain additional working capital, firms in bankruptcy may offer a lender postbankruptcy priority over all prebankruptcy creditors. Finally, for a reorganization plan to be accepted, creditors need not be in unanimous agreement, effectively blocking minority holdouts from preventing adoption of a plan. Otherwise, holdouts could make reorganization infeasible by demanding full repayment. The U.S. bankruptcy

---

9. Damage payments or penalties for nonperformance of contracts become unsecured claims against the firm, but these usually receive only a low payoff. However, firms that the bankrupt firm maintains contracts with are also allowed to reject contracts (see Che and Schwartz 1999). Weiss' (1990) study of large firms in Chapter 11 bankruptcy finds that nearly all reorganization plans are proposed by managers rather than creditors. See also LoPucki and Whitford (1990).

reorganization procedure even allows the bankruptcy judge to accept a reorganization plan when a majority of creditors in a particular class votes against it, a procedure known as cramdown.[10]

Bankruptcy Issues before Firms Are in Financial Distress

The possibility of financial distress and bankruptcy also affects whether creditors make loans to firms, because creditors' returns depend on the probability of default and on how much creditors receive if default occurs. An efficient bankruptcy policy must take account of its effects on incentives at this early time period.

Consider a model developed by Bolton and Scharfstein (1996). In their model, one or more creditors lend to the firm in period 1, and the firm's manager promises to repay creditors a fixed amount in period 2. In period 2, the firm may have either positive or zero cash flow, but—because cash flow cannot be verified—the manager and creditors cannot contract over a schedule of payments based on cash flow. Managers always default if cash flow is zero ("liquidity default"), and they may also default if cash flow is positive ("strategic default"). If managers default, creditors have the right to initiate a bankruptcy procedure. A market-based bankruptcy procedure follows, in which the firm's assets are offered for sale to the highest bidder, who is either the old manager or a new buyer who would install a new manager. If the default is a liquidity default, the existing manager has no cash, so the new buyer purchases the assets, and the manager is replaced. If the default is strategic, managers have cash and they outbid the buyer for the firm's assets. Bolton and Scharfstein argue that the firm's assets are best put to use when the existing manager continues to run the firm, making a sale of the assets to a new buyer inefficient. Regardless of whether or not the firm defaults in period 2, none of its cash flow in period 3 goes to creditors.

Two sources of inefficiency occur in the model: transferring firms' assets to new managers following default and strategic default, which unnecessarily puts firms into bankruptcy. Bolton and Scharfstein calculate the most efficient contract. It sometimes, though not always, involves putting firms into bankruptcy following default, regardless of whether the default was strategic- or liquidity-based. Putting some firms into

---

10. See Bebchuk and Chang (1992) for a model of bargaining in Chapter 11 reorganization that incorporates several of these features.

bankruptcy following default reduces managers' gain from defaulting strategically; while not putting firms into bankruptcy with certainty following default reduces the efficiency cost of bankruptcy. Under the optimal contract, managers never default strategically, so that creditors' return is higher and lending increases.[11]

The above analysis contains several implications for bankruptcy policy in the Asian countries in crises. First, current bankruptcy policy in these countries gives existing managers enormous power because, even when they default, creditors are unable to collect from the firm by seizing its assets. Bolton and Scharfstein's model shows that favoring managers to this extent is costly, for it encourages managers to default strategically and, therefore, discourages creditors from lending. Second, the model reflects an unrealistic aspect in arguing that the best use of firms' assets is always for existing managers to remain in control. As many firms that default are inefficient and their assets would be more valuable in alternative uses, this assumption becomes unrealistic in normal times. The assumption becomes more realistic for the Asian countries in financial crisis because economic disruption and lack of bank financing means that few buyers would have the money to purchase the assets of firms in bankruptcy.

Applying these considerations to Bolton and Scharfstein's model suggests that an efficient bankruptcy procedure for the Asian crisis countries might involve appointing a professional bankruptcy official to oversee each firm that defaults. The bankruptcy official would be instructed to make a determination as to whether individual firms in bankruptcy fall into any of four classes: (a) strategic default/efficient, (b) liquidity default/efficient, (c) strategic default/inefficient, or (d) liquidity default/inefficient. (Here, efficient versus inefficient refers to whether firms' assets are worth more in their current use or in an alternative use.) Firms in the first class would be put into bankruptcy with a probability between zero and one to penalize managers for strategic default. Firms in the second class would never be put into bankruptcy, because managers did not default strategically and the current use of the firm's assets is efficient. Firms in the third and fourth classes and are inefficient and should be put into bankruptcy in order to allow their assets to be transferred to better use. However, the probability

---

11. The model assumes more efficiency is derived from liquidating all of a firm's assets following default with a low probability than to liquidate some of firm's assets with a higher probability. This is because assets are subject to economies of scale.

of putting these firms into bankruptcy would depend on whether or not the country was in a financial crisis. In the absence of a financial crisis, the probability of bankruptcy would be one. If a financial crisis is taking place, the probability could be as low as zero. This is because, in a financial crisis, few new buyers exist in the market, meaning there is little to be gained from offering firms' assets for sale on the market.

Because a fraction of firms that defaulted strategically would be put into bankruptcy, managers would be deterred from behaving strategically. A fraction of firms whose managers defaulted for liquidity reasons would also be put into bankruptcy, but this would not affect incentives. The fraction of inefficient firms put into bankruptcy following default could be set based on the number of buyers and the amount of their bids at bankruptcy sales, because there would be fewer buyers who would make lower bids in times of financial crisis.

Bankruptcy officials will inevitably make mistakes in determining firm types. For example, if many strategic defaults (by both inefficient and efficient firms) were misclassified as liquidity defaults, there would be a lower probability of bankruptcy following a strategic default, and managers' incentives to default strategically would increase. If the opposite occurred, managers would be strongly deterred from defaulting strategically, but the costs of bankruptcy would be inefficiently high. These distortions, however, could be offset by varying the probability of putting firms into bankruptcy following default.

The law relating to secured credit also affects creditors' incentives to lend. As discussed earlier, having a security interest in a particular asset increases creditors' payoff when default occurs and reduces the probability of default. It therefore increases creditors' expected payoff and makes them more willing to lend.

However, secured credit has offsetting disadvantages. For instance, firms normally have a mixture of secured and unsecured loans. When some creditors are secured, the remaining unsecured creditors receive less following default, because they are repaid from the liquidation value of the assets not subject to security interests. The more secured claims the firm possesses, the fewer assets it has left to repay unsecured claims. This means that creditors are less willing to lend to firms in the form of unsecured loans. Furthermore, when firms are in financial distress, managers have an incentive to use assets not already subject to security interests as security for new loans that can be used to gamble on risky projects that might save the firm. Unsecured creditors cannot prevent this, because their only recourse against the firm involves taking legal action, which is costly and time-consuming.

Thus, if managers try to obtain unsecured loans by promising not to use the firm's assets to obtain secured loans in the future, these promises are noncredible because they are unenforceable. Having a mixture of secured and unsecured loans raises the probability that managers will act in ways that reduce the value of unsecured creditors' claims.[12]

The industrial countries' laws governing security vary in the degree to which they protect the interests of secured creditors. The laws of the United Kingdom strongly protect a single secured creditor (the floating charge creditor), who is allowed to prevent the firm from entering bankruptcy. In the United States, secured creditors can seize assets subject to security interests, regardless of whether or not the firm is in bankruptcy. However, if firms file under Chapter 11 to reorganize in bankruptcy, secured creditors' rights to seize assets are suspended during the reorganization. Instead, they receive cash payments, but these may be less than the value of the assets. Other countries provide less protection for secured creditors. Canada and France subordinate secured creditors' claims to workers' claims for wages and governments' claims for taxes, which are both unsecured. In Germany secured creditors receive only partial repayment of their claims from the sale of the assets subject to security interests, with the remaining amount of the claim being unsecured. Because stronger protection of secured creditors increases creditors' willingness to lend on a secured basis but reduces their willingness to lend on an unsecured basis, and vice versa, a single, economically efficient arrangement may not be possible.

In the Asian countries, providing strong protection for secured creditors may be worthwhile because it allows creditors to avoid the judicial system. As many of crisis countries' courts are corrupt, unsecured creditors have little protection against strategic default by managers. Secured creditors, however, can seize assets subject to security interests without going to court.

Bankruptcy and Entrepreneurial Activity

Another important aspect of bankruptcy relates to its effect on incentives for potential entrepreneurs to start and operate small businesses. In most

---

12. Unsecured claims are often involuntary (such as claims for taxes or tort judgments). Other claims are unsecured because they are too small to justify the cost of registering a secured interest, such as trade credit (see Bebchuk and Fried 1996; White 1989).

countries, small businesses, particularly small startups, are unincorporated. This means that the debts of small businesses are legally obligations of their owners. If a small firm fails, its owner could incur high debts (note that small firms are rarely reorganized in bankruptcy).

Bankruptcy law for individuals and small firms varies widely across countries. In the United States, individuals and married couples who own small firms can file for personal bankruptcy under Chapter 7 and both the firm's debts and the individual's personal debts will be discharged. Individuals do not have to use any of their postbankruptcy earnings to repay their debts, but they must give up all of their nonexempt assets to repay creditors. A key difference between bankruptcy procedures for individuals and for corporations is that individuals who file for bankruptcy are allowed to keep some assets, while corporations that file for bankruptcy are not. Each state in the United States sets exemption levels applicable in bankruptcy and individuals may keep any assets below the relevant exemption. Most states have separate exemptions for home equity (the homestead exemption) and for other types of assets, such as personal property, vehicles, and retirement accounts. Homestead exemptions vary widely, from only a few thousand dollars in some states to unlimited amounts in Florida, Texas, and five other U.S. states. Entrepreneurs in these states can file for bankruptcy if their firms fail and keep an unlimited amount of wealth, as long as the wealth constitutes home equity. Other exemptions are generally much smaller. Other countries' bankruptcy procedures for individuals entail much harsher penalties. Germany disallows discharge of debt in bankruptcy for individuals until many years after the bankruptcy filing, and then only if the individual makes a reasonable effort to repay the debt from postbankruptcy earnings. Therefore, German entrepreneurs whose businesses fail face the obligation to repay their business debts from future earnings. This deters entrepreneurship and prevents individuals from starting a new business if an earlier business failed.

From an economic standpoint, personal bankruptcy can be thought of as providing partial wealth insurance. Individuals have a choice between working for others, which generates a fairly steady stream of earnings and wealth, and starting a business, which generates a stream of earnings and wealth at high risk. Under U.S. bankruptcy law, individuals who choose to be entrepreneurs have partial wealth insurance because, if the business does badly, they can file for bankruptcy and their wealth will increase because their debts will be discharged. The higher the bankruptcy exemption, the greater the partial wealth insurance that bankruptcy provides. Clearly an increase in the bankruptcy exemption level raises the expected utility of running a business relative to working at a job, assuming that potential entrepreneurs are risk averse and that they borrow. By contrast, higher exemption levels reduce lenders' incentive to lend to small businesses, because debtors are more likely to default when the exemption is higher. Therefore, lenders are predicted to ration credit more tightly in states with higher bankruptcy exemptions.

In contrast, bankruptcy law in Germany does not provide any wealth insurance at all, because debts are not discharged in bankruptcy and there is no exemption. This means that, relative to the United States, potential entrepreneurs in Germany are more likely to choose to work for others rather than become self-employed. Lenders in Germany, however, presumably ration credit to small businesses less tightly, because individuals that become entrepreneurs are less likely to default than in the United States. Overall, differences in bankruptcy laws may partly explain why U.S. households are four times more likely to run businesses as households in Germany.[13]

No empirical research explains differences in the levels of entrepreneurial activity internationally. Two recent studies make use of cross-state differences in U.S. states' bankruptcy exemption levels to investigate, first, how bankruptcy laws affect small firms' ability to borrow small-business loans and, second, how bankruptcy laws affect the level of entrepreneurial activity.

In the first study, Berkowitz and White (1999) examine whether owners of small firms are more likely to be turned down for credit when they live in states that have higher bankruptcy exemptions, controlling for other factors. The study uses a dataset of small firms collected by the Federal Reserve Board of Governors that includes both noncorporate and corporate small firms. The dataset controls for the demographic characteristics of owners, firms' size and profitability, and the history of firms' relationships with their main lenders. The findings demonstrate that when noncorporate firms locate in states with unlimited homestead exemptions, rather than average homestead exemptions, their probability of being turned down for business loans rises from 21 percent to 33 percent, and the relationship has statistical significance. Otherwise, similar corporate firms are also more

---

13. The probability of running a business is 8.6 percent for U.S. households and 2.2 percent for German households, according to "Compliant German, Assertive American: Siblings as National Symbols," *New York Times*, Nov. 7, 1999, p. 14. Besides differences in bankruptcy law, other possible reasons for the lower rate of entrepreneurship include Germany's more generous system of support payments for the unemployed.

likely to be turned down for business loans when they locate in states with unlimited rather than average homestead exemptions: the figures are 17 percent versus 45 percent, and the relationship is statistically significant. This suggests lenders see through the corporate veil for small firms, and they recognize that assets can easily be shifted between small firms and their owners, regardless of whether or not the firm is incorporated.

In the second study, Fan and White (2000) use data from three different household surveys to examine whether individuals are more likely to start, run, and shut down small businesses if they live in states with higher bankruptcy exemptions. Households are categorized as running a business if they respond yes to a question asking whether anyone in the household runs a business or if they report having positive earnings from self-employment (farming is excluded). In the regressions, the study controls for household demographics, the predicted amount that the workers in the household could earn if they work at a job, and business cycle factors such as the unemployment level and the rate of growth of income in the individual's state of residence.

In one dataset, the probability of individuals being self-employed rises from about 10 percent if individuals live in states with low bankruptcy exemptions, to 11.5–12 percent if individuals live in states with high or unlimited bankruptcy exemptions. In two other datasets, the figures increase from about 12 percent if individuals live in states with low bankruptcy exemptions, to about 15 percent if individuals live in states with unlimited bankruptcy exemptions. The study also finds evidence that individuals are more likely to start businesses if they live in states with high bankruptcy exemptions. In one dataset, the probability of starting a business rises from about 4.0 percent per year to about 5.1 percent per year if individuals live in states with unlimited rather than low bankruptcy exemptions. In a second dataset, the figure increases from about 2.2 percent to about 3.3 percent. (All these relationships are statistically significant.) The study did not find evidence that the bankruptcy exemption level affects households' probability of shutting down existing businesses.

Overall, the evidence from these two studies suggests that adopting a higher bankruptcy exemption level increases the probability of individuals starting and running small businesses, but handicaps the businesses by reducing their probability of obtaining credit in the form of small-business loans. The results suggest that more attention needs to be paid to the issue of how bankruptcy laws affect levels of entrepreneurial activity internationally.

Conclusion

Bankruptcy law affects economic efficiency not just after firms enter financial distress, but also when potential entrepreneurs are thinking of setting up new businesses and when potential lenders decide whether to extend credit. Thus, bankruptcy law needs to be considered together with other aspects of commercial law, contract law, securities regulation, property law, and legal procedure. Even if potential lenders have identified a profitable investment opportunity in a country with an efficient bankruptcy law, they are unlikely to lend if the local manager can bribe the court to look the other way when the manager defaults on obligations to the foreign lender. With uncertain enforcement of contracts, potential investors or lenders cannot accurately evaluate investment opportunities. This means that less lending and investment occurs, and projects that do go ahead may not be the most efficient ones. Bankruptcy law is just one aspect of the general business environment in a particular country that affects lenders' incentives to lend to firms in that country.

References

Aghion, Philippe, Oliver Hart, and John Moore. 1992. "The Economics of Bankruptcy Reform." *Journal of Law, Economics, and Organization* 8(3): 523–46.

Aghion, Philippe, Patrick Bolton, and Steven Fries. 1999. "Optimal Design of Bank Bailouts: The Case of Transition Economies." *Journal of Institutional and Theoretical Economics* 155(1): 51–70.

Baird, David. 1986. "The Uneasy Case for Corporate Reorganizations." *Journal of Legal Studies* 15(3): 127–47.

Bebchuk, Lucian. 1988. "A New Method for Corporate Reorganization." *Harvard Law Review* 101(2): 775–804.

Bebchuk, Lucian, and H. Chang. 1992. "Bargaining and the Division of Value in Corporate Reorganization." *Journal of Law, Economics, and Organization* 8(2): 253–79.

Bebchuk, Lucian, and Joel M. Fried. 1996. "The Uneasy Case for the Priority of Secured Claims in Bankruptcy." *Yale Law Journal* 105(4): 857–934.

Berkowitz, Jeremy, and Michelle J. White. 1999. "Bankruptcy and Small Firms' Access to Credit." Department of Economics, University of Michigan, Ann Arbor, Michigan. Processed.

Bolton, Patrick, and David Scharfstein. 1996. "Optimal Debt Structure and the Number of Creditors," *Journal of Political Economy* 104(1): 1–25.

Che, Yeon-Koo, and Alan Schwartz. 1999. "Section 365, Mandatory Bankruptcy Rules and Inefficient Continuance." *Journal of Law, Economics, and Organization* 15(2): 441–67.

Fan, Wei, and Michelle J. White. 2000. "Personal Bankruptcy and the Level of Entrepreneurial Activity." Working paper no. 2. Department of Economics, University of Michigan, Ann Arbor, Michigan.

Gilson, Stuart C. 1989. "Management Turnover and Financial Distress." *Journal of Financial Economics* 26(2): 241–62.

_____. 1990. "Bankruptcy, Boards, Banks and Blockholders." *Journal of Financial Economics* 27(2): 355–87.

Gilson, Stuart C., and Michael R. Vetsuypens. 1993. "CEO Compensation in Financially Distressed Firms: An Empirical Analysis." *Journal of Finance* 48(2): 425–58.

Hotchkiss, Edith. 1995. "Postbankruptcy Performance and Management Turnover." *Journal of Finance* 50(1): 3–21.

Jackson, Thomas H. 1986. *The Logic and Limits of Bankruptcy Law*. Cambridge, Massachusetts: Harvard University Press.

Jensen, Michael C., and William Meckling. 1976. "Agency Costs and the Theory of the Firm." *Journal of Financial Economics* 3(4): 305–60.

LoPucki, Lynn. 1983. "The Debtor in Full Control: Systems Failure under Chapter 11 of the Bankruptcy Code?" *American Bankruptcy Law Journal* 57(4): 99–126 (part I), 247–73 (part II).

LoPucki, Lynn, and William Whitford. 1990. "Bargaining over Equity's Share in the Bankruptcy Reorganization of Large, Publicly Held Companies." *University of Pennsylvania Law Review* 139(3): 125–96.

Roe, Mark J. 1983. "Bankruptcy and Debt: A New Model for Corporate Reorganization." *Columbia Law Review* 83(1): 527–602.

Schwartz, Alan. 1997. "Contracting about Bankruptcy." *Journal of Law, Economics, and Organization* 13(1): 127–46.

Stiglitz, Joseph E. 1975. "Some Aspects of the Pure Theory of Corporate Finance: Bankruptcies and Take-Overs." *Bell Journal of Economics* 6(2): 552–79.

Webb, David. 1987. "The Importance of Incomplete Information in Explaining the Existence of Costly Bankruptcy." *Economica* 54(216): 279–88.

_____. 1991. "An Economic Evaluation of Insolvency Procedures in the United Kingdom: Does the 1986 Insolvency Act Satisfy the Creditors' Bargain?" *Oxford Economic Papers, New Series* 43(1): 139–57.

Weiss, Lawrence C. 1990. "Bankruptcy Resolution: Direct Costs and Violation of Priority of Claims." *Journal of Financial Economics* 27(2): 285–314.

White, Michelle J. 1989. "The Corporate Bankruptcy Decision." *Journal of Economic Perspectives* 3(2): 129–51.

_____. 1994. "Corporate Bankruptcy as a Filtering Device: Chapter 11 Reorganizations and Out-of-Court Debt Restructurings." *Journal of Law, Economics, and Organization* 10(2): 268–95

_____. 1996. "The Costs of Corporate Bankruptcy: A U.S.–European Comparison." In J. Bhandari and L. Weiss, eds., *Corporate Bankruptcy: Economic and Legal Perspectives.* Cambridge, U.K.: Cambridge University Press.

3

Systemic Corporate Distress: A Legal Perspective

Jay Lawrence Westbrook, The University of Texas at Austin

With reform of insolvency law a major policy issue in many countries, this volume performs a great service in highlighting the need for attention to the special case of systemic corporate distress; that is, widespread financial difficulties encompassing a large percentage of a country's or region's commercial community.[1] Such distress, traditionally called a recession or depression, relates to the ordinary ups and downs of capitalism like an epidemic resembles ordinary medical practices. Every public health authority understands the need for special medical rules and practices to deal with epidemics, but the need for special insolvency mechanisms invoked to treat widespread financial distress had received scant attention.

While epidemic control starts with a fundamentally sound system of public health, effective management of systemic corporate distress rests

---

1. In North America, the term bankruptcy often describes insolvency proceedings of all kinds, including those applicable to consumers and to businesses and to natural as well as legal persons. Many in the English-speaking world use insolvency to refer to enterprise cases and bankruptcy to refer to cases involving natural persons. Regardless of terminology or the nature of the debtor, the central idea concerns a collective legal proceeding responding to the circumstance of general default, actual or threatened (see, for example, United Nations General Assembly (1997), paragraph 50). Because this chapter addresses financially distressed businesses, it generally uses the term insolvency.

on an existing insolvency regime with well-developed institutions administering appropriate legal rules and practitioners with experience handling more routine commercial cases. This chapter primarily analyzes the key legal elements of insolvency regimes generally, which is a variation on the theme of systemic distress. The chapter then turns to the special issues presented by systemic distress.

The Reform Movement

Although the literature takes relatively little notice, governments around the world continue to ponder insolvency reform, and within the last decade, some have adopted new laws. In 1992 Canada substantially revised its insolvency laws, adding important amendments in 1997. Most Eastern European countries created new insolvency laws after the fall of the Berlin Wall. China, Germany, and Russia have adopted new insolvency laws.[2] Japan's insolvency reform commission has already adopted a new unified corporate reorganization law to replace the previous insolvency reorganization statutes.[3] The United States established a commission to consider extensive changes in its bankruptcy law. Following its report, the U.S. Congress nearly passed important changes last year, including the United Nations Commission of International Trade Law's Model Law on Cross-Border Insolvency.[4] The United Kingdom is actively considering further changes in its Insolvency Act, Mexico has passed a new insolvency statute in one house of its congress, New Zealand is studying new legislation, and the European Union is on the verge of adopting as a regulation its Cross-Border Insolvency Convention.

This wave of worldwide reform reflects the age of most insolvency laws in industrial and developing countries. Until the 1980s, few insolvency laws underwent substantial revision in this century. Even the Great Depression produced only changes in detail in most countries, or the addition of emergency measures, but not complete recodifications.

The globalization of enterprise and finance has increased the potential volatility of economic affairs even as it has enhanced wealth. Massive flows

---

2. For information on Germany, see "Insolvenzordnung" (Insolvency Law), art. 102, reprinted in *Gesetzesbeschluß des Deutschen Bundestages*, Drucksache 12/2443, April 21, 1994. Also see Balz (1997); Kamlah (1996).

3. Minjisaiseiho (Civil Rehabilitation Law), Law No. 225 of 1999.

4. The proposed legislation contained important changes to business bankruptcy provisions, although its most controversial provisions were on the consumer side.

of capital, often seeming to move in or out of regions or industries with irrational exuberance or panic, exaggerate the effects of economic change. Rapid and severe change sometimes makes otherwise healthy businesses subject to financial distress. Accelerated change can ravage a particular industry or corporate group, or it can create wider systemic corporate distress in a country or region. A globalizing economy requires a constant reshuffling and readaptation of economic enterprises. When those changes bring financial distress, as they often do, insolvency reorganization becomes the natural tool of economic repair.

"Degovernmentalization," a worldwide phenomenon closely related to globalization, describes the combination of deregulation and privatization, trends that have dominated governments' policies around the world for the last two decades. Most countries' policies in the 1930s emphasized regulation and nationalization to prevent a general default by an economic enterprise, a fact that is sometimes used to explain the reason the Great Depression produced revision, but not fundamental reform of most insolvency laws. When those policies were reversed in favor of market controls, it became necessary to adopt modern insolvency laws to manage the inevitable defaults in a system based on competition and risk.

The so-called stranger syndrome, which is particularly relevant to the recent emphasis on reorganization or rescue in insolvency reform, has also emerged in the globalizing economy. When economies were dominated by relatively small groups of people, often of the same background and social class, reorganization of a troubled but viable enterprise was possible on a relatively informal basis. Even if official intervention proved necessary (as with the London approach), the commonalties among the relevant people often made possible a consensual adjustment without the need for extensive formal proceedings. As economies have joined to create a global market, for finance and management as well as trade, informal accords have become far more difficult to achieve. Reorganizing a company whose equity and debt holders represent investors and institutions from many different worldwide commercial cultures appears more difficult. Because of the lack of common conventions and shared understandings, reorganization often requires a more formal and more rule-bound approach. That context also leads to an emphasis on notice, participation, and transparency. The U.S. Chapter 11 mechanism received such attention in reform discussions because it provides that sort of rule-bound, participatory approach, because it was developed in a continental economy lacking a single, cohesive commercial class.

Finally, in a number of countries, notably the United States, economic growth rests increasingly on massive corporate borrowing. The growing importance of debt in corporate financial structures naturally and properly leads to a greater concern with insolvency laws as mechanisms of adjustment.

Elements of Reform

This global laboratory of reform experiments, many of them based on the lessons learned from prior periods of economic difficulty, begins to produce certain elements commonly understood as central to an effective insolvency system. The following are the major elements of recent reforms:

- Emphasizing reorganization or rescue rather than liquidation
- Reducing priorities, except for those favoring workers and secured creditors
- Including secured creditors in the insolvency process, especially in reorganization
- Providing for cooperation in transnational cases.

However, two areas of great importance have been neglected, namely:

- Institutional reform
- Reform of related areas of law and administration.

Reorganization

The emphasis on reorganization constitutes the most striking aspect of worldwide reform.[5] The new German law, whose centerpiece entails modernizing the reorganization mechanism, imposes a decision period at the start of every proceeding to determine whether to liquidate or attempt to reorganize the business (Balz 1997; Kamlah 1996). Although based squarely and explicitly on U.S. Chapter 11, the German law differs distinctly in choices on many specific issues. The extensive Japanese reform program

---

5. See, for instance, Kamlah (1996). Once again, there are variations in terminology. Reorganization refers to a process by which a business activity continues as a going concern, in whole or significant part, rather than the assets being sold either piecemeal or as an assets-only package. It may or may not mean that the business organization—the company—continues. Rescue, restructuring, and rehabilitation signify other common terms in English. These procedures relate to the traditional legal procedure of composition. In Spanish, traditional procedures of this sort are often called *suspension de pagos* and in French *regalment*.

passed a new reorganization statute without waiting for the development of the remainder of the reform proposals. Most of the Japanese reforms and reform proposals place similar emphasis on reorganization.

As noted earlier, reorganization becomes central because the global economy puts otherwise healthy businesses at risk for financial distress. If that is true, the well-known fact that liquidation tends to destroy value means that a large amount of value might be destroyed unnecessarily without a mechanism for enabling viable businesses to weather an externally triggered storm. Reorganization would result in some group of beneficiaries retaining substantially greater value. Obviously, this point is closely related to the emerging concern with systemic distress.

In a number of countries, reorganization reform also reflects a new preoccupation with the role of entrepreneurs in economic growth. Although reorganization does not necessarily benefit entrepreneurs and their equity investors, it can have that purpose and effect. Those countries encouraging start-up companies and promoting entrepreneurial activity have seen reorganization as part of that program.

Priorities

In many countries, after the claims of priority creditors have been satisfied in an insolvency proceeding, little remains for distribution to general unsecured creditors. Consequently, a movement has arisen to reduce or eliminate priorities and return to the traditional insolvency ideal, equality of distribution. In recent years, notable examples include the new Australian, Canadian, and German statutes. In those statutes and in a number of reform proposals, however, the priorities accorded secured creditors and employees remain in place.

Inclusion of Secured Creditors

While the distribution priority of secured creditors has been preserved, a strong trend subjects those creditors to the insolvency process, especially in reorganization proceedings (IMF 1999). The inclusion of creditors reflects a realization that reorganization rarely occurs without the cooperation of secured creditors, and that compelling such cooperation often becomes necessary. Imposition of the insolvency stay or moratorium on secured and unsecured creditors' enforcement rights constitutes the most common mechanism for including creditors, making the claims of secured creditors a part of the overall reorganization plan.

Internationalization

Multinational enterprise leads necessarily to multinational default. United Nations Commission of International Trade Law has now promulgated a widely supported Model Law on Cross-Border Insolvency that is being seriously considered in a number of jurisdictions.[6] Even prior to the Model Law, several countries adopted special provisions for cross-border cooperation.[7] Most future reform legislation will likely contain such provisions.

Institutional Reform

By contrast, two other elements of reform—institutional and related areas of law and administration—remain largely ignored. This neglect partly results from the fact that much reform has occurred in industrial economies where the necessary institutions and related legal regimes already exist. Those countries saw less need for reform in these two areas, possibly causing reformers in other countries, where institutional reform and reform of related areas is still greatly needed, to misconstrue the lack of emphasis on institutional reform in the reforms adopted by developed countries.

Administration of insolvency laws requires strong, independent institutions. Insolvency, especially of large enterprises, can create enormous political ramifications and invite political intervention in individual cases. While political decisions necessarily and properly govern the macroeconomic directions of an economy, experience shows that political intervention in individual enterprises produces inefficiency and corruption (Lam and Kan 1999).[8] Creation of an independent mechanism to manage financial distress, with overall policy choices in place, lends the insolvency process a perception of fairness and economic efficiency, as well as other societal values. Only an administration in which the administrators (typically judges) receive reasonable compensation and remain insulated from political pressures can achieve those results.

---

6. It passed both houses of Congress in the United States at different times and passed the Senate in Mexico. It reportedly has been incorporated, in principle, into the new Japanese reorganization statute and is under active consideration in the legislatures of a number of other countries.

7. Australia: §29, Insolvency Act (1966); Germany: Insolvenzordnung §102; United Kingdom: §426 Insolvency Act (1986); United States: 11 U.S.C. §304 (1994).

8. China serves as an example of a country with excessive executive involvement and too little judicial independence.

Institutional independence alone is insufficient. Administrators must also be competent. Competence entails not only legal competence, but also some combination of academic and practical knowledge of business affairs. If the judges in a particular system lack business competence, other competent officials—trustees or consultants—must be included in the process, or the system must rely on creditors and other interested parties to make the necessary economic judgments. Competence comes from the employment of qualified people with the requisite educational and specialized credentials. Although extremely important, these attributes often receive scant attention. Educational programs frequently make more difference in the actual function of a legal system than the incentives and disincentives so carefully included in the law itself.[9] Specialization has two benefits: it enables educational programs to be targeted efficiently and, equally important, enables the various actors in a system (judges, administrators, lawyers, and others) to become repeat players, gaining both experience and mutual confidence over time. Where specialization appears too expensive because of the limited number of insolvency cases in good times, it can be limited to a portion of the system to be used in normal times to provide a cadre of experienced officials in times of systemic distress; for example, specialized panels of judges residing only in a country's largest city. These judges could handle commercial cases generally, taking charge of all insolvency cases and developing sustained expertise.[10]

Related Laws

Insolvency laws do not exist in isolation. On the contrary, reforms of an insolvency code may be useless if unaccompanied by necessary changes in related areas of the law and public administration. There are many such areas, but the most important are individual debt collection, bank regulation, and taxation.

Of these three, individual debt collection ranks the highest in importance. Many falsely view insolvency law as the simplest and best solution to the problem of a nonpayment commercial culture. For a variety of reasons,

---

9. A notable example was the dramatic increase in payout plans for individual bankruptcies under Chapter 13 of the U.S. Bankruptcy Code, an increase that probably resulted much more from educational programs than from the reforms that gave rise to the programs (see Sullivan, Warren, and Westbrook 1994).

10. Both Canada and Mexico have insolvency specialization in Toronto and Mexico City, respectively.

insolvency law alone is an inefficient method of debt collection. Insolvency laws provide a collective procedure, meaning that it is rarely in the interest of any one creditor to undertake the expense and risk of initiating such proceedings when that creditor will be only one of many beneficiaries (a collective action, free-rider problem). To solve that problem by establishing an easy standard for an involuntary proceeding creates a more serious problem: extortionate power in creditors and the risk of a great loss of value for all concerned because of the irresponsible actions of a single creditor.

The second key point is that the debtor ordinarily has much more information about its financial state than any creditor. Therefore, the debtor occupies a much better position in determining the need for an insolvency proceeding. However, the debtor possesses substantial disincentives for acting on that information even when creditors and other interested parties would be best served by an insolvency proceeding. Because of lack of information, creditors are seriously handicapped in making an accurate determination about the value of initiating an insolvency. They are likely to do so too soon or too late.

Hence, an effective system of debt collection becomes the best method for initiating appropriate insolvency and avoiding it when inappropriate. Such a system must embrace enforcement of both secured and unsecured debts. The former permits the seizure of collateral in the first instance, whether by self-help or judicial action, while the second normally provides summary methods for ascertaining liability for indisputable debts and then a process of asset seizure and sale for satisfaction of the debts. While both systems must provide for reasonable protection of debtors against improper demands, they should permit an efficient and cost-effective method of seizing assets. If they do, debtors will pay debts rather than seek insolvency when they find themselves in or near general default and, when in default, will initiate insolvency proceedings. If, by contrast, a legal system permits, through inefficiency or corruption, long periods of delay in individual debt collection, no insolvency system is likely to work effectively because of the problems associated with initiation. As discussed later, this point becomes even more important in the context of reorganization than of liquidation.

The scope of this chapter prevents a discussion of bank regulation and taxation policy as they relate to insolvency laws. It is important, however, to emphasize the interrelatedness of these legal regimes. For example, a regulatory scheme that requires a complete write-off of a debtor's loans upon insolvency may leave a bank lender little incentive to cooperate in a resolution. However, if regulations require a partial write-off, the bank may more easily accept reduction of debt in a plan of repayment by the amount the debt has been written off already. The issue of taxation provides an important example in the forgiveness of indebtedness income in a country with an income tax on corporations. If debt forgiveness (the reduction of debt under a reorganization plan) is treated as income, which it certainly is in economic terms, and payment of tax on that income is required in the usual way, the chances for reorganization in that jurisdiction become greatly reduced. Retrospective income is by definition far removed from the cash to pay the related tax, especially in the case of an insolvent taxpayer. By contrast, corporate tax law aids reorganization. If, for example, the tax law permits tax-free exchange of debt and equity, such exchanges become far more useful tools in the restructuring process.

Policy Choices

Insolvency cuts across many areas of law and policy, so no standard model will be satisfactory for every society. Each jurisdiction must make a series of policy choices about an insolvency code. Although some frequently make sweeping statements about the best approach to insolvency, there are remarkably few data to support any of them.[11] Thus, the policy choices to be made are largely a function of normative views about preferred outcomes, without a clear idea of the best methods of achieving those outcomes. Notwithstanding the shortage of data, experience provides a rough sense of the choices to be made. A report of the International Monetary Fund offers a good general discussion of policy choices (IMF 1999), but a brief summary seems appropriate here.

General agreement exists on the central purposes of insolvency law: maximizing asset values, providing equality of treatment for creditors and other parties with similar legal rights, preventing and undoing fraud, and providing commercially predictable results and transparent legal procedures. From a macroeconomic viewpoint, recapitalization of assets that are unproductively frozen by a surrounding mass of illiquid liabilities becomes the goal in each instance. Some systems recapitalize by selling the assets or the going-concern business to a buyer with the necessary capital to redeploy them, while others emphasize recapitalizing the existing business by debt reduction and refinancing. Endless variations apply to each approach, and many systems allow for either approach in particular cases. The key

---

11. Studies in the United States begin to provide some empirical data, see for example LoPucki and Whitford (1990, 1993).

point is that assets—tangible, intangible, and organizational—are separated from liabilities and thus become productive.

However, much more divergence resides in other policy choices, the three most important being the choice of beneficiaries of the insolvency process, the means of managing the insolvent business and the accompanying proceeding, and the need for early initiation.

QUI BONO? No clear, universal consensus exists for the proper beneficiaries of whatever value-maximizing results may be obtainable. The problem of priorities discussed earlier reflects the great variation in choice of beneficiaries, even in liquidation cases (IMF 1999, pp. 18–19). Reorganization proceedings present an even more profound and yet more subtle problem. Insolvency discussions often refer only to creditors as interested parties, yet on examination virtually every system reveals a complex configuration of beneficiaries.

A key question in reorganization procedures concerns whether the debtor interests (management and equity holders) possess a legitimate stake in any insolvency case and, if so, whether that interest persists if the company is by some measure insolvent. The question is often framed as "Do we want to save the business or the company?" If the business can be sold or continued as a going concern, who should get the resulting value? In some societies, it seems self-evident that any value, up to the exceedingly rare payment of 100 percent with interest, should go to creditors, and that the debtor interests have no claim. In others, it is axiomatic that the owners, management, employees, and other parties possess important interests, and that all interested parties should share in the losses and gains of the bankruptcy process.[12] As noted earlier, some countries deeply commit themselves to encouraging entrepreneurs and the venture capitalists who support them. Those countries are more likely to favor including debtor interests as beneficiaries. The United Kingdom traditionally represents the creditors only, and the United States takes a mixed view between creditors and debtors.[13]

Even a consensus that creditors should be the primary or exclusive beneficiaries of insolvency proceedings ignores the crucial distinctions among

---

12. Some of the debate in the United States is nicely captured in several articles (see Baird 1987; Warren 1987).

13. Note that both these countries, routinely cited as poles apart on this question, comprise common law jurisdictions, demonstrating that this legal heritage is not dispositive of policy choices in debtor-creditor law. Of course, the same is true for antitrust policy and a number of other legal fields.

creditors. Secured and other priority creditors often have interests different from each other and different from general unsecured creditors. In most countries, the latter routinely recover little or nothing in liquidations,[14] so they often support a reorganization in the hope that it may provide them some meaningful recovery of their investment. There are also divisions among general creditors. For example, suppliers (trade creditors) may be more concerned with future business from a revitalized enterprise, while bondholders want only to be paid as much as possible as soon as possible.

MANAGEMENT OF THE INSOLVENT COMPANY. The management issue often becomes blurred with the debate about the right of debtor interests to benefit from a reorganization. The management issue contains elements in common with that debate,[15] but it remains quite distinct. One obvious difference is that management might be left in control even if equity interests receive nothing. The best approach to managing the struggling enterprise reflects the central policy point. Whoever might benefit from a reorganization, someone has to attempt it. The choices seem to be the existing management, a trustee, existing management plus a trustee, or the creditors and a trustee. Of course, these are all points on a smooth continuum of possible approaches.[16]

The United States and a number of other countries use a Debtor in Possession concept. Existing management is retained, generally with a good deal of court control and supervision, at least in theory. The United States Chapter 11 differs from most of these regimes, however, in that most other laws have fairly rigid time limits for approving a plan and often strict minimum-payment requirements.[17] Other countries prefer management by a court-appointed trustee or by a trustee controlled by creditors. Canada has adopted a hybrid system, with a trustee combining with existing management.

To oversimplify grossly, the debate centers on which of two mistakes to make: to put a desperately struggling company under a new,

---

14. There seems to be a consensus on this point, although few data are available, see for instance Balz 1997; Herbert and Pacitti 1988.

15. For example, preexisting management and ownership remaining in place may better serve the interests of a local community.

16. There is a further alternative—reorganization by secured creditor. Although many conceive of the debenture-receiver system in the United Kingdom and elsewhere as a liquidation device, it could serve to reorganize as well.

17. The old German law, copied in many countries, remains exemplary (see Kamlah 1993).

unknowledgeable management often viewed with suspicion and hostility by existing employees or to leave the fox (or the lout) in charge of the hen house.

EARLY INITIATION. Experts nearly unanimously agree on early initiation as an important goal in any insolvency system. The problem arises from the conjunction of two facts: information asymmetry and debtor resistance to insolvency proceedings. Debtors have far greater information about their financial affairs than creditors, even large, secured creditors. Debtors thus occupy a far better position to judge the necessity or appropriateness of an insolvency filing. However, debtors have substantial disincentives to initiate such a proceeding, largely because of the potential for loss of control and loss of value, in addition to admission of failure. Businesses therefore often do not file insolvency petitions until little value remains to sustain reorganization or distribute in liquidation (IMF 1999, pp. 21–25, 53–56; LoPucki 1982). Thus, every modern insolvency system must include incentives or sanctions to promote earlier initiation by debtors.

The carrot and stick approaches are used to promote early initiation by debtors. In the United States and many other countries, the debtor in possession concept encourages management to file because they then assume control, and the shareholders receive at least a hope of salvaging their investment. The United Kingdom, among many other nations, favors the stick approach, in which devices like the rules on fraudulent trading attempt to force debtors to file bankruptcy promptly to avoid personal responsibility of officers and directors.

The use of incentives or sanctions relates to beneficiary and management issues, but constitutes a different question. For example, a system could leave management in control, but deny any benefit to owners. Conversely, a system could provide an incentive to owners to demand insolvency filings by offering the hope of some recovery of equity, albeit at the price of accepting outside management. By contrast, a system that denies both benefit and control to debtor interests may be compelled to use sanctions to encourage earlier initiation.

Special Rules for Systemic Distress

Every reason exists to believe that systemic distress—at its worst, distress like the Great Depression—changes the context of insolvency in a variety of important ways. For example, in normal times a business's financial distress frequently results from poor management. When businesses generally have been stricken by a widespread collapse, many competent managers will be caught in the wreckage. In ordinary times, a reasonable assumption (pending data) is that most businesses filing for bankruptcy should be liquidated, because they are likely to be worth little as going concerns, and liquidation value is probably the most that can be obtained for them. In the midst of systemic distress, however, those assumptions often prove wrong, because the collapse of the relevant markets, and the presence of panic in those markets, make obtaining any real return from liquidation difficult.

In addition, systemic corporate distress creates social and political imperatives that must often override other considerations. The need to restore economic and social order quickly and reassure populations about their economic systems may require necessary short-term measures even though they appear inefficient in more normal circumstances.[18]

Until recently, this problem received minimal study. Any serious approach requires an examination of historical examples and the contemporary evidence, especially in East Asia. This chapter can only offer some initial thoughts and proposals for a research agenda.

From a legal perspective, the two main questions concern (a) how to fashion a trigger for special insolvency rules, and (b) how those rules should change the normal insolvency procedures. The answer to the first question requires a nice balance between objectivity and an avoidance of predictability. Special rules must be beyond the power of short-term abuse for the benefit of some badly managed enterprises. That goal suggests some objective standard; for example, when insolvencies exceed a certain level based on historical experience, such as a stated percentage of incorporated businesses or of listed companies. At the same time, the existence of a set line may encourage strategic behavior at the margins. For example, creditors might rush to close businesses as the "special rules" margin approaches, hoping to avoid the rule change, thereby exacerbating the problem.[19] Incorporating enough discretion at the margin to make short-term predictability difficult represents one way to ameliorate that problem. Some political distance could still be maintained by giving limited discretion to a central bank or other institution with some institutional independence.

The most important special rule to be implemented in a period of systemic distress may be to increase delay. Normally, delay is all too available in any legal system, and indeed, represents one of its greatest failings, but where liquidity constitutes the central problem, along with

---

18. On proposals for emergency measures, see chapter 1 in this volume

19. Ordinarily legal scholars assume that predictability is a fundamental value in commercial law. This example illustrates one exception to that rule.

markets in disarray, delay may be just what is needed. However, excessive delay may leave financial institutions unable to resolve their balance sheets and, therefore, incapable of resuming normal funding, which is necessary for the resumption of normal economic activity. Perhaps the usual requirement that insolvency should practice a live off the land approach, that is, pay for its expenses from the assets of insolvents, should be modified to permit public expenditures on a large, expedited triage effort, so that hopeless cases can be identified and mercifully terminated, while the benefit of the doubt is given to the rest. As with any physical disaster, this funding might permit the introduction of outside experts (typically, accountants) to augment the ranks of local experts during a crisis. The usual time limits for proposing reorganization plans or terminating enforcement moratoria might be extended or suspended. There might also be a special category of core companies that would be prevented from being liquidated, and might even be nationalized or subsidized until containment of the crisis. The policy need not be "too big to fail," but rather "too big to fail quickly." If the law is structured so that the equity owners and creditors nonetheless find themselves involuntarily closed down or bought out by the government or a court-selected purchaser, moral hazard concerns ex ante would be minimized.

Cross-Disciplinary Research

Some useful work is currently being done (Claessens, Djankov, and Klapper 1999; La Porta and others 1998; see also chapters 1 and 10 in this volume), but a major research effort is necessary, precisely because so little work has been devoted to systemic distress. Relevant studies available from the Great Depression should be explored, but, even more important, contemporary data should be examined. Researchers must keep in mind two divergent thoughts: economic activity demonstrates recurring themes over the past several hundred years, and modern conditions are in some ways unique.

Most important, future research must be cross-disciplinary. It remains insufficient that people from many disciplines work on these problems; the problems must be addressed by multidisciplinary teams. Experts in one area cannot fully understand data from other fields, nor can they keep abreast of rapidly developing knowledge in related areas. Only experts working closely together and examining each other's analyses can achieve the necessary results. Insolvency studies in the United States offer a good example of the results when this sort of cooperation is lacking. The finance and economic journals, on the one hand, and the law reviews, on the other, abound with theories and data about insolvency questions, but these articles almost entirely ignore the findings and theories from the other side of the academic divide. The parable of the blind men and the elephant seems all too apt.

Some interesting recent work in the international field illustrates the kind of necessary creativity, but also makes apparent the pitfalls of doing the work without a cross-disciplinary team. This work links legal systems to economic performance. It necessarily relies on accurate characterizations of the key legal points. Although this work represents a good start, accurate characterization of the functioning of a particular legal system as to a particular economic phenomenon remains a difficult process, requiring the functional approach to comparative law now emerging in the legal literature (for surveys and critiques of developments in the field see Curran 1998). Among other things, that approach includes a substantial empirical component focusing not merely on what the law in a jurisdiction says, but on the actual results observed in the legal system.

The analysis in one interesting paper describes variation among debtor-creditor laws by legal families, identified as the English, the German, and the French (La Porta and others 1997; La Porta and others 1998, table 3). These categories reflect the traditional comparative literature, but even traditionalists warn that they are general and mask a host of jurisdiction-specific variations. More functionally-oriented comparativists assert that these categories are too broad and vague in context to be useful for most purposes.

That Dutch law is characterized as part of the French family illustrates the difficulties even from a traditional perspective. Although that is a traditional characterization of Dutch law as a whole, Dutch law clearly embodies a dynamic combination of French and German law, with a distinct leavening of pre-Enlightenment local doctrine, especially in the commercial section (Blankenburg 1998; Chorus and others 1993; Koopmans 1996). Indonesian law, also characterized in the referenced paper as part of the French family, derives directly, with few changes, from Dutch law (Wessels 1999).

Similarly, the paper describes Spanish, Philippine, and most Latin American law as being part of the French family. Spanish law derives from French law,[20] but in the bankruptcy field the *suspension de pagos* first appeared in the Code of 1885, before France adopted a much weaker composition law.

---

20. However, Portuguese, Spanish, and most Latin American bankruptcy laws may make up a special circle, distinct from other French-derived systems.

The *suspensión de pagos* procedure subsequently spread throughout Latin America, where today it remains a primary barrier to effective debt collection in Mexico and other Latin American countries. In key respects, it is not at all clear that Spanish and Latin American bankruptcy laws can be usefully included in a French family of laws.

Based on evidence presented by experts on both sides in a recent judicial proceeding in the United States, Philippine law is a combination of U.S. and Spanish law, the latter contributing the *suspensión de pagos* with a number of U.S.–influenced modifications. Thus, the French element seems attenuated if it exists at all.

These examples illustrate that identification of legal families can be a tricky business. Because traditional categories are too broad and are based more on historical and conceptual factors than functional ones, these difficulties appear pervasive. At a minimum, however, they retain importance in the bankruptcy and debtor-creditor field.

The problems inherent in the use of legal families as a unit of analysis are not unique. Other characterizations of legal rules and regimes remain problematic. Another example concerns characterization of countries as debtor-friendly or creditor-friendly. Although the recent literature contains some commendable efforts to characterize legal regimes as procreditor or prodebtor, this work is very new and fraught with difficulties. For instance, these characterizations often ignore the distinction between secured and unsecured creditors. Those distinctions are always important, but their importance may be emphasized in situations in which the division between secured and unsecured creditors roughly coincides with that between domestic and foreign creditor groups, while underlining the risk that differences in treatment may be influenced by parochial considerations.

Many analogous difficulties hamper the legal work in the field, with concepts from finance and economics too rarely reflecting the nuances of expert understanding and too often lagging behind the latest work. The pervasive difficulties suggest the use of cross-disciplinary teams. Yet academic customs and norms often discourage such work, in practice if not in theory.[21] The Bank could perhaps make a real contribution in that regard by providing a context in which such work could be done.

---

21. The author of this chapter has done a good deal of cross-disciplinary empirical work in bankruptcy and can certify to the numerous academic and institutional barriers to such work.

References

Baird, Douglas G. 1987. "Loss Distribution, Forum Shopping, and Bankruptcy: A Reply to Warren." *University of Chicago Law Review* 54(2): 815–34.

Balz, Manfred. 1997. "Market Conformity of Insolvency Proceedings: Policy Issues of the German Insolvency Law." *Brooklyn Journal of International Law* 23(1): 167–79.

Blankenburg, Erhard. 1998. "Patterns of Legal Culture: The Netherlands Compared to Neighboring Germany." *American Journal of Comparative Law* 46(1): 1–41.

House of Commons. 1986. *Insolvency Act*. London.

Chorus, J. M. J., P. H. M. Gerver, E. H. Hondius, and A. K. Koekkoek. 1993. *Introduction to Dutch Law for Foreign Lawyers*. Amsterdam: Elsevier.

Claessens, Stijn, Simeon Djankov, and Leora Klapper. 1999. *Resolution of Corporate Distress: Evidence from East Asia's Financial Crisis*. Policy Research Working Paper no. 2133. World Bank, Washington, D.C.

Curran, Vivian. 1998. "Cultural Immersion, Difference, and Categories in U.S. Comparative Law." *American Journal of Comparative Law* 46(1): 43–92.

Herbert, Michael, and Dominic Pacitti. 1988. "Down and Out in Richmond, Virginia: The Distribution of Assets in Chapter 7 Bankruptcy Proceedings Closed in 1984–1987." *Richmond Law Review* 22(1): 303–23.

IMF (International Monetary Fund). 1999. *Orderly and Effective Insolvency Procedural Principles: Key Issues*. Washington, D.C.

Kamlah, Klang. 1993. "Vergleichsverfahren: A German Reorganization Procedure." In Harry Rajak, ed., *Insolvency Law and Practice*. London, United Kingdom: Oxford University Press.

———. 1996. "The New German Insolvency Act: Insolvenzordnung." *The American Bankruptcy Law Journal* 70(3): 417–35.

Koopmans, Thijmen. 1996. "Comparative Law and the Courts." *The International Comparative Law Quarterly* 45(7): 545–56.

Lam, Joseph, and Carmen Kan. 1999. "Rules and Regulations on Insolvency and Restructuring in China." *Journal of International Banking Law* 14(11): 351–59.

La Porta, R., F. Lopez-de-Silanes, A. Shleifer, and R. W. Vishny. 1997. "Legal Determinants of External Finance." *Journal of Finance* 52(3): 1131–50.

_____. 1998. "Law and Finance" *Journal of Political Economy* 106(6): 1113–55.

LoPucki, Lynn. 1982. "A General Theory of the Dynamics of the State Remedies/Bankruptcy System." *Wisconsin Law Review* 26(1): 311–72.

LoPucki, Lynn, and William Whitford. 1990. "Bargaining over Equity's Share in the Bankruptcy Reorganization of Large, Publicly Held Companies." *University of Pennsylvania Law Review* 139(3): 125–96.

_____. 1993. "Corporate Governance in the Bankruptcy Reorganization of Large, Publicly Held Companies." *University of Pennsylvania Law Review* 141(1): 669–800.

Sullivan, Teresa A., Elizabeth Warren, and Jay L. Westbrook. 1994. "The Persistence of Local Legal Culture: Twenty Years of Evidence From the Federal Bankruptcy Courts." *Harvard Journal of Law and Public Policy* 17(2): 801–65.

United Nations General Assembly. 1997. *Guide to Enactment of the UNCITRAL Model Law on Cross-Border Insolvency.* Document No. A/CN.9/442. New York.

Warren, Elizabeth. 1987. "Bankruptcy Policy." *University of Chicago Law Review* 54(2): 775–814.

Wessels, Bob. 1999. "New Indonesian Bankruptcy Law, International Report." *International Bar Association*, Washington, D.C. Processed.

4

Creditor Protection and Bankruptcy Law Reform

Rafael La Porta and Florencio Lopez-de-Silanes, Harvard University

Recent research on corporate governance documents large differences in the breadth and depth of debt markets and in firms' access to credit in various countries. This chapter suggests that part of these differences can be explained by how well creditors are protected by law from expropriation by firms' managers and controlling shareholders. The chapter describes the differences in bankruptcy laws and the effectiveness of their enforcement across a sample of 49 countries, summarizes the consequences of these differences, and advances potential strategies for bankruptcy law reform. It further analyzes some of the recent failed reform attempts and suggests a more viable option to reform bankruptcy law that relies on a market-run procedure using auctions. This option may be particularly appropriate in countries with weak judicial systems.

The recent turmoil in international financial markets, starting in Thailand, spreading throughout East Asia and Latin America to reach even Brazil and Russia, reveals some key differences about access to credit around the world. While countries such as South Africa and the United Kingdom have broad markets for private and public debt, other countries such as Colombia and the Philippines have very narrow debt markets relative to their national economies. These differences also exist among industrial nations. For instance, debt markets are small in Belgium and Italy but large in Germany and Japan. This chapter shows that creditor protection, measured by the effective rights afforded to creditors through bankruptcy laws and their enforcement, explains these differences across countries.

When creditors finance firms, they face a risk that the returns on their investments may never materialize because the controlling shareholders or managers simply keep them and default on debt contracts. Extensive expropriation severely undermines the effectiveness of a financial system. When potential investors expect the insiders to expropriate their investment, investors do not finance firms through either debt or equity, making it difficult or impossible for entrepreneurs to fund even the most attractive investment projects.

Protection of creditors through the legal system constitutes the most effective way to limit expropriation. Creditors finance firms to a significant extent because their rights are protected by the law. However, as argued in La Porta and others (1997, 1998, forthcoming), legal rules and the effectiveness of their enforcement shape these rights. When reorganization and creditors' liquidation rights are extensive and well enforced by regulators or courts, creditors will finance firms. When the rules and their enforcement do not protect investors, corporate governance and external finance fail to work. Effective bankruptcy procedures may also be essential to allow banks to exercise their creditor rights appropriately. Furthermore, in a corporate debt crisis, the inability to repossess collateral may trigger a cascade effect of debtor defaults, deepening the economic crisis.

The beginning of this chapter demonstrates that to have large debt markets, countries must provide creditors with rights and the enforcement mechanism to exercise those rights. The chapter then argues that the consequences of poor creditor protection may extend beyond the size and breath of capital markets and affect the real economy through lower growth rates and higher likelihood of severe recessions.

These results raise an important policy question: how can countries develop an efficient bankruptcy procedure when the current options are not working? This chapter addresses that question by proposing, that emerging markets in particular move away from court-intensive bankruptcy procedures and adopt market-based bankruptcy/reorganization processes similar to those outlined in Hart and others (1997). Market-based processes reduce the role of discretionary decisions throughout a protracted judicial procedure and yield fair outcomes. The chapter concludes with some thoughts on the importance of improving creditor rights and their enforcement, particularly following a corporate debt crisis.

Content of Bankruptcy Laws around the World

In theory, a good bankruptcy procedure strikes a balance between reorganization and liquidation and meets the other criteria outlined earlier. What would be a reasonable checklist for measuring the strength of creditors' rights when examining an existing law? Such a checklist would benefit policymakers trying to define a code of best practice in creditors' rights if such rights can be shown to result in larger capital markets.

When a loan is in default, the right to repossess and then liquidate or keep collateral constitutes the most basic right of a senior collateralized creditor. In some countries, the law makes it difficult for such creditors to repossess collateral, partly because such repossession leads to liquidation of firms, which is viewed as socially undesirable. In these countries, creditors may still possess powers against borrowers, namely, their votes in the decision of how to reorganize the company. From a social viewpoint, the wisdom of reorganization versus liquidation raises extensive debate (Aghion, Hart, and Moore 1992; White 1993), posing the question of whether both or just one of the procedures are needed to protect creditors. Thus, a country with a perfect liquidation procedure but totally ineffective reorganization procedure might be extremely protective of creditors simply because reorganization never needs to be used. Because protecting the rights of some classes of creditors may reduce the rights of other classes, an additional conceptual difficulty arises when analyzing creditor rights.

Because almost all countries rely to some extent on reorganization and liquidation procedures, this chapter, in an attempt to undertake a cross-country analysis of creditor rights, scores rights in both procedures, totaling the scores to create an aggregate creditor rights index. In assessing creditor rights, the authors take the perspective of senior secured creditors, partly for concreteness and partly because much of the world's debt retains that character. A list of some of the most significant creditors' rights follows.

In some countries the reorganization procedure imposes an automatic stay on the assets, preventing secured creditors from taking possession of loan collateral. This rule obviously protects managers and unsecured creditors against secured creditors and prevents automatic liquidation. In Greece, for example, secured creditors have the right to foreclose on their property when their claim matures, not when the borrower defaults. In other economies such as Hong Kong (China) and Singapore, however, secured creditors can pull collateral from firms being reorganized without waiting for completion of reorganization, a right obviously of value to them.

Some countries do not assure secured creditors the right to collateral in reorganization. In these countries, secured creditors get in line behind the government and workers, who have absolute priority over them. In the Philippines, for example, various social constituencies must be repaid before the secured creditors, often leaving the latter with no assets to back up their claims.

Moreover, in some countries such as Thailand and the Republic of Korea, management can seek protection from creditors unilaterally by filing for reorganization, without creditor consent. Such protection is called Chapter 11 in the United States, and gives management a great deal of power, because, at best, creditors can get their money or collateral only with a delay. In contrast, in other economies like Hong Kong (China) or the United Kingdom, filing for reorganization requires creditor consent and, hence, managers cannot escape easily creditor demands. In countries like the Philippines, management stays pending the resolution of the reorganization procedure, whereas in other countries, such as Malaysia, a team appointed by the court or the creditors replaces management. This threat of dismissal may enhance creditors' power.

Table 4.1 shows the results of a cross-country study undertaken by La Porta and others (1997, 1998) to analyze bankruptcy procedures for a sample of 49 countries (the appendix details the sources of data). The results on creditor rights for the whole sample of countries show that nearly half do not have an automatic stay on assets, 81 percent pay secured creditors first, more than half restrict managers' rights to seek protection from creditors unilaterally, and 45 percent remove management in reorganization proceedings.

A closer look at the results reveals interesting patterns. The 49 have been classified into four different groups (or families) according to the origin of

Table 4.1. *Creditor Rights around the World*

Country	No automatic stay on assets	Secured creditors paid first	Restrictions for reorganization in place	Management does not stay in reorganization	Creditor rights index
Panel A: creditor rights (1 = creditor protection is in the law)					
Australia	0	1	0	0	1
Canada	0	1	0	0	1
Hong Kong (China)	1	1	1	1	4
India	1	1	1	1	4
Ireland	0	1	0	0	1
Israel	1	1	1	1	4
Kenya	1	1	1	1	4

(table continues on following page)

Table 4.1 continued

Country	No automatic stay on assets	Secured creditors paid first	Restrictions for reorganization in place	Management does not stay in reorganization	Creditor rights index
Malaysia	1	1	1	1	4
New Zealand	1	0	1	1	3
Nigeria	1	1	1	1	4
Pakistan	1	1	1	1	4
Singapore	1	1	1	1	3
South Africa	0	1	1	1	4
Sri Lanka	1	0	11	1	3
Thailand	1	1	0	1	3
United Kingdom	1	1	1	1	4
United States	0	1	0	0	1
Zimbabwe	1	1	1	1	4
English-origin average	0.72	0.89	0.72	0.78	3.11
Argentina	0	1	0	0	1
Belgium	1	1	0	0	2
Brazil	0	0	1	0	1
Chile	0	1	1	0	2
Colombia	0	0	0	0	0
Ecuador	1	1	1	1	4
Egypt	1	1	1	1	4
France	0	0	0	0	0
Greece	0	0	0	1	1
Indonesia	1	1	1	1	4
Italy	0	1	1	0	2
Jordan	n.a.	n.a.	n.a.	n.a.	n.a.
Mexico	0	0	0	0	0
Netherlands	0	1	1	0	2
Peru	0	0	0	0	0
Philippines	0	0	0	0	0
Portugal	0	1	0	0	1
Spain	1	1	0	0	2
Turkey	0	1	1	0	2
Uruguay	0	1	0	1	2
Venezuela	n.a.	1	n.a.	n.a.	n.a.
French-origin average	0.26	0.65	0.42	0.26	1.58
Austria	1	1	1	0	3
Germany	1	1	1	0	3
Japan	0	1	0	1	2

(table continues on following page)

Table 4.1 continued

Country	No automatic stay on assets	Secured creditors paid first	Restrictions for reorganization in place	Management does not stay in reorganization	Creditor rights index
Korea, Rep. of	1	1	0	1	3
Switzerland	0	1	0	0	1
Taiwan	1	1	0	0	2
German-origin average	0.67	1.00	0.33	0.33	2.33
Denmark	1	1	1	0	3
Finland	0	1	0	0	1
Norway	0	1	1	0	2
Sweden	0	1	1	0	2
Scandinavian-origin average	0.25	1.00	0.75	0.00	2.00
Sample average	0.49	0.81	0.55	0.45	2.30
Panel B: tests on means (t-statistics)					
Common vs civil law	2.65[a]	1.04	1.86[c]	4.13[a]	3.61[a]
English vs French origin	3.06[a]	1.75[b]	1.89[c]	3.55[a]	3.61[a]
English vs German origin	0.25	−1.46	1.74[c]	2.10[b]	1.43
English vs Scandinavian origin	1.83[c]	−1.46	−0.11	7.71[a]	1.71[c]
French vs German origin	−1.85[c]	−3.20[a]	0.37	−0.32	−1.29
French vs Scandinavian origin	0.05	−3.20[a]	−1.18	2.54[b]	−0.62
German vs Scandinavian origin	1.27	0.00	−1.26	1.58	0.38

n.a. Not available.
a. Significant at 1 percent
b. Significant at 5 percent
c. Significant at 10 percent.
Source: La Porta and others (1997, 1998).

their corporate and bankruptcy laws: (a) English common law, (b) French civil law, (c) German civil law, and (d) Scandinavian civil law. The results show that the legal origin matters. Common law countries offer creditors stronger legal protections against managers. They have the highest (72 percent) incidence of no automatic stay on assets; with two exceptions, they guarantee that secured creditors get paid first (the German civil law and Scandinavian families have no exceptions); they frequently (72 percent, behind only Scandinavia) preclude managers from unilaterally seeking court protection from creditors; and they have by far the highest (78 percent) incidence of removing managers in reorganization proceedings. The United States remains one of the most anticreditor common law countries: it permits automatic stay on assets, allows unimpeded petition for reorganization, and lets managers keep their jobs following reorganization. The average aggregate creditors' rights score for common law countries is 3.11, by far the highest among the four families, but the United States scores only 1 on creditors rights.

The French civil law countries offer creditors the weakest protection. Few of them (26 percent, the same as Scandinavia) have no automatic stay on assets; relatively few (65 percent) assure that secured creditors get paid first; few (42 percent, although still more than German civil law countries) place restrictions on managers seeking court protection from creditors; and relatively few (26 percent) remove managers during reorganization proceedings. The average aggregate creditors' rights score for the French civil law countries is 1.58, or roughly half of that for the common law family.

On some measures, countries in the German civil law family are strongly procreditor. For instance, 67 percent of them have no automatic stay, and secured creditors in all of them get paid first. By contrast, relatively few of these countries (33 percent) prevent managers from getting protection from creditors unilaterally, and most (67 percent) allow managers to stay following reorganization. The evidence reveals that the German civil law countries respond positively to secured creditors by not allowing automatic stay and by letting them pull collateral. As a consequence of making liquidation easy, these countries rely less on reorganization of defaulting firms, so being soft on such firms by letting managers stay may not be a major problem. The average creditors' rights' score of 2.33 for the German family may therefore understate the extent to which secured creditors are protected.

Finally, Scandinavia has an overall average score of 2.00, a bit lower than the German family, but higher than the French.

To summarize, bankruptcy laws differ a great deal across countries, particularly because they come from different legal families. Common law countries provide the most relative protection to creditors, and French civil law countries provide the least protection. German civil law countries fall in the middle. The one exception is the strong protections that German civil law countries afford secured creditors.[1]

Enforcement of Laws around the World

Although enforceable rights may look good on paper, that may not translate into actual enforceable rights. For example, table 4.1 shows Argentina and the Philippines to be countries with good creditor protection, but creditors in these countries actually complain bitterly about the lack of effective creditors' rights. A corrupt or inefficient legal system can render legal rules ineffective. The opposite case may also occur if a strong system of legal enforcement substitutes for weak rules, as active and well-functioning courts can step in and rescue creditors abused by managers and/or shareholders.

To address these issues, this chapter examines proxies for the quality of enforcement of these rights, namely, estimates of law and order in different countries compiled by private credit risk agencies for foreign investors interested in doing business in the respective countries. Table 4.2 uses one of these measures—the rule of law.[2] This measure results from an assessment of the law and order tradition in the country produced by the country-risk rating agency, International Country Risk. The scale for this variable runs from 0 to 10, with lower scores indicating less of a tradition for law and order in a given country. In addition, table 4.2 shows an estimate of the quality of a

Table 4.2.   *Creditor Rights and Debt Markets*

Country	Creditor rights index	Rule of law	Rating on accounting standards	Debt/ GNP	GDP growth	Log GNP
Panel A: means						
Australia	1	10.00	75	0.76	3.06	12.64
Canada	1	10.00	74	0.72	3.36	13.26

(table continues on following page)

---

1. When studying the relationship between per capita income and creditors' rights, the evidence indicates that these results are not the consequence of richer countries having stronger investor rights. If anything, the results for creditors' rights show the reverse.

2. Some of these measures have been previously shown to affect national growth rates (Keefer and Knack 1995).

Table 4.2 continued

Country	Creditor rights index	Rule of law	Rating on accounting standards	Debt/ GNP	GDP growth	Log GNP
Hong Kong (China)	4	8.22	69	n.a.	7.57	11.56
India	4	4.17	57	0.29	4.34	12.50
Ireland	1	7.80	n.a.	0.38	4.25	10.73
Israel	4	4.82	64	0.66	4.39	11.19
Kenya	4	5.42	n.a.	n.a.	4.79	8.83
Malaysia	4	6.78	76	0.84	6.90	11.00
New Zealand	3	10.00	70	0.90	1.67	10.69
Nigeria	4	2.73	59	n.a.	3.43	10.36
Pakistan	4	3.03	n.a.	0.27	5.50	10.88
Singapore	3	8.57	78	0.60	1.68	11.68
South Africa	4	4.42	70	0.93	7.48	10.92
Sri Lanka	3	1.90	n.a.	0.25	4.04	9.28
Thailand	3	6.25	64	0.93	7.70	11.72
United Kingdom	4	8.57	78	1.13	2.27	13.86
United States	1	10.00	71	0.81	2.74	15.67
Zimbabwe	4	3.68	n.a.	n.a.	2.17	8.63
English-origin average	3.11	6.46	69.62	0.68	4.30	11.41
Argentina	1	5.35	45	0.19	1.40	12.40
Belgium	2	10.00	61	0.38	2.46	12.29
Brazil	1	6.32	54	0.39	3.95	13.03
Chile	2	7.02	52	0.63	3.35	10.69
Colombia	0	2.08	50	0.19	4.38	10.82
Ecuador	4	6.67	n.a.	n.a.	4.55	9.49
Egypt	4	4.17	24	n.a.	6.13	10.53
France	0	8.98	69	0.96	2.54	14.07
Greece	1	6.18	55	0.23	2.46	11.25
Indonesia	4	3.98	n.a.	0.42	6.38	11.84
Italy	2	8.33	62	0.55	2.82	13.94
Jordan	n.a.	4.35	n.a.	0.70	1.20	8.49
Mexico	0	5.35	60	0.47	3.07	12.69
Netherlands	2	10.00	64	1.08	2.55	12.68
Peru	0	2.50	38	0.27	2.82	10.92
Philippines	0	2.73	65	0.10	0.30	10.44
Portugal	1	8.68	36	0.64	3.52	11.41
Spain	2	7.80	64	0.75	3.27	13.19
Turkey	2	5.18	51	0.15	5.05	12.08
Uruguay	2	5.00	31	0.26	1.96	9.40
Venezuela	n.a.	6.37	40	0.10	2.65	10.99
French-origin average	1.58	6.05	51.17	0.45	3.18	11.55

(table continues on following page)

Table 4.2 continued

Country	Creditor rights index	Rule of law	Rating on accounting standards	Debt/ GNP	GDP growth	Log GNP
Austria	3	10.00	54	0.79	2.74	12.13
Germany	3	9.23	62	1.12	2.60	14.46
Japan	2	8.98	65	1.22	4.13	15.18
South Korea	3	5.35	62	0.74	9.52	12.73
Switzerland	1	10.00	68	n.a.	1.18	12.44
Taiwan	2	8.52	65	n.a.	11.56	12.34
German-origin average	2.33	8.68	62.67	0.97	5.29	13.21
Denmark	3	10.00	62	0.34	2.09	11.84
Finland	1	10.00	77	0.75	2.40	11.49
Norway	2	10.00	74	0.64	3.43	11.62
.Sweden	2	10.00	83	0.55	1.79	12.28
Scandinavian-origin average	2.00	10.00	74.00	0.57	2.42	11.80
Sample average	2.30	6.85	60.93	0.59	3.79	11.72
Panel B: tests of means (t-statistics)						
Common vs. civil law	3.61	−0.77	3.12[a]	1.33	1.23	−1.06
English vs. French origin	3.61	0.51	4.66[a]	2.29	1.97	−0.28
English vs. German origin	1.43	−1.82	2.22[b]	−1.88	−0.78	−2.31
English vs. Scandinavian origin	1.71	−15.57	−1.05	0.71	1.81	−0.44
French vs. German origin	−1.29	−2.55	−2.10[b]	−3.39	−1.96	−2.48
French vs. Scandinavian origin	−0.60	−20.80	−3.32[a]	0.82	0.97	−0.33
German vs. Scandinavian origin	0.63	−11.29	−2.66[b]	2.71	1.32	2.11

GNP Gross national product.
n.a. Not available.
a. Significant at 1 percent
b. Significant at 5 percent
Source: La Porta and others (1997, 1998).

country's accounting standards. Accounting plays a potentially crucial role in corporate governance. To understand and compare company disclosures, investors and others need basic accounting standards upheld. Even more important, contracts between managers and creditors typically rely on some measures of firms' income or assets being verifiable in court. If a bond covenant stipulates immediate repayment when income falls below a certain level, for the bond contract to be enforceable, that income level must be verifiable. Accounting standards are necessary for financial contracting, especially if investors' rights are weak. The measure of accounting standards in table 4.2, like the rule of law measures, is a privately constructed index based on examination of company reports from different countries.

Table 4.2 also arranges countries by legal origin and presents tests of equality of means between families. The table suggests that quality of law enforcement differs across legal families. In law enforcement, Scandinavian countries are clearly first, with German civil law countries a close second. Of all families, these families score the highest in efficiency of the judicial system, rule of law, corruption, risk of expropriation, and risk of contract repudiation by the government. On all the rule of law measures, common law countries place behind the leaders but ahead of the French civil law countries. The statistical significance of these results varies from variable to variable.

With regard to quality of accounting, Scandinavia still comes first, although common law countries score second (statistically significantly) ahead of the German civil law countries. The French family has the weakest quality of accounting.

These results do not support the conclusion that the quality of law enforcement substitutes or compensates for the quality of laws. Both the laws and the system that enforces them poorly protect investors in a French civil law country. On average, the reverse is true for an investor in a common law country. Poor enforcement and accounting standards aggravate, rather than cure the difficulties faced by investors in the French civil law countries.[3]

---

3. By every measure, richer countries have a higher quality of law enforcement. Nonetheless, even controlling for per capita income, French civil law countries still score lower on every single measure and, statistically, significantly lower for almost all measures than the common law countries. The regression results continually show that legal groups with investor-friendlier laws also have stronger enforcement of laws (see regression results in La Porta and others 1998).

Consequences of Creditor Protection in Financial Markets

The broader question, of course, concerns whether countries with poor creditor protection also have inferior opportunities for external financing and, thus, smaller capital markets. For this chapter, the authors collected data on the total bank debt of the private sector in each country, as well as on the total face value of corporate bonds in each country. The aggregate of these two variables relative to the gross national product (GNP) is a plausible measure of the overall ability of the private sector to access debt finance.[4]

Table 4.2 shows that aggregate debt as a share of GNP comprises 68 percent for common law countries, 45 percent for the French civil law countries, 97 percent for the German civil law countries, and 57 percent for the Scandinavian countries. Again, debt finance is more accessible in the English-origin group than in the French-origin group. The German civil law countries (sometimes described as countries with bank-focused financial systems) possess even higher indebtedness. Low creditor rights line up with small markets when we compare French and English origin, but German civil law countries appear somewhat of a mystery. Rajan and Zingales (1995) suggest a possible explanation in a finding that German companies have high overall liabilities, though not necessarily high debt per se (maybe as a result of their large liquid assets).

Table 4.3 presents regression results for the aggregated indebtedness measure. In the first specification, which does not include legal-origin dummies, both the level of the nation's GNP and the historical growth of gross domestic product (GDP) are associated with higher total debt relative to GNP; however, the statistical significance of these results does not carry over once legal origin is controlled for. In the specification without legal-origin dummies, the coefficient on the creditor rights index is also statistically significant, but this result loses significance and the coefficient falls sharply once origin is controlled for. The effect of rule of law is more robust, as it has a large and statistically significant effect on the size of the capital market: the move from world mean to a perfect 10 is associated with a 20 percentage point increase in debt to GNP ratio, or 0.7 of a standard deviation. The origin effects prove interesting. Relative to common law countries, French legal-origin countries have a lower ratio of debt to GNP (which becomes insignificant with the inclusion of creditors' rights,

---

4. The fact that this analysis considers the entire private sector rather than just corporations may actually be an advantage, because in many countries entrepreneurs raise money on their personal accounts to finance their firms by, for example, mortgaging their properties (see La Porta and others 1997).

Table 4.3. *Debt/GNP Regressions*

(ordinary least squares regressions of the cross-section of 49 countries around the world)

Independent variables	Dependent variable: debt /GNP		
GDP growth	0.0310[c]	0.0251[c]	0.0197
	(0.0171)	(0.0134)	(0.0152)
Log GNP	0.0667[b]	0.0370	0.0404
	(0.0252)	(0.0255)	(0.0250)
Rule of Law	0.0615[a]	0.0698[a]	0.0694[a]
	(0.0132)	(0.0147)	(0.0148)
French origin		−0.1516[b]	−0.1163
		(0.0740)	(0.0825)
German origin		0.1080	0.1082
		(0.1010)	(0.0982)
Scandinavian origin		−0.2764[b]	−0.2618[b]
		(0.1037)	(0.1075)
Creditors' rights	0.0518[c]		0.0270
	(0.0267)		(0.0298)
Intercept	−0.8621[a]	−0.3496	−0.4414
	(0.2579)	(0.2524)	(1.341)
Number of observations	39	39	39
Adjusted R²	0.5522	0.5191	0.5984

Note: The dependent variable is "Debt/GNP." The independent variables are (a) GDP growth, (b) log GNP, (c) rule of law, (d) French origin, (e) German origin, (f) Scandinavian origin, and (g) creditor rights index (White 1980). Corrected standard errors are shown in parentheses.

a. Significant at 1 percent.
b. Significant at 5 percent.
c. Significant at 10 percent.
Source: Authors' calculations.

perhaps because of a high negative correlation between creditors' rights and the French dummy). French-origin countries have a 12 to 15 percent lower ratio of debt to GNP, where the overall sample mean is 59 percent. German-origin countries again have a higher ratio of debt to GNP, but the effect is not statistically significant. Finally, Scandinavian-origin countries have a large (almost one standard deviation) lower ratio of debt to GNP, a difference not much diminished by the inclusion of the creditors' rights index. In summary, French and Scandinavian civil law countries have more narrow debt markets than common law countries.

Overall, the results on debt suggest that legal rules influence external finance. The results find that good laws and good enforcement have a considerable effect on the size of debt markets. The analysis also finds large systemic differences in the size and breadth of capital markets in countries from different legal origins. Common law countries have larger debt markets than civil law countries, particularly French civil law countries. The differences in creditor protection capture some of these differences. The results consistently reveal that the quality of the legal environment significantly affects the ability of firms in different countries to raise external financing.

Real Consequences of Creditor Protection

As more countries transition to market economies, the public policy debate, with its current focus on macroeconomic stability, will broaden to include the design of institutions that sustain growth. This should, in turn, encourage countries to take actions to facilitate growth and prevent crises. Thus, the development of capital markets deserves the attention of policymakers for the reasons included earlier and described later, even though empirical research remains incomplete.

A growing literature links large capital markets with growth. La Porta and others (1997) show that countries with poor investor protection have significantly smaller debt and equity markets. King and Levine (1993) and Levine and Zervos (1998) find that developed debt and equity markets contribute to economic growth. Levine (1998) addresses the endogenous nature of the relationship between growth and the development of capital markets using the legal origin variables in La Porta and others (1998) and confirms the King and Levine findings that financial development promotes economic growth. Lastly, Beck, Levine, and Loayza (2000) find that the degree of development of the banking sector significantly affects total factor productivity growth. This impact remains when using legal origin as an exogenous component of banking development. Similarly, Rajan and Zingales (1998) find that industries in capital-intensive sectors grow faster in countries with developed financial systems than in countries with small capital markets, presumably because capital-intensive firms depend more on external financing than labor-intensive firms. Taken together, this evidence links legal systems, capital markets, and economic development. Note, however, that while the shortcomings of creditor protection described previously have adverse consequences for financial development and growth, they are unlikely to be an insurmountable bottleneck. After all, Belgium and Italy are rich countries even though they have weak creditors' rights and small capital markets.

Reasons exist to believe that good institutions become particularly valuable in bad times and may reduce the likelihood of a severe and protracted recession. Rationally or irrationally, investors are less fearsome of the deadweight loss introduced by a bad bankruptcy procedure during good times than bad times. When bankruptcy becomes a tangible possibility, investors demand a high premium on risky debt. Because of the asymmetry of a bad bankruptcy law, it may disproportionately lower economic activity in bad times. Johnson and others (2000) draw an ingenious connection between investor protection and financial crises by examining the depreciation of currencies and the decline of stock markets in 25 countries during the East Asian crisis of 1997–98. They found that governance variables, such as investor protection indexes and measures of the quality of law enforcement, constitute powerful predictors of the extent of market declines during the crisis. These variables explain the cross-section of declines much better than the macroeconomic variables that have been the focus of the policy debate.

If accounting standards are unreliable, monitoring financial institutions becomes difficult, and investors find it harder to assess the true risk characteristics of various corporate borrowers. For example, a devaluation may not only reveal the existence of previously unknown, large, unhedged foreign debts of a prominent corporate borrower, but the bad news may also rationally trigger a downgrade of the whole corporate sector debt as investors fear (and cannot verify) that the problem may be global. Without transparency in financial reporting, too many bad projects may be initiated and too many initially good projects may be pursued even after changes in circumstances indicate that they should be abandoned. Wurgler (2000) attempts to explain cross-country differences in the efficiency of investment allocation across manufacturing industries. He found that countries with less developed financial systems allocate investment across industries less in line with industry growth opportunities than financially developed countries. Beck, Levine, and Loayza's (2000) paper suggests these results demonstrate that financial development improves allocative efficiency and, through this channel, investor protection benefits productivity and output growth.

Good financial institutions may provide a useful tool to deal with the effects of a crisis once it has set in. The length of the recession may be related to the amount of time it takes the system to eliminate the debt hangover problem. Without an effective bankruptcy procedure, financially distressed firms may stay in limbo, unable to restructure debt and get the required resources for new projects. In a big crisis, a country needs a reliable bankruptcy mechanism to clean up the aftermath and quickly restore financial viability to firms in need of new capital. When firms become unable to raise external finances while in financial distress, a bankruptcy system that allows bad debts to fester can only prolong the macroeconomic downturn. Krueger and Tornell (1999) found some evidence supporting this scenario. In analyzing the impact of Mexico's 1994 crisis on the recovery of firms in tradeable and nontradeable sectors, they report that firms in the tradeable sector found access to financing in international capital markets, resulting in a remarkably quick recovery. Meanwhile, firms in the nontradeable sector found virtually no access to international funding and faced a severe domestic credit crunch resulting from the steady increase in nonperforming loans of the Mexican banking system. The lack of financing meant that nontradeable goods firms recovered only sluggishly. Mexico's bankruptcy system ranks among the worst in protecting creditors' rights and does not provide an efficient mechanism for banks to perform their financing role.

Reforming Bankruptcy Procedures

In the absence of a bankruptcy law, creditors may engage in a socially wasteful race to be the first to seize their collateral or to obtain judgement against the debtor. This race may lead to the dismemberment of the debtor's assets and to a loss of value to all creditors when the assets are worth more as a whole than as individual components. Therefore, it is in the collective interest of creditors to ensure the orderly disposition of the debtor's assets.

A good bankruptcy procedure not only assures the orderly disposition of the debtor's assets, but, in protecting creditors' rights, it should also meet the following four conditions:

- It should try to achieve an outcome that maximizes the total value of the proceeds received by the existing claimants. Clearly, all creditors would benefit if the bankruptcy procedure could be modified to deliver a higher than expected ex post value of the firm.
- It should neither be too soft on "bad" companies nor too hard on "good" firms. Debt can serve an important role in disciplining management by, for example, limiting their discretion to engage in wasteful projects. Accordingly, a good bankruptcy procedure should preserve the ex ante bonding role of debt by penalizing managers adequately in bankruptcy states. Even economically viable firms run into financial distress, however, and bankruptcy law should provide a way to preserve them.
- It should maintain the absolute priority of claims; that is, the most senior creditors should be paid off before the next most senior creditors receive anything, and so on. Two basic reasons exist for this. First,

senior creditors would be reluctant to lend if the previously contracted structure of debt priority is violated within the framework of the bankruptcy procedure. Second, having different rules for dealing with creditors inside and outside of bankruptcy can result in perverse incentives, with some creditors wasting resources to try to induce management to either forestall or precipitate bankruptcy.

- It should try to minimize the amount of discretion that the judiciary can exercise. For example, allowing the judge to make business decisions may not be desirable if the judge does not have the qualifications or the appropriate incentives. In addition, discretion may facilitate corruption.

Most countries rely on two basic procedures to address problems of financial distress: cash auctions and structured bargaining. A discussion of each of these two procedures follows.

Cash auction (for example, Chapter 7 in the United States) closes down the firm's operations and appoints a trustee or receiver to organize a cash auction of the firm's assets. The firm may be sold as a going concern or piecemeal. The receipts from the auction are distributed among claimants according to absolute priority. If capital markets were perfect, selling the firm to the highest bidder would guarantee an efficient outcome. However, when capital markets are inefficient, the best managers may not be able to raise the cash necessary to buy the firm. Capital market imperfections may have dire consequences if firms are inefficiently dismantled and their assets sold off cheaply at fire sale prices.

Structured bargaining (for example, Chapter 11 in the United States) encourages creditors and shareholders to bargain about the future of the company. Under the judge's supervision, claimants develop a plan to liquidate or reorganize the firm and divide its value among themselves. A suitable majority of each claimant class must approve the plan for implementation. A well-functioning structured bargaining procedure requires a sophisticated legal system. In practice, Chapter 11-type procedures have been criticized for being time-consuming, involving significant legal and administrative costs, causing considerable loss in company value, being relatively soft on management, and granting abusive powers to the judge. Although legal reform could, in principle, address these difficulties, two inherent problems occur with any structured bargaining process. First, knowing what fraction of the firm should be allocated to each class of claimants is difficult, because objective valuation exists for the restructured firm. Second, and more important, structured bargaining processes address two questions simultaneously: (a) Who should get what? and (2) What should be done with the firm? The coupling of these issues introduces conflicts of interest and may not put assets to their most productive use. For example, a senior creditor may press for a speedy liquidation (as that individual will then be paid off for certain), whereas junior claimants may encourage protracted bargaining (because they enjoy the upside, not the downside, of any changes in the firm's value).

Most emerging markets have liquidation and/or structured bargaining procedures similar to those in industrial countries. Thus, the critique of Chapter 7- and Chapter 11-type procedures also applies to emerging markets. In addition to these critiques, bankruptcy procedures in developing countries may present further problems. Because capital markets in emerging economies are less developed, the deficiencies outlined for liquidation procedures may be more severe. Note also that the effectiveness of court procedures is impaired by the low efficiency of the judicial system and widespread corruption, which characterize emerging markets (Keefer and Knack 1993). Court procedures in some of these nations remain slow not only as a result of less efficient courts, but also because of undeveloped and vague laws. Many of these countries have poor systems for registering property, causing long and uncertain court bankruptcy procedures because title to property is difficult to ascertain. Finally, the deficient accounting standards that characterize financial reporting of companies in emerging economies make it harder to sort out the claims and determine if bond covenants have been breached (see Center for International Financial Analysis and Research 1994).

These deficiencies mean that creditors in countries like Indonesia, Mexico, Russia, and Thailand can recoup a very small fraction of their claims at the end of a protracted procedure, resulting in those countries having very small debt markets.[5] Given the high costs of current procedures, few court-sanctioned reorganizations occur, as firms typically prefer informal solutions to their financial problems. In some countries, personal property, which can be seized more easily because it is not subject to the provisions of the bankruptcy law, is commonly used as collateral in commercial transactions. Unfortunately, personal property can back only so much debt. Moreover, although out-of-court settlements can be an effective way to cope with financial distress, the creditors' bargaining

---

5. The resolution of a bankruptcy procedure may take anywhere from three to seven years in countries like Mexico or Peru, and even decades in Thailand.

positions are compromised by the lack of an effective collective procedure. Furthermore, in some cases the parties may not achieve an out-of-court settlement, particularly when many creditors exist.[6]

This scenario becomes more evident during a corporate debt crisis, such as the recent one in East Asia. In the aftermath of that episode, investors demanded better creditors' rights, triggering some attempts of bankruptcy law reform in several countries in the region. The solution adopted in those countries involved modifying some procedural features of the existing court-run bankruptcy and reorganization laws. In Indonesia, for example, bankruptcy reform became a condition for more loans from the International Monetary Fund. To carry out the reforms, a government committee was formed under the supervision of officials from the International Monetary Fund. The committee decided to carry out the reforms based on the Netherlands' bankruptcy and reorganization procedures. Unfortunately, the reforms ended up leaving investors in a situation similar to their previous one. Although some lending institutions are still assessing the effectiveness of the changes, statistics show that the reform has not succeeded. As the reforms took place in 1998, there have only been 50 filings for reorganization in the whole of Indonesia, even though many regard it to be in severe financial crisis. Under the new law, a common complaint concerns the judge still retaining a great deal of discretion, regularly throwing out petitions for reorganization on the grounds that the creditors should give more time to the debtors or that creditors have not proven they are owed money.

This discussion suggests that court-intensive bankruptcy procedures may impose substantial deadweight loses as assets dissipate throughout the process and out-of-court settlements prove expensive. The deadweight loss associated with bad bankruptcy procedures may be significant in emerging markets and may prevent solvent firms from undertaking some positive net present value projects. Therefore, developing countries may welcome the search for alternative bankruptcy procedures to reduce reliance on the judiciary.

In the absence of a well-functioning judicial process, as seen in most emerging markets, it may be worth considering the following two alternative reorganization procedures. First, one could allow creditors, for example,

---

6. In a study of the New York and American stock exchanges companies in severe financial distress during 1978–87, Gilson, John, and Lang (1990) found that workouts failed more than 50 percent of the time, and the larger the number of creditors, the greater likelihood of failure (see also John 1993).

secured creditors, the right to appoint an administrative receiver in charge of both running the firm in default and disposing of its assets piecemeal or as an ongoing operation. This method would parallel the U.K.'s administration procedure. Once the assets of the firm had been disposed of, the receiver would distribute the proceeds in accordance with absolute priority, marking the end of the process. This mechanism allows implementation quickly, thereby minimizing the firm's loss of value. In addition, the immediate transfer of control to creditors minimizes intervention from the court, whose main role is to police the procedure to avoid fraud. Unfortunately, no reason exists to believe that a creditor-appointed receiver would be interested in maximizing the firm's value. Not only might the receiver favor some creditors over others, but also may fail to act in the interest of shareholders while the firm remains economically viable.

Second, another departure from court-intensive procedures leaves market forces to decide whether the distressed firm will be restructured or liquidated. Introducing market forces in bankruptcy proceedings entails taking steps akin to those in a privatization. Hart and others (1997) developed such a bankruptcy procedure using auctions. Specifically, both firm insiders and outsiders may place cash and noncash offers for the assets of the firm. In other words, the assets of the bankrupt firm are auctioned off to the highest bidder, and the proceedings are used to cancel the existing claims according to absolute priority. Although the firm is stripped of its assets, in preparation for the auction, claimants retain control and cash flow rights (bankruptcy rights) over the firm's assets. The holders of such bankruptcy rights decide among the bidders' competing offers and retain all the proceeds from the auction. To eliminate conflicts of interest among different classes of claimants, this procedure transforms the capital structure of the firm into an all-equity firm through a mechanism that preserves absolute priority of claims. This goal is achieved by canceling all debts, allocating all bankruptcy rights to the most senior class of claimants, and allowing more junior classes to acquire these rights only if they retire all senior claims to them.

This mechanism's potential drawback is that capital market imperfections may preclude junior claimants from exercising their right to buy bankruptcy rights from senior creditors. In such cases, this procedure delivers allocative efficiency, but not a fair outcome, because senior creditors benefit at the expense of other classes of claimants. However, Hart and others (1997) show that the basic procedure can be enhanced to avoid liquidity constraints through the introduction of an outside market for bankruptcy rights. A public cash auction for bankruptcy rights may be organized to sell all bankruptcy rights that could not be assigned to claimants and to purchase bankruptcy rights held by claimants if outside investors were willing to offer a price so that the claims of its holders are paid in full.[7]

Several advantages result from the introduction of market forces into bankruptcy through this procedure. First, the ability for firm insiders and outsiders to make offers in cash and/or noncash securities, for the firm as a whole or for parts of it, makes it more likely that the firm's assets will be put to their most productive use.[8] Second, it eliminates conflicts between different classes of claimants regarding the future of the firm, because all holders of bankruptcy rights are equal and have only one objective: to maximize the value of firm. Third, while increasing creditor rights, this procedure allows for debtor protection by giving shareholders and management the opportunity to propose offers for the firm, which may include reorganization plans, and permits them first priority in exercising their right to acquire the bankruptcy rights from creditors.[9] Fourth, the procedure is simple and quick, reducing uncertainty and minimizing the loss of value created by financial distress and the depletion of assets that usually follows the declaration of bankruptcy and reorganization. The preservation of the firm's value increases the probability of a successful reorganization, translating into higher cash flows for the claimants entitled to the assets. Finally, the procedure minimizes the reliance on and room for discretion of the judicial system, yet it achieves a fair outcome in terms of absolute priority.[10]

Conclusion

This chapter suggests that improving creditors' rights amounts to a sound strategy to develop credit markets. Unfortunately, reforming creditors'

---

7. Note that in contrast to current liquidation schemes, this proposal mitigates liquidity constraints by requiring claimants to raise cash to cover only a fraction of the value of the firm.

8. Allowing outside bids for the firm holds a related advantage in that it reduces the probability of strategic behavior of debtors by making it harder for them to declare bankruptcy and buy the firm cheaply.

9. This preferential treatment protects shareholders when bad luck rather than poor management performance causes financial difficulties.

10. An additional advantage of this procedure over existing options is that contentious claims need not hold up the reorganization process. This feature makes the proposal particularly attractive for emerging markets with a poor registry of property and/or lengthy court proceedings. For more details of the procedure, see Hart and others (1997).

rights can prove politically treacherous. Extending improved creditors' rights to preexisting credits is likely to cause wealth transfers from debtors to creditors. In addition, banks may be uninterested in facilitating bankruptcy reform if it means having to write down the value of bad loans in their portfolio and, as a result, injecting fresh capital into their operations. Bankruptcy reform may be further complicated by the need to reach compromise between the conflicting interests of secured and unsecured creditors (see Hart 1999).

Political expediency, as well as fairness, suggest that changes in creditors' rights should apply only to new credits. One could take this idea further and allow firms to opt for a more protective creditor regime by specifying irrevocably in their charters whether the new creditor-friendly rules apply in the event of financial distress. If the new set of rules for creditor protection is superior to the old ones, firms should voluntarily adhere to higher standards of creditor protection enticed by the prospect of lower interest rates.

The reform of creditor rights must be grounded on those rights that can be enforced. Even if Chapter 11 were optimal, it probably would not work effectively in countries with slow and ineffective judicial systems. The auction mechanism described in this chapter may be particularly appropriate in countries with weak judicial systems. The success of the Mexican escrow system (*fideicomiso*) illustrates the practical importance of creating out-of-court mechanisms for dealing with financial distress. Mexican *fideicomisos* allow, for example, a real estate developer to raise financing while putting the property in escrow with a financial institution. The financial institution retains title of the property so long as the credit is not fully paid. This allows the financial institution to sell the property (without court interference) for the benefit of the creditor when the debtor defaults on his or her obligation. *Fideicomisos* have been successful in some sectors precisely because they are beyond the reach of bankruptcy law. Their success illustrates the importance of thinking about changes in creditor rights that can be enforced in environments with weak courts and of allowing debtors to opt for the more protective creditor regime. However, more extensive legal reform of the sort advocated here is likely to be necessary to allow for broad access to credit.

Appendix 4A. Definitions of Variables

This appendix describes the variables collected for the 49 countries included in our study.

Table A.4.1. *Definitions of Variables*

This appendix describes the variables collected for the 49 countries included in our study.

Variable	Description	Source
Legal origin	Identifies the legal origin of the company law or commercial code of each country. Equals 1 if the origin is English common law; 2 if the origin is the French commercial code; and 3 if the origin is the German commercial code.	Foreign Law Encyclopedia Commercial laws of the world
Restrictions for going into reorganization	Equals 1 if the reorganization procedure imposes restrictions, such as creditors' consent, to file for reorganization. It equals 0 if there are no such restrictions.	Bankruptcy and reorganization laws
No automatic stay on secured assets	Equals 1 if the reorganization procedure does not impose an automatic stay on the assets of the firm upon filing the reorganization petition. Automatic stay prevents secured creditors from gaining possession of their security. It equals 0 if such a restriction exists in the law.	Bankruptcy and reorganization laws
Secured creditors first	Equals 1 if secured creditors are ranked first in the distribution of the proceeds that result from the disposition of the assets of a bankrupt firm. Equals 0 if nonsecured creditors, such as the government and workers, are given absolute priority.	Bankruptcy and reorganization laws
Management does not stay	Equals 1 when an official appointed by the court or by the creditors is responsible for the operation of the business during reorganization. Also equals 1 if the debtor does not keep the administration of its property pending the resolution of the reorganization process, and 0 otherwise.	Bankruptcy and reorganization laws
Creditors' rights index	An index aggregating different creditor rights. The index is formed by adding 1 when (a) the country imposes restrictions, such as creditors' consent or minimum dividends to file for reorganization; (b) secured creditors are able to gain possession of their security once the reorganization petition has been approved (no automatic stay); (c) secured creditors are ranked first in the distribution of the proceeds that result from the disposition of the assets of a bankrupt firm; and (d) the debtor does not retain the administration of its property pending the resolution of the reorganization. The index ranges from 0 to 4.	Bankruptcy and reorganization laws

(table continues on following page)

Table A.4.1 continued

Variable	Description	Source
Rule of law	Assessment of the law and order tradition in the country produced by the country-risk rating agency, International Country Risk. Average of the months of April and October of the monthly index between 1982 and 1995. Scale from 0 to 10, with lower scores for less tradition for law and order. (We changed the scale from its original range going from 0 to 6).	International Country Risk Guide
Accounting standards	Index created by examining and rating companies' 1990 annual reports on their inclusion or omission of 90 items. These items fall into seven categories (general information, income statements, balance sheets, funds flow statement, accounting standards, stock data, and special items). A minimum of three companies in each country was studied. The companies represent a cross-section of various industry groups where industrial companies numbered 70 percent while financial companies represented the remaining 30 percent.	International accounting and auditing trends, Center for International Financial Analysis and Research, Inc.
Debt/GNP	Ratio of the sum of bank debt of the private sector and outstanding nonfinancial bonds to GNP in 1994, or the last available.	International Financial Statistics, World Bondmarket Factbook.
GDP growth	Average annual percentage growth of per capita GDP for the period 1970–93.	*World Development Report 1995*
Log GNP	Logarithm of GDP in 1994.	*World Development Report 1996*

Source: Authors.

References

Aghion, Philippe, Oliver Hart, and John Moore. 1992. "The Economics of Bankruptcy Reform." *Journal of Law, Economics, and Organization* 8(3): 523–46.

Beck, Thorsten, Ross Levine, and Norman Loayza. 2000. "Finance and the Sources of Growth." *Journal of Financial Economics* 58(1): 261–300.

Center for International Financial Analysis and Research, Inc. 1994. *International Accounting and Auditing Trends*. New York, New York.

Gilson, Stuart, Kose John, and Larry Lang. 1990. "Troubled Debt Restructurings: An Empirical Study of Private Reorganization of Firms in Default." *Journal of Financial Economics* 27(12): 315–53.

Hart, Oliver. 1999. "Different Approaches to Bankruptcy." Cambridge, Massachusetts: Harvard University. Processed.

Hart, Oliver, Rafael La Porta, Florencio Lopez-de-Silanes, and John Moore. 1997. "A New Bankruptcy Procedure that Uses Multiple Auctions." *European Economic Review* 41(3): 461–73.

John, Kose. 1993. "Managing Financial Distress and Valuing Distressed Securities: A Survey and Research Agenda." *Financial Management* 2(3): 60–78.

Johnson, Simon, Peter Boone, Alasdair Breach, and Eric Friedman. 2000. "Corporate Governance in the Asian Financial Crisis, 1997–98." *Journal of Financial Economics* 58(1): 141–186.

Keefer, P., and S. Knack. 1993. "Why Don't Poor Countries Catch Up? A Cross-Country National Test of an Institutional Explanation." Working Paper no. 60. University of Maryland, Center for Institutional Reform and the Informal Sector, College Park, Maryland.

_____. 1995. "Institutions and Economic Performance: Cross-Country Tests Using Alternative Institutional Measures." *Economics and Politics* 7(13): 207–27.

King, Robert, and Ross Levine. 1993. "Finance and Growth: Schumpeter Might Be Right." *Quarterly Journal of Economics* 108: 717–38.

Krueger, Anne, and Aaron Tornell. 1999. "The Role of Bank Restructuring in Recovering from Crises: Mexico 1995–98." Working Paper No. 7042. National Bureau of Economic Research, Cambridge, Massachusetts.

La Porta, R., F. Lopez-de-Silanes, A. Shleifer, and R. W. Vishny. 1997. "Legal Determinants of External Finance." *Journal of Finance* 52(7): 1131–50.

_____. 1998. "Law and Finance." *Journal of Political Economy* 106(4): 1113–55.

_____. Forthcoming. "Investor Protection: Origins, Consequences, and Reform." *Journal of Financial Economics*.

Levine, Ross. 1998. "The Legal Environment, Banks, and Long-Run Economic Growth." *Journal of Money Credit and Banking* 30(3): 596–613.

Levine, Ross, and Sara Zervos. 1998. "Stock Markets, Banks and Economic Growth." *American Economic Review* 88(3): 537–58.

Rajan, Raghuram, and Luigi Zingales. 1995. "What Do We Know from Capital Structure: Some Evidence from the International Data." *Journal of Finance* 50(5): 1421–60.

_____. 1998. "Financial Dependence and Growth." *American Economic Review* 88(3): 559–86.

White, Halbert. 1980. "A Heteroskedasticity-Consistent Covariance Matrix Estimator and a Direct Test for Heteroskedasticity." *Econometrica* 48(4): 817–38.

White, Michelle. 1993. "The Costs of Corporate Bankruptcy: The U.S.-European Comparison." University of Michigan, Department of Economics, Ann Arbor. Processed.

World Bank. 1995. *World Development Report.* Washington, D.C.

_____. 1996. *World Development Report.* Washington, D.C.

Wurgler, Jeffrey. 2000. "Financial Markets and the Allocation of Capital." *Journal of Financial Economics* 58(1): 187–214.

5

Corporate Debt Restructuring: Auctions Speak Louder Than Words

Donald B. Hausch, University of Wisconsin, and
S. Ramachandran, World Bank

In many countries, courts neglect to enforce bankruptcy laws and creditors' rights, even when they are adequate. Those countries' courts that can handle the ordinary failure of firms would still be overwhelmed by the sheer number of firms adversely affected by a general economic crisis of the magnitude of the recent East Asian crisis.

This chapter proposes a market-based scheme to swiftly reduce claims to levels creditors deem serviceable. The Auction-Based Creditor Ordering by Reducing Debts (ACCORD) involves creditors making noncash bids through debt forgiveness to vie for places in a line. Any existing hierarchy of claims is respected, and places within this hierarchy are auctioned. Creditors are serviced sequentially: the creditor at the head of the line gets paid from the operating cash flows as and when the firm chooses, and only when the creditor's (reduced) debts are fully discharged does the line move up to the next creditor in line. Owners remaining last in line continue to operate the firm. This chapter shows that this type of auction sufficiently reduces claims to give owners an incentive to operate the firms efficiently.

While such a scheme has general applicability, it serves particularly well the current East Asian situation in which ownership rarely separates from management, creditors are ill-suited to be owners, and existing owners balk at any dilution of ownership or loss of control. The recent attempts to improve bankruptcy laws failed to hasten the resolution of corporate indebtedness, and delay has eroded values when the owner-managers' overwhelming indebtedness saps incentives. Furthermore, by guaranteeing the deposits in domestic banks with a negative net worth, governments, either directly or through agencies they control, implicitly become unsatisfied creditors of private firms, which risks politicizing the resolution. Under these circumstances, market-based bankruptcy alternatives seem attractive.

The basic approach in bankruptcy involves creditors negotiating with debtors and with each other to reorganize a viable firm's liabilities or, if not viable, liquidating the firm in an orderly manner. Countries' laws differ in the specified pecking order of claims. For example, must secured creditors wait to give reorganization a chance? Do workers' claims come ahead of them in line? They all rely on negotiations to resolve bankruptcy. While all courts try to prevent individual creditors from seizing assets or garnering proceeds out of turn, only a few countries, such as the United States under Chapter 11, require courts to nudge negotiations directly. When courts only entertain liquidation petitions, ruling on them quickly and predictably, they encourage financial reorganizations through negotiations, without courts' direct involvement. This chapter argues that negotiations have become stymied in East Asia not because of the laws or courts, although these could doubtless be improved, but because of more fundamental incentives, making a market-based alternative more appropriate. The authors of this chapter propose a specific scheme using noncash auctions.

Firms in the crisis countries of East Asia find themselves heavily indebted (table 5.1). Despite weak creditor protection, they were highly leveraged before the crisis, partly because the even weaker protection accorded to outside equity holders (La Porta, Lopez-de-Silanes, and Shleifer 2000). These firms' leverage has since increased because debts were often denominated in foreign currency, even for nonexporters, and sharp rises in interest rates and falls in their currencies' values in the foreign exchange market accompanied the economic crisis. Their debts have now mushroomed to possibly unserviceable levels.

Despite heavy indebtedness, East Asian firms have been generally well run. While total factor productivity appears to have declined in recent years, making East Asia's growth less miraculous than earlier believed, few doubt that firms' managers are generally competent and able to adapt to the new situation. Despite vigorous attempts to restore the firms' profitability, unserviceable debts must be renegotiated, which has failed to occur rapidly. The status quo erodes the owner-managers' incentives to operate the firm efficiently, because any increase in firm value accrues almost entirely to the creditors.

Table 5.1.   *Salient Corporate Statistics, East Asian Crisis Countries*

Statistic	Indonesia	Korea	Malaysia	Philippines	Thailand
Real GDP ratio (1988–96)	0.88	1.00	1.00	1.05	0.92
GDP (1998, US$ billions)	105	309	69.4	68	121
Nominal exchange rate ratio (mid-1999 to mid-1997)	2.75	1.31	1.5	1.43	1.44
Capacity utilization[a] (mid-1998), percent	58	71	65	68	60
Total corporate debt (US$ equivalent)	118.0	444.0	120.2	47.5	195.7
External debt	67.1	64.0	40.0	23.3	32.5
Domestic debt	50.9	380.0	80.2	24.2	163.2
Banking sector's external debt (US$ billions)	50.3	72.4	23.0	17.8	46.8
Debt to equity ratio (1996)	2.0	3.5	1.1	1.4	2.4

a. World Bank survey of firms (mid-1998).
Source: Hausch and Ramachandran (1999).

In the recent crisis, all five East Asian countries promulgated new bankruptcy laws or amended old ones and began improving their courts' functioning. It nevertheless seems clear that the courts are—and should be—designed to deal with the normal failure rate of firms, not economywide financial distress, or systemic crisis. Furthermore, for most creditors to take over and attempt operation of the affected firms would be foolhardy, because they lack the skills and cannot oversee the managers who do. In the aggregate, a large-scale reshuffling of owner-managers, even if possible through widespread bankruptcies, only destroys firm-specific managerial human capital.

The debts must be quickly reduced to sustainable levels while existing owners remain in control. Bankruptcy negotiations remain slow partly because owners stall, fearing loss of control, and courts seem unable to prevent such delay. Moreover, the governments have intervened heavily in the banking system and, by guaranteeing the deposits, have become liable for banks' losses that far exceed bankers' equity. As a result, governments, either directly or through various agencies, have become major creditors of privately owned firms. Consequently, debt negotiations could become a political issue; but even if this were averted, bureaucrats would be unwilling to reduce the face value of the claims—even if their market value were the same or higher—lest they be accused of corruption or favoritism. Although owners are often blamed for the slow pace of negotiations to resolve the firms' excessive debts, the creditor agents' unwillingness to accept "haircuts" (practitioner parlance for partial forgiveness) would also be a hurdle. Market-based debt reduction provides an objective yardstick for creditor bureaucrats to defend their actions, and such alternatives to court proceedings therefore appear attractive.

Market-Based Bankruptcy

In recent years academics (Bebchuk 1988; Aghion, Hart, and Moore 1992) have proposed market-based alternatives to often seemingly protracted negotiations. Using Black and Scholes' (1972) original insight that equity is a call option on the firm's assets with an exercise price equal to the debt owed, Bebchuk proposes working up the hierarchy of claims. Starting with the most junior claimant, namely, equity, each claimant class is given a choice of either fully paying off all the more senior claimants or having its own claims extinguished. Whichever class pays off, all the more senior claimants become the firm's new owners. Bebchuk's proposal respects the absolute priority of claims and results in an all-equity firm.[1]

Bebchuk's proposal allows only existing claimants (shareholders and creditors) to bid for a settlement. However, outsiders may run the firm better, thereby raising its value, so Aghion, Hart, and Moore proposed allowing outsiders to bid also and to specify different means of paying the existing claims. Creditors may offer to restructure the existing debt, while an outside bidder, a firm in a similar business, for example, may offer to merge and replace debt with equity in the merged entity.

These proposals may be ill-suited to East Asia, where credit markets work poorly, especially in a financial crisis. Domestic banks are largely bankrupt (governments are restructuring them) and access to foreign credit has been disrupted.[2] With potential domestic bidders' cash constrained,

---

1. The firm could borrow through a separate transaction that may occur simultaneously if all the claimants in that class agree to accept *pro rata* fractions of each class of liabilities in the desired new financial structure.

2. Hart and others (1997) extend the Aghion, Hart, and Moore proposal to accommodate cash-constrained creditors, but the difficulties of cash constraints on the firms' bidders persist.

foreigners could outbid those better suited to maximize firm value. Furthermore, large-scale sales to foreigners could generate a backlash of public sentiment, especially in countries with recent and unpleasant colonial experiences. Even if surmountable, these problems present outsiders (whether domestic or foreign) with an acute information-asymmetry problem: firms have been remarkably coy about divulging their finances to their own creditors let alone to unrelated parties, even if they were potential bidders. Schemes relying on outside bidders (as in the Aghion, Hart, and Moore proposal), or having junior claimants raise additional cash (as in the Bebchuck proposal), are therefore unworkable.

The Proposed ACCORD

This chapter proposes a scheme that assures existing owners' continued control of the firm and compels creditors to reveal their valuations in a noncash auction in which they accept a reduction of the face value of their claims. Concerns that this needlessly or unfairly favors existing owners would be assuaged in the scheme's offering of an additional alternative whose adoption requires creditor consent. Creditors in the noncash auction bid the reduction in the claims they are willing to accept, and their bids arrange them in a line to be serviced in sequence. Those willing to accept the greatest proportionate reduction would be placed ahead of the others in the line to be serviced sequentially from the firm's operating cash surplus, which owners continue to control and operate. The firm does not promise a schedule of cash payments, and pays creditors only as and when it feels able. Also, unlike conventional seniority in which junior and senior claimants get paid simultaneously and seniority only affects the distribution of liquidation proceeds, other creditors get nothing until full discharge of the (reduced) debts of the creditor at the head of the line. When this happens, the line moves up, and the next creditor in line awaits payment.

All creditors remain creditors, but those that forgive a greater proportion have their (reduced) debts fully discharged before others who forgave less, leaving them further behind in the creditor line. Creditors who attach a low value to the firm and doubt if they would be repaid would be willing to forgive a larger proportion of their claim to ensure obtaining at least something before the firm's operating cash flows are exhausted. Conversely, those perceiving the firm's difficulties as temporary would forgive little, waiting patiently in line for their turn. The original equity holders, that is, the most junior claimants, would not bid, but would continue to own and operate the firm, obtaining any leftover residual. So until all the creditors' reduced claims are fully discharged, the owners receive no cash flows, such as dividends.

This process may be thought of as auctioning places in a creditor line. Creditors essentially bid the fraction of debt they will forgive: the more they forgive, the sooner, and more likely, they will be repaid. The creditor trades off between a higher amount and a higher probability of being repaid, and by this means prices overcome the free-rider problem.

The free-rider problem makes negotiations difficult in a conventional financial reorganization in which creditors are asked to forgive some of their claims. The dominant strategy often entails not forgiving, because the creditor would be entitled to a larger fraction of the resulting claims when others forgive. Furthermore, creditors in all classes simultaneously receive the periodic payments made. Junior creditors thus have a greater incentive not to forgive. Experienced judges could prevent negotiations from stalling, although in the crisis-affected East Asian countries, that remains unlikely, especially on the required scale.

In contrast to such negotiations, ACCORD makes nonforgiving creditors wait longer for the payments, as they would remain behind others in the line. ACCORD deals with the free-rider problem through the noncash auction: creditors are motivated to forgive because, although their claims will be lower, they will receive payment sooner and, hence, with a higher probability.

Hausch and Ramachandran (1999) solved the equilibrium bidding strategy of the creditors. If the value of the firm is certain, in equilibrium creditors with the same initial seniority bid the same proportionate reduction in their claims to share the value among themselves and leave nothing for the owners. For example, if the firm is worth US$160 (unobservable, but known to the creditors), and only two creditors exist, each owed US$100, then each would offer to forgive 20 percent in equilibrium. As the creditors make identical offers, they are randomly chosen to be at the front or back of the line. In this certainty case, both creditors eventually obtain US$80, regardless of their place in the line. This is an equilibrium (the unique pure-strategy equilibrium), because—given that one creditor forgives 20 percent—the other would be worse off forgiving more than 20 percent (and being first in the line) and no better off by forgiving less (and being second in the line).

Uncertainty about the value of the firm provides each creditor an incentive to be near the front of the line, leading to greater forgiveness. For instance, consider the above example of two creditors, but now suppose that the value of the firm could be either US$120 or US$200 (a two-point distribution), both equally likely. As before, the expected value of the firm is US$160, but some uncertainty exists about the actual value. Both creditors forgiving 20 percent no longer creates an equilibrium, because if they did, they are equally likely to be at the front and the back of the line. The one at the front definitely receives US$80, but the one behind gets an expected value of US$60 (receiving US$80 if the firm value turns out to be worth US$200 and only US$40 if the firm value is US$120). As the two creditors are equally likely to be positioned at the front and the back of the line if both forgive 20 percent, each creditor's expected payoff is one-half (US$80) plus one-half (US$60), equaling US$70. Clearly, each creditor has an incentive to forgive a bit more (say, up to 21 percent), because that would put the creditor at the front of the line, thereby being assured of obtaining US$79.

Each creditor has this incentive to forgive a bit more than in the certainty case, and the resulting equilibrium results in greater forgiveness (than the 20 percent) and results in the owner obtaining some residual value. The result is driven by the fact that creditors near the back of the line get little when the firm's value turns out to be low. Thus, owners in equilibrium obtain a strictly positive residual return—an important feature of the equilibrium—if they are to have the incentive to operate the firm more efficiently.

Implementing ACCORD

ACCORD does not require a complex bureaucracy, and the auction could be conducted either outside of or by the bankruptcy courts. While the details should be tailored to the circumstances of each country, the outline given here shows how it could be implemented under the aegis of the bankruptcy court, however inadequate it may otherwise be in overseeing complex negotiations.

The judge's role is modest and, by splitting the oversight role among others, the scheme cannot be easily subverted through incompetence or corruption. The judge announces the rules for participation in the ACCORD scheme and the auction procedures (bidding forms, deadlines, and so forth). The court appoints (a) an ACCORDer and (b) a recorder, whose roles become far more modest than that of a conventional administrator or receiver under bankruptcy. Each could therefore handle a large number of firms. Only one of them, perhaps the ACCORDer, need be an official of the court. The recorder might be an accounting firm with an incentive to maintain an international reputation for honesty and trustworthiness.

As the ACCORD scheme requires the firm's consent, that is, managers/controlling owners and a significant majority of creditors, no coercion is involved. A refusal entails no adverse repercussions beyond the existing "threat" of conventional bankruptcy, which already exists. Also, the preparatory steps are nonbinding; the parties commit themselves irrevocably to the ACCORD rules only just before the auction is conducted.

Preparatory Steps

Any of the parties involved—a creditor (for instance, a bank restructuring agency that has inherited the claim), a shareholder, or the firm's managers—can approach the bankruptcy judge to suggest the firm for the ACCORD scheme. This does not constitute a filing for bankruptcy, and at this stage the court serves simply as a sort of post office.

The judge informs the firm's managers about the rules of the ACCORD scheme and asks if they are interested in submitting within 30 days (a) a list of creditors and the amounts they are owed, and (b) a business plan. Official notification is only made to the party who suggested the firm to inform that person that the request was heeded, but the publicity of a bankruptcy filing is avoided. The firm's owner-managers may prefer the ACCORD scheme to conventional financial reorganization under bankruptcy in which their ownership may be diluted and they may lose control. Thus they are likely to provide the court with the creditor list and business plan, perhaps even contacting the major creditors directly to canvass the requisite majority support for the plan to ensure the ACCORD can proceed. As in a conventional financial reorganization, the creditors may form a committee to discuss the plan with the firm's managers, but the court would not be involved. As creditors may not approve a skimpy plan, the firm's owners have an incentive to supply information to satisfy the creditors.

If the firm declines, or fails to respond by the specified deadline, the matter ends without prejudice. If, however, the firm submits a plan, the court conveys it to all the creditors involved without examining its viability or fairness and alerts any claimants not listed by publishing its intent to conduct an auction of the firm's claims under ACCORD rules. The court notes that it will do so within two weeks if no disputes arise about the creditor list and the amounts owed and the requisite supermajority of creditors approve the plan.[3]

---

3. The requisite supermajority would be the same as that required for a cramdown under the bankruptcy law: generally, a simple majority within each class and two-thirds or three-quarters of the aggregate. This would also bind any new creditors who subsequently lend the firm money (suitable clauses could be inserted into the loan contract).

After the two weeks, the judge ascertains the above two steps in a hearing. If the judge is not satisfied, for example, because new claimants emerge, the matter ends with no prejudice against any party involved. In other words, the parties are free to either live with the status quo or file any suit under the bankruptcy or other laws, or to try to enter the ACCORD at a later date. If the judge is satisfied, the parties commit to ACCORD's binding rules.

The Binding ACCORD Rules

At this stage, just prior to conducting the auction, the judge binds the parties to the ACCORD rules. All creditors forfeit their right to file bankruptcy or liquidation petitions for, say, five years.[4] Owners agree to forgo any cash dividends or payouts during this period and, if the reduced debts are not fully discharged by the end of five years, to forgo automatic liquidation.[5] Box 5.1 outlines some of the auction's procedural details intended to make collusion among participants difficult.

By allowing bidders to hide their true identity, bidder collusion becomes more difficult and corruption less likely when the ACCORDer and the recorder divide this information between themselves. Limiting the judge's discretion, both before and after the auction, makes success less vulnerable to any shortcomings of the court. The judge only rules on disputes of fact, not questions of fairness. Once creditors approve the plan and bid in the auction, only fraud or egregious misconduct, not mundane business decisions, for instance, whether some asset should have been sold, would come up before the court.

One likely dispute may involve creditors' belief that the firm could pay out more cash faster. Cash is often needed to operate, or even expand, the business. While unlikely, some owners may accumulate a cash horde needlessly, but having the judge adjudicate this contingency would tie the courts and the parties involved into endless knots. Such fears are easily exaggerated: owners, eager to operate unfettered by the rules of the ACCORD, may discharge their debts sooner rather than later. Having interest at specified rates accrue on deferred debts, and automatically liquidating the firm

---

4. As the requisite supermajority needed for any cramdown under conventional bankruptcy has approved both the plan and the decision to enter the AC-CORD scheme, this can be made binding on the dissenters.

5. Depending on the company law, a shareholder meeting may have to ratify the management decision to undertake ACCORD. This protects the board of directors and managers against subsequent shareholder suits (although few countries are as litigious as the United States).

Box 5.1.   Details of the Auction Procedure

Bidding

Creditors submit bids in double envelopes to the recorder, who opens only the outer envelope. The envelope contains (a) a slip with only the bidder's name, address, and so on; and (b) another sealed envelope containing the bid, which the recorder does not open. The outside of this inner envelope and the accompanying slip contain the claim's priority and face value.

The recorder generates a unique identifying code and stamps it on the outside of the inner envelope (which does not otherwise identify the creditor) and on the accompanying slip. The recorder notes this code in his or her own records, with the bidder's name and face value of the claim and, knowing the list of original claims, also ensures that no bids are submitted in excess of what is owed. If the amount that has been (cumulatively) bid exceeds what the creditor is owned, the bid is rejected; if not, each bidder gets the slip back immediately as proof of the bid (it has each bidder's name and identifying code).

Creditors may submit multiple envelopes, perhaps bidding different reductions for different face values, or just splitting the bid to hide their identity (because the list of original claims is publicly known).

When the date for accepting bids ends, the recorder also submits envelopes on behalf of creditors who did not bid (an identifying code and amount outside with a zero reduction bid inside). There are therefore sealed envelopes totaling the aggregate claims outstanding (publicly known), and all these unopened inner envelopes are passed on to the ACCORDer on the date when bids are opened.

Opening the Bids

On the appointed day, the ACCORDer opens the sealed inner envelopes in public and reads out the identifying code, the face value of the claim, and the proportionate reduction bid. The aggregate reduction in the debt could be immediately calculated and announced. Each creditor can verify that his or her bid has not been tampered with, his or her position in the line, and (if the creditor keeps track of all bids) the (reduced) amount owed ahead of (and behind) the creditor. However, because of the identifying codes, the creditor does not know the true identity of those ahead or behind, nor how much any other creditor forgave, thereby making bid collusion difficult.

The ACCORDer knows those in line by their identifying codes, but not their true identities. The recorder (who is not present at the opening) knows the creditor identity of each code and the aggregate auction result (public information), but not what each creditor forgave. The firm (the owner) knows the original claims of each creditor and the aggregate reduction in debt, but does not know where any creditor is in line or the individual amounts of the deferred (or reduced) claims.

The ACCORDer sends a written confirmation of each bidder's result in a sealed envelope, with the identifying code outside, to the recorder by the end of the day, and the recorder forwards it to the creditor within another three days.

Periodic Payments

The firm places periodic payments into an escrow account (which the recorder administers) and informs the ACCORDer. When told the cash balance, the ACCORDer tells

(box continues on following page)

Box 5.1 continued

the recorder whom (identifying code) to pay and how much. (Only then does the recorder discover the bid amount.) In addition to paying the amounts promptly, the ACCORDer sends all creditors a quarterly statement of how much (face value) is still outstanding ahead of them, so they know how the line is moving.

Secondary Market

The deferred claims are transferable, but as they are not uniform, trading will only be sporadic with negotiated rather than quoted prices. The latest quarterly update forms the basis for the price, but a trade requires the seller to register the change in the claim ownership with the recorder. The secondary trade does not concern the ACCORDer or the firm.

---

if the (reduced) debts have not been fully discharged by the end of the specified five years, may provide sufficient incentives.[6] (Liquidation, too, could be accomplished by auction, with the owners and creditors free to bid.) Regardless of their position in the line, however, creditors may trade their claims at any time, as well as cash in their claims, albeit at a price different from their reduced claim.[7]

While firms may not distribute cash (except to the head of the creditor line as specified under ACCORD), they are free to raise additional funds through asset sales, new equity, or borrowings. These new claims cannot come ahead of existing claims and may not be serviced before full discharge of all the deferred claims outstanding. Any new equity would be in the same class as the old equity (at the very end of the line), but a new loan would come after all other loans (although ahead of the equity). This differs from conventional bankruptcy filing, in which new loans come before prefiling loans, because the old creditors have already reduced their claims.

Putting new borrowings at the back of the creditor line would not be detrimental to the continued operations of the firm or disadvantageous to

---

6. Interest accrual does not benefit creditors per se, as the bids compensate for this, but if interest did not accrue, firms would have an incentive to accumulate cash and only pay just before the five-year deadline to avoid liquidation. It is not onerous for the ACCORDer to calculate interest, which must be near market rates, permitting loans in foreign currency to accrue interest at a different rate. The automatic liquidation clause protects creditors against the firm accumulating cash surpluses (which may have genuine business reasons) instead of discharging the (reduced) debts.

7. When they do trade, they must inform the auditor so the check can be sent to the correct claimant, but neither the firm nor the court need be informed.

the new creditor, because the firm is not obligated to make any cash payment. Thus, its ability to finance its continued operations is considerably greater. The firm may also discharge all its outstanding debts at any time, so if the new lenders or investors find the restrictions onerous, the firm could use the proceeds to discharge the outstanding debts to the deferred creditors and operate unfettered by the ACCORD rules.

Additional Considerations

It appears initially that ACCORD hurts creditors by reducing their debts without giving them an equity stake or curtailing the owners' control. Despite laws, however, creditors are already hurt because they have little legal protection, and in most countries seem unable to seize control of the firm if they wanted to (though not all creditors seek this alternative). Offering ACCORD as an additional alternative to the status quo could therefore only benefit creditors, whose consent is still needed. ACCORD would only be used in the case of a Pareto improvement. That remains possible if the transaction costs, with the inevitable but wasteful threats, bluffs, and other inefficiencies of multiparty negotiations are reduced, or if increased efficiency results from eliminating the corporate debt overhang. The following section anticipates and answers some questions about the ACCORD scheme.

Preexisting Seniority of Claims

While ACCORD is best explained by beginning with creditors of equal initial seniority jockeying through their bids to become more senior, that is, to get ahead of other creditors in the line, the scheme can easily handle a preexisting hierarchy of claims by having an auction for each class.

A hierarchy of existing claims simply means that a creditor line already exists—albeit one that only applies to the distribution of liquidation proceeds. The scheme could nevertheless respect this priority of creditor classes when the new line gets formed: claimants could only bid for their relative positions within their class or segment of the creditor line. Thus, no matter how much a junior creditor forgives, that creditor could never get ahead of a senior creditor. As before, payments go only to the head of the line—that senior creditor who forgave the greatest proportion—and the line moves up. All the senior creditors are paid before any of the original junior creditors receive anything; however, within the class of senior creditors, the one who forgives the greatest proportion is paid before the others.

ACCORD begins with the most senior class of creditors, asking each of them to bid a level of forgiveness. The new aggregate debt level of this senior class is then publicly announced, after which the next most senior class bids, and so on until the lowest creditor class bids, knowing the new (reduced) aggregate debt senior to them. The analysis follows closely the discussion under the above heading "The Proposed ACCORD." Specifically, if the more senior classes are certain to be paid, that is, the range of possible firm values is such that they incur no uncertainty, they will forgive no part of their claims. Only when payment is uncertain for any creditor class will they offer to forgive, but as each will try to move ahead in that segment of the creditor line, they would forgive enough to leave a residual value to the class below them. This residual diminishes for every subsequent creditor class, but continues down to the owners, producing the desired outcome.

What if Forgiveness Were Insufficient?

While ACCORD reduces debts, no guarantee exists that subsequent cash flows will prove sufficient. This commonly occurs in conventional bankruptcy. Gilson (1997) reports that one-quarter to one-third of financially distressed firms that reorganize experience financial distress again within a few years. The expectation of another opportunity to reorganize could alter bidding strategies: creditors would bid a smaller forgiveness, thereby increasing the likelihood of subsequent bankruptcy. However, creditors realize that such uncertainty is detrimental to the firm and to the value of their claim, so they may bid more aggressive forgiveness.

Owner/Manager Effort

The ACCORD scheme results in creditors giving owners some residual value (they forgive more than seems absolutely necessary), but conventional financial reorganization under Chapter 11 also has this feature. Such seemingly "excessive" forgiveness provides the owner/managers with the incentive to operate the firm efficiently, especially when creditors are unable to closely oversee them.

If, as seems reasonable, owner/managers' effort is an increasing function of their residual return, more forgiveness does not just mean a smaller slice of the pie for creditors, but a smaller slice of a larger pie. The pie gets larger because, with the restoration of managerial incentives, managers operate the firm better. The assumption decrees that because creditors forgive less with Chapter 11, the owner/managers' effort remains lower, reducing the likelihood of creditors being repaid.

Government-Creditor and Noncompetitive Bids

Many East Asian governments now hold, directly or indirectly, substantial claims against financially distressed private firms. The governments have either taken over or substantially control the domestic banks whose nonperforming loans far exceed their capital. Banks' claims on private, financially distressed firms, whether residing in the intervened banks, bank restructuring agencies, or asset management companies, are substantial, but they may be influenced by the governments, or by various regulatory rules on capital and/or provisioning. While such government agents could bid like other creditors, given their size and vulnerability to making politically motivated bids, this chapter argues that they not be allowed to; instead, these claims should be reduced by the weighted average of the other bids.[8] Such noncompetitive bids (to use the misleading term derived from the auction for U.S. Treasury bills) would avoid politicizing the auction, and may also be permitted for other small creditors who may be at an informational disadvantage.

Nonparticipating Creditors

If a creditor fails to bid, one response would interpret this as a refusal to forgive and place the creditor at the end of the relevant segment of the line. Knowing this, other creditors would be emboldened to forgive less, because they would be certain to be ahead of the inactive creditor. Depending on the number of nonbidders, the result might be insufficient reduction in the aggregate debts of the firm. Of course, this imposes a penalty on those who did not participate and now find themselves at the back of the line with the firm's debt level difficult to sustain, possibly motivating their participation.

An alternative would treat nonbidders like the noncompetitive bidders, and reduce their claims by the weighted average forgiveness. While this

---

8. It could also be that the government's claims and positions in line are assigned to match perfectly the proportionate reductions and positions in line of the other creditors. Thus, rather than the government's claims appearing as a bulge in the middle of the queue, its claims could be uniformly spread over the queue.

may be reasonable, it might increase the incentive to corrupt the auction process by providing an incentive for bids "to go missing."

Conclusion

A common question posed in response to an unusual solution is "Has it been done before?" Some may find the absence of a precedent disconcerting. Systemic bankruptcy on the East Asian scale is unprecedented, and tailor-made solutions obviously cannot have been tried elsewhere. While the proposed ACCORD now only exists as an idea, auctions of analogous importance and complexity are increasingly widespread. In 1996 the U.S. Federal Communications Commission auctioned part of the spectrum suitable for cellular telephone use.

Besides its theoretical attraction, auction-based schemes such as AC-CORD prevent politics and venal courts from distorting the renegotiations of debt. East Asian governments and courts already have a reputation for being susceptible to the influence of powerful and wealthy business interests. With taxpayers bearing much of the losses through the government guarantee of banking deposits, some of the well-connected debtors may enjoy an unwarranted reduction in debts in negotiations with government agents; for example, the asset management companies or bank restructuring agencies that hold the claims. Even if this does not prove to be the case, the fear of such an accusation would stymie any bureaucrat negotiating unpaid claims. An auction protects the honest civil servant, because the government-controlled claims could be reduced by the weighted average of other bids. The ACCORD dispenses with a complex bureaucracy, and the auction could be conducted either by or outside the bankruptcy courts.

References

Aghion, P., O. Hart, and J. Moore. 1992. "The Economics of Bankruptcy Reform." *Journal of Law, Economics, and Organization* 8(3): 523–46.

Bebchuk, Lucian A. 1988. "A New Approach to Corporate Reorganizations." *Harvard Law Review* 101(2): 775–804.

Black, Fischer, and Myron S. Scholes. 1972. "The Valuation of Option Contracts and a Test of Market Efficiency." *Journal of Finance* 27(2): 399–417.

Gilson, S. 1997. "Transaction Costs and Capital Structure Choice: Evidence from Financially Distressed Firms." *Journal of Finance* 52(1): 161–96.

Hart, Oliver, Rafael La Porta Drago, Florencio Lopez-de-Silanes, and John Moore. 1997. "A New Bankruptcy Procedure That Uses Multiple Auctions." *European Economic Review* 41(3): 461–73.

Hausch, Donald D. B., and S. Ramachandran. 1999. "Bankruptcy Reorganization through Markets: Auction-Based Creditor Ordering by Reducing Debts." Policy Research Working Paper no. 2230. World Bank, Washington, D.C.

La Porta, Rafael, Florencio Lopez-de-Silanes, and Andrei Shleifer. 2000. "Investor Protection and Corporate Government." *Journal of Financial Economics* 58(1): 3–27.

6

Alphatec Electronics PCL

Perry Fagan, C. Fritz Foley, and Stuart Gilson,
Harvard Business School

> *It is better to eat dogs' dung than to go to court.*
> —Thai saying[1]

On the morning of July 28, 1997, Robert Mollerstuen, president and chief operating officer (COO) of Alphatec Group, received a call from the Alphatec Electronics Public Company Limited (ATEC) board of directors asking him to take over as interim chief executive officer (CEO). Based in Thailand, ATEC was part of the Alphatec Group, a sprawling network of technology-intensive businesses, ranging from semiconductors to telephones, plastics, and life insurance. ATEC had been a high tech pioneer in Thailand, starting out as a sub-contract semiconductor packager with assembly and test operations in Bangkok, Shanghai, and two locations in the United States. At an emergency session of ATEC's board, Charn Uswachoke, ATEC's charismatic founder and CEO, had resigned after a Price Waterhouse (PW) financial

1. William Gamble, "Restructuring in Asia—A Brief Survey of Asian Bankruptcy Law," *Emerging Market*, Volume III, No.1, January 25, 1999.

review uncovered several years of falsified financial statements and unauthorized disbursements to other companies controlled by him. Three weeks earlier Thailand had let its currency float, triggering a devaluation that set off a financial crisis across Asia.

The transactions PW discovered masked widening operating losses at ATEC, which left the company unable to service its $373 million debt. After it missed payments on two of its bond issues, a restructuring effort was launched in June 1997 under the direction of ATEC's management and creditors. An initial attempt at restructuring failed when Charn, ATEC's largest shareholder, rejected a plan that would have significantly diluted his ownership interest in the firm.

The failure of ATEC's first attempt at restructuring coincided with an April 1998 amendment to the Thai bankruptcy code that for the first time offered debtor companies like ATEC the option to seek reorganization under the Thai equivalent of Chapter 11 protection found in U.S. bankruptcy law. The prior law had provided only for the liquidation of distressed companies. Creditors could spend as long as 15 years in court arguing their rights, and their prospects for significant recovery were dim. As a result, creditors were reluctant to seek the intervention of the courts.

In the wake of Charn's refusal to approve the first restructuring plan, ATEC and its creditors initiated bankruptcy proceedings under the new law. Under court supervision creditors devised a second plan to restructure the company, one that did not require shareholder approval.

However, certain key creditors voted down this plan because of the large write-off involved and because they believed it would not guarantee their right to pursue legal action against Charn and ATEC's former auditors, KPMG Peat Marwick Suthee Ltd. (KPMG). Negotiations over a revised plan commenced between ATEC's Creditors Steering Committee, two potential equity investors, the court appointed Planner, and ATEC management. A final vote on the plan was scheduled for February 2, 1998.

For Mollerstuen, a "yes" vote would prove his longstanding faith in ATEC's underlying business, and would allow ATEC to emerge as the first firm to be reorganized under Thailand's amended bankruptcy code. A rejection by creditors would lead to further delays and risk the defection of the plan's two equity investors, who had agreed to inject $40 million of fresh capital into the cash-starved company.

For over 18 months Mollerstuen had served as ATEC's head cheerleader (with bodyguards for protection), confronting anxious creditors, angry shareholders, and impatient customers against the backdrop of Thailand's economic collapse. He felt strongly that with the new business plan the company could roar out of bankruptcy and could be profitable enough to go public within five years. With the vote less than one week away, he reflected on the events surrounding ATEC's bankruptcy and wondered what more he could do to end the protracted crisis.

History of Alphatec Electronics and The Alphatec Group

Born to a middle-class ethnic Chinese family in Bangkok, Thailand, Charn Uswachoke graduated from North Texas University. After graduating, he joined Honeywell in the United States, and soon returned to Thailand to work for a division of the company. Thailand's economy was booming, and Charn wanted to set out on his own. When Philips NV decided to sell a portion of an integrated circuit (IC) packaging plant, Charn borrowed money to make the purchase from Philips and build a new factory in Chachoengsao province (about 40 km southeast of Bangkok) in 1989. As part of the deal, Philips agreed to purchase 90% of the output for the next five years.

The company, named Alphatec Electronics, began production in 1991. ATEC's objective was to provide fully integrated "turnkey" IC packaging and testing services at competitive rates and high quality. Packaging involved the sealing of an IC in a plastic or ceramic casing. Packaged ICs were then tested to meet customer specifications. The company hoped to develop long-term strategic relationships with leading semiconductor manufacturers and offer a broad mix of packaging services. Some important early customers included Cypress Semiconductor Corporation and Microchip Technology, Inc.

Charn hoped to capitalize on two significant trends in the semiconductor industry. First, more semiconductor companies worldwide were subcontracting some or all of their packaging and testing operations to independent companies such as ATEC. Independents could offer significant cost savings due to their longer production runs and superior operating flexibility (e.g., they were better able to extend the useful lives of their equipment by migrating older machines to the testing of less complex products). Second, Southeast Asia was an increasingly attractive place to locate IC packaging and testing, due to the region's low operating costs and the heavy local concentration high-tech manufacturing.

Nineteen ninety-three was a pivotal year in the company's development. The company went public in Thailand through an initial public offering (IPO), and in the process increased its borrowings from banks and public debt markets. Charn acquired a major semiconductor assembly and test plant from National Semiconductor, as well as telephone assembly and testing plants from AT&T. He also entered the tool and plastic die industry.

The following year Charn began pursuing a longer-term strategy of developing a competitive cluster in the IC industry. He wanted to do design work, wafer fabrication, IC assembly and testing, and product manufacturing. His first major act under this expanded growth strategy was to launch a $1.1 billion venture called Submicron that would become Thailand's first state-of-the-art wafer fab. The project's initial financing included $350 million of debt with 26 local banks and finance companies.

The fab industry had played a significant role in the development of fellow Asian tiger countries Taiwan and Singapore, but it required reliable sources of water and power. Since these were generally wanting in Thailand, Charn decided to develop AlphaTechnopolis, a 4,000-acre high tech industrial park that would be located 9km from Alphatec Electronics. This park was intended to include Alpha Power, a $400 million 400-megawatt power facility, a $150 million water plant, and $200 million in other assets. Long range plans called for the development of housing and retail establishments, a hospital and school, an R&D center, and a technical university.

During 1994–1996, a string of acquisitions and investments followed. These included a joint venture with China's state-owned Shanghai Industrial and Electronic Holding Group Co. (SIEHGC) and Microchip Technology of Arizona to produce high volumes of low-tech chips (named Alphatec Shanghai). Charn purchased the U.S. firm Indy Electronics for $30 million (renamed Alphatec USA). He founded several new businesses, including two life insurance companies, an equipment leasing company, and a telephone equipment company. He took a majority equity stake in Alpha Memory Co. Ltd., a joint venture between Texas Instruments (TI) and Acer that would provide assembly and testing services for semiconductor memory products and would require $100 million in capital expenditures. And in late 1995 he and TI broke ground on a new $1.2 billion semiconductor manufacturing facility at AlphaTechnopolis, even though little progress had been made in completing the Submicron plant.

"Mr. Chips"

Although Charn was a significant shareholder in all of the companies he founded or acquired, he kept the businesses separate legal entities. Each company had its own board and reported separate financial information. Many of Charn's family members supported his efforts to build a competitive IC group of companies in Thailand, and they had important management positions at AlphaTechnopolis, AlphaComsat, and other group affiliates.

To manage all of his operations effectively, Charn united Alphatec Electronics and all of the other companies in which he held major stakes into what became known as the "Alphatec Group" (see figure 6.1). The Group was an informal entity without any legal basis. Charn ran this centralized management group from ATEC headquarters in downtown Bangkok.

Figure 6.1.   The Alphatec Group

The "Alphatec Group" consisted of over 11 companies, including ATEC, its subsidiaries, and Alphatec Shanghai. There was no legally recognized holding company, so the Alphatec Group was not a group of companies in the generally accepted sense of sharing a common parent. The companies were linked by a number of common shareholders, which together held a controlling interest in each of the Alphatec Group companies. The interests of individual common shareholders varied from company to company. A chart showing the interrelationships of the companies within the group is presented below.

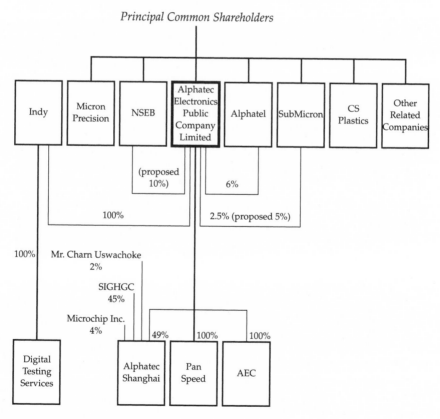

Source: Alphatec Electronics.

Group managers were split across several departments, including public relations, finance, and operations. Charn had the financial organizations in each company report directly to himself.

The operations department was actively involved in improving the efficiency of Charn's various businesses. Mollerstuen was an important member of this group. He was an American with more than 30 years of experience in the computer industry in both the United States and Asia, and had held top-level operational management positions at National Semiconductor and Philips Semiconductor. As chief operating officer he was responsible for all group assembly and test operations. He also had a significant role in building and maintaining ATEC's customer base. Working closely with Mollerstuen was Willem de Vries, executive vice president for production. De Vries had previously been the managing director of Philips Semiconductors Thailand, and also had more than 30 years of industry experience, working in England, the Philippines, Germany, France, Brazil, and the United States.

The ATEC board of directors was headed up by Waree Havanonda, a former deputy governor of the Bank of Thailand (BOT), and Charn's former finance professor. She countersigned for all of the major ATEC checks written by Charn. The 11-member board consisted of 6 bankers, the chairman of a trading company, the vice president of Bangkok Coil Center, Co. Ltd., and the Dean of the Institute of Industrial Technology at Suranaree University. "At that time the board had a bunch of bankers on it," Mollerstuen recalled. "They did not know the electronics industry well and relied on Charn for a lot of guidance. People in operations and from the factory were never allowed to attend meetings. Charn insisted that the meetings be conducted in Thai." As a result, Mollerstuen, de Vries, and other expatriate executives in the operations department had very little interaction with the directors.

By the mid-1990s ATEC had won much praise for its financial management practices and performance. Charn was considered by many as a pioneer of Thailand's electronics industry, earning him the nickname "Mr. Chips." In 1995, Alphatec received the prestigious Financial Management Award from the Manila-based Asian Institute of Management, in a ceremony attended by the Prime Minister of Thailand. In 1996, *Electronic Business Asia* magazine named Charn one of Asia's top business executives,[2] and some observers compared him to Bill Gates. In 1996 ATEC employed

---

2. *The Bangkok Post*, December 20, 1996.

over 1,700 workers and accounted for roughly 1% of Thailand's total exports. By 1997, seven of the top 10 North American IC producers were ATEC customers, including Advanced Micro Devices, Cypress Semiconductor, Microchip Technology, Inc., Philips Semiconductor, and TI.[3]

Alphatec in Distress

In 1995, coinciding with a general slowdown in the global semiconductor industry, ATEC's profit fell by 35%, from 699 million baht to 452 million baht. (Historical financial statements appear in table 6.1.) The Group came under increasing pressure to raise new financing. The initial phases of investment in AlphaTechnopolis, Alpha-TI, and the Submicron wafer fab plant had required large infusions of cash. However, businesses that could have provided positive cash flow for investment were slow in getting off the ground. For example, although Charn had hired a staff for his two life insurance companies, he had not yet been able to obtain licenses to operate them.

Charn turned to Lehman Brothers for advice on funding his numerous ventures. One proposal considered was to merge six of the group companies including ATEC and then raise money through an offering of American Depository Receipts. During the due diligence process, however, Lehman noted significant inconsistencies in ATEC's historical financial statements, and it terminated its relationship with Charn. Concerned by this development, ATEC's board hired PW to conduct a financial review of the company.

In March 1997 Charn made a proposal to the Prime Minister of Thailand asking the government to make investments in electronics companies, in a program similar to that used in Malaysia, Singapore, Taiwan, and Korea. On June 3 and June 10 the Thai cabinet issued proclamations confirming support of the electronics industry in general, and The Group in particular. The cabinet committee appointed to study ATEC's request for funds said it felt the firm's debt was excessive and should be restructured. The committee appointed Krung Thai Bank (owned by the government and controlled through the Ministry of Finance) to work with ATEC on the

(text continues on page 119)

---

3. ATEC's contracts with semiconductor manufacturers were denominated in U.S. dollars, as were the majority of its direct material purchase contracts. Roughly 40% of factory spending was baht based. About 35% of ATEC's total debt was in U.S. dollars.

Table 6.1. Alphatec Electronics Public Company Limited and Subsidiaries: Consolidated Balance Sheets, 1991-1996 (at December 31)[a]

(million baht)	1991	1992	1993	1994	1995	1996
Assets:						
Cash in hand and at banks	6.27	77.71	503.38	1,621.19	474.61	506.48
Short-term investment	—	0.97	1.00	4.25	3.67	3.21
Promissory notes—finance companies	—	—	—	—	2,167.00	1,927.00
Accounts receivable—other	3.54	512.33	1,109.33	609.95	1,359.81	2,004.87
Accounts receivable and loans to subsidiary companies	—	—	—	74.15	18.27	251.82
Inventories	745.11	1,033.97	1,100.40	1,216.73	1,423.14	2,203.37
Other current assets	74.51	58.77	42.41	15.17	48.31	101.72
Advance to employees	2.46	3.00	5.61	15.71	17.44	383.60
Investments in Subsidiary and related companies	3.64	—	—	195.00	518.28	520.04
Deposits	—	—	—	250.40	805.32	1,094.52
Property, plant and equipment—net	527.20	583.78	1,055.51	2,197.10	2,319.09	4,007.06
Other assets	93.89	449.54	574.42	780.18	937.62	577.73
Total Assets	1,456.62	2,719.97	4,392.06	6,979.83	10,092.56	13,581.42
Liabilities						
Bank overdrafts and loans from banks	251.64	620.91	1,536.98	2,370.99	3,308.36	5,381.60
Short-term loans	118.61	203.40	690.43	901.00	201.92	798.22
Accounts payable	582.82	895.79	189.02	187.24	182.88	455.62
Current portion of long-term loans	122.10	283.43	18.40	150.25	160.20	630.76
Other current liabilities	22.62	286.55	349.29	154.45	197.81	435.74
Loans from Directors	—	2.27	70.00	42.00	—	—
Long-term loans	193.83	80.79	329.62	394.73	320.71	556.71

(table continues on following page)

Table 6.1 continued

(million baht)	1991	1992	1993	1994	1995	1996
Convertible debentures	—	—	—	1,101.61	1,101.61	1,101.61
Total Liabilities	1,291.62	2,373.14	3,183.74	5,202.27	5,473.49	9,360.26
Shareholders' Equity:						
Share capital—common shares at baht 10 par value:						
Authorized and fully paid up	150.00	220.00	300.00	300.71	369.71	369.71
Premium on share capital	—	19.60	587.60	620.18	3,094.24	3,094.24
Retained earnings:						
Appropriated	15.00	111.62	30.00	54.00	74.00	100.00
Unappropriated	—	(4.39)	289.34	699.37	1,077.35	656.43
Foreign currency transaction adjustment	—	—	1.38	3.30	3.77	0.78
Total shareholders' equity	165.00	346.83	1,208.32	1,677.56	4,619.07	4,221.16
Total Liabilities and Shareholders Equity	1,456.62	2,719.97	4,392.06	6,979.83	10,092.42	13,581.42
Sales and services	2,152.43	4,477.77	8,017.69	10,031.07	11,274.44	12,241.32
Other income	59.54	9.40	21.71	45.01	7.25	89.48
Total Revenues	2,211.97	4,487.17	8,039.00	10,076.08	11,281.69	12,330.80
Cost of sales and services	2,070.88	4,090.53	7,318.35	8,910.73	9,825.54	10,891.27
Selling and administrative expenses	58.27	162.88	256.84	374.78	480.30	575.97
Interest expenses	67.81	135.02	201.43	300.76	273.95	445.66
Income tax	—	0.09	0.06	1.25	3.21	3.83
Total Costs and Expense	2,196.96	4,388.52	7,776.68	9,587.52	10,583.00	11,916.73
Income before extraordinary item	15.01	98.65	262.72	488.56	698.69	414.07

(table continues on following page)

Table 6.1 continued

(million baht)	1991	1992	1993	1994	1995	1996
Add extraordinary item			—	—	—	125.47
Add net loss in subsidiaries companies before acquisition date	—	—	—	—	—	60.73
Net result from investments in associated companies by equity method	—	—	—	—	—	(22.70)
Net profit for year	15.01	98.65	262.72	614.03	698.69	452.10

	1996 Baht	1995 Baht
Cash flow from operating activities:		
Net profit	452,100,499	698,685,826
Adjustment to reconcile net income to net cash provided by (used in) operating activities:		
Depreciation and amortization	557,723,599	273,296,121
Allowance for obsolete goods	(6,391,711)	6,978,799
Loss on exchange rate	15,884,610	9,034,411
Change in assets and liabilities		
Foreign currency translation adjustments	(2,988,924)	466,491
Increase in accounts receivable—others	(640,973,916)	(748,412,912)
Decrease (Increase) in accounts receivable and loans to related companies	(230,413,349)	56,979,810
Decrease (Increase) in advance to related company	163,475,000	(160,550,000)
Increase in inventories	(773,836,888)	(213,387,257)
Increase in other current assets	(53,410,691)	(33,139,331)
Increase in advances to director and employees	(366,148,331)	(1,736,844)

(table continues on following page)

Table 6.1 continued

	1996 Baht	1995 Baht
Decrease (Increase) in other assets	205,275,783	(74,231,183)
Increase (Decrease) in accounts payable—other	167,097,482	(5,443,258)
Increase in accounts payable—related companies	105,156,311	—
Increase in other current liabilities	223,513,014	43,364,965
Increase in other liabilities	14,423,050	—
Net loss in subsidiary before acquisition date	(60,729,350)	—
Net result from associated companies by equity method	22,701,341	—
Net cash provided by (used in) operating activities:	(207,542,471)	(148,094,362)
Cash flows from investing activities:		
Decrease (Increase) in short-term investments	460,000	(540,000)
Decrease (Increase) in notes receivable—financial companies	240,000,000	(2,167,000,000)
Decrease (Increase) in share subscriptions deposit	444,718,560	(444,718,560)
Increase in investments in associated and related companies	(127,202,178)	(159,807,555)
Cash received from (paid for) machinery deposits	(284,078,746)	(200,400,000)
Paid for land deposits	(450,000,000)	(310,600,000)
Increase in property, plant, and equipment	(2,091,089,905)	(291,442,790)
Land not using in operation	—	(187,045,380)
Paid for goodwill	(440,345,310)	—
Net cash used in investing activities	(2,707,537,579)	(3,360,754,285)

(table continues on following page)

117

Table 6.1 continued

	1996 Baht	1995 Baht
Cash flows from financing activities		
Increase in bank overdrafts and loans from banks	2,057,491,072	925,069,664
Increase (Decrease) in short-term loans	594,698,020	(699,080,000)
Increase in current portion of long-term loans	470,560,000	9,950,334
Increase (Decrease) in long-term loans	230,878,436	(74,019,474)
Repayments on loans from director	—	(42,000,000)
Proceeds from share capital	—	2,543,060,390
Dividend paid	(406,677,799)	(300,707,090)
Net cash provided by financing activities	2,946,949,729	2,362,273,824
Net increase (Decrease) in cash and cash at banks	31,869,679	(1,146,574,823)
Cash and cash at banks at January 1	474,610,609	1,621,185,432
Cash and cash at banks at December 31	506,480,288	474,610,609
Cash at banks under commitments	(80,860,888)	(50,000,000)
Cash and cash equivalents as at December 31 (Note 2)	524,619,400	424,610,609
Supplemental disclosures of cash flows information:		
Cash paid during the years:		
Interest expenses	569,026,792	385,648,232
Income taxes	4,007,386	3,268,012

Note: Consolidated financial statements since 1992.

a. Includes ATES and Alphatec Electronics USA, but not other Alphatec Group companies.

Source: Company Annual Reports.

restructuring. The envisioned restructuring would include write-offs, debt-to-equity conversions, and conversions from short-term to long-term debt.

In early May, TI announced it was pulling out of both Alphatec-TI and Alpha Memory. Although the factories were nearing completion, neither had the financing necessary to start production. "What was clear was that Charn was not infusing the capital he promised into the ventures," explained a spokesman for TI. "Nor was the area's infrastructure coming together."[4]

Later that month, ATEC failed to make a $34 million debt payment to a syndicate of banks led by ING Bank, and in late June it failed to come up with $45 million for a put option on its U.S. dollar-denominated Euro Convertible Debentures. Under the company's loan covenants, any formal declaration of default on either claim would have placed its entire $373 million in debt in default.

In response to these developments, in August ATEC appointed a provisional creditors' steering committee (CSC) to intermediate between the company and its various creditors. The group met multiple times per week in Bangkok and had 12 members representing more than 60% of the total loans outstanding. Members included Thai banks, foreign banks, Japanese banks, bill of exchange holders, bondholders, and finance companies. Of ATEC's 1,277 listed creditors, 1,025 were company employees, 176 were trade creditors, 31 were bondholders, and 44 were financial institutions. Krung Thai Bank held the largest debt of 4.23 billion baht (32%), followed by Bangkok Bank with 1.47 billion baht (11%), and Union Bank of Bangkok with 390 million baht (3%). (See table 6.2 for a list of financial claims.)

The company's share price dropped from over 300 baht in early May to less than 100 baht in late June. "Even though the Alphatec Group was not a legal entity," Mollerstuen complained, "the press reported its collapse. People confused group problems with problems at ATEC, and this was very bad for our marketing efforts and employee morale."

The July 2, 1997 Currency Crisis

Nevertheless, Mollerstuen remained optimistic. "We believe the restructuring will work and by August it will be business as usual," he wrote in an update distributed to ATEC customers and employees on July 2. The

---

4. Crista Hardie Souza, "Alphatec chairman quits; scandal grows," *Electronic News*, Vol. 43, August 4, 1997, pp. 6(1).

Table 6.2.   *List of Major Claims against ATEC*

	Currency	Baht	U.S. Dollars
Financial Claims (number)			
Claims for which amounts had been agreed (37)		5,990,149,393	137,881,818
Convertible Debentures (31)	USD	2,018,003,728	47,082,187
Claims for which amounts still had to be agreed (7)			
Bangkok Bank Plc	Baht	1,477,691,581	34,476,126
Bangkok Metropolitan Bank	Baht	853,068,249	19,902,995
GE Electric	USD	133,757,979	3,120,717
Krung Thai Bank	Baht	4,227,918,135	98,641,855
Nakornthon Bank	Baht	313,395,394	7,311,850
Pacific Finance & Securities Plc	Baht	128,241,095	2,992,002
Union Bank	Baht	390,663,444	9,114,596
Subtotal		7,524,735,878	175,560,141
Total		15,532,888,998	362,524,146
Employees (1,025)		63, 545,793	1,482,591
Trade and Other Creditors (176)		548,884,877	12,806,072
Contingent Liabilities (1)[a]		2,611,165,815	60,921,293

Note: 1 U.S. Dollar = Baht 42.8613

a. Amount owed Custom Department and Revenue Department.

Source: Alphatec Electronics Public Company Limited Business Reorganization Plan, January 7, 1999. Based on ADR claim filings as part of ATEC's rehabilitation process.

very same day, the Bank of Thailand allowed the baht to float in international money markets. It had previously been tied to a basket of foreign currencies. By September, the baht had fallen by 25%, to 32.75 to the dollar (figure 6.2), plunging firms with significant amounts of U.S. dollar-denominated debt into financial distress. Foreign capital fled the country, causing an extreme liquidity crisis. Banks and finance companies suddenly found themselves burdened with huge numbers of nonperforming loans. The government directed 16 finance companies to cease operations for 30 days and merge with stronger companies. Table 6.3 and figure 6.3 provide data on Thailand's economic and stock market performance.

The Price Waterhouse Audit

On July 24, 1997 PW issued its preliminary report to the ATEC board. The accounting firm raised two areas of concern. The first was that ATEC had maintained two distinct sets of financial records: a set of internal

Figure 6.2.   *Exchange Rate, Thai Baht to U.S. Dollar (January 1, 1990-*
January 1, 1999)

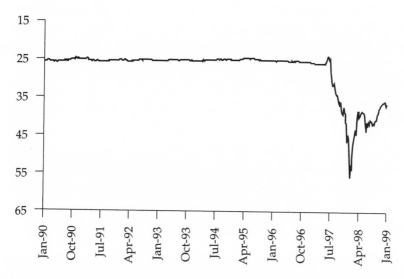

Note: Scale has been inverted to show the Baht's strength.
Source: Datastream.

Table 6.3.   *Selected Economic Indicators for Thailand*

I. Comparative Indicators, 1998

	Thailand	Malaysia	Indonesia	United States	Japan
GDP ($ billion)	116.1	71.1	88.3	8,511.0	3,782.7
GDP per capita	1,899	3,204	435	31,522	29,885
Consumer price inflation (avg; %)	8.1	5.3	57.5	1.6	0.7
Current-account balance($ billion)	13.2	9.1	4.0	−233.7	121.0
% of GDP	11.4	12.8	4.6	−2.7	3.2
Exports of goods fob ($ billion)	53.05	73.2	50.7	673.0	373.3
Imports of goods fob ($ billion)	−38.59	−58.3	−31.6	−919.0	−251.2
Foreign trade[b] (% of GDP)	78.9	185.0	93.2	18.7	16.5

a. Official estimate.
b. Merchandise exports plus imports.
Sources: Economist Intelligence Unit Country Profile of Thailand, 1999-2000.

(table continues on following page)

Table 6.3 continued

II. Stockmarket Indicators

	1994	*1995*	*1996*	*1997*	*1998*
Companies quoted (no.)	389	416	454	431	418
Total capitalization at market value (Baht billion)	3,300.8	3,564.5	2,559.5	1,133.3	1,268.1
Daily average turnover (Baht million)	8,628.0	6,239.7	5,340.7	3,763.5	3,504.8
SET index (year-end)	1,360.1	1,280.8	831.6	372.7	355.8

Source: Bank of Thailand, *Key Economic Indicators,* as reported in Economist Intelligence Unit Country Profile of Thailand, 1999-2000.

III. Nonperforming Bank Loans (Baht billion)

	December 1998		*January 1999*	
	NPLs	*% of total credit*	*NPLs*	*% of total credit*
Commercial banks	2,356.08	43.0	2,356.57	44.3
Eight private banks	1,245.15	40.7	1,281.38	42.0
State-owned banks	1,036.69	62.5	1,008.21	66.3
Foreign banks	74.24	9.8	77.98	10.1
Finance companies	2,681.45	45.1	2,700.67	46.5

Source: Bank of Thailand, as reported in Economist Intelligence Unit Country Report on Thailand, second quarter, 1999.

"management accounts," and a set of "financial accounts" for the public. Analysis of these accounts revealed that the company's reported profits and net assets had been overstated. PW concluded:

> As at 24 May 1997…our current best estimate is that the net assets of the company per the "financial accounts" were approximately Baht 3.6 billion higher than those per the "management accounts." In addition, our current best estimate is that reported profits of the company have been overstated by Baht 500 million in the first quarter of 1997, by Baht 1.8 billion in the year ended December 1996, by Baht 1.8 million in the year ended December 1995 and by lesser amounts in prior years. The company's reported profits in the first

Figure 6.3.   *Daily Closing Prices for Bangkok SET Index and Thailand SE Electric Products/Computer Indices, January 1, 1990-January 1, 1999*

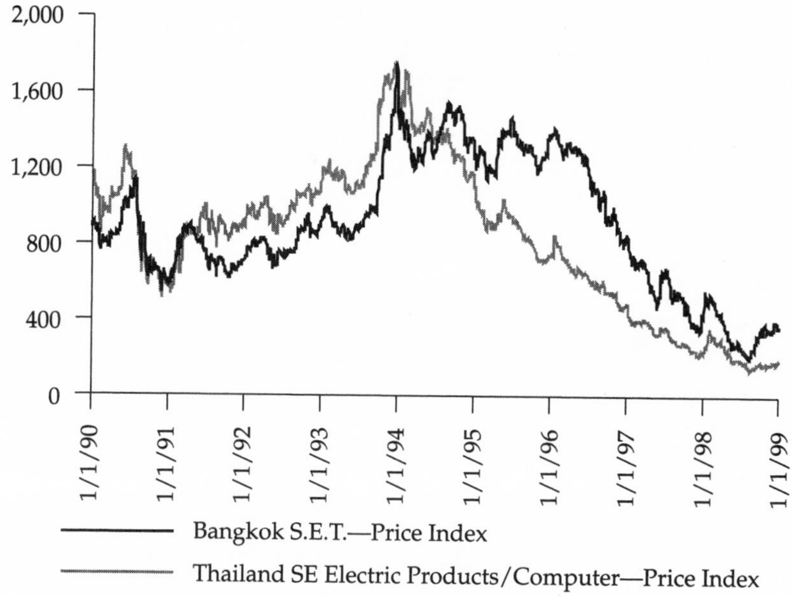

Bangkok S.E.T.—Price Index

Thailand SE Electric Products/Computer—Price Index

Source: Datastream.

quarter of 1997 and in prior years should have been reported as significant losses.

PW's second concern was that Charn had withdrawn money from ATEC without proper authorization. "From December 1994 to July 1997," the report stated, "amounts totaling Baht 3.95 billion have been paid out of the company to related persons apparently without the prior approval of the directors of the shareholders. A substantial portion of the payments have been initially recorded as being advanced to an executive director of the company, but subsequently recorded as transactions with companies under his control."

When ATEC's board questioned him about these accusations, Charn denied that he had used the money for personal gain. He told *The Bangkok Post* that he was "a determined guy who wanted to get things done quickly," and that was "one of the many reasons his ambitious project fell apart."[5]

---

5. Busaba Sivasomboon, "'Determined guy' runs into storm clouds," *The Bangkok Post*, August 3, 1998.

On July 28 the Alphatec board issued a press release announcing that it had asked the Thai stock exchange (SET) to suspend trading in its shares. It also announced it had accepted Charn's resignation as CEO, although as ATEC's largest shareholder with over 13% of the firm's outstanding shares he remained a member of the board.[6] In the months following his resignation Charn remained secluded, out of sight of the press.[7] In a subsequent telephone interview with *The New York Times*, he was reported as saying that ATEC was a victim of Thailand's imploding economy.[8]

New Management Takes Charge

On the same day that Charn resigned, the board named Mollerstuen Acting CEO (figure 6.4 shows Alphatec's organization chart). When Mollerstuen arrived at headquarters the next day he found finance executives shredding documents. He barricaded them in a conference room and later suspended the whole financial management team. Mollerstuen had occupied the office next to Charn for years, and recalled the difficult situation he faced stepping in as Acting CEO:

> As of August 1, 1997, the company had sales of about $50 million and debt of about $373 million. It was obvious that we needed to restructure. We put together a quick business plan and decided that $35 million was the most debt we could service. This meant that the banks would need to take more than a 90% write-off. They were shocked. The banks were facing their own liquidity problems because of the growing levels of non-performing loans. Even though we tried to get them to help us to restructure, they were primarily focused on their own problems.

---

6. Alphatec's board filed a complaint against Charn with Thai police, accusing him of damaging the company's finances. The police and the SET began an enquiry into doubtful accounting practices surrounding Alphatec's buying of land from its executives at above market prices, as well as at its procedures for acquiring foreign subsidiaries.

7. The compound consisted of eight houses near the ATEC factory. According to an August 3, 1998 report in *The Bangkok Post*, in the months after the Alphatec crisis erupted Charn lost over 20 pounds due to stress. However, the press reported that "he never thought of escaping from the problems or committing suicide, something his secretaries and associates were concerned about." Soon thereafter reports surfaced in the press that Charn was hard at work trying to revitalize Submicron.

8. Mark Landler, "No. 1 in Its Bankruptcy Class, A Company in Thailand Starts to Get Its Act Together," *The New York Times*, June 11, 1999.

Figure 6.4. Alphatec Organization Chart at November 25, 1997

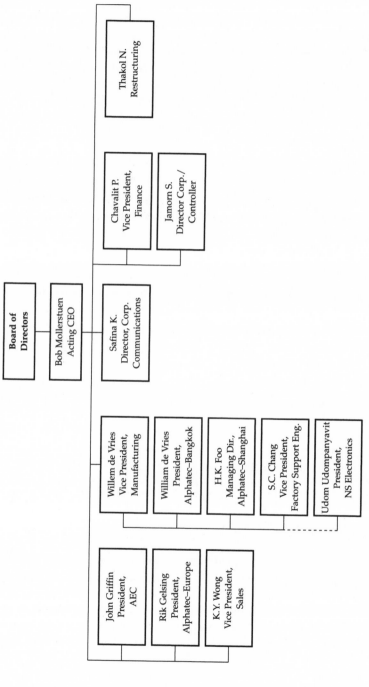

Board of Directors

Bob Mollerstuen
Acting CEO

Safina K.
Director, Corp.
Communications

Chavalit P.
Vice President,
Finance

Jamorn S.
Director Corp./
Controller

Thakol N.
Restructuring

Willem de Vries
Vice President,
Manufacturing

William de Vries
President,
Alphatec–Bangkok

H.K. Foo
Managing Dir.,
Alphatec–Shanghai

S.C. Chang
Vice President,
Factory Support Eng.

Udom Udompanyavit
President,
NS Electronics

John Griffin
President,
AEC

Rik Gelsing
President,
Alphatec–Europe

K.Y. Wong
Vice President,
Sales

Source: Alphatec Electronics.

125

In mid-August Crédit Agricole Indosuez filed a claim against ATEC in the Thai Civil Court for $8.2 million for failure to service an outstanding loan. "We wanted to assure our customers and creditors that this was an isolated claim," said Mollerstuen. "The provisional CSC had informed us that they continued to support us in our restructuring effort. We tried to convince the bank to withdraw its claim and participate with the other creditors under the umbrella of the CSC." Although the court ordered ATEC to pay the debt, the bank was persuaded to temporarily forbear.

In mid-September, Charn resigned from Alphatec's board of directors. He explained:

> Now that I've fulfilled my responsibility to ensure the successful start toward implementation of the restructuring plan, I think it's time for me to leave the board. I'm very grateful that the bondholders and the creditors have supported Alphatec in its goal of restructuring. This company does have a very bright future, once the financial problems are solved.[9]

In a company press release announcing Charn's departure, ATEC's board chairman stated, "Prior to his departure, we have been assured by Charn that it's his intention and his commitment to repay to the company all the moneys which were transferred out without the proper authority." On October 10, de Vries and Mollerstuen were appointed to ATEC's board of directors.

Running the Plant

Even though negotiating with creditors was an arduous, time-consuming process, Mollerstuen and de Vries faced the additional challenge of keeping the productivity and morale of the employees high.

"The first time most people at the plant knew there was a problem was when they read about the breakdown of the Alphatec Group in the newspaper," said Nonglak Phungsom, director of human resources at the Alphatec Thailand plant. She continued:

> People had viewed Alphatec as a great place to work. The stock price quickly went from the offering price of 10 baht to 400 baht. The

---

9. "Two board directors resign from Alphatec," *The Bangkok Post*, September 13, 1997.

situation was very difficult for factory employees from a psychological perspective. Khun[10] Charn, whom most had looked up to, was being attacked in the press. Employees would read news stories that were sometimes only partially true. Employees were shocked and there was not much they could do. The average employee did not know that numbers in the annual report had been misstated.

Willem (de Vries) told us to remain calm, and that he would not lay people off so long as he was here. Since he is a European, and not an American, we thought that he would have a longer-term perspective, and we trusted him on this point. Finding another job during the crisis would have been difficult. Many employees just did not have outside opportunities. Also, if people left [voluntarily] during the crisis, it would have been a sign that they did not care, that they were ignoring the problems, or maybe even that they were guilty.

De Vries recalled: "I took over plant operations from the start and I was very open with people, even more so in this time of crisis. I told them that I would not leave, that I would be the last one to turn off the light. We lost some expatriates, but most people stayed on." De Vries and Mollerstuen believed that firing people at the plant would bring ATEC to its knees. Mollerstuen also explained that firing a worker in Thailand meant paying him or her six months' severance. Because he estimated that the restructuring would take five months, and that he would need to rehire people let go during the restructuring, he saw no point to firing people.

Nonglak described some of the actions taken at the plant during the restructuring:

> The crisis forced us to learn new things. We were given the opportunity to challenge ourselves. We understood that we needed to make the factory more efficient if we wanted to survive. Our suppliers had stopped extending trade credit to us. We took a 20% salary cut at the management level. Employees were encouraged to find ways of saving cash and to write these up as suggestions. Many of their ideas were implemented. We started printing on both sides of each page. There was no more free coffee. We provided cheaper rice at the canteen. We carefully looked at all steps of the production process. We reduced the waste of gold wire and plastic compound. We consolidated the bus service lines that we provided to employees.

---

10. The term "Khun" was a polite form of address in Thailand.

We began to give the employees all of the details about our cash position and our earnings. We never missed a payroll payment, but we came close. We tried to make it clear that we all needed to work together to survive.

During the restructuring, ATEC's Thailand plant was running at one-third its capacity. "During the slowdown at the plant, we tried to get QS 9000 and ISO 14000 certification so that we would be ready for the future," Nonglak explained. "This international quality standard would give us more credibility in export markets." Plant management also reduced cycle time from six to three days, and increased yield from 99% to 99.7%.

The First Restructuring Plan

On February 2, 1998 the CSC and the ATEC board circulated the first formal restructuring plan.[11] The plan included a number of provisions that would enable the company to finance its short-term working capital requirements and make necessary capital improvements. First, cash could be raised through the pre-financing[12] of accounts receivable and a drastic reduction in receivables payment terms to less than 10 days. Second, some of ATEC's creditors could form a trading company ("NewCo") to collect receivables, take customer orders, pay trade creditors, and supply materials on consignment to the existing Alphatec factory ("OldCo"). An extension of this proposal had NewCo also fund capital expenditures by financing and/or leasing equipment. Under this scenario NewCo would supply OldCo equipment on consignment or through operating lease, with service or lease payments remitted by OldCo to NewCo (see figure 6.5).[13]

In the medium term, all lenders would participate as shareholders in a new private company that would take over the assets of the old ATEC. The existing liabilities would remain with Old ATEC, while the new company would become a platform for raising new debt and equity.

---

11. In August, ATEC had appointed a formal CSC comprised of eight financial institutions: ING Bank, Bangkok Bank, Bankers Trust, Dresdner Bank, Krung Thai Bank, Nakornthon Bank, Standard Chartered Bank, and The Sumitomo Bank.

12. Customers would send payment to one or more banks, which would extend a loan for the same amount to ATEC.

13. No approval from ATEC's shareholders would be needed for this proposal. However, ATEC would need approval from 75% of shareholders in the event that the trading company controlled funds flowing into ATEC.

Figure 6.5.   *Proposals for a New Alphatec at November 25, 1997*

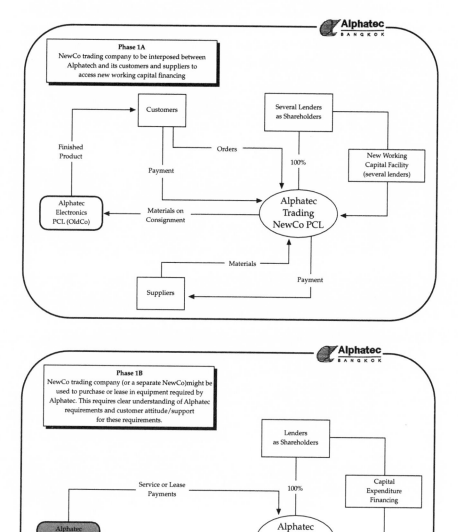

(figure continues on following page)

Figure 6.5 continued

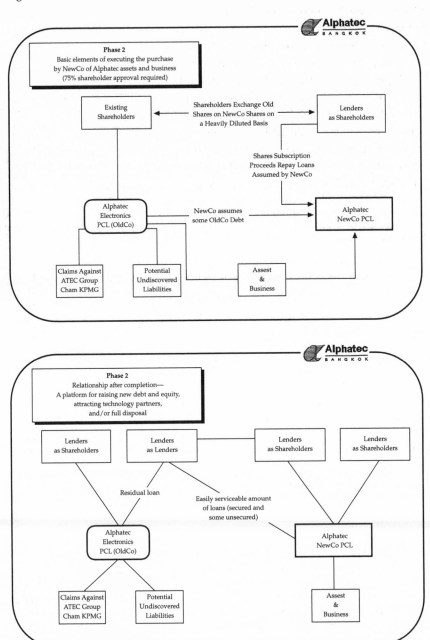

Source: Alphatec Electronics.

In the long term, the plan described options to consolidate various Group affiliates, and to open a new factory in early 1999, called "Alphatec II." Revenue projections were based on significant growth in unit volume (see table 6.4 for financial projections under the plan and table 6.5 for comparative data).[14] The company claimed it had already cut corporate overhead by 50 percent by reducing headcount in its Bangkok headquarters, and would realize additional cost savings by restructuring sales offices in Japan and the United States, and by selling U.S.-based assembly and test operations, which had continued to be unprofitable.

The plan required that creditors convert 95% of their outstanding debt into equity, with senior unsecured creditors expected to receive 12 to 13 cents on the dollar.[15] The plan also proposed a $30 million equity infusion

Table 6.4.   *First Restructuring Plan Financial Projections (US$'000s)*

Totals, 1998–2002	Alphatec I	Alphatec I and II	Alphatec I and II and Alphatec Shanghai	Alphatec I and II, Alphatec Shanghai and NSEB
Volume (units)	1,529,468	1,877,218	4,982,418	11,259,091
Revenue	668,776	1,799,366	2,162,313	3,212,063
EBIT	139,425	399,721	492,003	717,949
Cumulative depreciation	67,432	NA	NA	NA
EBITDA	206,856	543,600	683,332	1,029,707
Capex	(66,318)	(375,318)	(471,927)	(485,623)
Free Cash Flow	140,538	186,282	229,405	438,845

Note: The restructuring plan valued businesses of this type at multiples of 1x Revenue, 6x Free Cash Flow, and 10x EBIT.

14. The IC contract assembly and test market was expected to grow at 28% in 1997; 29% in 1998; 30% in 1999; 35% in 2000; and 16% in 2001. ATEC's top five customers accounted for roughly 95% of revenues; including TI (37%), Cypress Semiconductor (30%), and Advanced Micro Devices (10%). It was estimated that a delay of one month during restructuring would delay anticipated production volumes by at least two months due to reduced customer confidence and qualification procedures.

15. In contrast, creditors' returns from liquidation were estimated at between 20%-25% for secured creditors, and zero for unsecured creditors.

Table 6.5. *Comparative Data for Selected IC Packagers (US$ million)*

Company Fiscal year Ended	Net Sales	Depreciation & Amortization	Net Income	Net Cash from Operations	Total Assets	Long-term Debt	Market Value Common Stock
Amkor Technology Ltd. (USA)							
Dec. 1995	932	27	62	53	NA	NA	NA
Dec. 1996	1,171	58	33	9	805	167	NA
Dec. 1997	1,456	82	43	250	856	197	NA
Dec. 1998	1,568	119	75	238	1,004	15	1,275
Advanced Semiconductor Engineering (ASE) (Taiwan)							
Dec. 1995	595	41	85	59	744	94	967
Dec. 1996	649	63	72	170	844	130	1,405
Dec. 1997	586	71	227	156	1,387	365	3,575
Dec. 1998	645	101	50	NA	1,460	380	2,984
ST Assembly Test Services (Singapore)							
Dec. 1995	NA	NA	NA	NA	NA	NA	NA
Dec. 1996	32	12	(7)	13	NA	NA	NA
Dec. 1997	88	25	(9)	10	225	—	NA
Dec. 1998	114	42	(1)	48	237	54	NA

Note: Amkor was the world's largest independent provider of semiconductor packaging and test services. It was also a leading developer of advanced semiconductor packaging and test technology. ASE was the largest independent IC packaging company in Taiwan, and one of the largest IC packagers in the world, with operations in Taiwan and Malaysia. ST Assembly Test Services was a Singapore-based independent provider of a full range of semiconductor test and assembly services.

Source: Global Access, Datastream.

from two foreign investors. Equity would be invested in $6-$10 million tranches for agreed projects keyed to plan milestones.

The plan required the approval of 75% of the company's shareholders (by value) plus 100% creditors' approval. It also needed approval of 66% of bondholders (in number). The plan was contingent on ratification by shareholders of PW as the company's new auditor. Management believed ATEC's debt could be restructured by March 2. "We are getting close!" Mollerstuen wrote to customers. "The next few weeks will tell."

Negotiations Falter

Progress in the plan negotiations was interrupted when PW presented its year-end audit of ATEC's 1997 results to a meeting of shareholders on February 27, 1998. It recommended that ATEC record a net loss of 15.4 billion baht ($381 million) for the year—in dramatic contrast to the profit of 452 million baht reported in 1996. PW believed the company needed to take write-offs and write-downs totaling more than 11 billion baht against accounts receivable, loans to directors and related companies, unusable fixed assets, and falsified inventories.

Charn rejected the report, and the appointment of PW as ATEC's new auditor. According to *The Wall Street Journal*, shareholders believed "[PW's] assessment of how much of the company's assets should be written off was too harsh."[16] Given the voting requirements of the plan, this meant that an out-of-court restructuring would not be possible under the current terms. Within a few days, Cypress Semiconductor announced that it was canceling its testing contract with ATEC.

On March 16, ATEC announced that it was "clearly insolvent" at the end of 1997. In a report to the ATEC board, PW expressed "substantial doubts" about ATEC's ability "to continue as a going concern."[17] According to Mollerstuen, the company had only enough cash to last into May, as it continued to reduce plant operating costs and sell excess equipment.

The next day Mollerstuen wrote to customers: "The word for today: Don't Panic! Bankruptcy is our contingency plan. Bankruptcy is the way we want to go! We will come out of this a lot leaner and meaner—much better able to meet your ongoing cost requirements."

---

16. "Thai Alphatec Posts Massive Loss, Appears Headed for Bankruptcy," *The Wall Street Journal*, March 17, 1998.

17. *The Wall Street Journal, op. cit.*

The New Thai Bankruptcy Law

For months the CSC and ATEC's management had been watching the slow progress of Thailand's government in amending the country's bankruptcy code. The existing law provided only for liquidation. After several delays, and under pressure from the International Monetary Fund, the new legislation was finally signed into law by Thailand's King on April 10, 1998.[18] By giving debtors and creditors more flexibility in renegotiating debt repayment and reorganizing troubled businesses, the government hoped to help the country's many ailing financial institutions and corporations. (See figure 6.6 for a comparison of the old and new laws.)

Under the new law, a creditor, debtor, or government agency could file a petition with the court to initiate the in-court restructuring process. A hearing was scheduled to determine whether the court would issue an "order for business rehabilitation." During the hearing, the court examined whether there was a reasonable way to rehabilitate the business. The petitioner also needed to establish that the company was insolvent. Insolvency required that the book value of assets be less than the book value of debt.

If granted, the order triggered an automatic stay on creditors' ability to seize assets. The new law also enabled firms to obtain working capital financing by granting certain lenders "preferential creditor" status, giving them first claim over other creditors. An Official Planner was selected by creditors and approved by the court as part of the petition. The restructuring procedures gave the planner the control rights of the former managers and shareholders of the debtor. The planner had three months to submit a rehabilitation plan to the Official Receiver for a vote by creditors. Only two one-month extensions were allowed.

Once he or she had received the plan, the Receiver would send copies to all creditors with voting ballots. The Receiver would then convene a meeting of creditors and call for a vote on the plan. If approved by 50% of the creditors in number and 75% of creditors in value, the plan would be submitted to the court for approval. The law did not recognize different classes of creditors. Existing shareholders had no voice in the rehabilitation process. A final plan had to be approved by the court within five months of the original order for rehabilitation.

The company would then be placed under reorganization by the court. The company had five years to implement the plan under the supervision

---

18. Ameneded bankruptcy laws were one requirement the IMF attached to its $17.2 billion bailout of the Thai economy.

Figure 6.6. *Thai Bankruptcy Process*

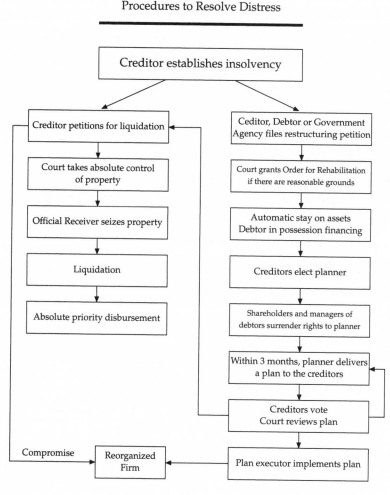

Procedures to Resolve Distress

Creditor establishes insolvency

Creditor petitions for liquidation

Court takes absolute control of property

Official Receiver seizes property

Liquidation

Absolute priority disbursement

Ceditor, Debtor or Government Agency files restructuring petition

Court grants Order for Rehabilitation if there are reasonable grounds

Automatic stay on assets Debtor in possession financing

Creditors elect planner

Shareholders and managers of debtors surrender rights to planner

Within 3 months, planner delivers a plan to the creditors

Creditors vote Court reviews plan

Compromise

Reorganized Firm

Plan executor implements plan

Thai Bankruptcy

Source: C. Fritz Foley.

of a Plan Administrator. During implementation, the Plan Administrator maintained the control rights of the managers of the debtor and the shareholders, but day-to-day management responsibilities were delegated to company executives. If the company did not meet targets established under the plan, its assets could be liquidated by the court, or creditors could attempt to restructure the company again.

ATEC Files for Bankruptcy

On May 12, 1998 ATEC's management and creditors filed a petition for rehabilitation with the Bangkok Civil Court, the first such filing under the new law. On June 4, the petition was approved, and ATEC officially entered rehabilitation. The petition named Price Waterhouse Corporate Restructuring Ltd. (PWCR) as the Official Planner. Crédit Agricole Indosuez was named as international financial advisor to the CSC. The bank and PWCR would be responsible for securing additional equity investors and working capital for ATEC, advising the CSC on the soundness of the restructuring plan, and overseeing its implementation.

All Thai members of ATEC's board resigned, leaving de Vries and Mollerstuen as the only board members. All accounts payable were frozen. Payment of these amounts and other liabilities would be provided for in the rehabilitation plan. The company operated on a "pay-as-you-go" basis.

The Rehabilitation Plan

Reaching agreement with creditors and potential equity investors on the terms of ATEC's rehabilitation proved difficult. After a one-month extension, PWCR filed the rehabilitation plan with the Receiver on November 5.

Under the plan assets of the old ATEC would be transferred to a new company, Alphatec Holding Co. Ltd. (AHC). AHC would own 99.9% of Alphatec Semiconductor Packaging Co. (ASP), which would be set up to take over the core operating assets and employees and run the business of ATEC. The holding company would also own 51% of the Alphatec Shanghai joint venture, and 100% of ATS Services Company. Based in San Jose, California, ATS provided worldwide sales and marketing support for all companies under the AHC umbrella.

The Bankruptcy Law of Thailand prohibited claims from being made if an application for the repayment of debt was not filed within a prescribed time period. However, the law did not cover overseas claims. Investors feared that such claims might arise and believed that the new organizational form would protect them. In addition, investors wanted to invest in a company that had a known history that could provide a "clean vehicle" for a future stock listing. Because AHC and ASP were newly incorporated companies, investors believed there would be no unpleasant surprises.

At that point ATEC had total debt of $373 million (15.4 billion baht) and book value of assets of $82.7 million (3.4 billion baht) (a current balance sheet is shown in table 6.6). ATEC owed $363 million to financial institutions, and another $10 million to nonfinancial institutions. Under

Table 6.6. ATEC Financial Position at June 4, 1998 (Baht millions)

	Submitted to Court	Unaudited Management Accounts	Note
Current Assets:			
Cash and deposits	61	61	
Investments	8	8	1
Accounts receivable – trade (net)	125	125	2
Accounts receivable, loans to related parties (net)	114	114	3
Inventory	210	210	
Other current assets	61	61	4
Total Current Assets	579	579	
Investments in subsidiaries and related co. (net)	234	234	5
Property, plant and equipment (net)	2,355	2,355	6
Other assets (net)	234	234	7
Total Assets	3,402	3,402	
Liabilities:			
Loans from financial institutions	14,593	14,654	8
Accounts payable	314	314	8
Other current liabilities	446	446	8
Investment in subsidiary	0	183	9
Total Liabilities	15,353	15,597	
Net deficiency	(11,951)	(12,195)	10
Contingent liabilities	314		11

Notes: (Assume US $1.00 = Baht 41.16)

1. Comprise short-term deposits and investments in marketable securities, adjusted by management to reflect market prices.
2. Includes amounts owned by existing customers of Alphatec, in addition to a net amount of approximately Baht 1.4 billion owed by Pan Speed Limited, a wholly owned subsidiary of Alphatec, which has been fully provided against. It has subsequently been discovered that this amount was overstated by approx. US$ 750,000 as a result of bona fide price adjustments agreed with a customer that had not been reflected against recent invoiced amounts.
3. Comprises as follows:

	Baht Million
Alphatec Electronics Corporation Co., Ltd. (registered in USA)	27
Alphatec Electronics Corporation of Shanghai (registered in People's Republic of China)	11
Alpha Technopolis Company Limited	553
NS Electronics Bangkok (1993) Limited	73
Micron Precision Company Limited	130
Micron Archin Company Limited	435
Other related companies	62
	1,291
Less: Allowance for doubtful accounts	(1,177)
Total	114

(table continues on following page)

Table 6.6 continued

4. Primarily consists of prepayments.
5. Comprises as follows:

	Baht Million	Baht Million
Subsidiaries:		
Alphatec Electronics Corporation Co., Ltd.		
(registered in USA)		17
Alphatec Electronics Corporation of Shanghai		
(registered in People's Republic of China)		214
Pan Speed Limited (Registered in Hong Kong)	139	
Less: Allowance for diminution in value of investment	(139)	
	0	231
Investments in other companies:		
C.N.C. Building Company Limited	4	
Alphasource Manufacturing Solutions Public		
Company Limited	174	
Submicron Technology Public Company Limited	50	
	228	
Less: Allowance for diminution in value of investment	(228)	
Bangkok Club Co., Ltd.		3
Total	0	234

6. Comprise the land and buildings occupied by Alphatec at Chachoengsao, Thailand, and all machinery and equipment owned by Alphatec. Amounts represent book value. Valuations of land, buildings, machinery and equipment indicate that book value exceeds the current market value of these assets.
7. Other assets (net) were:
   - Freehold vacant land located adjacent to land and buildings occupied by Alphatec at Chachoengsao (at purchase price): 201 Baht million
   - Refundable deposit: 26 Baht million
   - Advance and loan to directors and employees: 7 Baht million
8. Includes both secured and unsecured creditors, and convertible debentures.
9. At March 31, 1998, Alphatec USA, Inc., a wholly owned subsidiary of Alphatec, had a capital deficiency of US$ 4.4 million. Alphatec accounts for this as a negative investment under the equity method.
10. Indicates there is a substantial deficiency in shareholders equity.
11. Consist of outstanding purchase orders issued by Alphatec, against which materials or services had not been provided as at 4 June 1998

Note on Contingent Assets:
Contingent assets of Alphatec include claims against certain parties as follows:
   - A civil lawsuit was filed in the Central Labour Court on 17 July 1998 in the amount of approx. Baht 14 billion against the former CEO, certain former employees of the company and other companies in respect to alleged misappropriation of Alphatec funds, falsification of Company records and other actions causing detriment to Alphatec.

(table continues on following page)

Table 6.6 continued

- A lawsuit filed in the Civil Court on 23 July 1998 in the amount of approx. Baht 20 billion against the previous auditors of Alphatec up to the time that the financial irregularities were discovered in July 1997, in respect to alleged damages suffered by the Company as a result of a failure to detect and report on the misstated financial position of the Company.

Source: ATEC Rehabilitation Plan, January 7, 1999.

the plan, the $363 million debt would be restructured as follows: $10 million would be converted into equity, $35 million would be serviced after the restructuring (fully payable by 2003), $55 million would be payable contingent upon company performance, and $263 million would be written off or recovered through legal action against Charn and KPMG.[19] The company estimated that creditors would realize significantly lower recoveries under a liquidation (see table 6.7).

PWCR announced that AIG Investment Corporation (Asia) Ltd. (part of insurance giant American Insurance Group), and Investor AB (the largest Swedish industrial holding company and parent of Ericsson) were finalizing negotiations for a large infusion of equity into ATEC. Under the plan the investors would be required to inject an initial $20 million, followed by an additional $20 million to fund subsequent expansion of production capacity (table 6.8 shows financial projections).

AIG and Investor AB would own 80% of AHC, while creditors would own the remaining 20%. Existing shareholders of ATEC would have their claim reduced to one percent of registered capital, while creditors would become the principal shareholders.

Krung Thai Balks

On December 14, ATEC's creditors voted down the rehabilitation plan. While the majority of creditors in number supported the plan, the necessary approval by value of 75% of creditors was not obtained.[20] The vote was swung by Krung Thai Bank, which voted against it. The bank believed that the plan did not protect its right to seek recovery from ATEC's former management (primarily Charn, who had personally guaranteed the loans),

---

19. Creditors choosing not to write off their loans would be eligible to receive proceeds from the sale of noncore assets of ATEC. Creditors choosing to write off their loans would receive a tax credit but not proceeds from the disposal of noncore assets.

20. The vote was approximately 50% in favor and 50% opposed on a value basis.

Table 6.7. *Estimated Realizations from Alternative Strategies under the Rehabilitation Plan*

	Amount Outstanding (US$mil)	Restructured (US$mil)	%	Liquidation (US$mil)	%	Note
Financial creditors:						
Interest in						
Alphatec's						
Senior Secured						
Debt	178	20		20		1
Junior Secured						
Debt	185	15		8		2
Shares in						
Holdco	—	10		—		
Performance-	—	Not known		—		3
linked		(55)				
obligation						
Noncore assets	—	Not known		Not known		4
Legal claims	—	Not known		Not known		4
TOTAL	363	45	12	28	8	
Employee creditors	1	1	100	—	—	2
Trade and other						
unsecured						
creditors	9	3	33	1	10	2
TOTAL	373	49	13	29	8	

Notes:
1. In addition to the secured portion of Senior Secured Debt, approximately USD 2.6 million (liquidation value) of noncore assets can be realized for the benefit of secured creditors.
2. The liquidation value of unencumbered assets approximates USD 10 million based on a valuation received in July 1998. In the event of liquidation, this amount would be shared between unsecured financial creditors, trade creditors, and employees.
3. In the Plan, financial creditors will receive a performance-linked obligation with a face value of USD 55 million. However, as this does not mature for 10 years and is contingent on future profit performance, realization from this instrument is not included in the above analysis.
4. Recoveries from noncore assets and legal claims are not possible to estimate with any certainty at this time.

Source: ATEC Rehabilitation Plan, January 7, 1999.

Table 6.8. *Financial Projections Contained in the Rehabilitation Plan*

The financial projections prepared by management for distribution to potential investors indicated the following for Thailand operations:

USD'mil	1999	2000	2001	2002	2003	2004	2005	2006	2007	2008
Revenue	73	164	241	303	332	381	439	505	580	668
Cost of sales	(36)	(84)	(123)	(156)	(174)	(194)	(220)	(255)	(299)	(355)
Gross profit	37	80	118	147	158	187	219	250	281	313
Net profit	2	12	30	57	72	102	138	116	134	151
CAPEX	62	71	54	22	20	40	40	40	404	40

Note: Excludes any contribution from ATES, but includes reimbursement of AEC costs.

The results of work undertaken by CAI in seeking additional equity investment indicated that, given the existing state of the semiconductor market, potential investors were willing to invest significantly less than the amounts originally sought by ATEC to fund more conservative growth projections. Revised financial projections were prepared by the Investor based on a lower level of initial investment and lower capital expenditure levels going forward. The more conservative projections for Thailand operations indicated the following:

USD'mil	1999	2000	2001	2002	2003	2004	2005	2006	2007	2008
Revenue	36	66	102	120	131	135	140	145	153	163
Cost of sales	(19)	(37)	(57)	(68)	(75)	(78)	(81)	(84)	(89)	(96)
Gross profit	17	29	45	52	56	57	59	61	64	67
Net profit	—	4	13	14	13	18	15	15	18	20
CAPEX	14	20	17	19	11	8	8	10	10	10

(table continues on following page)

Table 6.8 continued

Notes:
1. Includes royalty from ATES, and includes reimbursement of AEC or similar costs.
2. Management believed these projections were conservative, particularly for 2000 onwards; however, these revised projections formed the basis for the restructuring assumptions included in the second plan.
3. Working capital requirements were estimated as follows (US$ millions):

1999	10
2000	10
2001	14
2002	17
2003	19

Source: ATEC Rehabilitation Plan, January 7, 1999.

142

and KPMG. The bank feared that it would give up this right if it wrote down its debt.[21]

Creditors appointed a different division of PWC as planner, and gave the firm 45 days to present a modified plan. ATEC management forecasted that the company would deplete all available cash (including cash that had been reserved for traditional year-end employee bonuses) in mid-January 1999. As before, an offshore holding company would be created, AHC, and ATEC's assets would be transferred to a new Thai operating company, ASP.

Financial creditors of ATEC were offered an option in how they would hold their claims in the restructured company. Creditors could hold their claims directly in AHC or indirectly through ATEC. If a creditor exercised the option to hold its claim in AHC, it could write off any residual debt claims from ATEC immediately and realize any tax-related benefits. In writing off claims against ATEC, creditors would leave the pursuit of claims against Charn and KPMG to the plan executor (see figure 6.7). The plan did provide for creditors who took write-offs to share in future recoveries if they contributed to the legal fees the plan executor would incur pursuing such claims. Finally, AIG and Investor AB agreed to commit up to $5 million of their investment proceeds for working capital, if required. All other material aspects of the plan remained unchanged.

PWCR distributed the revised plan to creditors, and another vote was scheduled for January 27, 1999. "In the Planner's view," wrote PWCR in its preamble to the revised plan, "it is highly unlikely that Alphatec would be able to secure a more attractive restructuring alternative."

Another Deferral

On January 27, 1999 Krung Thai Bank asked fellow creditors to delay the vote while it considered its options. The Receiver agreed to delay the vote by three working days. AIG and Investor AB also agreed to the delay, but said that if the decision were prolonged indefinitely, they would stop their plans to invest in ATEC, and would shift their investment to Malaysia.[22]

Meanwhile, Charn had resurfaced in the press. He claimed the creditors' plan to rehabilitate ATEC was unacceptable because it effectively

---

21. Under the amended Thai bankruptcy law, there was no legal recourse against alleged fraud involving personal guarantors if a rehabilitation plan was approved by the majority of creditors.

22. "Krung Thai Bank defers final decision," *Bangkok Post*, January 28, 1999.

Figure 6.7.   *Transaction Structure under the Revised Rehabilitation Plan*

Under the terms of the original rehabilitation plan, each creditor was to have received directly its portion (the "Entitlements") of restructured debt, performance-linked obligation, and shares in Holdco.

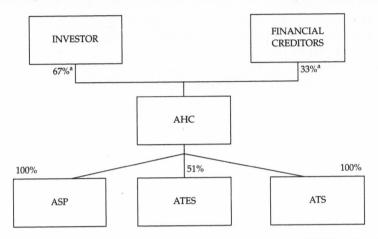

a. Percentage ownership following the Investor's initial investment of US$20 million. Once the Investor made its subsequent US$20 million investment, the percentage ownership applicable to the Investor and Financial Creditors would be 80% and 20%, respectively.

In the revised plan, each creditor would have the option of (1) receiving its Entitlement via a distribution such that it held its Entitlement directly, as proposed in the original plan, or (ii) retaining its Entitlement via a continuing stake in Alphatec.

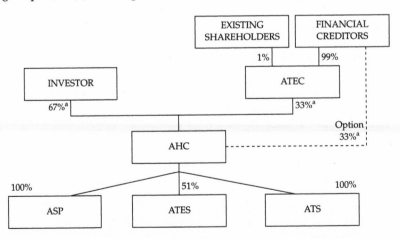

a. Percentage ownership following the Investor's initial investment of US$20 million. Once the Investor made its subsequent US$20 million investment, the percentage ownership applicable to the Investor and Financial Creditors would be 80% and 20%, respectively.
Source: ATEC Rehabilitation Plan, January 7, 1999.

established a new company and because it valued the company at only $40 million. He said the company's land, buildings, and machinery were worth more than $40 million, and that he was confident that the electronics industry would pick up by the fourth quarter of 1999 and would once again become profitable.[23] He was rumored to be considering taking legal action to stop the rehabilitation plan from proceeding.

In the event the revised rehabilitation plan failed, Mollerstuen and de Vries intended to pursue ATEC's restructuring through a management buyout. "The company has managed to survive thanks to the efforts of employees, management, suppliers and the loyalty and patience of customers," he said. "But time, patience, and cash are running out."[24]

Postscript

On February 2, 1999, creditors of Alphatec Electronics approved the company's revised restructuring plan, producing the first successful reorganization under Thailand's new bankruptcy law.

Under the plan, which became effective on April 24, the U.S. insurance company American International Group and Sweden's Investor AB (parent of Ericsson) invested a total of US$40 million for 80% of the equity of newly incorporated AHC. Foreign and domestic creditors of Alphatec received the remaining 20% of AHC's equity.

Based in the Cayman Islands, AHC owns 100% of the equity of Alphatec Semiconductor Packaging Co. (which was created to take over Alphatec's operations in Thailand), 51% of the joint venture Alphatec Electronics Corporation of Shanghai, and 100% of Alphatec Services Co. (representing Alphatec's U.S sales and marketing operations).

Under the plan, Alphatec's foreign and domestic creditors wrote off the firm's US$379 million debt, in exchange for the 20% interest in AHC. In addition, they were given secured debt of US$35 million in Alphatec Semiconductor Packaging and a performance-linked 10-year bond in AHC that could pay as much as $55 million. Alphatec's former shareholders were effectively wiped out.

The plan was approved by 85% of Alphatec's 1,200 creditors, representing 75.2% of the outstanding debt. Thus the plan just narrowly satisfied the 75% voting majority requirement in the new law. The outcome hinged on the vote of Alphatec's largest creditor, Krung Thai Bank PCL, which

---

23. *Ibid.*
24. "Alphatec Creditors File Rehabilitation Plan," *The Nation*, May 13, 1998.

had rejected the previous plan proposed in December 1998. The bank finally voted for the plan on the condition that it would retain the right to pursue legal action against former Alphatec managers, including Charn Uswachoke, who had personally guaranteed the firm's debt.[25]

Less than two weeks after the plan was approved, Charn, who was still a major shareholder of record, objected in civil court that the plan was unfair and that it mainly benefited foreign investors. Charn also argued that the plan was illegal under the bankruptcy law because it proposed to alter Alphatec's basic corporate structure (through the creation of AHC). The judge rejected Charn's arguments, however. Among other things, the judge noted that the primary goal of the new bankruptcy law was to encourage the reorganization of troubled businesses, which did not necessitate keeping a firm's corporate structure intact.[26]

Some observers predicted that on the basis of Alphatec's success in reorganizing its debts, many other troubled Thai companies would soon make use of the new law. After one year, however, only 18 firms had sought bankruptcy court protection. Of these cases, the court rejected eight because the debtor was deemed not to be insolvent. Of the remaining 10 cases, only two ultimately resulted in a final court-approved plan of reorganization.

To address several perceived defects in the 1998 statute, in April 1999 a revised bankruptcy law was passed (Bankruptcy Act B.E. 2541). The new law made it easier to approve a plan of reorganization, by recognizing several distinct classes of claims and relaxing the voting requirements for approving a plan. Under the 1998 law all creditors, regardless of seniority or security, were treated as a single class. The revised 1999 law recognizes four different classes of creditors: large secured creditors (who each hold more than 15% of the company's total debt), small secured creditors, unsecured creditors, and subordinated creditors. Each class votes separately. A plan can now be approved if creditors holding at least 75% of the debt *in any one class* vote affirmatively, provided at least 50% of all the company's debts are voted in support of the plan. (As under the 1998 law, a plan can also be approved if creditors holding at least 75% of all the firm's debts vote affirmatively.) The 1999 law also provides for a form of post-petition

---

25. "Alphatec Restructuring Gets Go Ahead," *The Asian Wall Street Journal*, February 3, 1999.

26. "Thai Court Rules in Favor of Alphatec's Restructuring," *Associated Press Newswires*, February 15, 1999.

"debtor in possession" financing, which in principle should improve bankrupt firms' access to capital.

According to a Thai government official, during the three months that followed enactment of the 1999 law, eleven new cases were filed, and in seven of these cases creditors approved the rehabilitation plan.[27] In June 1999, Thailand's first specialized bankruptcy court began operations.

Despite the legal charges facing Charn, Alphatec's former CEO remained chief executive of SubMicron and maintained control of a number of other businesses that had been part of the Alphatec group. In January 2000, the Central Bankruptcy Court froze his assets and those of SubMicron after ruling that both he and the company were insolvent.[28] However, the charges that he faced with respect to misappropriation of funds and falsification of company records were still pending in June 2000.

In the time that has passed since Alphatec emerged from bankruptcy, the company's operations have experienced a significant turnaround. Benefiting partly from a recovery in the worldwide semiconductor market,[29] the company was able to boost its capacity utilization from 35% at the beginning of 1999 to more than 85% by the end of January 2000.[30] The company's key Alphatec Semiconductor Packaging subsidiary generated positive earnings before interest, taxes, depreciation, and amortization in the second quarter of 2000, and the company has planned investments in several new factories to increase manufacturing capacity.

---

27. "More Thai Companies Seek Rehab After New Bankruptcy Law Enacted," *Dow Jones International News*, August 9, 1999.

28. "Thailand's 'Wafer Fab Man' Close to Losing His Plant," *Business Times*, January 31, 2000.

29. In 1999 worldwide industry revenues grew by 19% and are expected to grow by over 30% in 2000.

30. "Alphatec on the Comeback Trail," *The Nation*, January 31, 2000.

7

Corporate Debt Restructuring in a Systemic Financial Crisis: Mexico's Experience, 1996–98

Alberto Mulás, Fondo Bancario de Protección al Ahorro

In 1995, Mexico's gross domestic product (GDP) dropped 6.2 percent in real terms, with actual decreases closer to 10 percent in the second and third quarters of the year. GDP dropped even more in those sectors focused on the domestic marketplace, such as consumer goods, retail, construction, real estate, and other sectors. Overall consumption deteriorated, while inflation, interest and exchange rates, labor costs, and prices for raw material increased sharply. The combination of these factors led to an extremely difficult economic situation that significantly affected Mexico's corporate and financial sectors.

The resulting crisis created an environment in which most corporations either faced insolvency or a significant reduction in corporate value. The combined effect of reduced sales and revenues, higher operating costs from inflation, increased interest expense, and reduced cash flows characterized this environment. Many corporations could not meet their financial obligations, be they interest or principal payments, and had to stop payments to creditors, leading them to restructure such obligations. As expected, creditors reacted by threatening to legally enforce their contractual rights, which resulted in corporations and shareholders filing for counterprotection under the Suspensión de Pagos Law.

Shareholders of large, highly visible, distressed companies sought to solve their problems with creditors, mainly Mexican banks, through nonmarket-based solutions, including using the Suspensión de Pagos or seeking government support and subsidies. Equivalent to the U.S. Chapter 11, the Suspensión de Pagos Law gives troubled companies a temporary moratorium on debt service and payments. It offers the debtor a chance to solve the problem of a cash flow crunch. This law, however, also provides corporate shareholders the opportunity to remove significant corporate assets from creditors' control. Under the law, shareholders can continue to control the company. It also allows shareholders the right to stop payments, convert dollar-denominated loans to pesos at a fixed exchange rate, and accrue interest at court-determined noncommercially low interest rates.

The significant exposure of the financial sector to large, troubled corporations (estimations suggest that the largest 50 debtors represented an aggregate amount of about US$8 billion dollars in debt, equal to the total equity in the financial system) combined with the internal turmoil financial institutions were experiencing, forced bankers to first concentrate on solving the largest corporate restructuring cases at the expense of delaying the restructuring of smaller corporations.

Meanwhile, shareholders of small- and medium companies who could not initiate their restructuring process also threatened bankers with the Suspensión de Pagos in an attempt to force banks to focus on their case and, in some instances, to grant them favorable restructuring terms. Both large and small corporations used the law as a weapon to force concessions from creditors.

During the crisis, banks were also subject to strong pressures from the development of a highly leveraged and poorly performing client base, making banks' loan portfolios extremely risky and requiring larger amounts of reserves. Banks, however, were unable to maintain the reserve and capital levels established by the regulator, as they were also affected by marking to market their short-term securities, their dollar-denominated liabilities, and their derivatives trades, while also paying higher funding costs. Banks sought to keep their asset base current by aggressively collecting or restructuring their loan portfolios and avoiding costly bad loan loss provisions. However, the general corporate and shareholder threat of the Suspensión de Pagos Law kept banks from aggressively seeking to take possession of their guarantees, creating an indefinite, quasi-bankruptcy status.

In this environment, the government launched three programs to improve confidence in the financial system and avoid a run on bank deposits. First, a foreign-exchange liquidity support program offered short-term dollar credits to banks experiencing problems with renewing their foreign currency liabilities. Second, a temporary capitalization program provided banks extra time to reorganize in an orderly fashion. In this program, banks with capital ratios below the 8 percent threshold had to issue subordinated debentures that were bought by the central bank. These securities automatically converted into equity after five years and precluded banks from paying dividends or issuing additional capital unless they were repaid in full. The program aimed to provide incentives for shareholders to raise new equity for their bank, or risk losing their institution to the government. Third, a loan purchase program in which the central bank offered to buy two dollars of loans for every dollar of new equity invested by shareholders. The purchase of loans was done on a 75-percent risk basis, that is, the selling bank transferred 75 percent of the economic risk, keeping the other 25 percent, while also remaining responsible for administrating the loan.

The latter program, known as the Loan Purchase Program, improved capital and reserve ratios and resulted in the financial system's exposure to a single entity of troubled corporate borrowers, a central bank trust called the Fondo Bancario de Protección al Ahorro (FOBAPROA). This provided the opportunity to centrally supervise the asset recovery process and to facilitate the corporate debt restructuring process.

Concurrent with these programs, the government implemented the takeover (intervention) of six mismanaged and seriously troubled financial institutions, representing approximately 15 percent of the financial system. The regulator, the National Banking and Securities Commission (CNBV) was responsible for interventions. When the CNBV detects operational irregularities, encompassing anything from banking law deviations to outright fraud, it uses the intervention mechanism to protect the interests of depositors. While the CNBV is responsible for the intervention, FOBAPROA is the entity that bears the final risk and cost of all intervened banks' assets, thus adding the loans from these banks to its portfolio. The CNBV appoints the manager of the intervention (the interventor) who reports back to the CNBV. The interventor estimates the real value of the bank's assets, defines the cost of the bank's rescue, and identifies any illegal activities of previous managers or shareholders.

Corporate Debt Restructuring, 1995–97

Debt restructuring during Mexico's crisis turned into a painful process in which stakeholders feared losing their investments. Shareholders, lenders, suppliers, and workers were subjected to enormous pressure, resulting in a tense atmosphere not conducive to dialogue. Lenders felt betrayed and lost their confidence in lending money. Shareholders worried about losing all they owned. Workers faced the risk of losing their jobs and were, therefore, concerned with the operational status of their employers. In addition, suppliers were preoccupied with keeping their clients in operation to continue selling or to recover past due receivables.

In the face of this crisis, suppliers and workers insisted on being paid in cash, clients exercised their privilege to pay upon product delivery, and lenders and shareholders moved to protect their rights. For example, secured lenders tried to exercise their guarantees and obtain their collateral, and shareholders sought legal protection through the Suspensión de Pagos Law to prevent the collapse of their businesses. These aggressive and uncoordinated procedures led to a vicious cycle in which corporate value was not protected.

In addition, the characteristics of Mexico's banking loan portfolio further complicated the restructuring process for three reasons. First, loans were documented on a short-term, variable interest rate basis that was linked to the interbank cost of borrowing. This made amounts due grow as interest payments capitalized at increasingly higher interest rates or at higher exchange rates. Second, the lack of common market practices and of a syndicated loan format resulted in loan fragmentation. Each financial institution independently arranged loans, generating a mass of differing assets (loans) in terms of borrower type, loan type, payment terms, security, and loan documentation. Third, Mexico's complex corporate structure, whereby corporations generally consisted of holding companies with various levels of subsidiaries, had loans outstanding at both the holding and the subsidiary levels, creating structural subordination issues.

Combined with adverse economic conditions, the complexity of the restructuring process led to tremendous friction both among banks and between banks and corporations (or their shareholders). The delay of the restructuring process not only prolonged the crisis, but also generated mistrust between bank executives and company officers, as the constantly changing economic environment caused frequent changes in the terms of restructuring agreements.

Recognizing that wide use of the Suspensión de Pagos Law would have resulted in major bank losses, regulators and banks sought to promote constructive debt negotiations to prevent bankruptcy. For these reasons the government created the Unidad Coordinadora para el Acuerdo Bancario Empresarial (UCABE), a restructuring support and mediation committee. UCABE, a four-member interdisciplinary committee, acted as mediator and facilitator in those corporate debt restructurings that suffered from the previously described decisionmaking vacuum in the financial system.

UCABE's four members complemented each other's professional experience, and together these members provided the basis for recommending to banks, corporations, and the government the means to proceed with each debt-restructuring process. This interdisciplinary committee was comprised of a prominent businessman, the chief credit officer from Nafin (Mexico's national development bank), a senior officer from the banking regulator (the CNBV), and a senior investment banker.

UCABE's mandate and operating procedures were outlined in a set of bylaws that were included in the agreement signed between the CNBV and the National Bankers Association. The heads of the 18 largest commercial banks also signed this agreement, providing a basis for UCABE's activities within the banking community. This document described the objectives of the unit: to facilitate dialogue among banks and between banks and corporate shareholders and to work as a third-party broker, focusing on two goals, restructuring corporate debt and preserving the ongoing concern value of viable corporations facing solvency problems. By so doing, UCABE enabled shareholders to solve their debt solvency crisis and return to the design of new corporate strategies appropriate for the new economic environment. It also allowed banks to restructure their troubled loans.

UCABE's Operating Rules

UCABE's bylaws also outlined a series of simple rules to facilitate its mediation efforts. These rules applied at two levels of interaction: interaction among banks and interaction between banks and corporations. The rules governing interactions among banks were as follows:

- Banks would organize a creditor's committee (the restructuring committee) in every restructuring case.
- Every restructuring case would have a lead bank, generally the bank with the highest share of bank debt. The lead bank would be allowed to receive a restructuring commission of 1 percent of the restructured amount and would share with all other banks the expenses incurred during the recovery process. If the bank with the largest exposure was unable, or unwilling, to become the lead bank, another bank would be appointed with approval from banks holding at least 60 percent of the total debt outstanding.
- Banks would agree to sign a stand-still agreement. In the agreement, banks would pledge to avoid legal proceedings, providing certainty

to all parties during negotiations. The agreement would mandate that banks not collect principal or interest and not take legal action until either the restructuring was finalized or the stand-still agreement was terminated. The agreement included a time limit to prevent companies from seeking to perpetuate their stand-still status.

- Banks would accept decisions taken in any formally convened meeting attended by at least three banking institutions, including the lead bank, that represent 60 percent or more of the outstanding debt.
- Restructuring proposals would always respect guarantees. Banks with cash-flow-generating guarantees would have priority over banks without cash-flow guarantees.
- In the event that a participating bank authorized new money loans to the company, other banks would accept that these new funds would have payment priority over all other debt and could be given new guarantees by the borrower.

The rules governing interactions between banks and corporations were as follows:

- Negotiations would be based on maximizing corporate value and on maintaining the highest amount of sustainable debt possible under the new cash flow generation conditions. Corporate value would be calculated on the basis of the net present value of the company's cash flows, using discounted rates of return mutually agreed on by the banks and the borrower.
- Banks and shareholders would agree to consider debt capitalization on the basis of a mutually agreeable corporate value. Capitalized amounts would include any debt remaining after deducting from the firm's total indebtedness both the amount of sustainable debt to be left in the company and any debt amount settled with assets. The resulting equity positions would carry minority-right protections for banks or shareholders. The price for debt-to-equity conversion would be determined by the net present value of cash flows, or on the basis of a formula mutually established by the restructuring committee and the shareholders. It would necessarily include exit options.
- Shareholders would agree to respect each of the bank's legal guarantees prior to signing a stand-still agreement.
- Shareholders would agree to reject the Suspensión de Pagos option, because it was likely to negatively affect negotiations and recovery of value.

UCABE's Function in Corporate Debt Restructuring

The UCABE committee focused on corporate value, using its third-party, honest-broker position to influence the discussions on corporate value assessments and their distribution among corporate stakeholders.

Participation in UCABE was not mandatory for banks or corporate shareholders, and its recommendations were not enforceable on either party. However, once banks and corporations accepted UCABE's mediation process, both had to adhere to the guidelines and principles of UCABE's arbitration process.

All negotiations were held at UCABE's offices. To make the process as efficient and speedy as possible, negotiations were generally held in the absence of lawyers. In every negotiating session, all attendees signed a two-page summary outlining the discussions, agreements, and compromises reached by each party. This provided a guideline for future sessions and enhanced the commitment of all parties to reaching a solution.

UCABE became the information center for all major restructurings. It provided a forum for discussions and served as a unique platform for the fair hearing of business leaders and for building relationships among the bankers, advisors, and consultants dedicated to the restructuring process. UCABE also promoted the creation of workout units within each bank to deal with distressed loans and acted as a clearinghouse.

In 1996, the amount of corporate debt requiring restructuring amounted to about 15 percent of the total debt outstanding in the system, or approximately US$15 billion. Of that amount, approximately 60 percent came from large corporations with US$20 million or more in sales. From November 1995 to April 1997, UCABE helped to restructure approximately 90 companies, assuming full responsibility for 51 of them, with the remainder being supervised by other entities. Of these 51 corporations, UCABE successfully restructured 41 companies, worth approximately US$6 billion in loans. These companies either agreed to a signed contract or a letter of understanding defining the terms of the restructuring with their lenders.

UCABE's Value-Focused Restructuring Process

UCABE focused on a limited number of borrowers (originally 50, although it reviewed close to 90), while considering each company's unique financial condition. UCABE recognized that a successful mediation of the restructuring process needed to strike a balance between commercial discussions and the exercise of legal rights. Thus, UCABE designed a corporate restructuring process that grouped stakeholders into two distinct groups, internal and external, revolving around the interaction of two restructuring procedures, the legal and the value methods. UCABE always favored the value method.

Internal stakeholders included workers, suppliers, and shareholders. External stakeholders included lenders, tax authorities, and regulators. During the negotiations, two different patterns of interaction emerged. One involved suppliers, workers, and clients who required cash payments; the other involved lenders and shareholders, who shared the remaining economic value of the company after cash costs were adequately provided for.

While UCABE widely recognized the need to maintain a constructive dialogue with and among all internal stakeholders, UCABE expended most of its efforts working with banks and shareholders. UCABE left negotiations among internal stakeholders to the equity holders, whose subordinated position provided them with the incentive to keep suppliers, workers, and clients informed and satisfied.

In executing its honest-broker role, UCABE identified a set of five dynamics (see figure 7.1 for a depiction of the interactions among these dynamics). UCABE monitored these dynamics carefully to maintain the thrust of its efforts on the value dynamic. These five dynamics include the intralender dynamic, which occurs among the various lenders. The stakeholder dynamic functions among a corporation's stakeholders (other than its lenders), namely, suppliers, clients, workers, tax authorities, and shareholders. Third, the lender-company dynamic occurs among the stakeholders of the company, particularly its shareholders and the group of lenders. The fourth dynamic is the legal dynamic, which helps lenders and corporate stakeholders to focus on and negotiate about the use of legal procedures. Finally, the value dynamic serves as UCABE's approach to develop, foster, and promote negotiations on the assessment and distribution of corporate value between lenders and shareholders.

The Value Dynamic

UCABE's restructuring process focused solely on value and restricted discussions to commercial terms only (defined as the value dynamic), as it considered the introduction of legal interests a deterrent to the restructuring process. Furthermore, the legal dynamic enhanced the emotional tone of negotiations. UCABE's process thus focused discussions between shareholders and lenders on the sharing of future cash flows and value and

Figure 7.1.   *Interactions among the Five Restructuring Dynamics*

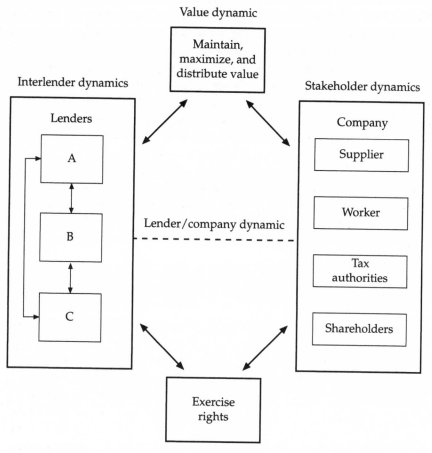

Source: Author.

helped both sides realize that value recovery was maximized through the continuity of operations.

The value dynamic required that creditors and debtors accept that the two sides lost value because of the crisis, and not because one party took advantage of the other. The key to properly managing the constructive value dynamic is to analyze, assess, and distribute corporate value. Initially, stakeholders must question the company's worth as an ongoing concern with respect to its liquidation value. The key question concerns whether the company can generate operating profit and cash flow. If it cannot, creditors should seek to optimize their repayment by selling the company's assets either in one package or piecemeal. If the company generates cash and, therefore, value, structuring a mechanism to assess and distribute such value among stakeholders becomes useful.

The value dynamic begins by generating a realistic business plan and a cash-flow projection and proceeds with determining the net present value of the company at an agreed-on discount rate (corporate value). Once corporate value is agreed on, discussions focus on the fair way to distribute such value among stakeholders. Figure 7.2 describes UCABE's value-restructuring process, which was organized around the three phases described in the following paragraphs.

DEFINING CORPORATE VALUE. In the midst of Mexico's economic crisis, defining value became a difficult task. Judging value implied projecting a

Figure 7.2.   UCABE's Restructuring Process

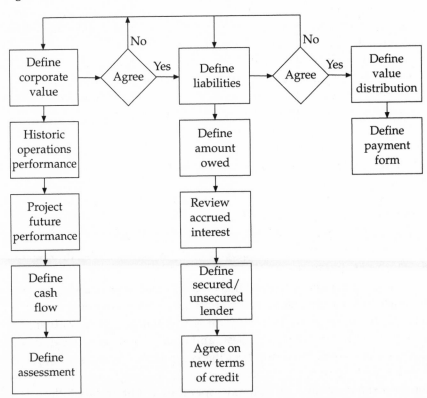

Source: Author.

company's performance (revenues, costs, and so on) and determining an adequate discount rate to apply to its future cash flows. To estimate a fair set of projections, satisfying both shareholders and creditors, the efforts of a third-party, honest broker became necessary. The honest broker assessed the merit of each party's position and supervised the adequate implementation of the value assessment techniques. UCABE became a key link in this process.

DEFINING LIABILITIES AND THE TOTAL OUTSTANDING AMOUNT. Once corporate value was agreed upon, UCABE then mediated between banks and shareholders on how such value would be allocated among them. To do so, UCABE first had to define the amount of corporate liabilities and then seek to avoid the disruptive environment created when each lender acts separately to enforce its legal rights and recover its investment, thereby placing the company in a bureaucratic limbo, delaying value recovery, and possibly destroying a potentially viable business. UCABE therefore directed lenders to a constructive dynamic in which consensus helped define claim priorities and presented a common front to the company. This meant that structured teams reviewed amounts due and guarantee rights. Among other things, they analyzed the legal documentation of guarantees and security interests in an organized manner. UCABE first reviewed loan contracts and grouped creditor claims by their credit quality. It then sought to normalize the interest rate charged by all equal quality creditors (from the first day of nonpayment through closing), and for each institution eliminate from the outstanding amount any moratorium interest or nonpayment penalties, which differed greatly, thereby normalizing the value of all claims.

DEFINING VALUE DISTRIBUTION AMONG LENDERS. With such a normalized outstanding amount (debt amount), shareholders and lenders revised cash flow projections and agreed on a debt amount the company could service (the sustainable debt). The sustainable debt was then subtracted from the debt amount, negotiating the settlement of any remaining debt amount in either equity (capitalization) or physical assets (payment in kind).

In the case of settling the difference with equity, negotiations turned toward the equity value at which debt would be converted and to issues like minority shareholders' rights and protection, equity repurchase agreements, management considerations, and so forth. In cases where the debt amount was significantly higher than the corporate value, negotiations focused on the amount of equity to be granted to shareholders. In this situation, UCABE assisted shareholders and creditors in negotiating the value of matters such as their management abilities, intangible contributions (know-how), willingness to forgo a legal proceeding to turn over corporate assets, and so on. The sharing of value was generally designed on a pro rata basis to each bank's exposure. However, when appropriate, it also considered granting premiums to those lenders that had better guarantees or payment priorities. Such premiums went against the share of unsecured creditors. Company value remaining after settling the outstanding amount flowed to holders as equity.

FOBAPROA's Role as a Restructuring Agent through its Corporate Asset Recovery Unit

As described previously, FOBAPROA became the entity through which the government implemented the banking rescue programs. In Mexico, the liabilities of the banking sector carry the central bank's implicit guarantee. The Mexican government thus established a trust for the protection of bank savings, FOBAPROA, in which the central bank acted as fiduciary trustee. FOBAPROA was not intentionally created to aid in the systemic crisis of 1995. Because of its savings protection mandate (similar to that of the Federal Deposit and Insurance Corporation in the United States), it became the vehicle that implemented the rescue program with the objective of achieving orderly capitalization of the banks.

As Mexico's 18 largest banking institutions went through the different phases of the banking rescue plan in 1995–96, FOBAPROA's responsibilities for Mexico's financial system grew substantially. FOBAPROA's size and exposure increased as a result of three main processes: (a) the government's intervention in financial institutions whose fraudulent management left them technically bankrupt (Union, Cremi, and Banpais, for instance), making FOBAPROA the de facto owner of their loan portfolios; (b) the sale of seriously undercapitalized institutions, such as Probursa, Inverlat, and Mexicano, whose shareholders would not commit more equity to their rescue, to foreign financial institutions through a good bank-bad bank structure, in which FOBAPROA agreed to acquire low-quality loan portfolios through the bad bank; and (c) the Loan Purchase Program in which a group of banks (mainly Banamex, Bancomer, Serfin, Banorte, and Bital) transferred a significant amount of their loan portfolios to FOBAPROA. (Note that under the Loan Purchase Program loans were not directly purchased from banks. Rather, the banks transferred the right to the loan's cash flows into loan trusts in which the selling bank retained 25 percent of the collection risk.)

Thus FOBAPROA held a significant amount of the country's banking loan assets (estimated at more than 50 percent of the loans in the system) and concentrated a vast amount of the system's nonperforming corporate loans stemming from the crisis. By early 1998, FOBAPROA's risk exposure had reached nearly US$60 billion. Given the substantial change in the nature of its original activities, FOBAPROA's mandate expanded from its objective of deposit protection to include supervising the administration of the loan portfolios of the intervened banks and the loan trusts, expediting the resolution of FOBAPROA's assets by selling those to which it had direct title and coordinating the sale of those in the loan trusts, and accelerating the debt restructuring process.

As a consequence of these expanded activities, in late 1996 FOBAPROA created two supporting entities: the Comité de Crédito Central (CCC) and the Valuación y Venta de Activos (VVA). The CCC coordinated the collection and restructuring activities among the various loan trusts, the intervened banks, and the remaining exposures within commercial banks. From November 1996 through April 1997, the CCC participated in Mexico's corporate debt-restructuring process, substantially interacting with UCABE, the mediation unit formed a year earlier by the government and the private sector.

By contrast, the VVA acted as agent in the sale of FOBAPROA's assets. However, the VVA's activities were hindered by the following obstacles: (a) the VVA could not directly sell the loans acquired by FOBAPROA through the Loan Purchase Program, because the selling bank remained the loan's legal owner, and because it had a 25 percent stake in the recovery and kept all the documentation, the VVA had to coordinate with the selling banks; (b) the large amount of debt restructuring, being either negotiated or implemented, made the transfer of loans difficult until such restructuring ended, thereby limiting the amount of assets (loans) to be sold; (c) the VVA's compilation and completion of the loan's documentation for due diligence purposes became a highly complex and lengthy process because such documentation remained in the files of the financial institution that administered or held the loans; and (d) the responsibilities of the VVA and FOBAPROA were poorly defined, complicating the relationship between the two agencies.

In April 1997 FOBAPROA instituted a new management team, marking a new phase in the organization's development. This team sought to consolidate the corporate loan recovery process (defined as its administration, transformation, and sale) into a single entity, merging the activities of the VVA and FOBAPROA. This step created the Dirección de Activos

Corporativos (DAC), which in June 1997 assumed leadership in coordinating corporate debt restructurings, thus terminating the operations of the CCC, VVA, and UCABE.

By early 1998, political issues relating to the size and cost of the financial rescue program diminished FOBAPROA's effectiveness. The exposure of the banking sector rescue plan had reached almost 15 percent of the country's GDP, making the potentially high cost of rescue the center of political discussions in the Mexican Congress. By this time, however, Mexico's economy had moved toward recovery, spearheaded by a strong export boom resulting from the North American Free Trade Agreement. The Mexican economy grew by 7 percent in 1997 and 4.6 percent in 1998, and the efforts of both UCABE and DAC had paid off.

The Corporate Asset Recovery Unit

In 1997 FOBAPROA promoted the resolution of corporate debt through DAC. This organization oversaw and coordinated the corporate debt-resolution process of FOBAPROA's loan portfolio through three basic functions: administering, transforming, and selling the loans in either their existing or their restructured format. These three functions were implemented for FOBAPROA's own loans, that is, for those from intervened banks and for those acquired through the Loan Purchase Program, in which FOBAPROA had rights only to the loans' underlying cash flows. In the latter instance, FOBAPROA's role required coordination with the bank that sold the loan and maintained its title. In accordance with FOBAPROA's new mandate, DAC defined its purpose as maximizing the recovery of FOBAPROA's corporate debt (asset) portfolio.

For this purpose, DAC considered four key elements as follows:

- DAC's successful recovery could only be achieved when FOBAPROA received cash in return for its loan or for its rights to the cash flows of a loan.
- Cash could only be received through two processes, either collecting monies owed under the underlying loan contract (returning the loan to a performing standard) or selling the loan in its pre- or postrestructuring format.
- Recovery had to be maximized for the full amount of FOBAPROA's exposure.
- Recovery values must be first analyzed with respect to the company as a going concern.

Initially DAC organized its inventory by debtor instead of by the selling bank. However, this task proved highly complex and timeconsuming, given that FOBAPROA's loan portfolio comprised thousands of different credits resulting from the lack of a syndicated loan format and the complexity of Mexican corporate structures (most companies have a holding company with numerous subsidiaries, and in many cases each subsidiary had outstanding loans).

Once it organized its loans by debtor company, DAC then grouped the loans into so-called economic groups in which one economic group included all outstanding amounts owed to FOBAPROA from debtors (companies) that had the same shareholder base. DAC then pursued its debt recovery function by seeking to collect or sell its loans by economic group.

To collect the loans of an economic group, the loans had to be current. If loans were nonperforming, they had to be transformed into a different asset type that could be either collected or sold. DAC called this process "transformation."

DAC subsumed these four resolution functions under one single entity, enabling it to view them as simultaneous rather than sequential steps. The administration, transformation, supervision, and sale of assets therefore became harmonious activities, optimizing the recovery of assets, reducing inefficiencies and delays, and consolidating all recovery activities.

Restructuring corporate debt constituted the heart of the transformation function. Transformation of a nonperforming loan could lead to three new asset types: (a) physical assets such as buildings, land, and machinery, referred to as payments in kind; (b) new restructured debt, called restructuring; or (c) equity, termed capitalization. These three new asset types could then be sold or collected. DAC created a structure whereby the restructuring activity paralleled the efforts of the bank, if any, administering the loans. DAC's director previously headed UCABE's restructuring function and, therefore, DAC's approach to debt restructuring incorporated similar rules, guidelines, and ideas into UCABE's procedures.

To optimize the work out of its loan portfolio, DAC followed an elaborate case-by-case process for each economic group. Once all the necessary information on the loans outstanding from one economic group was obtained, DAC and the banks administering the loan analyzed recovery alternatives.

DAC oversaw the recovery of assets totaling about US$16 billion, representing 28,000 credits from more than 4,000 companies.

DAC generally succeeded in the resolution process with its administration, transformation, and supervision functions. It failed, however, in its sales function. Although during its first six to eight months DAC prepared an adequate inventory of loans and other sale assets, including equity and debt positions obtained from lengthy transformations and loan files ready for due-diligence procedures, the political environment suddenly shifted dramatically against FOBAPROA's activities, causing DAC to halt its sales process.

Key Lessons from Mexico's 1996–98 Restructuring Experience

The main lessons learning from Mexico's restructuring during 1996–98 can be summarized as follows:

- Corporate debt restructuring of viable companies requires a constructive approach in which attention focuses on value (the value dynamic). Building an adequate process for corporate debt restructuring requires the capability to analyze, define, and distribute corporate value.
- Debt restructuring requires a case-by-case approach, for that is the only way to treat both shareholders and lenders fairly in the definition of corporate value and in its distribution.
- During systemic financial distress, with the accompanying significant frictions and tensions between corporations and banks, a third-party, honest broker, such as UCABE, is key to maintaining focus on the value dynamic.
- Both lenders and shareholders must agree to work together with the honest broker to achieve successful restructuring.
- When loans are concentrated among a relatively small number of companies, consolidating bad loans in a single entity—capable of controlling or supervising their administration and transformation (restructuring)—eases the recovery process. A single holder achieves economies of scale, makes majority decisions quicker, and maintains fairness and quality control along strict guidelines.
- Concentrating bad loans in a government entity, however, risks a situation in which significant political pressures derail or affect the recovery process.
- The debt recovery, or resolution, process must be administered by an experienced, capable, and unbiased group of professionals who can help reduce the time required for restructuring or selling the assets to prevent additional economic costs. Focusing on value and maintaining market standards achieves this goal.

- The effort to restart the economy requires the confidence of investors, lenders, and depositors. This can only happen with the proactive management of the crisis, overcoming the downfall as quickly as possible and putting in place new mechanisms that prevent similar future experiences.
- In hindsight, analysis of the Mexican banking crisis reveals several weaknesses in the financial system that should be addressed to reduce future risks. Such weaknesses include the following:

  - *Poor legal protection for lenders.* The Suspensión de Pagos Law, which allows companies to stop making payments and fix their interest and foreign exchange rates at nonmarket levels, prevented lenders from recovering their investments in a simplified manner and complicates borrowers' access to the debt market to fulfill their working capital needs.
  - *Loan documentation homogeneity.* Loan homogeneity, particularly in their documentation format, permits banks to exchange (swap) loans on the basis of standardized documentation. This leads to a simplified process of loan trading, which can significantly facilitate the resolution process by setting market value levels and allowing banks to trade their positions. Regulators should promote the use of syndicated loans or common market practices for loan documentation.
  - *Absence of a secondary loan market.* The absence of a secondary market that allows banks to trade their loan positions hindered Mexico's debt resolution process by precluding the market from setting reference terms for value and hampered the possibility of concentrating exposures in interested institutions.
  - *Lack of a credit bureau.* After privatization of the banking sector, shareholders pursued asset (loan) growth strategies at the expense of risk exposure. In the aftermath of the crisis, bankers and regulators recognized that several institutions had engaged in imprudent lending. The lack of a credit bureau that rigorously monitors the degree of leverage and the performance of corporate borrowers and consumers limited the risk control of banks' balance sheets. Such a bureau also could have contributed to the standardization of loan formats.
  - *Lack of bankruptcy expertise.* Inadequate bankruptcy laws hindered the restructuring process, not only because of reduced protection offered to lenders, but also because of the lack of experienced judges

and trustees to effectively manage bankruptcies. Such lack of experience lengthened the crisis, because the time to solve each corporate restructuring or outright bankruptcy case increased. The government and the banking sector must develop a contingency plan to prepare professionals knowledgeable in corporate restructuring to act as arbiters in the restructuring process.

— *Coordinated actions to maximize recovery.* A widespread crisis can sometimes lead to rash decisionmaking that sacrifices value. To maximize recovery and reduce its financial burden, a systemic crisis must be handled in as orderly a fashion possible. With its complexity and interdependency, a financial crisis becomes highly difficult to manage, and individual decisions affecting the remainder of the system can result in general systemic indecision. An adequate government-sponsored program can fill the decisionmaking vacuum created by the crisis. However, basic regulation and legislation should be established to control banking institutions, as well as to address corporate governance.

8

Reconstruction Finance Corporation Assistance to Financial Intermediaries and Commercial and Industrial Enterprises in the United States, 1932–37

Joseph R. Mason, Drexel University, LeBow College of Business

Economic historians and others have attempted to distill lessons on combating economic crises from the experiences of the U.S. Reconstruction Finance Corporation (RFC) during the 1930s. However, the resulting policies have engendered widespread doubts and criticisms. Many economic historians doubt that RFC assistance to financial intermediaries and commercial and industrial firms contributed a great deal to stabilizing the U.S. economy during the Great Depression. RFC assistance probably did not form a significant basis for the general economic recovery following the depression of the 1930s. Although this chapter does not dispute that conclusion, between 1932 and 1937 the RFC experimented with a wide variety of programs targeted at resolving systemic distress. It attempted to stimulate credit and capital market activity by acting as a lender of last resort, recapitalizing the banking industry and providing direct credit to commercial and industrial enterprises.

Although no single one of these programs achieved unmitigated success, important lessons can be learned by comparing the structures of

The author expresses his gratitude to Charles Calomiris and Daniela Klingebiel for valuable comments and criticism of the manuscript of this chapter.

successful programs with unsuccessful ones. The first section of this chapter compares the objectives, operations, and outcomes of four major RFC programs. The lessons to be learned from the experiences of these four programs revolve around two guiding principles. First, successful RFC programs restricted credit or other assistance to reasonably sound institutions. This strategy seems simple in theory, but may be quite difficult in practice. During economic and financial crises, conditions of high asymmetric information may result in markets that do not reflect true fundamental asset values. Therefore, the RFC often evaluated firm solvency and soundness on the basis of future market expectations or favorable environmental conditions that were (and still are) difficult or impossible to quantify. Second, successful RFC programs often took a measure of control over institutions to assuage junior creditors and nurse firms to profitability and recovery over the long run.

RFC Background: Politics, Funding, and Operations

Before evaluating individual RFC programs, it is important to have some understanding of the structure and function of the RFC itself. President Herbert Hoover grudgingly established the RFC only after strong moral suasion and the failure of an experiment with private sector cooperative alternatives, the National Credit Corporation and the Railroad Credit Corporation. Hoover never favored government intervention in private markets, but accepted that markets were beginning to fail as a result of the severity of the Great Depression. Therefore, Hoover resuscitated the U.S. War Finance Corporation that had so successfully motivated human and financial capital during World War I to stimulate general economic activity during peacetime.[1]

At the time the RFC was established, the Great Depression was primarily attributed to overleverage and debt deflation:

> As business everywhere slowed down, the banks began to feel the pressure of curtailed activity. Credit was contracted by the paying down of business loans, and bank profits were reduced. For a time, these developments were not serious, but soon bankers began

---

1. Hoover and the chairman of the Federal Reserve Board, Eugene Meyer, had been instrumental in the success of the War Finance Corporation and modeled the RFC directly on that institution, with the same organizational structure and many of the same people in charge.

to realize that trade advances that had been amply secured by the pledge of marketable securities and commodities were no longer fully protected when the market value of those commodities was rapidly falling (Waller 1934, pp. 7–8).

Banks therefore slowed lending to reduce further exposure to declining asset values and accumulate loan loss reserves that could offset the capital depletion resulting from expected defaults. The combined reduction in bank credit and debt deflation led policymakers to believe that the relief of bank credit stringency would increase capacity utilization and, therefore, asset values, stimulating general economic recovery (Olson 1972, p. 268).

At the same time, policymakers also believed that the Depression would soon end.[2] This belief was widely held from 1929 until after 1935, when several studies of low credit activity concluded that the perceived credit stringency may have actually been a lack of demand for rather than a lack of supply of business credit (Hardy and Viner 1935; Kimmel 1939). Until this realization became apparent, the RFC's focus remained conservative, extending primarily fully secured short-term credit at penalty rates as a lender of last resort. Once the RFC made that realization, its programs substantially broadened in scope, recapitalizing the banking sector and making loans to a broad base of commercial and industrial enterprises (Agnew 1945; Locker 1943; Olson 1972; Spero 1939).

The RFC served an agency of the Executive Branch of the U.S. government. Therefore, expansion of the scale or scope of the RFC's powers could be enacted by Executive Order rather than congressional legislation (Waller 1934, p. 20). In an economic emergency, this contained obvious implications for organizational and institutional flexibility. Furthermore, the RFC was immune from civil service regulations on hiring and promotion as well as audits of the congressional General Accounting Office (Delaney 1954, p. 12).[3]

The freedom that was advantageous to organizational and institutional flexibility, however, also raised issues of accountability and misallocation of government funds. Indeed, in reaction to widespread allegations of political favoritism, five months after passage of the RFC Act, Congress added an amendment that made public the names of recipients of monetary assistance from the RFC and the amounts received. As with

---

2. Indeed, the original RFC Act contained a sunset clause that gave the agency a life span of one year. This was extended by Executive Order on December 8, 1932.

3. As a true corporation, the RFC could also sue and be sued in a court of law.

any political entity, the RFC's distributions may have been affected by political influence and favoritism. Unlike other New Deal programs, however, no evidence exists to substantiate systematic political influence among RFC credit and capital distributions.[4]

At least three elements of the RFC's structure probably mitigated political influence over the RFC's credit and capital assistance programs. First, the original RFC Act stipulated that all "loans made by the corporation be fully and adequately secured," and this stipulation was extended to nearly all the RFC's credit and capital programs to which this chapter refers (RFC *Circular no. 1* 1932, p. 1). Once the RFC received an application for assistance from a financial institution or commercial and industrial enterprise, the agency only had the power to evaluate whether asset values were sufficient to secure assistance.[5] Companies sometimes challenged whether their industry sector was appropriate for RFC investment under the law. However, a staff consisting primarily of displaced bank loan officers instructed to keep asset valuations rather liberal underwrote RFC loans. Therefore, RFC decisions about collateral were rarely, if ever, challenged (Delaney 1954; Simonson and Hempel 1993).

Second, the RFC's funding assured a minimum of political interference. Because the operation was too large to fund directly out of federal budget allocations, the RFC was founded as a government-owned corporation with an initial appropriation from Congress and the right to borrow more money from the public at large. On behalf of the U.S. government, the Secretary of the Treasury subscribed the original capital stock of the RFC. Additionally, the RFC was initially authorized, with the approval of the Secretary of the Treasury, to have outstanding at any one time subordinate notes, debentures, bonds, or other such obligations in an amount aggregating not more than three times its subscribed capital stock.

The U.S. Treasury marketed these additional notes, debentures, and bonds using all the facilities of the Treasury Department authorized by law for the marketing of obligations of the United States. The Secretary of the Treasury was authorized, at his discretion, to purchase or sell any

---

4. See Wallis (1998); and Anderson and Tollison (1991) for analyses of New Deal programs in general. See Mason (1996) for an analysis of RFC credit and capital programs.

5. Although political influence and positioning certainly took place with respect to RFC grants for state-level unemployment relief and development, these programs were not the original focus of the RFC and are not dealt with in this chapter (see Olson 1972, 1988).

obligations of the RFC. The United States fully and unconditionally guaranteed these notes, bonds, or other obligations of the RFC as to the interest and principal, and such guaranty was expressly noted on the face of all RFC obligations. Rates paid by the RFC approximated those of other U.S. government obligations with similar maturity (Waller 1934, pp. 43–44). As the RFC was an executive agency, the limit on additional notes and debentures and, therefore, the scale of the agency, could be (and was) raised unilaterally by Executive Order (Waller 1934, p. 41; Walk 1937, p. 229). Because RFC officials did not have to appeal to Congress for this additional funding, the potential for political influence that otherwise would be apparent was eliminated.

Third, wherever possible, RFC decisionmaking devolved to the regional level. The RFC functioned through a principal office in Washington, D.C., and loan agencies (or field offices) were established in principal cities throughout the country. Field office managers had authority to approve loans up to US$100,000, though unusual loans required clearance by the Board of Directors in Washington.[6] In practice, each field office was almost autonomous, and only major problems were taken up with Washington (Delaney 1954, p. 7).

The field offices possessed "the sole right to fix a valuation on the securities put up for collateral with each application" (Waller 1934, pp. 61–62). If a field office showed a profit, everything was fine; if not, someone would be detailed from Washington to see what was the matter and, possibly, a new field office manager would be appointed" (Delaney 1954, pp. 47–48). These profitability yardsticks seem to have effectively constrained inefficient credit or capital allocation that may have arisen from ineptitude or local political influence.

In summary, at least three factors constrained influence over RFC officials that could channel assistance to inefficient applications. First, RFC credit and capital programs were specifically required to be "fully and adequately secured" extensions. Second, the RFC's primary budgetary reliance on an established capital base (rather than the congressional budget process) reduced contact between RFC officers and directors and the vast majority of elected officials. Third, the independence of regional field offices in the credit and capital allocation processes constrained the extent to which influence could be exercised. In addition, the RFC's status

---

6. Washington interventions were therefore often the subject of widespread journalistic scrutiny.

as an Executive Branch agency led to a great deal of organizational and institutional flexibility that could be brought to bear on resolving systemic distress among financial institutions and firms. However, policymakers' perceptions regarding the depth and severity of the economic crisis constrained these activities of the RFC. These perceptions significantly lagged behind the reality. Having outlined the overall objectives of the RFC and its operating procedures, the next section analyzes the four main RFC credit and capital programs, and the principal similarities and differences that led to their individual success or failure.

RFC Assistance to Financial Institutions and Commercial and Industrial Enterprises

Throughout this section, there are two guiding principles. First, successful RFC programs restricted credit or other assistance to reasonably sound institutions, but sometimes evaluated soundness rather liberally due to unresolved, high asymmetric information in markets during the financial crisis. Second, successful RFC programs often assumed a measure of control over institutions to calm junior creditors and nurse firms to profitability and recovery over the long run.

The Financial Intermediary Loan Program

The creators and initial board members of the RFC attributed the ongoing Depression largely to the effects of a debt deflation, and believed that the effects of this debt deflation need not be persistent. Such beliefs led policymakers to believe that if they could relieve the existing credit stringency, economic recovery would follow quickly (Olson 1972, p. 268). Providing liquidity to the financial institutions that extended credit in the private sector constituted the simplest way to relieve the credit stringency. Therefore, it is not surprising that the first RFC program provided for loans to financial institutions.

Under the provisions of section 5 of the original RFC Act, the RFC was authorized to make loans on full and adequate security to any bank, savings bank, trust company, building and loan association, insurance company, mortgage loan company, credit union, federal land bank, joint-stock land bank, federal intermediate credit bank, agricultural credit corporation, or livestock credit corporation, organized under the laws of any state, territory, or possession of the United States. These provisions also included the ability to make loans secured by the assets of any bank, savings bank, or building and loan association that was closed, or in the process of liquidation, or to aid in their reorganization or liquidation upon application of the receiver or liquidating agent of such institution (Waller 1934, pp. 27–28).

OPERATIONS OF THE FINANCIAL INTERMEDIARY LOAN PROGRAM. Three main aspects of the RFC loan program deserve attention. First, loans under section 5 could be made with a maturity not exceeding three years, and the RFC could renew or extend the time of payment up to a maximum of five years from the dates on which the loans were made originally (Waller 1934, pp. 28–29). Despite this authority, the RFC limited loan maturities to less than six months to effect greater control over borrowers than would otherwise be possible.

Second, the RFC board initially set loan interest rates at 6 percent for all types of financial institutions. The board lowered rates to 5 percent in mid-1932, then to 4 percent in 1933. Despite these decreases, RFC rates were always above those at the Federal Reserve Bank discount windows, whose collateral requirements were always kept on a par with those accepted at the RFC. The highest rate at the Federal Reserve Bank of New York during this period was 3.5 percent during 1932 and 1933. The rate dropped to 2 percent in 1934 and 1.5 percent in 1935 and 1936 (U.S. Department of Commerce 1975, p. 1001). The RFC consciously kept its rates well above the market rate to ensure that RFC financing would not crowd out private sector alternatives. In doing so, however, the RFC seems to have priced itself out of the market for loans that may have actually helped weak institutions in need of liquidity.

Third, financial institutions, not regulators or the RFC itself, initiated the assistance process. Banks initiated the assistance process by submitting an application form and recent examination reports to any of the RFC's regional loan offices. The loan agency could then ask for any additional information it deemed necessary. Once a loan was granted, even private financial institutions consented to any examinations the RFC required (RFC *Circular #1* 1932, p. 2).

After July 1932, the RFC made public any loan amount it authorized, and these were typically carried in local newspapers and trade journals. In addition, in 1933 the law prohibited the RFC from making or renewing loans to borrowers (a) if at the time any officer, director, or employee of the applicant received compensation at a rate that appeared unreasonable to the RFC and (b) unless the applicant agreed to the satisfaction of the RFC not to increase compensation beyond such reasonable levels for the life of the loan (Waller 1934, p. 29). As these later conditions were somewhat subjective, these additional provisions gave the RFC implicit control over bank operations after the loan was granted.

OUTCOME OF THE FINANCIAL INTERMEDIARY LOAN PROGRAM. Short maturities, high interest rates, and the possibility of publicity and RFC control probably dissuaded financial institutions from taking advantage of the liquidity offered through the financial institution loan program. These aspects represented substantial disincentives to apply for a loan in the first place. Nonetheless, figure 8.1 shows that during the first year of the RFC, loans to financial intermediaries composed the primary form of assistance offered by the agency. Figure 8.1 also shows a decline in loans to financial intermediaries as other RFC programs were established.

Figure 8.2 illustrates that open banks almost immediately switched out of the RFC loan program and into RFC preferred stock when that program became available after March 1933. There is a good reason banks switched out of the loan program. Olson maintains

> The RFC helped only those basically sound enterprises that needed temporary liquidity... For weaker banks the conditions of an RFC loan often brought more problems than solutions. The [RFC's] collateral requirements were so high that an RFC loan forced a bank to deposit its most valuable and liquid assets as security for the Corporation's advance. All to often, the Corporation would advance a loan, take over the bank's best assets for collateral, and leave the bank unable to meet demands by depositors once those demands exceeded the amount of the loan (Olson 1972, pp. 177–78).

By statute, the RFC could not make any loans or advances that were not considered fully secured (Waller 1934, p. 49). Initially, the RFC accepted as collateral only 80 percent of the market value of the highest grades of securities, and no more than 50 percent of the market value of other assets (Olson 1972, p. 88). In practice, therefore, the RFC often took a bank's most liquid assets as security for loans, increasing the risk of default on remaining bank debt and undermining the stabilizing effect of assistance.

Mason (1999a) also shows that a nontrivial portion of RFC lending can be accounted for by repeated rollover of the short-term debt. Of the more than US$1 billion lent to banks prior to the March 1933 banking holiday, nearly 70 percent went to banks borrowing more than once and 15 percent to banks borrowing more than five times (see table 8.1). The RFC therefore appeared to be lending a lot of money during this period, but in reality a lot of this activity resulted from merely rolling over loans it had already extended.

Figure 8.1. *RFC Authorizations under Four Corporate Assistance Programs, Quarterly, 1932–37*

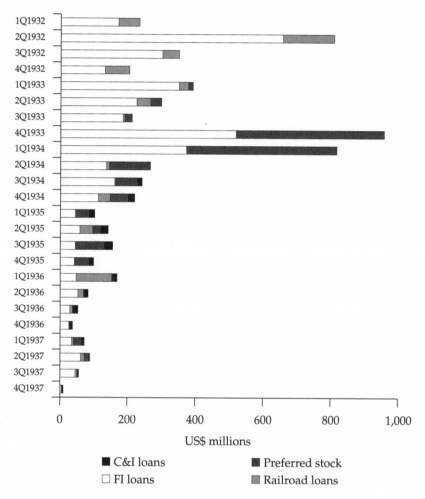

Q Quarter.
Source: Reconstruction Finance Corporation, *Quarterly Reports* (various issues).

While maintaining short maturities to keep collateral values on par with market conditions and charging high interest rates represent sound lending practices, especially during a deflationary period, they do not necessarily form the basis for effective assistance to banks constrained by liquidity. Mason (1999a) also uses individual bank balance sheet, income statement, and other data to construct a bank-failure model to test the effects of individual RFC loans on subsequent survival. The RFC loans in Mason's sample,

Figure 8.2.   *Amounts Authorized to Open Banks under the RFC Loan and Preferred Stock Programs, Monthly, 1932–36*

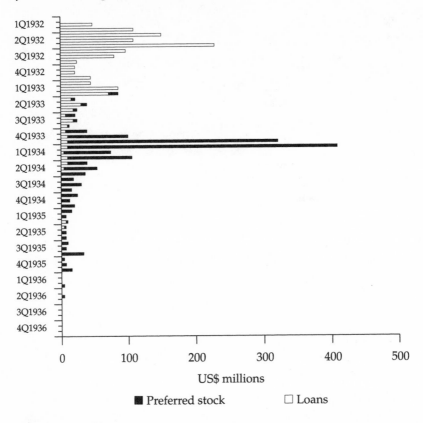

Q Quarter.

Note: Figure includes only loans to open banks. It does not include loans to receivers or those made on preferred stock. The RFC preferred stock program began in March 1933. Preferred stock includes investments made through notes and debentures to banks in states that prohibited preferred stock investments.

Source: RFC monthly reports to Congress (various issues).

however, are associated with increased ex post probability of failure. Furthermore, RFC loans are most strongly associated with increased failure probabilities during the earliest periods of RFC activity in early 1932, when RFC collateral requirements were most strict. RFC publicity requirements enacted after July 1932 had no effect on whether a bank failed or survived after a loan. Though the deleterious effect of RFC loans eases with the gradual relaxation of collateral requirements and rates up to March 1933, loans never have a positive effect on bank survival in Mason's analysis.

Table 8.1.   *Borrowing Behavior of Banks, February 1932–March 1933*

Number of loans authorized to the Bank	Number of banks	Total amount of bank borrowing from the RFC (US$)	Average bank loan amount from the RFC (US$)
1	4,481	358,077,401	79,910
2	1,342	325,464,728	242,522
3	434	125,427,278	289,003
4	175	97,681,758	558,181
5	66	31,357,926	475,120
6	38	42,665,018	1,122,764
7	18	104,056,173	5,780,898
8	4	3,517,862	879,466
9	3	1,448,438	482,813
10	2	1,065,099	532,550
>10	4	6,806,276	126,042
Total	6,567	1,097,567,957	167,134

Note: Table includes only loans to open banks. Does not include loans to receivers or those made on preferred stock.

Source: RFC monthly reports to congress (various issues); author's calculations.

Because deposits in closed banks represented decreased consumer and business illiquidity, the closed bank loan program had tremendous potential to relieve debt deflation and restore economic activity. The closed-bank lending program was severely constrained from the start and was unpopular among RFC officials. Under section 5 of the RFC Act, the outstanding stock of loans to closed banks, savings banks, and building and loan associations was limited to US$200 million (Agnew 1945, p. 34). The stock of deposits in closed national banks alone averaged more than US$285 million on a monthly basis throughout the period 1932–37, peaking at close to US$1.2 billion in March 1934 (Mason, Anari, and Kolari 1999).[7] RFC officials viewed closed-bank loans as long-term loans that were secured only in the speculative judgement of asset values in five to eight years' time. As the RFC Act stipulated that all loans be "fully and adequately secured," RFC officials thought closed-bank lending was outside the legislative scope

---

7. Mason, Anari, and Kolari (1999) further conjecture that state bank assets added significantly to this stock not only because there were more failed state than national banks, but also because of the relative illiquidity, and consequent slower liquidation, of state bank assets.

of the agency. Furthermore, such risky, long-term lending had the potential to place a significant amount of their capital at risk. Therefore, the Deposit Liquidation Board was created on October 15, 1933, to continue the closed-bank loan program outside the RFC.

In summary, neither the RFC's closed- or open-institution loan programs alleviated the succession of financial crises of the early 1930s. By the time the RFC was established, many financial institutions were already technically insolvent, or close to insolvent, due to the pernicious effects of the debt deflation spiral. The available evidence suggests that the RFC was too conservative in its open-institution loan structures to help these marginal institutions. These financial intermediaries needed long-term assistance based on collateral values that more accurately reflected the probable future price of the underlying assets, if not outright recapitalization. That is, they needed an institution to bridge the asymmetric information gap that depressed market values and constrained capital flows. The additional temporary liquidity offered by RFC loans was insufficient to rescue the economy from crisis and depression.

The Railroad Loan Program

The railroad loan program served two purposes over the life of the RFC. When the RFC began operations, the railroad loan program's only objective was to directly augment the financial intermediary loan program. Federal and state governments had recapitalized or otherwise bailed out weak railroads since the late 19th century. Because of this implicit bailout provision, nearly all railroad bonds were rated AAA. With the retirement of U.S. government securities stock during the 1920s, banks and other financial intermediaries increasingly relied on railroad bonds as safe liquid investments that were a close substitute for reserves. When railroads were not bailed out in the early 1930s, however, the value of railroad bonds and, thus, bank reserves fell precipitously. Helping out railroads could theoretically increase the value of bank reserves and stimulate credit activity, relieving the perceived credit stringency and pulling the economy out of the debt deflation spiral. After 1933 the railroad loan program shifted its objective, becoming a means of stabilizing general business activity and maintaining employment. This objective, however, did not significantly differ from that of traditional New Deal programs in that the loans were not specifically for the relief of corporate distress. This evaluation of the railroad loan program focuses only on the first objective—the degree to which the program relieved corporate distress in the railroad sector and, consequently, relieved the perceived credit stringency and debt deflation spiral.

OPERATIONS OF THE RAILROAD LOAN PROGRAM. Under the provisions of section 5 of the RFC Act, the RFC could make loans, upon approval of the Interstate Commerce Commission, to railroads and railways engaged in interstate commerce, and the RFC could aid in the temporary financing to railroads and railways in the process of construction. The RFC could also lend to receivers of railroads and railways when they were unable to obtain funds upon reasonable terms through banking channels or from the general public, guaranteeing that the corporation would be adequately secured.[8]

In contrast with loans to financial intermediaries, only loans to railroads in receivership had to be adequately (though not fully) secured. Spero, who wrote the definitive history of the RFC railroad loan program, maintains that the RFC initially paid "little attention to the financial position and structure of [railroad and railway] applicants and their earning potentiality" (Spero 1939, p. 2). Between February 1932 and October 1937, more than US$638 million was authorized to 75 railroads (see Spero 1939, p. 33 for a complete list). "Of the twenty-one largest railroad borrowers from the RFC, nine were ultimately forced to file for bankruptcy, four underwent capital reorganization and judicial readjustment of their interest charges to avoid bankruptcy, and one was absorbed by a larger line. Only seven survived the depression and the RFC's loans unscathed" (Olson 1972, p. 182) (see table 8.2).

Furthermore, rather than pricing themselves out of the relevant market as with loans to financial intermediaries, between 1932 and 1935 the RFC actually priced themselves into the market for railroad loans by setting rates below even benchline common stock yields. Like loans to financial institutions, railroad loans were set at 6 percent in 1932, 5.5 percent in 1933, and 5 percent for 1934 and beyond. Over this period, Moody's common railroad stock yields amounted to more than 7 percent in 1932 and almost 6 percent in 1933 and 1934 (U.S. Department of Commerce 1975, p. 1,003).[9] RFC debt was therefore cheaper than a typical railroad equity issue between 1932 and 1934. The incentive to finance with RFC debt rather than equity and the moral-hazard implications of less-than-secured lending to railroads mandated under the RFC Act soon placed RFC capital at risk, as the RFC was forced into litigation to recover loan proceeds in large-scale, widely publicized bankruptcy proceedings.

---

8. And later, trustees of railroads that reorganized under section 77 of the Bankruptcy Act of March 3, 1933.

9. During 1935 and thereafter, common railroad stock yields were below RFC rates.

Table 8.2.   *Major RFC Railroad Loans and Corporate Outcomes*

Railroad	Loan amount (US$)	Result	Date
Baltimore & Ohio	82,125,000	Judicial Readjustment of Debt	9/3/38
Boston & Maine	7,569,000	Judicial Readjustment of Debt	1/4/40
Chicago & Northwestern	46,589,000	Bankruptcy	6/28/65
Chicago, Milwaukee, & St. Paul	15,840,000	Bankruptcy	6/29/35
Chicago & Rock Island	13,718,000	Bankruptcy	6/8/33
Colorado and Southern	29,000,000	Judicial Readjustment of Debt	12/19/40
Denver & Rio Grande	8,300,000	Bankruptcy	11/1/35
Erie	16,582,000	Bankruptcy	1/20/38
Ft. Worth & Denver	8,176,000	Merger	4/4/32
Great Northern	105,422,000	OK	
Illinois Central	35,312,000	OK	
Lehigh Valley	9,500,000	Judicial Readjustment of Debt	10/11/33
Missouri-Pacific	23,134,000	Bankruptcy	4/1/33
New York Central	27,500,000	OK	
New York, Chicago, & St. Louis	18,200,000	OK	
New York, New Haven, & Hartford	7,700,000	Bankruptcy	10/23/35
Pennsylvania	29,500,000	OK	
St. Louis & San Francisco	8,000,000	Bankruptcy	11/1/32
St. Louis & Southwest	18,790,000	Bankruptcy	5/17/33
Southern Pacific	23,200,000	OK	
Southern Pacific	19,610,000	OK	

Source: Loans data from Spero (1939, p. 33); Olson (1972, p. 207).

Table 8.3 details the major purposes of railroad loans. Between February 1932 and October 1933, most RFC loans to railroads aimed to pay debt interest and principal. Between November 1933 and October 1934, RFC loans predominantly paid off short-term maturity debt principal. Both of these types of loans helped preserve the value of railroad securities, thereby aiding banks.

Between February 1932 and October 1933, the RFC also dedicated a substantial amount of resources to purchasing equipment trust certificates,

Table 8.3. Purposes and Amounts of Authorized RFC Loans to Railroads, January 22, 1932–October 31, 1937 (US$)

Purpose	Jan. 22, 1932–Oct. 31, 1932	Nov. 1, 1932–Oct. 31, 1933	Nov. 1, 1933–Oct. 31, 1934	Nov. 1, 1934–Oct. 31, 1935	Nov. 1, 1935–Oct. 31, 1936	Nov. 1, 1936–Oct. 31, 1937
Bond interest	68,815,734	34,399,942	7,028,475	8,906,800	0	0
Bond maturities	54,144,460	15,073,000	10,597,575	6,757,000	—	218,861
Retirement of bonds	—	—	—	—	12,405,667	18,007,500
Equipment trust maturities	21,829,181	16,212,305	4,611,000	—	5,000,000	573,000
Equipment trust interest	5,115,054	545,316	—	—	—	—
Short-term maturities	40,702,413	—	43,000,000	—	—	—
Short-term obligations, interest	—	—	—	280,800	—	—
Payment of short-term loans (notes)	—	—	—	—	—	310,639
Debenture maturities	—	3,177,500	4,143,000	—	—	—
Debenture interest	—	—	1,281,910	—	—	—
Purchase of carriers' securities	—	—	—	28,978,900	111,445,400	—
Mortgage sinking fund payments	—	—	—	622,000	—	—
Purchase of stock of subsidiary company	—	—	—	3,182,150	—	—
Interest on leased line stock certificates	—	—	—	195,200	—	—
Additions and betterments	53,964,007	2,674,000	3,286,254	205,748	150,000	27,000
Bank loans	39,803,100	—	—	—	—	—
Taxes	20,467,204	5,937,811	5,823,891	1,918,000	—	—
Audited vouchers for materials, supplies, etc.	14,080,492	560,689	2,500,000	200,000	—	—

(table continues on following page)

Table 8.3 continued

Purpose	Jan. 22, 1932– Oct. 31, 1932	Nov. 1, 1932– Oct. 31, 1933	Nov. 1, 1933– Oct. 31, 1934	Nov. 1, 1934– Oct. 31, 1935	Nov. 1, 1935– Oct. 31, 1936	Nov. 1, 1936– Oct. 31, 1937
Rentals	7,050,059	—	—	—	—	—
Preferential claims	6,986,742	1,500,000	—	—	—	—
Judgments	—	6,959,943	—	—	—	—
Equipment repairs	—	2,500,000	—	—	—	—
Purchase of property of lessor company	—	—	—	—	—	900,000
Working capital	—	—	—	—	—	—
Miscellaneous	13,870,733	35,838	686,467	134,200	140,000	61,805
Total	346,829,179	89,576,344	82,958,572	51,380,798	129,141,067	20,098,805

— Not applicable.
Source: Interstate Commerce Commission, *Annual Report* (various years).

that is, debt instruments for the purchase of operating equipment such as locomotives and freight cars and secured by the same. The purchase of equipment trust certificates maintained business activity and employment in ancillary industries. As it later turned out, support to this sector significantly smoothed production of railroad equipment on the eve of a high-demand period during World War II.

During November 1934 through October 1936, the principal purpose of RFC assistance became the repurchase of railroad securities in order to reduce firm leverage ratios. In January 1935, the agency was further empowered to purchase and guarantee directly the general obligations of railroads and railways (Spero 1939, p. 27). In this way, RFC railroad loans, in practice, were initially used to help out with bond interest payments and finance equipment, but were eventually used as a substitute for railroad capital. As mentioned earlier, this extension of the RFC's powers acknowledged that the Depression was expected to last much longer than previously believed. Therefore, the operations of the agency adapted to this philosophical shift by providing long-term capital (or debentures) rather than short-term secured debt.[10]

OUTCOME OF THE RAILROAD LOAN PROGRAM. As RFC railroad loans were not fully secured under the original statute, many railroad loans failed shortly thereafter. There thus existed a set of perverse incentives whereby railroads could borrow from the RFC to pay favored creditors and investors in full before defaulting. More important, because railroad capital levels were not regulated and rates on railroad loans, unlike those on the RFC's loans to financial intermediaries, were favorable, railroads gained an incentive to borrow from the RFC to finance a public capital flotation. This could then be used to replace private debt (sometimes held primarily by insiders) with a mix of equity and RFC debt before default.

---

10. Loans for additions and improvements were important during February–October 1932, but diminished in significance afterward. These loans primarily sought to maintain or increase employment rather than maintain or restructure the firm's finances. Although these loans did not require approval from the Interstate Commerce Commission, they carried two additional requirements: (a) the railroad had to repay the loan before granting any dividends, and (b) 75 percent of the money had to be spent rehiring furloughed labor (Jones 1951, p. 118; Spero 1939, pp. 27, 38–41). By 1933, a substantial portion of lending for unemployment relief, including loans to railroads for additions and improvements, was spun off to other New Deal agencies.

Once RFC officials recognized this problem, they demanded changes in the original statute. In June 1933, Congress amended the RFC Act so that the agency could no longer make a loan to any railroad or railway in need of financial reorganization. In 1935, as policymakers became further convinced of the long-term nature of the economic downturn, the RFC railroad loan program was further restricted to only those applicants "who could demonstrate the fundamental soundness of their financial position and their ability to survive a reasonably prolonged period of depression" (Spero 1939, p. 2).

Loans made before the more stringent provisions still placed RFC capital at risk. Therefore, as the RFC became concerned with the effects of its loans to the railroads, it also worried about the quality of the management of those railroads (Jones 1951, p. 145). As time passed, the RFC directly intervened more often in response to imprudent financial management and corrupt activities with other creditors.

The Missouri-Pacific railroad line offers a good example of the manipulations the RFC faced. Investment bankers lent to the Missouri-Pacific to arrange a capital flotation for the railroad at high interest rates and fees with a notion that the RFC would be called in to bail out the railroad with cheap debt and support the issue. Through these and other manipulations, the Missouri-Pacific line was eventually drained of cash by its holding company, the Alleghany Corporation, and its principal holders, the Van Sweringen family. Indeed, after bailing out the Missouri-Pacific, the RFC, as the principal creditor, was repaid only after wresting control of the line from Allegheny in a protracted bankruptcy and reorganization of the line between 1935 and 1937 (Sullivan 1951).

After the Missouri-Pacific debacle, the RFC exercised a great deal more caution by constraining management from the outset. Eventually, the RFC insisted on management changes as a condition of support. When the Southern-Pacific Railroad borrowed US$23.2 million in early 1937, the RFC "ordered reduction of executives' salaries [ranging] from ten percent to sixty percent" (Sullivan 1951, p. 43). During this period, the RFC also strictly enforced its requirement that railroads repay RFC loans before granting dividends. The "Pennsylvania Railroad borrowed seventy-five million dollars from the Corporation to electrify the lines between Boston, Massachusetts, and Washington, DC. When the debt was only a few months old and the dividend period was approaching, Pennsylvania Railroad, being proud of its [long, continuous] dividend record, paid off the Reconstruction Finance Corporation loan instead of stopping the payment of dividends" (Sullivan 1951, p. 23).

Even with such conditions, RFC loans to railroads only prevented temporarily a large number of insolvencies, prolonging the agony of impending bankruptcy. "Prices of railroad bonds moved generally downward, intensifying the economic, banking, and credit difficulties" (Spero 1939, p. 143). Like the corporation's loans to banks, the underlying problems of the railroads, declining revenue, increased competition, and burdensome debt structures, were left untouched" (Olson 1972, p. 181).

The problem with RFC railroad loans was almost exactly the opposite of the experience with loans to financial intermediaries—the program was too liberal instead of too conservative.[11] Over time, however, RFC officials learned that the less secure interest resulting from these more liberal policies could be mitigated by strictly enforced, detailed covenants and greater involvement with day-to-day management. These provisions, especially the intimate involvement with management, were effective not only at making loans that were repaid, but also at resolving asymmetric information about management quality at marginally solvent firms. Over time, both these provisions became integral features of the financial institution preferred stock program and the commercial and industrial (C&I) loan program.

The Preferred Stock Program

The objectives of the preferred stock program were twofold. First, the establishment of the preferred stock program in March 1933 marked the further evolution in policymakers' perceptions of the Great Depression. Before this period, policymakers largely believed that the depression was a the manifestation of a temporary debt deflation spiral. If they provided liquid funds to relieve the credit stringency that perpetuated the spiral, they believed the economic pressures would lift. After March 1933, policymakers began to realize that the debt deflation spiral was caused by something much more complex than a simple lack of liquidity. They began to believe it was caused by a general lack of bank capital to support additional lending, even in the face of added liquidity through the RFC loan program. The preferred stock program would add capital to banks and trust companies to relieve this constraint.

---

11. Part of this was most likely due to the different institutional structure of the railroad industry as well as the involvement of the Interstate Commerce Commission in the lending process.

A second de facto objective of the preferred stock program became apparent around October 1933. All banks were required to be solvent in order to reopen following the nationwide Bank Holiday of March 1933. Authorities believed that such a requirement would relieve public fears about the incidence of solvency in the banking sector that could lead to panics. With some 15,000 banks in the United States at this time, accurately evaluating the soundness of all of these within the allotted week was impossible. In trying to restore confidence in the majority of institutions, regulators and policymakers consciously erred toward reopening marginal banks in hopes that their condition would improve.

Though public sentiment was immediately relieved by this strategy, a few months later it was again shaken. In March 1933, Congress passed a bill to provide Federal Deposit Insurance Corporation (FDIC) coverage to depositors at all banks that were solvent on January 1, 1934. By October 1933, it became apparent that several thousand banks that reopened following the Bank Holiday still were not solvent, and therefore could not qualify for FDIC coverage. The RFC preferred stock program became an important mechanism through which these banks could be quickly and effectively recapitalized so their number and condition would not be exposed.

OPERATIONS OF THE PREFERRED STOCK PROGRAM. After the Bank Holiday decreed by President Franklin Roosevelt, the RFC was authorized on March 9, 1933, to subscribe for preferred stock, exempt from double liability, in any national or state bank or trust company. The RFC was also authorized at this time to make loans secured by the preferred stock of national or state banks as collateral. In cases where a state bank or trust company was not permitted to issue preferred stock exempt from double liability, or if state laws permit such issue only by unanimous consent of the stockholders, the RFC was authorized to purchase legally issued capital notes or debentures. The RFC was authorized to sell in the open market the whole or part of its preferred stock, capital notes, or debentures of any national or state bank or trust company.[12]

---

12. On June 10, 1933, the RFC was further authorized to purchase preferred stock of insurance companies, but the size of insurance company authorizations never grew to any substantial prominence. Such equity could only be purchased if (a) the applicant had unimpaired capital stock or promised that it would furnish new capital unimpaired; and (b) no officer, director, or employee received total compensation in excess of US$17,500 per year. The total amount outstanding of loans, preferred stock subscriptions, and capital notes in insurance companies could not exceed US$50 million at any time.

RFC preferred stock initially paid senior dividends of 6 percent per year. RFC officials quickly realized, however, that banks already considered this rate too expensive, causing the lowering of the rate to 5 percent within two months. Even at the reduced rate, however, RFC preferred stock was priced only slightly below the prevailing yield for Standard & Poor's corporate preferred stocks, which averaged around 5.75 percent in 1933.[13] As RFC officials more actively sought to recapitalize the banking industry, rates were lowered further still. In 1934, RFC rates were lowered to 4.5 percent, and in 1935 to 3.5 percent. Moody's benchmark preferred stock yields dropped to about 5.25 percent in 1934, and maintained about 4.5 percent thereafter, making RFC preferred stock attractive during this later period. (U.S. Department of Commerce 1975, p. 1003).

Unlike the first railroad loans, however, the preferred stock purchased by the RFC was subject to some important additional provisions. RFC preferred stock was senior to all other stock upon liquidation of the firm. All other stock dividends were limited to a specified maximum, and remaining earnings were devoted to a preferred stock retirement fund. These provisions were strictly upheld, and banks, like railroads during this period, often found them overbearing.

The stock also carried voting rights that were often used to direct the institution toward solvency and profitability. The RFC was prohibited from purchasing more than 49 percent of the total outstanding voting stock in any one bank. However, it often owned the largest voting block in the company. Thus, the RFC had effective control of many of the institutions in which it had investments (Cho 1953, pp. 29–34; *Commercial and Financial Chronicle* 1933, pp. 1625–26; Upham and Lamke 1934, p. 234).

In several situations, the RFC used this control to replace officers and significantly alter the business practices of the institution. The earliest and most prominent intervention involved Continental Illinois National Bank of Chicago. Agreement on selecting a new chair was a precondition of the investment in Continental Illinois. However, the current directors did not approve of the RFC's choice and visited Washington, D.C., to voice their objections. They finally acquiesced after eight other directors were replaced with RFC appointees.[14]

---

13. Banks were first allowed to issue preferred stock after March 1933 under the RFC preferred stock program.

14. Continental was actually quite weak at the time, and despite a rather large investment in the First National Bank of Chicago, a few weeks later the RFC did not intervene in the bank's management after the death of its chief executive, Melvin Traylor (Jones 1951, pp. 47–49).

A similar situation played out with the Union Trust Company of Cleveland. The RFC agreed to finance the reorganization of Union Trust by providing a loan of US$35 million to liquefy and write off the poor assets of the old bank and purchase US$10 million of preferred stock to guarantee the new bank's capital structure. However, these were contingent upon "the right of the RFC to select the new bank's officers and the ability of those officers to raise US$10 million more in common stock" from the private market (Olson 1972, p. 233). Other prominent banks were assured that the situations at Continental Illinois and Union Trust were due to a combination of unusual circumstances and would not be repeated without due cause, but the threat of such control kept many banks from availing themselves of the resources offered by the RFC for at least the first nine months of the program's existence (see figure 8.2).

OUTCOME OF THE PREFERRED STOCK PROGRAM. The RFC preferred stock program was an appropriate response to capital growth constraints that plagued the banking sector during the Great Depression. Indeed, since early 1931 bankers and federal legislators appealed for a recapitalization program like the RFC. By the time the preferred stock program went into effect, however, high adverse selection premiums—high bid-ask spreads for common stock and high dividend yields for preferred stock—made bank capital relatively expensive. Figure 8.3 illustrates that bid-ask spreads moved sharply upward at the end of 1929 and remained high until at least 1936. Figure 8.4 shows that New York Stock Exchange preferred stock dividend yields were at record levels in June 1932 and did not decline to their August 1931 low until February 1935. Therefore, although RFC dividends were always below New York Stock Exchange preferred stock dividend yields, they were by no means cheap by historical standards.

Figure 8.2 depicts the lack of demand for bank capital as it reflected on the RFC preferred stock program. Before the first quarter of 1934, demand for RFC preferred stock assistance was stagnant. As with RFC loans, banks petitioned the agency for preferred stock assistance. At this time, many banks felt that having their name published in conjunction with receiving assistance from the RFC was evidence of high default risk, which could precipitate deposit outflows. Furthermore, banks feared the sort of RFC intervention exhibited at Continental Illinois and Union Trust. Because banks felt that capital was costly, feared publicity about their financial condition, and did not want to be reorganized at the hands of RFC officials, they were understandably reluctant to apply to the preferred stock program.

Figure 8.3. *Calomiris-Wilson Bid-Ask Spreads for New York Banks, 1920–40*

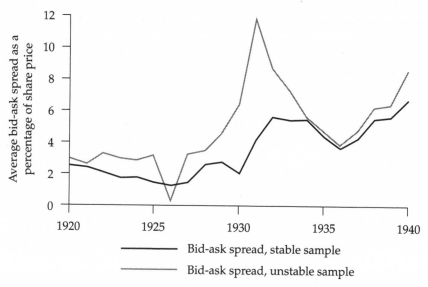

Bid-ask spread, stable sample

Bid-ask spread, unstable sample

Source: Calomiris and Wilson (1999).

Banks found themselves severely undercapitalized during this period. Wigmore points out that banks not feeling financial pressures during this period were rare. Even the largest banks in the country faced intense pressure on earnings and stock prices. Chase's stock hit a low of 13 percent of its highest 1929 price, and National City fell to 8 percent. However, during the first three weeks of the preferred stock program, the RFC made investments in only four banks, most as part of larger restructuring plans. During the second quarter of 1933, the RFC authorized preferred stock purchases in only 50 banks nationwide (Wigmore 1985, p. 468).

As the existing set of voting rights, price, and publication requirements proved to be substantial disincentives for banks to apply for preferred stock assistance, some leverage was needed to get weak banks into the program. Although the Glass-Steagall Act of 1933 did not alter the RFC's operating procedures, it provided just that leverage in the establishment of the FDIC. The FDIC would open on January 1, 1934, and only financially sound banks would be accepted for membership. However, Jesse Jones, chairman of the RFC, estimated that more than 5,000 banks that reopened after the holiday "required considerable added capital to make them sound" (Jones 1951, p. 27).

Figure 8.4.   *Dividend Rates on RFC and NYSE Preferred Stock,*
January 1921–December 1937

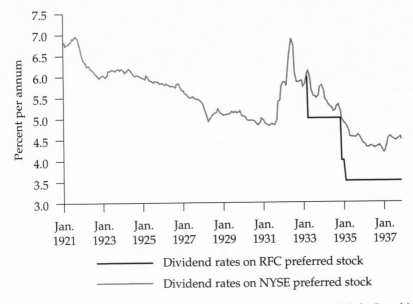

Source: Standard and Poor's *Trade and Securities Statistics: Security Price Index Record*, NBER Macro History Database, http://www.nber.org/databases/macrohistory/contents/chapter13.html.

Widespread opinion held that if all certified banks failed to join the FDIC after the Bank Holiday, a crisis of confidence would ensue and deposit outflows would again increase. Still, marginally solvent open banks were often unwilling to issue preferred stock to the RFC, and as they were not in reorganization, they could not be forced to join. For nearly three months, Jones harangued and cajoled bankers about the need for all banks to join the FDIC on January 1, 1934. At the American Bankers Association annual meeting in Chicago in September 1933, Jones strongly rebuked bankers for their reluctance to participate in the preferred stock program. In his speech, Jones urged all the leading U.S. banks to sell preferred stock to the RFC "so that depositors would not be induced to switch out of...banks when their names were published." The appeal to the American Bankers Association convention had an impact, and the number of applications received daily at the RFC increased substantially. In time, nearly all the banks, including those undeniably sound like the First National Bank of Chicago, the Continental Illinois Bank and Trust Company of Chicago, and National City Bank, sold stock to the RFC (Burns 1974, pp. 123–25; Jones 1951, pp.

26–27; Wigmore 1985, pp. 468–70). On January 1, 1934, the FDIC accepted 13,423 banks as members and rejected only 141, and the potential crisis of confidence was averted (Olson 1988, p. 81).[15]

By March 1934 the RFC had purchased preferred stock in nearly half the commercial banks in the United States (Jones 1951). By June 1935, these RFC investments made up more than one-third of all outstanding capital in the banking system (Olson 1988, p. 82). Mason (1999b) shows empirically that RFC preferred stock was associated with lower ex post probabilities of bank failure. Therefore, it appears that the preferred stock program was successful at helping banks withstand the economic depression.

In many ways, the preferred stock program addressed the inadequacies of the financial institutions' loan program while taking into account the valuable lessons learned from the railroad loan program. RFC capital was a cheaper, more junior (less secure), and longer-term claim than financial institutions' loans, but, as with railroad loans, it carried more detailed covenants and voting rights to effect greater corporate control. Preferred stock did not result in increased bank lending, as policymakers hoped. However, unlike previous programs, it did stabilize the business sector that it targeted for assistance.

The Commercial and Industrial Program

Banks avoided costly equity issues by reducing default risk elsewhere on the balance sheet. Calomiris and Wilson (1999, pp.22–23) explain that "in the wake of the loan losses produced by the Depression, high default risk was penalized with deposit withdrawals... To reduce deposit risk, banks increased their riskless assets and cut dividends," but avoided costly equity issues. By 1935, therefore, a dearth of new bank capital issues and bank programs to stabilize default risk by investing in safe liquid securities severely constricted the business lending pipeline. Figure 8.5 shows that bank lending continued to decrease after bank capital began to recover. Indeed, in Figure 8.5 bank lending does not turn up until at least late 1935.

---

15. Not all the banks were actually recapitalized by the time the FDIC opened for business. On December 15, 1933, more than 2,000 open banks were still in need of RFC capital to join the FDIC. Jesse Jones met with Secretary of the Treasury Henry Morgenthau to propose a compromise: if Morgenthau would certify these banks as solvent, Jones guaranteed they would be so within six months (Jones 1951, pp. 28–30). This bargain was instrumental in qualifying nearly all the open banks for membership in the FDIC on January 1, 1934.

Figure 8.5.   Bank Capital and Bank Lending, 1921–37

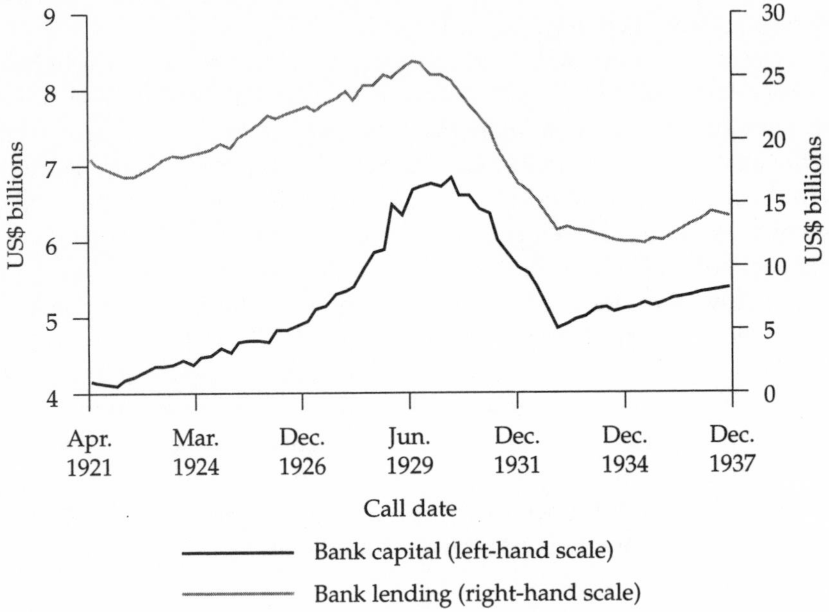

Source: Author's calculations.

Although preferred stock stabilized the banking sector, as long as banks were primarily concerned with their perceived default risk among depositors, they would not undertake new lending. RFC officials and other policymakers still believed that an ample supply of business credit represented the key to unwinding the debt deflation spiral at the heart of the economic downturn. Therefore, in June 1934 the RFC began making C&I loans directly to businesses in order to relieve the credit stringency and expand economic activity.

OPERATIONS OF THE COMMERCIAL AND INDUSTRIAL LOAN PROGRAM. The legislation passed in June 1934 allowed the RFC to make C&I loans with maturities "up to five years provided the applicant was sound, could supply adequate collateral, and could not get credit at banks. Loans could be advanced for working capital rather than equity or fixed capital, but could not exceed $500,000 per customer or be used to pay off existing indebtedness" (Olson 1972, p. 274).

In addition, section 1 of the same act that granted direct C&I loan authority to the RFC also amended the Federal Reserve Act to give equal authority to the Federal Reserve System (Walk 1937, p. 62). The legislation "allowed the RFC to loan up to $300,000,000 and the Federal Reserve Banks up to $280,000,000," in C&I loans. Of the US$280 million authorized to the Federal Reserve Banks, half was funded by their own surplus and half by the Treasury (Walk 1937, p. 65). Any future extensions of the US$280 million limit would be funded in the same manner.

Table 8.4 shows few differences between the terms of RFC and Federal Reserve C&I loans. Both could lend to any commercial or industrial firm, although the RFC could also lend to the fishing industry. Both required that credit be otherwise unavailable through conventional channels. The RFC required borrowers to be solvent, and both the RFC and Federal Reserve required that loans be backed by reasonable and sound, adequate security. Borrowing businesses had to be established concerns; that is, RFC and Federal Reserve loans could not be used to start new businesses (this provision was altered after 1937 to provide investment for the war effort). Both also required all borrowers to "consent to such examinations as the [RFC or Federal Reserve Banks] may require" (Agnew 1945, p. 48).

Federal Reserve C&I loan procedures were similar to general loan procedures already established at the RFC. Each set up local industrial loan committees composed of three to five industrialists, which passed on the merits of applications. As with RFC loans to financial intermediaries, only unusual RFC loans were reviewed by the Washington staff. Federal Reserve C&I loan applications were evaluated solely at the regional level, and were not subject to central review or pricing policies established in Washington (Walk 1937, p. 64).

RFC and Federal Reserve Bank C&I loans were granted to a similar mix of business types (see table 8.5). In particular, both granted the majority of their loans to the manufacturing and wholesale and retail trade sectors. As a matter of informal policy, however, the RFC did not lend to newspapers, radio stations, churches, the oil industry, and the automobile industry. This decision resulted from the potential political nature of the media and the moral suasion that could arise from religious organizations. Large industrial concerns, such as those in the oil and automobile industries, could usually obtain financing elsewhere on reasonable terms, which excluded them from the RFC or Federal Reserve credit programs.

To conserve capital and reintroduce banks into business credit arrangements, the RFC and Federal Reserve developed cooperative credit arrangements with banks by purchasing participations in C&I loans rather than originating the loans exclusively (Olson 1972, p. 276). Most of the RFC C&I assistance authorized after 1934 consequently took the form of loan participations with firms' existing banks (Agnew 1945, p. 78).

Table 8.4. *Legal Qualifications and Conditions for Direct C&I Loans*

Item	Reserve banks	RFC
Type of business	Any industrial or commercial business	Any industrial or commercial business, including the fishing industry
Age of business	An established business	Established prior to Jan. 1, 1934
Financial status	—	Solvent in the opinion of the Board of Directors of the RFC
Credit position	Unable to obtain requisite financial assistance on a reasonable basis from usual sources	"When credit at prevailing bank rates for the character of loans applied for is not otherwise available at banks"
Purpose of loan	For working capital	For maintaining and increasing the employment of labor
Maturity of obligation	Not over 5 years	Not over 5 years
Security required	"On reasonable and sound basis"	"Adequately secured in the opinion of the Board of Directors of the [RFC]"
Amount of funds available	US$139,299,557	US$300,000,000
Amount of any one loan	—	Not over US$500,000
Form of transaction	(a) Direct loan, or (b) Discount or purchase from financial institutions, or (c) Advance to financial institution on the security of such obligation, or (d) Commitments with regard to such loan or advance to financial institution (b, c, and d require 20-percent participation of financial institution in the risk)	(a) Direct loan, or (b) Loan in cooperation with bank, or (c) Purchase of participation

— Not applicable.
Source: Hardy and Viner (1935, p. 30).

Table 8.5. C&I Commitments Approved by the Federal Reserve Banks and RFC, Major Industrial Classifications

Type of industry	Number approved by the federal reserve banks, June 19, 1934– May 1, 1935	Amount approved by the federal reserve banks, June 19, 1934– May 1, 1935 (US$)	Number approved by the RFC, June 19, 1934– December 31, 1937	Amount approved by the RFC, June 19, 1934– December 31, 1937 (US$)
Manufacturing				
Autos, trucks, and accessories	17	7,732,500.00	43	5,320,500.00
Metals	27	2,798,000.00	249	20,562,998.34
Machinery and machine tools	33	3,285,000.00	145	12,863,123.43
Textiles	19	2,496,500.00	259	33,597,883.33
Lumber and builders' supplies	31	2,286,600.00	235	20,418,203.81
Furniture, office, and household equipment	31	1,964,500.00	84	4,680,600.00
Wholesale and retail trade				
Food products	30	1,985,900.00	42	536,050.00
Lumber and builders' supplies	42	1,630,700.00	34	983,000.00
Chain and department stores	15	689,000.00	13	2,391,000.00
Grain, feed, seeds, etc.	12	753,000.00	32	802,760.00
Miscellaneous				
Contractors and construction	19	1,572,000.00	*	*
Printing, publishing, and allied trades	22	953,000.00	84	2,499,450.00
Hotels, apartments, restaurants	8	188,500.00	*	*
Transportation	6	120,000.00	*	*

* Authorized under alternate RFC programs.
Source: Mason (1999a).

RFC C&I loan participations were either immediate or deferred. Immediate participations could cover any portion of the loan agreeable to both participants. These could consist of a bank purchasing part of an RFC-originated loan, or the RFC purchasing part of a bank-originated loan, upon disbursement. Either way, the RFC took a stake in the default risk underlying the investment, which instilled confidence in the firms and effectively insulated the banking sector from default.

In practice, immediate participations were often combined with deferred participations. Deferred participations allowed the banking sector to assume a larger proportion of a loan while holding a put option on a portion of the default risk. By definition, "a deferred participation is one in which the [RFC] and the bank execute an agreement under which the [RFC] will purchase upon ten days notice by the bank an agreed percentage of the unpaid balance of the loan"[16] (Sullivan 1951, pp. 15–16).

The price of the put option depended upon the amount of risk the RFC assumed. Deferred participations were priced as "two percent per annum when the local bank's participation is less than twenty-five percent of the loan; one and one-half percent per annum when the bank's participation is from twenty-five percent to fifty percent of the loan; and one percent per annum when the bank's participation is fifty percent or more," (Agnew 1945, p. 79).

A streamlined set of procedures for deferred participations was developed for small borrowers. In cases where the loan principal was less than US$100,000, the bank filed a one-page application to the RFC accompanied by supporting documents: identification of borrower, use of funds, and collateral. The RFC approved or denied on the basis of this application and any supporting material (Sullivan 1951, p. 17). The borrower never had to deal with the RFC directly in a small-loan participation. More than 85 percent of all RFC C&I loans were eligible for the small-loan program[17] (RFC *Report of the Reconstruction Finance Corporation*, Fourth Quarter 1937, p. 93).

Federal Reserve Bank and RFC C&I loans were also used in tandem with the other assistance programs outlined earlier. For instance, both RFC

---

16. Deferred participations by the RFC could not exceed 70 percent in loans of less than US$100,000, and 60 percent in loans of greater than US$100,000 (Sullivan 1951, pp. 15–16).

17. Although these made up only about 35 percent of the amount of RFC C&I lending, the wide base of these loans provided much-needed political capital. This program later formed the basis for the Small Business Administration, which was spun off from the agency upon its liquidation in 1953.

and Federal Reserve Bank participations could be used to limit a bank's exposure to any single borrower as per statutory loan limits. If a bank was limited to US$100,000 per borrower, a loan in which the RFC or Federal Reserve Bank took up the excess principal over US$100,000 would keep the bank within the regulatory limits (Walk 1937, p. 68). Alternatively, an RFC or Federal Reserve participation might also limit banks' exposure to credit risk. Sometimes, a bank that had previously refused to accommodate a borrower would later request to purchase or participate in the loan after the RFC or Federal Reserve decided to accept it (Walk 1937, p. 71). If all other methods failed, the Federal Reserve Bank or the RFC could make loans to financial intermediaries for the indirect purpose of funding particular C&I credit (Walk 1937, p. 68).

OUTCOME OF THE COMMERCIAL AND INDUSTRIAL LOAN PROGRAM. Like the railroad and preferred stock programs, the assistance provided to commercial and industrial firms afforded the RFC "a profound influence upon policies and organizations of borrowers to insure soundness of their equity" (Sullivan 1951, p. 7). As long as any portion of a [C&I] loan remained outstanding, no dividends could be paid by any corporate borrower, nor could distribution or withdrawal be made by a partnership or individual borrower without the consent of the RFC (Walk 1937).

The RFC sometimes used its influence or inserted managers directly in commercial and industrial concerns to ensure sound business practices, and thereby help provide earnings sufficient to repay C&I loans. Although no formal data exists on the extent to which the RFC intervened in business operations directly, Jones includes several examples (Jones 1951, pp. 183–92). One example describes how the RFC funded the reorganization of the National Department Stores, Inc., of New York City. The national subsidiary stores in major cities throughout the country were generally sound, but the parent company was in reorganization. The RFC put up US$2.25 million for a successful restructuring that allowed the company and its subsidiaries to remain in business.

Jones also describes the case of Botany Worsted Mills of Passaic, New Jersey. The owner of Botany sold products at unprofitable levels to keep 5,000 citizens of Passaic employed. The RFC loaned Botany US$1 million and inserted a representative on Botany's finance committee to ensure merchandise was sold at a reasonable profit. Although the loan had to be increased several times, Botany ultimately regained profitability, repaid the RFC, and subsequently hired the RFC's advisor as a consultant. These are just two examples of RFC intervention that helped improve business operating procedures and maintain employment, thereby stimulating local economic activity.

The C&I loan programs had the capacity to make up a substantial portion of C&I funding during the early to mid-1930s. RFC and Federal Reserve loan programs combined allowed the extension of almost US$600 million to C&I firms. Compared with total industrial capital flotations of only US$381 million in 1933, US$491 million in 1934, and US$2.3 billion in 1935, the programs had the capacity to fully cover new industrial capital investment in 1933 and 1934, and more than a quarter of new investment in 1935 (*Commercial and Financial Chronicle*, various issues). Despite this capacity, the C&I loan programs' performance was lackluster. The comparison of RFC and Federal Reserve direct loans outstanding in table 8.6 shows that by the end of 1937, the RFC had only authorized about US$140 million in its C&I loan program, and the Federal Reserve only about US$150 million.[18] Neither agency ever drew close to their statutory limits on C&I lending.

At least part of the explanation for this lackluster performance probably lies again with pricing. Even at their highest, in 1932, bank rates were only about 4.7 percent, and they continued to decline in subsequent years. When RFC rates were at 6 percent at the inception of the C&I loan program in 1934, comparable bank rates were about 3.5 percent. Although RFC rates were lowered to a range of 4.5 to 5.5 percent in 1935 and thereafter, comparable bank rates were less than 3 percent, reaching nearly 2.5 percent in 1937. Therefore, it appears that RFC C&I loans were grossly overpriced compared with bank rates on short-term business loans during the period (U.S. Department of Commerce 1975, p. 1,002).

Furthermore, in 1934, when Congress first authorized the RFC to make loans directly to industry, the law again provided that they should be adequately, although, again, not fully, secured. Although these loans could be made to insolvent firms, the RFC had already learned the value of close monitoring from their experience with the railroad loan program. As with loans to financial institutions, however, the adequate security greatly constrained the RFC's ability to affect a meaningful recovery. Therefore, "the provision respecting loans to industry was later, at [the RFC's] request, changed to read that such loans be so secured as 'reasonably to assure payment,'" (Jones 1951, p. 184).

---

18. Federal Reserve direct loans also included loans to financial intermediaries that supported specific C&I loans. Such extensions by the RFC were covered under the bank loan program.

Table 8.6. *Number and Amounts of Federal Reserve Bank and Reconstruction Finance Corporation Industrial Advances*

Date (last Wednesday of each month)	Federal Reserve Bank applications recommended for approval to date (with and without conditions)		Outstanding Federal Reserve Bank participations with financial institutions	RFC applications recommended for approval to date (with and without conditions)		Outstanding RFC participations with financial institutions
	Number	Amount (US$)	Amount (US$)	Number	Amount (US$)	Amount (US$)
Dec-34	1,122	54,531	1,296	519	25,477	0
Jan-35	1,341	73,470	1,764	632	28,840	0
Mar-35	1,521	79,490	2,472	826	37,557	0
May-35	1,734	90,799	4,228	977	46,999	0
Jul-35	1,907	109,603	5,611	1,135	63,623	20
Sep-35	2,009	121,837	7,060	1,263	79,064	26
Nov-35	2,134	130,502	8,893	1,386	85,937	26
Jan-36	2,212	134,243	8,699	1,506	93,996	26
Mar-36	2,294	138,450	7,550	1,605	99,879	26
May-36	2,374	141,749	7,641	1,704	104,746	26
Jul-36	2,413	143,978	7,534	1,782	111,296	25
Sep-36	2,463	147,191	7,276	1,840	118,511	25
Nov-36	2,482	148,312	7,435	1,900	122,359	24
Jan-37	2,506	149,527	6,977	1,958	128,690	24
Mar-37	2,543	150,561	6,767	2,002	132,328	24
May-37	2,577	153,720	7,114	2,049	134,334	134
Jul-37	2,590	155,023	7,330	2,105	138,899	141
Sep-37	2,610	155,902	7,304	2,134	140,029	129
Nov-37	2,624	156,533	7,145	2,152	142,087	129

Source: Mason (1999a).

Still, this relaxation in collateral requirements had little effect on the program. In 1935 Hardy and Viner concluded that "efforts to relieve [credit] stringency through direct lending on the part of the Federal Reserve Bank of Chicago and the Chicago agency of the Reconstruction Finance Corporation have so far had a negligible effect on the general state of credit" (Hardy and Viner 1935, p. vi). In a later study, Kimmel (1939) reached similar conclusions for the entire period 1933 through 1938:

> [B]oth the demand for loans and the soundness of [C&I] borrowers was not what [RFC officials] expected. By September [1934], the Corporation had authorized only 100 business loans totaling $8,000,000. Less than $400,000 had been disbursed. Either because of inadequate security, insolvency, excessive indebtedness, or lack of potential earning power, the RFC rejected the majority of applications. But the apparent lack of demand for credit by business provided the RFC with its greatest surprise. It was a direct contradiction of what both [the Hoover and Roosevelt] administrations had told the country since 1931 (as cited in Olson 1972, p. 277).

Policymakers and RFC officials thus discovered what banks knew all along: the perceived credit stringency did not exist. Commercial and industrial firms did not want loans because consumption was stagnant. As it turned out, bank lending remained below its 1921 levels until the 1940s, when fiscal programs stimulated by wartime production resuscitated economic activity. No amount of RFC C&I lending, preferred stock, or other assistance to the corporate sector would change these fundamental conditions.

Nonetheless, the C&I loan programs built on many of the lessons learned from the financial institution loan, railroad loan, and preferred stock programs. C&I loans included longer maturities and were eventually based on relatively liberal collateral and solvency requirements, while these attributes were balanced by strong covenants and, if necessary, active involvement in firm operations. The C&I loan program was not very effective, but it appears this was the result of restrictions that loan proceeds be used to maintain or increase employment, not to replace or roll over existing debt finance. C&I firms really needed a long-term replacement for their existing debt. That is, like banks, C&I firms needed long-term capital investment. However, in the United States, such a large-scale nationalization of the nation's commerce and industry probably conflicted too strongly with American philosophies and ideals.

Summary and Conclusions

The RFC operated a wide variety of recapitalization and lending programs for financial institutions, commercial and industrial enterprises, and individuals from 1932 to 1953. This chapter described the details of a few of those programs that are widely held as instrumental in America's emergence from the Great Depression and subsequent growth in the latter half of the 20th century.

Although results under these individual programs vary significantly, RFC programs converged over time into a set of operating principles that can guide prudent contemporary policy responses to systemic distress and economic crisis. First, assistance offered through such programs should be of a long-term nature, based on liberal collateral requirements or loose interpretations of current solvency. Second, and crucially, the security of assistance should lie in fixed-term, medium-to-senior-insider stakes and strict covenants that will promote relationships with management to guide eventual profitability and repayment. Those relationships should resolve asymmetric information so firms may once again obtain outside finance from normal markets and intermediaries and subsequently provide an avenue through which the assistance can be systematically phased out as economic growth resumes.

Two caveats deserve mention, however. First, the RFC programs above do not constitute a necessary and sufficient set of institutions to remedy economic downturn or crisis. One glaring omission lies in the RFC's reluctance to provide funds that could be used to purchase bank assets in liquidation, relieving asset market overhang and supporting reflation. Research suggests that this overhang results from rational behavior by trustees charged with maximizing creditor recovery during a systemic downturn, and this behavior was an important determinant of the persistence of the Great Depression (Mason 1999b; Mason, Anari, and Kolari 1999). The existing programs would probably have been more helpful with this support.

Second, any application of the lessons from the RFC must be tailored to the institutional context of the sovereign nations in which they are implemented. At the very least, this means there must be legal provisions for bankruptcy and registration of collateral claims. There should be economic provisions for an active market for corporate control, a profit motive for recovery, and a macroeconomic policy of reflation that promises long-term economic growth. There also should be cultural provisions that provide a credible threat of closure, asset seizure, and liquidation as a result of insolvency. Without at least adapting policies for these institutional preconditions, little impact can be expected from the reincarnation of RFC-like policies in contemporary crises.

References

Agnew, Richard L. 1945. *Loans to Financial Institutions by the Reconstruction Finance Corporation*. Master's thesis, University of Nebraska.

Anderson, Gary M., and Robert D. Tollison. 1991. "Congressional Influence and Patterns of New Deal Spending, 1933-1939." *Journal of Law and Economics* 34(1): 161–75.

Burns, Helen M. 1974. *The American Banking Industry and New Deal Banking Reforms, 1933–1935*. Westport, Connecticut: Greenwood Press.

Calomiris, Charles W., and Berry Wilson. 1999. "Bank Capital and Portfolio Management: The 1930's Capital Crunch and Scramble to Shed Risk." Working Paper No. W6649. National Bureau of Economic Research, Cambridge, Massachusetts.

Cho, Hyo Won. 1953. "The Evolution of the Functions of the Reconstruction Finance Corporation: A Study of the Growth and Death of a Federal Lending Agency." Ph.D. dissertation, Ohio State University, Columbus, Ohio.

Commercial and Financial Chronicle. 1933. Various issues, New York: William B. Dana Company.

Delaney, John A. 1954. "Field Administration in the Reconstruction Finance Corporation." Thesis: Washington, D.C.: George Washington University.

Hardy, Charles O., and Jacob Viner. 1935. *Report on the Availability of Bank Credit in the Seventh Federal Reserve District*. Washington, D.C.: U.S. Government Printing Office.

Interstate Commerce Commission. Various issues. *Annual Report*. Washington, D.C.: U.S. Government Printing Office.

Jones, Jesse H. 1951. *Fifty Billion Dollars: My Thirteen Years with the RFC (1932-1945)*. New York: The Macmillan Company.

Kimmel, Lewis H. 1939. *The Availability of Bank Credit, 1933–1938*. New York: National Industrial Conference Board, Inc.

Locker, Warren T. 1943. "The Reconstruction Finance Corporation and Its Effect on Banking." Master's thesis, American Bankers Association Graduate School of Banking, New York.

Mason, Joseph R. 1996. "The Determinants and Effects of Reconstruction Finance Corporation Assistance to Banks during the Great Depression." Ph.D. dissertation, University of Illinois at Urbana-Champaign.

_____. 1999a. "Do Lender of Last Resort Policies Matter? The Effects of Reconstruction Finance Corporation Assistance to Banks during the Great Depression." Working Paper. Drexel University, Philadelphia.

_____. 1999b. "What Do We Know about Asset Liquidation Rates? Evidence from Commercial Bank Liquidations during the 1930s and 1990s." Working Paper. Drexel University, Philadelphia.

Mason, Joseph R., Ali Anari, and James Kolari. 1999. "The Role of Failed-Bank Liquidation Rates in the Propagation of the U.S. Great Depression." Working Paper. Drexel University, Philadelphia.

Olson, James S. 1972. "From Depression to Defense: The Reconstruction Finance Corporation: 1932-1940." Ph.D. dissertation, State University of New York at Stony Brook.

_____. 1988. *Saving Capitalism: The Reconstruction Finance Corporation and the New Deal, 1933-1940*. Princeton, New Jersey: Princeton University Press.

Report of Activities of the Reconstruction Finance Corporation (Monthly, Published). Various issues. Washington, D.C.: U.S. Government Printing Office.

Report of the Reconstruction Finance Corporation (Quarterly). Various issues. Washington, D.C.: U.S. Government Printing Office.

RFC *Circular no. 1*. 1932. Washington, D.C.: U.S. Government Printing Office.

Simonson, Donald G., and George H. Hempel. 1993. "Banking Lessons from the Past: The 1938 Regulatory Agreement Interpreted." *Journal of Financial Services Research* 7(3): 249–67.

Spero, Herbert. 1939. *Reconstruction Finance Corporation Loans to the Railroads, 1932-1937*. New York: Bankers Publishing Company.

Standard and Poor's. *Trade and Securities Statistics: Security Price Index Record*. Obtained from National Bureau of Economic Research's Macro History Database, http://www.nber.org/databases/macrohistory/ contents/chapter13.html.

Sullivan, Francis J. 1951. "Reconstruction Finance Corporation and Corporate Financial Policy." Master's thesis, George Washington University, Washington, D.C.

Upham, Cyril B., and Edwin Lamke. 1934. *Closed and Distressed Banks: A Study in Public Administration*. Washington, D.C.: The Brookings Institution.

U.S. Department of Commerce, Bureau of the Census. 1975. *Historical Statistics of the United States, Colonial Times to 1970*. Washington, D.C.: U.S. Government Printing Office.

Walk, Everett G. 1937. "Loans of Federal Agencies and Their Relationship to the Capital Market." Ph.D. dissertation, University of Pennsylvania, Philadelphia.

Waller, Clyde. 1934. "The Administrative Powers of the Reconstruction Finance Corporation." Master's thesis, Southern Methodist University, Dallas, Texas.

Wallis, John J. 1998. "The Political Economy of New Deal Spending Revisited, Again: With and Without Nevada." *Explorations in Economic History* 35(2): 140–70.

Wigmore, Barrie A. 1985. *The Crash and Its Aftermath: A History of Security Markets in the United States, 1929-1933*. Westport, Connecticut: Greenwood Press.

9

Japan Confronts Corporate Restructuring

Arthur J. Alexander, Japan Economic Institute

Japanese businesses are restructuring at a faster pace than in past economic downturns. Mergers and acquisitions are occurring in numbers unprecedented for Japan, while the frequency and scale of bankruptcies also have hit new highs. Unemployment has reached a postwar peak, with more than a million jobs lost in 1998 and 1999 alone. Companies are shedding cross-held shares, and the role of private fixed, nonresidential economic investment shrank to a level not seen since the beginning of the economic miracle in 1956. Major corporations are shutting down subsidiaries and selling off unprofitable businesses.

Despite ongoing changes, continuing regulation of the economy; widely held norms that favor lifetime employment practices by big companies; traditional disdain for mergers, acquisitions, and bankruptcy; and reluctance to disrupt longtime business relations slow the adjustment process. While restructuring at an incremental pace may soften the pain, this approach most likely will prolong the negative fallout. Nonetheless, Japan's economy has embarked on an unprecedented transition.

Restructuring involves cutting costs, downsizing, and selling off assets. Corporations also reorganize through spinoffs, divestitures and carve-outs, mergers and acquisitions, bankruptcies, and securitization. The process of transforming business occupies minds both within and beyond the corporate sector. In March 1999, the government established the Competitiveness Commission, a group of cabinet ministers and business leaders tasked with recommending supply-side measures to address Japan's economic malaise. The members of the commission met weekly until March 2000, when they issued recommendations. As unemployment reached new monthly highs, policymakers considered the pace of recovery too slow. A special fall 1999 session of the Diet, the Japanese legislature, was the target date for finishing draft legislation. According to instructions Prime Minister Obuchi issued in early May 2000, the advisory panel completed a package of bills before the end of the regular 2000 legislative session in mid-June.

Such an acceleration of public policymaking in Japan is extraordinary. Just as incredible is the forcefulness of the political leadership driving a system that ordinarily would get bogged down in bureaucratic processes. Bureaucratic actions to facilitate restructuring accelerated during the past two years in the areas of bankruptcy, mergers and acquisitions, and debt securitization. Rather than acting as a barrier to change, the government now appears convinced of the need for thorough restructuring in the corporate sector.

Although judging ongoing initiatives on the parts of the business community, politicians, and the government is premature, this level of activity signals a historic shift in Japan's economy. Before proceeding with the restructuring issue, however, considering what the process is and what drives it may be useful.

The Case for Restructuring

Restructuring describes the effort to raise both profits and the rate of return on the assets a company uses in its business. The latter is important because profits alone are an imperfect yardstick of corporate success. However, raising the rate of return on assets is meaningful only in relation to the return it provides to investors. Indeed, in a capitalist economy, the ability of a company to generate benefits for other stakeholders—employees, managers, suppliers, and the host community—depends in the long run on its capacity to attract investment, which, in turn, hinges on meeting competitive rates of return on capital.

Several factors have combined to focus corporate Japan's attention on the bottom line. By international standards, Japanese returns on capital are low. Elevated rates of business investment throughout the postwar period have driven capital or output ratios higher than they are in most other advanced economies. By various measures, the capital intensity of production in Japan surpassed the U.S. level in the 1970s. Not unexpectedly, the marginal productivity of nonresidential capital in producing the country's gross domestic product (GDP) fell below the U.S. figure long before the bubble economy stimulated even more low-return investment. Economywide, by the early 1990s, returns on capital in Japan were one-third less than the U.S. value. Japan's average rate of return on equity has been lower than the U.S. level since at least 1980 and lower than European values since 1983. Another measure indicates that the average return on business capital in Japan fell below the averages for France, Germany, the United Kingdom, and the United States in 1974, with the gap widening in every subsequent year.

These demonstrably low returns provoke another set of questions. Why did Japanese companies continue to invest at such high rates at the same time that returns were falling? Force of habit is one explanation. During the high-growth phase of the economy's expansion, which lasted until the early 1970s, Japanese rates of return soared to almost 35 percent (Alexander 1998). Another explanation is that high rates of consumer savings supplied generous amounts of low-cost capital to the business sector. Although some of these savings began to flow abroad in the early 1980s, most remained within the county and fed investment. A third explanation is that, until the 1980s, financial sector regulation reinforced corporate and consumer habits by restricting household savings to bank accounts and by reducing competitive pressures on banks to seek the highest returns. The regulation of interest rates and the prevalence of a system in which no bank was allowed to fail created little incentive to maximize yields.

These conditions created a hazardous situation in which protected parties took greater risks than they would have in the absence of guarantees. Government policies insured lenders, borrowers, depositors, and bank creditors against failure. Neither lenders nor borrowers used expected rates of return as the governing criterion for investment. Instead, they based decisions on the profits that would accrue under the most optimistic scenario. If something less than the best occurred, a bank or its borrowers would be protected from failure; the government picked up the pieces.

What standard should policymakers use to judge the pace of restructuring? An examination of several areas of recent activity—investment, employment, mergers and acquisitions, and changes in cross-shareholding—may answer this question.

Investment. By 1999, private fixed, nonresidential investment had fallen to a level not seen since 1956. At 13.3 percent of GDP, business investment in the last quarter of 1998 was almost 7 percentage points below peak levels in early 1991 and 2.5 points behind the rate that characterized the aborted recovery attempted at the beginning of 1997. The June Bank of Japan survey of the short-term business outlook revealed that almost all sectors planned to continue their investment cutbacks.

The large size of Japan's corporate capital stock, estimated at approximately 3.4 times GDP, implies that companies must invest almost 13 percent of aggregate output annually just to make up for depreciation (Maddison 1995).[1] If investment drops below that level, the total value of capital will decline. Indeed, that eventuality may be appropriate, given the country's low rates of return. Reductions in investment may not be the best medicine for a stagnant economy, but such a development is consistent with a restructuring effort that would drive up returns and prepare Japan for more vigorous future growth.

EMPLOYMENT. A survey of March and April 1999 headlines in the online English edition of *Nihon Keizai Shimbun*, Japan's leading business daily, turned up 23 articles reporting reductions in corporate payrolls. In aggregate, unemployment rose to the historically high level of 4.8 percent in March 1999. During 1998–99, the seasonally adjusted number of people at work fell by more than 1 million, or 1.6 percent of the working population, even though more than 780,000 people joined the working-age population in the same period.

The difference between the 1998–99 period and the downturn in the early 1990s illustrates the changed circumstances. Between 1991 and 1993, employment continued to grow despite a 15 percent drop in industrial production. Indeed, despite sustained decline in factory output, total employment at the end of 1993 was slightly higher than in early 1991.

Compared with the U.S. history of big layoffs by major employers to cut costs, the slow pace of job reduction in Japan implies that unemployment will grow worse over the next few years unless the number of new companies, and even whole industries, grows quickly enough to fill the gap. The drop in investment, however, bodes ill for the early arrival of an entrepreneurial miracle to save Japanese jobs.

MERGERS AND ACQUISITIONS. Mergers and acquisitions serve several functions in raising returns. They can affect both the numerator and the denominator of the rate of return equation. When a company is acquired, the sale's price often places a new value on its capital. With a revalued, lower denominator, the same profit stream translates into a higher rate of return. In addition, new management with different expertise, plus the

---

1. Maddison assumes a 39-year life for structures and a 14-year life for machinery and equipment. The weighted average annual depreciation rate for Japan's capital stock is 3.8 percent.

combination of assets from various companies, usually raises expectations of higher profits, making a deal even more attractive.

The lack of transparency in the books of potential targets serves as another barrier to mergers and acquisitions. For example, Tokyo Department Store Company, Ltd. sought a buyer, but found no takers. On the surface, the company seemed a good buy. Its total market capitalization in October 1998 was estimated at only ¥ 20 billion (US$166.7 million),[2] while its Nihonbashi store and the land it occupied in the heart of downtown Tokyo was valued at ¥ 60 billion (US$500 million). The probable reason for the lack of interest in this seemingly guaranteed moneymaking investment was that Tokyo Department Store's off-balance-sheet loan guarantees for other companies in its group were thought to total at least ¥ 40 billion (US$333.3 million). However, potential buyers were uncertain about the scale of these hidden liabilities, making the company a less appealing takeover target.

One of the major impediments to mergers and acquisitions in Japan is the widespread practice of cross-shareholding. According to some accounts, mutual shareholding among companies started in the 1970s specifically to ward off undesired acquisitions, especially from foreign firms, at a time when international capital markets were liberalizing. Japan's relatively low number of mergers and acquisitions is even today an indication of the success of this practice.

Economic forces, however, are eroding the barriers against mergers and acquisitions erected by policies and attitudes. Many Japanese companies, especially family-owned businesses established in the early postwar period, are seeking injections of capital to preserve themselves after the departure of their founders. More generally, almost a decade of slow growth or recession has left many companies starved for capital because operating losses and write-offs of bad assets have been a drain. In addition, the same plunging asset prices that have created the need for new capital have converted previously overpriced companies into more attractive takeover options despite the continuing economic slump. At the same time, foreign corporations possess the capital and skills to turn underperforming Japanese firms around.

As a result of these pressures, mergers and acquisitions set new records in 1998. The estimated total of 847 mergers and acquisitions among domestic companies was two-thirds greater than the 1997 figure, which was one-third greater than 1996's total. Acquisitions by foreign companies also

---

2. The exchange rate used throughout this chapter is ¥ 120 = US$1.

reached a new high in 1998, with 61 acquisitions, up from 53 in 1997. In 1990, foreign acquisitions were in the single digits. The value of these deals totaled US$6.9 billion last year compared with US$1.1 billion in 1997. Moreover, the number shot up to US$7.1 billion in just the first quarter of 1999, confirming the rapid pace of foreign takeovers.[3]

The growing volume of foreign activity represents another reason for the removal of many of the regulatory constraints on business activities. As companies in formerly regulated sectors had neither the incentive nor the authorization to develop the experience that their unregulated foreign counterparts cultivated, overseas firms often possess capabilities that Japanese companies lack. Foreign competitors making inroads in such areas as finance, retailing, and telecommunications have taken advantage of expertise gained in less regulated markets abroad.

Several recent regulatory changes have made mergers and acquisitions activity cheaper and simpler. In 1997, the Diet amended the Commercial Code to reduce—or, in some circumstances, eliminate entirely—the number of shareholder meetings required to approve mergers. Moreover, the Holding Company Law, approved in December 1997, removed constraints on carving out subsidiaries for sale and allowed buyers more freedom in structuring their acquisitions.

CROSS-SHAREHOLDING. Surveys of the 2,388 companies listed on Japanese stock exchanges indicate that as of March 1998 other companies cross-held 18.2 percent of the value of corporate shares. Shares are defined as cross-held if company A holds shares in company B and B has shares in A. The cross-shareholding ratio is the proportion of a company's outstanding stock owned in this way summed across all publicly traded companies. Analysts defined a larger proportion of the stock market's capitalization, 35.7 percent, more broadly as representing long-term holdings—bank holdings of non-bank shares and vice versa—in which mutuality is not necessarily involved.

Both ratios have declined, although long-term holdings fell by a larger amount (see table 9.1). The sharpest drop in the narrow measure of cross-shareholding occurred as nonbank companies have dumped their bank shares. This figure fell by more than 2 percentage points between fiscal year 1995 and fiscal year 1997 and accounted for the entire decline in mutual shareholding.

The Tokyo Stock Exchange also surveys its members to determine who owns what shares. Its research showed that financial institutions held 42.1

---

3. International data is available at http://www.kpmg.com.

Table 9.1.   *Cross-Shareholding among Japanese Companies, 1987–97*
(percent)

Fiscal year	Long-term holdings	Cross-holdings
1987	41.5	21.2
1988	41.6	20.7
1989	42.5	20.2
1990	41.1	21.2
1991	41.1	21.2
1992	41.3	21.1
1993	40.6	20.8
1994	40.5	20.8
1995	39.0	20.6
1996	37.7	19.6
1997	35.7	18.2

Source: Tokyo Stock Exchange (1997).

percent of all shares by capitalized value in 1997 (Tokyo Stock Exchange 1997). Nonfinancial business corporations owned an additional 24.6 percent, and individuals owned 19 percent. Foreign owners, who increased their share from 11.9 percent in 1996 to 13.4 percent a year later, made up the fastest growing group.

A revealing aspect of the Tokyo Stock Exchange survey is the change in the average price of shares owned by the different groups of investors (Tokyo Stock Exchange 1997). Between 1996 and 1997, the average price declined 10.4 percent for all Tokyo Stock Exchange–listed shares. Stocks held by foreigners fell by only 0.6 percent, the smallest drop among all the groups. Nonfinancial corporations suffered the largest loss at 14.3 percent, significantly underperforming the market price. Brokerages' holdings fell 18.1 percent in value, but they owned less than 1 percent of all shares.[4] Falling prices are part of the reason that companies are tending to sell their shares to each other.

Managing Financial Distress

Low rates of return on capital do not necessarily lead to financial distress. However, if the returns on a firm's assets are less than the commitments to creditors, distress is sooner or later inevitable. If the problem is merely one

---

4. Measures based on capitalized value were quite similar to those based on the number of shares (see Tokyo Stock Exchange 1997).

of timing, that is, if cash is not immediately at hand but will be at a later date, a crisis can often be weathered. However, if the value of the firm's assets is less than the firm's debts, the structure of the firm's assets and liabilities must be changed to reflect their economic value. This restructuring can be accomplished through formal court-based proceedings, but less formal, private methods also are common. Noncourt-based activities gain their effectiveness from a formal court-based bankruptcy regime establishing a viable, accepted, and well-understood alternative to private negotiations.

Bankruptcy refers to the inability to meet debts as they mature. Insolvency usually means that the aggregate of the debtor's property, at a fair valuation, is insufficient to pay his or her debts. A debtor may be insolvent without becoming bankrupt and vice versa. Bankruptcy laws seek primarily to provide creditors with an equitable share of the debtor's assets that are available for the payment of liabilities in an orderly manner.

As used in Japan, the term bankruptcy includes private arrangements with creditors and formally recognized court-sanctioned proceedings. The term encompasses liquidation and reorganization. Until the 1990s, approximately 15 percent of broadly defined business failures involved formal proceedings. However, that percentage rose in the last few years to 30 percent mainly because larger firms have now experienced failure and are more likely to prefer the protections and safeguards of courts over the cheaper, faster, and simpler proceedings of private negotiations.

Companies can voluntarily liquidate themselves under the Commercial Code upon a decision by the board of directors and a vote of the shareholders. However, if a company cannot pay its creditors in a timely fashion, it may seek the protection of the court to prevent indiscriminate asset seizures during the liquidation process. If the firm believes it has a higher value as a going concern and can convince its creditors and a court that this is the preferred method of resolving its distress, it can request a court to protect its assets during reorganization. Five different statutes that cover liquidation and reorganization govern court-based business failure.

Bankruptcy originated when a statute governing the liquidation of insolvent firms was introduced in 1872. In 1893, a German advisor wrote new laws based on French concepts (the description of the different statutes is taken from the appendix to Packer and Ryser 1992). When the Commercial Code was revised in the 1920s to bring Japanese law closer to German practice, the bankruptcy law again was revised. The U.S. occupation introduced U.S. corporate law concepts in 1952 by way of a major revision of the bankruptcy statute. All debtors (individuals and corporations) are eligible for bankruptcy proceedings, and either the debtor or creditors may initiate petitions. An inability to pay creditors or an excess of liabilities over assets are required for the court to accept the petition The court may issue an order to prevent creditors from enforcing their claims immediately after filing the petition, but such a stay is not automatic. The court could wait until it examines whether the case meets the required criteria. In any event, secured creditors—those with a right to specified assets in case of nonpayment—may exercise their rights outside of the bankruptcy proceeding.

Special liquidation under the Commercial Code was introduced in 1938 to provide a less cumbersome process that was less costly and quicker than bankruptcy. The statute was modeled after British corporate law. Special liquidation was linked to the existing law that governed voluntary liquidation but sought court oversight during the liquidation process. The criteria are broader than under bankruptcy laws and can be invoked if liabilities are suspiciously excessive, and especially if multiple creditors make an orderly liquidation difficult. However, as a two-week notice to shareholders must precede a meeting on liquidation, creditors have a substantial window to seize assets prior to the court's intervention.

Composition is the Japanese law most similar to the U.S. Chapter 11 law governing reorganization. The word composition as used in corporate reorganizations takes its meaning from the definition of "mutual settlement or agreement." The law defining reorganization was enacted in 1923 at the same time that the bankruptcy liquidation law passed and derived from an Austrian law of the period. Bankruptcy was considered so humiliating that authorities sought a means to separate the law and procedure for companies that could be reorganized from those undergoing liquidation to enhance the future success of these reorganized companies. The prerequisites for filing a petition to reorganize are the same as for bankruptcy, which means that a firm must verge on failure. Courts may issue an order upon the filing of the petition to stay the actions of creditors to prevent panic and avert the suspension of bank transactions. The Tokyo and Osaka district courts traditionally conformed to disparate standards for issuing stays. The Osaka court was willing to grant stays immediately, while the Tokyo court usually required proof of agreement from a majority of creditors. The greater leniency of the Osaka court in granting protection from creditors has been explained as arising from the greater prevalence of organized crime in bankruptcy activities in the Osaka region, which tended to impede private arrangements. The absence of legal enforcement mechanisms with regard to payments to creditors outside the proceedings weakens reorganization procedures. Moreover, secured creditors are excluded from stay orders. Reorganization is accepted when a meeting of the creditors, representing at least three-quarters of the claims, produces a majority consenting to the plan with the court's approval.

Reorganization under the Commercial Code

Gatekeeping procedures in Japanese law and regulations act as a barrier to court action. For example, an advance payment of estimated court costs is required with a bankruptcy application in the form of deposits that vary with the scale of the firm's liabilities. Deposits under bankruptcy proceedings range from ¥ 0.7 million to ¥ 4 million (US$5,800 to US$33,000), the largest deposit required for liquidations worth more than ¥ 1 billion (US$8.3 million). In reorganization courts, the fees are somewhat higher, ranging from ¥ 2 million to ¥ 5 million (Packer and Ryser 1992). For firms on the edge of insolvency, the cash demands of advance payments often keep them out of the court system. Although the deposits are not an excessive burden for larger firms, bankruptcy specialists claim that a major challenge for a company applying for reorganization is to withdraw the cash from its account without alerting its banks, thereby setting off a creditor panic before the firm can get to court.

Because of a deliberate Japanese government policy of restricting the number of lawyers, judges, and courts, time delays are longer in official proceedings than in private workouts. In 1989, half of all liquidations required more than three years from application to conclusion, and 25 percent took more than five years. More than 75 percent of reorganization plans took more than five years from application to conclusion (Packer and Ryser 1992).

Japanese courts do not automatically accept bankruptcy petitions. Certain prerequisites must be met, and the court examines the application to determine if the firm meets the conditions. In the crucial first days after a firm applies for court protection from its creditors, protection by the courts is essential to prevent creditors from raiding the firm's assets and crippling future reorganization. In 1989, more than three months passed after initial application before the courts began their oversight in more than half of all cases. This delay in the approval process weakens the protection of the courts in preserving the assets of the company. The Tokyo District Court recently adopted a fast-track approach in significant reorganization cases. By appointing a special adviser to seek new funding sources, the first phase of the reorganization procedure was reduced from a year or more to two or three months.

The delay in commencing a case is compounded by the lack of automatic stay on the exercise of unsecured claims. In contrast, Chapter 11 of the U.S. bankruptcy code, which governs reorganization, automatically holds in abeyance creditor claims until they can be adjudicated in the bankruptcy proceeding. The lack of automatic stay on the exercise of unsecured claims in Japan allows alert creditors to seize assets while the court is deciding whether to accept the company's application.

Because secured creditors are not included in the group of creditors that the company is granted protection from, a disincentive to pursuing formal protection exists in all but one of Japan's laws governing bankruptcy. Therefore, secured creditors can exercise their right to the collateral underlying their claims outside of formal bankruptcy proceedings. Because much bank lending in Japan uses collateral to back up loans, a large share of a firm's debts may not be included under the umbrella of court protection.

Another impediment comes from the inexperience of Japanese judges in bankruptcy courts. Judges serve in a lifetime position with no prior private sector experience. They move from court to court on a generalist career path and are transferred to bankruptcy courts with little specific background knowledge. Consequently, they have not had exposure to business practice and law and reputedly act with extreme caution, particularly in granting preservative measures to foster the viability of the firm in reorganization.

The Dominance of Private Actions

Given the many impediments to formal bankruptcy in Japan, most business failures are handled privately and informally. The most common method is unique to Japan. Banks initiate an action by freezing the transactions of an individual or a corporation that issues a dishonored check or bill twice within six months. For the affected business, the resulting suspension of bank credit amounts to a death sentence. Some 70 to 85 percent of broadly defined bankruptcies follow from the suspension of bank credit.

Most Japanese business failures are messy affairs because of the informal means for squaring accounts. Specialized trucking companies, for example, make a business of removing assets quickly and quietly from a company's place of operations in the dead of night before creditors descend on the premises to seize whatever is available. Creditors also use specialized firms to break into premises to take movable equipment, furnishings, and whatever else can be plundered and sold. Since small firms often go into debt with loan sharks in desperate attempts to survive, the failure to repay a loan on time can mean visits from *yakuza*-related collection experts.

Not all business dissolutions end up as bankruptcies, no matter how they are defined. Many companies simply cease operations. For example, the demise of Yamaichi Securities Co., Ltd. in November 1997 was self-initiated and did not result in formal bankruptcy until the final books were examined in June 1999, 18 months after the firm announced its failure. In the interim period it was never included in the bankruptcy statistics.

Another example is the net decline of some 86,000 manufacturing establishments that took place between 1991 and 1996. This contraction amounted to 10 percent of all manufacturing establishments. During the same period, Tokyo Shoko Research listed 11,531 bankruptcies in manufacturing, accounting for only 13.4 percent of the disappearing establishments. The rest vanished without a statistical trace. In addition to the loss of some 86,000 production establishments, employment in manufacturing fell by more than 1.2 million workers between 1991 and 1996.

Bankruptcy Trends

No official measures of business failure exist in Japan, but several companies that evaluate business credit also record failures when liabilities exceed ¥ 10 million (US$83,300). Tokyo Shoko Research Co., Ltd. and Teikoku Databank, Ltd. publish monthly figures on business failures and the liabilities of failed companies. In addition, the Federation of Bankers' Associations of Japan collects information on suspensions of business transactions with banks, which is a less inclusive figure than other business failure data.

Figure 9.1 shows annual, broadly defined bankruptcies as reported by Tokyo Shoko Research and the number of private bank suspensions reported by the Federation of Bankers' Associations. The number of formal, court-related cases represents the difference between these figures. Business failures declined steadily after the 1985 recession, especially during the bubble economy expansion in the latter half of the 1980s (see table 9.2). The following recession drove the number of bankruptcies up to around 1,200 per month from the low of 500 in 1990. By the end of 1997, they averaged 1,600 a month. Total business failures reached 16,464 in 1997. Business failures were well on their way to reaching a postwar record in 1998 when the government intervened by guaranteeing bank loans to companies. This rescue package enabled banks to continue to support companies that may have looked less than credit-worthy without such guarantees. The total number for 1998 came to just less than 19,000, just shy of the 1984 peak of 20,841.

Figure 9.1. *Business Failures in Japan, 1984–98*

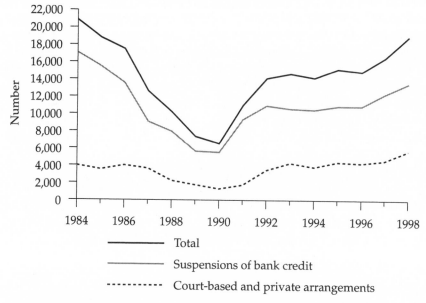

Source: Tokyo Shoko Research Co., Ltd. and Federation of Bankers' Associations of Japan data.

The increase in the total number of business failures in 1998 came from both privately negotiated and court-adjudicated cases. However, the proportion of formal proceedings has almost doubled since the Japanese economic slowdown began in 1991, increasing from 15 percent to 30 percent. This increase in formal bankruptcies indicates that larger companies now enter the ranks of the financially distressed.

Even more dramatic than the larger number of bankruptcies is the sharp rise in liabilities (figure 9.2). Bigger companies now leave larger amounts of debt. The total monthly value of liabilities of failed companies, which fluctuated around ¥ 600 billion (US$5 million) between 1992 and 1995, started to surge in late 1996. The surge became an explosion the following year. In both 1997 and 1998, liabilities of business failures climbed to ¥ 14 trillion (US$117 billion).

The more rapid growth in liabilities than in the number of failures implies that the average debt of failed companies expanded rapidly. Average liabilities remained stable during the period of declining bankruptcy rates in the second half of the 1980s, but they shot up by a factor greater than three during the postbubble recession. The jump in average liabilities since

Table 9.2. Business Failures in Japan by Statute and Process, 1980–98
(number)

Year	Hasan	Tokubetsu Seisan	Kaisha Kosei	Kaisha Seiri	Wagi	Private arrangements	Suspensions of bank credit	Total
1980	277	—	41	59	261	251	16,635	17,524
1981	281	—	33	52	294	236	15,683	16,579
1982	330	—	26	46	292	245	14,824	15,763
1983	513	14	23	35	282	339	15,848	17,054
1984	637	13	33	30	325	329	16,976	18,343
1985	717	23	21	30	336	407	15,337	16,871
1986	856	14	35	35	385	513	13,578	15,416
1987	696	12	13	14	228	450	9,040	10,453
1988	536	10	5	9	119	364	7,819	8,862
1989	381	19	7	2	60	244	5,550	6,263
1990	388	4	6	4	46	238	5,292	5,978
1991	657	15	12	18	122	833	9,066	10,723
1992	1,156	29	26	18	196	2,014	10,728	14,167
1993	1,289	25	34	22	225	2,094	10,352	14,041
1994	1,459	32	12	20	161	2,033	10,246	13,963
1995	1,604	66	21	32	178	2,443	10,742	15,086

(table continues on following page)

Table 9.2 continued

Year	Hasan	Tokubetsu Seisan	Kaisha Kosei	Kaisha Seiri	Wagi	Private arrangements	Suspensions of bank credit	Total
1996	1,683	62	10	25	175	1,868	10,721	14,544
1997	1,990	81	24	10	215	1,997	12,048	16,365
1998	2,617	110	56	19	308	2,705	13,356	19,171

— Not available.
Hasan Bankruptcy.
Tokubetsu seisan Special liquidation.
Kaisha kosei Corporate reorganization.
Kaisha seiri Corporate arrangement.
Wagi Composition.
Note: Tokubetsu seisan failures were not recorded before 1983. Because of reporting inconsistencies, the number of private arrangements, suspensions of bank credit and total vary by small amounts in different sources.
Source: Teikoku Databank, Ltd., and Federation of Bankers' Associations of Japan for suspensions of bank credit.

Figure 9.2.   *Liabilities of Business Failures in Japan, 1984–98*

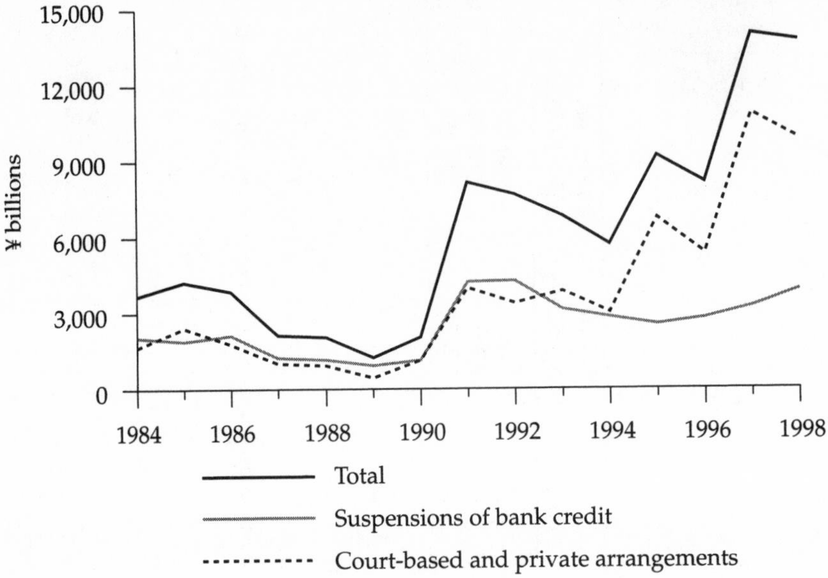

Source: Tokyo Shoko Research Co., Ltd. and Federation of Bankers' Associations of Japan data.

1996 (figure 9.3) resulted from the larger number of big firms in trouble and from the greater size of each failure.

Another indication that larger companies are experiencing financial difficulties is apparent in the fact that of the more than 19,000 total bankruptcies in 1998, the five largest failures accounted for ¥ 3.5 trillion (US$29.1 billion), or 25.7 percent of all liabilities. The year before, the five largest represented a slightly smaller share, 24.9 percent of the total, up sharply from the 1996 share of 18 percent. At the top of the 1998 list was Japan Leasing Co., Ltd., whose liabilities of ¥ 2.18 trillion (US$18.2 billion) were not only the biggest of the year, but also an all-time high. The trend continued in the first four months of 1999, at which time the liabilities of the top five failures accounted for 31.3 percent of the total.

Because of differences in laws and legal systems and Japanese values that imbue business failure with a powerfully negative emotional and moral tone, making direct comparisons between Japan and the United States is difficult. Until U.S. bankruptcy law was liberalized in the late 1970s, the number of business failures was similar in the two countries. However,

Figure 9.3.   *Average Liabilities of Business Failures in Japan, 1984–98*

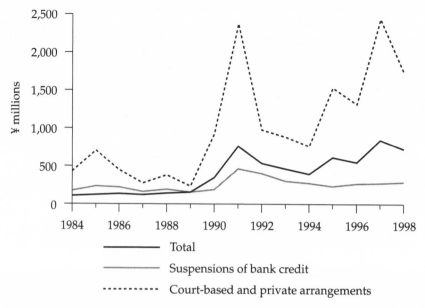

Source: Tokyo Shoko Research Co., Ltd. and Federation of Bankers' Associations of Japan data.

because the Japanese economy has fewer business concerns, the failure rate was higher in Japan. Since the late 1970s, bankruptcy has increased sharply in the United States. Dun and Bradstreet reported 83,384 business failures in 1997 and almost 73,000 in 1998. The number of court-managed cases was about 10 times higher in the United States than the corresponding number was in Japan.

Considering liabilities rather than the number of failures and adjusting for the scale of the two economies, Japanese broadly defined liabilities as a share of GDP averaged 1.22 percent from 1980 to 1997, whereas the U.S. figure was some 40 percent smaller at 0.72 percent (figure 9.4). In the last few years, Japanese liabilities as a share of GDP have been four to five times higher than the U.S. rate.

The elevated level of liabilities in Japan is frequently explained by the high leverage of Japanese companies, which typically raise a much greater share of financing through bank borrowing than do U.S. firms. The danger of financing through borrowing is that the interest payments are contractually obligated, whereas dividends to equity capital holders are paid at

Figure 9.4.   *Percentage of Liabilities of Business Failures to GDP in Japan and the United States, 1970–98*

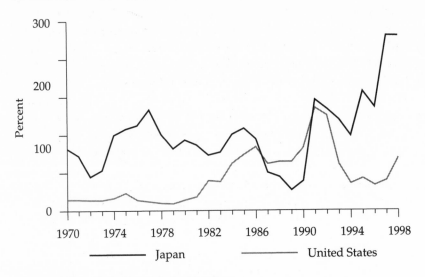

Source: Tokyo Shoko Research Co., Ltd. data.

the discretion of the company. Therefore, when revenues and profits decline, highly leveraged companies are more likely to default on their interest payments or other credit obligations.

Workouts in Japan

Workouts can be defined as informal arrangements that mimic formal bankruptcy proceedings in which creditors and the debtor company privately negotiate debt restructuring. One method to restructure debt is to convert hard contracts into soft ones by exchanging debt for equity. In addition, new financing can be provided to increase liquid assets, enable the distressed company to carry through on worthwhile investment projects, or pay for reorganization. Often the new funds will be in the form of new equity shares. Existing shareholders may be required to write down the value of their equity in the workout negotiations; even if this does not occur, the issue of new shares for debt will dilute the value of the old ones.

In the United States, specialized investors have arisen to take advantage of the opportunities offered by the increasing use of workout equity. The market for workout securities includes investors bargain hunting for assets priced below what they estimate to be their inherent value. These investors will earn a return if the value of the equities grows to their estimated long-run value. Another type of investor specializes in turnarounds. Turnaround investing involves hands-on management such as reorganizing, strategic planning, enhancing efficiency, restructuring operations, and disposing of excess and low-return assets (Mueller 1997). According to one expert, both kinds of investors seek minimum returns of 30 percent, reflecting the U.S. market for investments of similar risk.

The practice of workouts has been almost totally absent from the Japanese experience. As a result, neither the expertise nor the ready capital to facilitate the easing of financial distress exists. Japanese banks, for example, hold on to their nonperforming loans at book value for years after writing down and reserving against their balance sheet value. As a consequence, borrowers continue to face the original payment obligations. Any funds that emerge from restructured operations flow directly to the bank, dulling the incentives to make poorly performing assets more profitable. Although banks often provide additional loans to cover unpaid interest and principal, financing is not offered to allow a debtor to return to profitability. Partially constructed apartment buildings, for example, tend to remain unfinished and without rent-paying tenants due to the absence of completion financing.

Despite the absence of generalized workout expertise, workouts in fact have been undertaken as a matter of course within corporate families. Core banks or other leading financial members of corporate families traditionally assisted troubled group members with all the things that workout specialists do. Companies in trouble have had their debt to their main corporate family bank reduced or extended, other group members have taken new equity in the troubled firm to provide working capital, and subsidiaries have been sold to other group firms. An example of this behavior was the Long-Term Credit Bank of Japan, Ltd.'s intention to cancel several billion yen of loans for its subsidiary Nihon Leasing. This plan was canceled when a U.S. shareholder in the bank threatened a lawsuit for inappropriate behavior if the deal went through.

Another element missing from the Japanese experience is a market-driven motivation and rationale for reorganization and bankruptcy activities. As a consequence, group workouts have been episodic and ad hoc, and, as a result, techniques and instruments have not developed. Group firms tended to support each other as a matter of group solidarity. Because the motivation has been missing, the kind of market-based methods and finance characteristic of London or New York have been missing in Japan. Moreover, Japanese banks are reluctant to engage in workouts with nongroup companies. This attitude has interfered with financial reconstruction in the Asian crisis countries.

Despite the taboo against taking losses, Japanese banks have begun to engage in debt workouts. In late 1998, several construction companies on the verge of insolvency requested that their lenders forgive portions of their debt. Haseko Corporation, a major condominium construction company, began negotiations with its banks in November 1998 to restructure its loans. A month later, 38 banks canceled 48 percent of the ¥ 800 billion (US$6.7 billion) of loans lacking collateral.

The following March, financial institutions came to an agreement to forgive the debts of another troubled construction company. Led by Asahi Bank and the Industrial Bank of Japan, 29 creditors agreed to waive some 30 percent or ¥ 200 billion (US$1.7 billion) of their claims on Aoki Corporation. This deal was said to be the first case of a bailout of a construction firm by debt forgiveness (*Japan Times* 1999a).

That same month, supermarket chain operator Seiyu, Ltd. announced it had reached an agreement with a group of 17 banks to forgive about ¥ 210 billion out of ¥ 500 billion in loans to its nonbank financial subsidiary, Tokyo City Finance Company. A motivating factor in Seiyu's strategy was to avoid putting its own consolidated accounts into capital deficit under the new consolidated reporting mandated for the fiscal year ending March 31, 2000. This workout was described as the first major loan waiver for a retail business in Japan (*Japan Times* 1999b).

The rush to conclude debt restructuring in March coincided with the end of the Japanese fiscal year on March 31, 2000, when companies closed their books. Tokai Bank announced on the last day of the month that it was forgiving a total of ¥ 220 billion worth of debt owed by construction company Fujita and property company Towa Real Estate Development.

A government-affiliated loan collection body got into the workout mood in May 1999 when the Resolution and Collection Corporation (RCC) offered to forgive part of its claim on the Hokkaido department store operator Marui Imai, Inc. The RCC was established to take over nonperforming loans of troubled banks. If concluded, this deal would be the first time the RCC forgave a claim. The RCC bought the department store company's loans with a face value of ¥ 36 billion from the defunct Hokkaido Takushoku Bank for a reported ¥ 16 billion. Through a combination of selling off ¥ 21 billion of claims to other investors for ¥ 10 billion and recovering ¥ 8 billion from the borrower, the RCC could end up with a profit despite the writedown of ¥ 7 billion. This move by the Japanese version of the U.S.

Resolution and Trust Corporation, which acted to clean up the U.S. savings and loans mess a decade ago, represents a welcome development in the Japanese cleanup effort.

Legal and Regulatory Changes

The move by banks to forgive debts of distressed borrowers led to a rise in the share prices of several similarly stricken construction companies. These increases focused policy discussions on the apparent rewards to shareholders at the expense of banks. The seeming unfairness of this wealth transfer stimulated consideration of debt-for-equity swaps in which commitments would not be reduced but converted into shares held by the bank. Such a move preserves the banks' assets but converts them into soft contracts. The dilution of company shares would reduce the value of the existing shares and not confer an advantage to shareholders.

Several changes are being proposed to make bankruptcy procedures more efficient and effective. In April 1998, the Ministry of Justice proposed revisions to integrate the five laws governing corporate bankruptcy into a single law. Many of the changes are aimed at making the formal bankruptcy process easier for small firms. Officials sought to enhance the prospects for reorganization, especially given the worsening economic climate. One goal is to move cases out of the unprotected realm of private negotiations, where they often end in dissolution, and under the umbrella of legal procedures, which government officials believe is more conducive to reorganization and the preservation of the ongoing business.

The proposed legislation also includes changes to shorten the period of asset assessment from the current three to seven months to one month. This shortening of the procedural process is intended to smooth the process of locating rescuers and promoting reorganization. A motivating factor in this particular revision is the concern that undue delay leads to a deterioration of the human assets and a weakening of working relations that the firm has with other companies. Other changes call for greater disclosure and removal of barriers to selling parts of a company. The original plan was for these changes to be implemented in 2003. As the economy declined, however, authorities thought they could speed up the revisions by submitting a bill to the Diet in fiscal year 2000.

Concerned with the rising tide of business failures in early 1999, the Ministry for International Trade and Industry proposed bankruptcy law revisions to speed up reorganization of bankrupt companies. The ministry suggested procedures to allow the sale of failed businesses even before the start of the legal reconstruction process. To preserve the value of a going business, it suggested allowing sale of business units before the approval of a reconstruction plan at a shareholders' meeting if the creditors approve the plan.

Recognizing that problems were accumulating before they could be dealt with by a comprehensive revision of the bankruptcy laws, the Ministry of Justice drafted more limited revisions in the spring of 1999 to be submitted to the next session of the Diet in late 1999. The current law permits applications for reorganization only after a firm becomes virtually insolvent. It generally looks for a change in management, and business leaders have to file reorganization plans at about the same time as they apply to the court. Business legal experts believed that these requirements prevented distressed companies from seeking resolution of their problems in a timely fashion and resulted in unnecessary business failures. Under the proposed approach, companies could apply to the courts for protection with more of their assets intact, keep the management team in place, and later draw up a turnaround plan. The new law would prevent creditors from forcing the sale of assets before the distressed debtor could initiate legal processes to gain protection.

Conclusions

Economists in the 1950s developed the concept of the turnpike theorem. They posited that under certain conditions it would make sense for a nation to reconfigure its economic structure to emphasize rapid investment and production growth while sacrificing current consumption. It might pay to make a detour to get on the turnpike, zoom along at high speed, and then take the exit ramp to the path of increasing consumption. What economists did not foresee in the case of Japan, however, was that the turnpike to growth could easily become a treadmill to nowhere, with the exit ramps blocked by structural inertia and political barriers protecting the status quo.

Economic obsolescence is an unwelcome fact of life and one that policymakers would rather avoid, especially when resources are still quite capable of performing their former tasks. Markets are the usual means for assessing the value of assets in changing circumstances, but the results are often troublesome when they imply economic hardship. Adjustment inevitably imposes economic and political costs. When government is involved in a hard-hit sector, when firms and workers are regionally concentrated, or when firms or workers have enjoyed high returns (often as a result of protection or regulation), the political pressures to provide good jobs for good people become particularly difficult to resist.

Moreover, the ordinary workings of business decisionmaking and economic rationality could block adaptations when it is not obvious that conditions have changed sufficiently and permanently enough to make old methods obsolete. When the natural tendency to persist with successful strategies combines with the conservatism of institutions developed to respond to rapid growth, delayed response ensues.

However, countermeasures to delayed response exist. A feature of recent Japanese experience that has promoted greater sensitivity to shifting patterns of demand is the deregulation of the financial sector and the increasing role of foreign businesses free of the obsolete lessons and methods of Japan's past. In particular, liberalized financial markets and the loss of government guarantees of financial institutions have introduced a missing appreciation for profitability.

The seemingly wasteful destruction of firms and the dissipation of their resources, workers, and career experiences by the mysterious actions of market forces often seems to be a high price to pay for growth and productivity. The counter to this response is the awareness that not making the changes is not a sustainable long-term policy, although it can buy time for several years. Ultimately, the choices are deeply political. The promotion of vigorous financial markets—itself a political choice—can go a long way toward bringing economic forces to bear on business and political judgements. This is what is happening in Japan today as business restructures at a rate that may look slow in some quarters, but that could cumulatively change the landscape of Japanese society.

References

Alexander, Arthur J. 1998. "Transpacific Aviation Pact Yields Extensive Opportunities." *JEI Report 7A* 10(4): 4–12.

Japan Times. 1999a. "29 Institutions to Forgive Aoki's ¥ 200 Billion in Debts." March 16.

_____. 1999b. "Banks to Forgive Loans to Seiyu Finance Unit." March 27.

Maddison, Angus. 1995. *Explaining the Economic Performance of Nations.* Brookfield, Vermont: Edward Elgar.

Mueller, John. 1997. "Workout Investing for Fun and Profit." *The Secured Lender* 48(2): 68–89.

Packer, Frank, and Marc Ryser. 1992. "The Governance of Failure: An Anatomy of Corporate Bankruptcy in Japan." Working Paper no. 62. Center on Japanese Economy and Business, Columbia University, New York.

Tokyo Stock Exchange. 1997. *Corporate Share Ownership Survey.* Tokyo.

10

Financial Restructuring in East Asia: Halfway There?

Stijn Claessens, Simeon Djankov, and Daniela Klingebiel, World Bank

One of the most difficult tasks confronting policymakers is the management of systemic banking and corporate distress. This chapter reviews bank and corporate restructuring efforts up to September 1999 in the four crisis-affected East Asian countries (Indonesia, the Republic of Korea, Malaysia, and Thailand) and identifies remaining priority areas for reform. Not surprisingly, the analysis indicates that two years into the process, much has been done, but much still remains to be accomplished. While governments have spent substantial resources to clean up the balance sheets of financial intermediaries, restructuring is still incomplete, and in most cases new private owners have yet to be found. Progress with corporate restructuring is less advanced, and many corporations are still overindebted. Durable economic recovery depends on further progress in these dimensions. In particular, decisive improvements in the allocation of investible funds will require better-capitalized banking systems and deeper institutional reforms in financial regulation and supervision, corporate governance, and bankruptcy procedures.

Was the East Asian Crisis Unique?

The East Asian crisis began in Thailand in mid-1997, when an ailing financial sector, an export slowdown, and large increases in central bank credit to weak financial institutions triggered a run on the baht. The crisis then spread to other countries in the region as common vulnerabilities and changes in international sentiment triggered large capital outflows.

Whether these sudden shifts in market expectations and confidence entailed the primary source of the financial turmoil has been hotly debated. Proponents of the sudden shift view argue that while macroeconomic and other fundamentals worsened in the mid-1990s, the extent and depth of the crisis cannot be attributed to a deterioration in fundamentals, but rather to the panic reaction of domestic and foreign investors (Radelet and Sachs 1998). Others argue that the crisis reflected structural and policy distortions in the region—including weak macroeconomic policies—and that fundamental imbalances spurred the crisis (Corsetti, Pesenti, and Roubini 1998). A third group of observers points to weak corporate governance and the risky investment strategies of corporations as the main cause of the crisis (Claessens, Djankov, and Ferri 1999; Johnson and others 1998; Krugman 1999). Causes of the crises most likely lie with foreign panic, interacting with misguided macroeconomic policies and structural weaknesses in the financial and corporate sectors (Caprio and Honohan 1999; Harvey and Roper 1999).

East Asian Crisis: Similar Origins to Previous Crises, but Difference in Scale

While debates on the exact causes of the crisis continue, it might be more informative to ask whether the East Asian crisis was systematically different from previous financial crises. Here, cross-country comparisons show that the causes of the East Asian crisis were not systematically different from those underlying other financial crises. Rather, the depth of the crisis' financial systems and the leverage of its corporations make East Asia's crisis unique. In Korea, Malaysia, and Thailand, private sector claims equal or exceed 140 percent of gross domestic product (GDP) (figure 10.1). And because of the high leverage, corporate distress—as measured by the share of nonperforming loans in GDP—is much higher. Moreover, East Asian economies are dominated by banks, making it difficult for corporations to find alternative sources of funding.

Steep Decline and Rapid Recovery

GDP growth in East Asia's crisis countries turned sharply negative in 1998 (table 10.1). The steep decline in output was driven by a severe drop in private capital investment and, to lesser degree, by a reduction in private consumption. The largest drops in investment occurred in Indonesia and

Figure 10.1. *Comparative Scale of the East Asian Crisis*

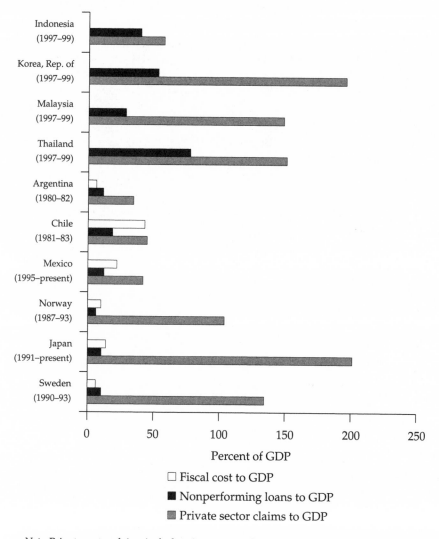

Percent of GDP

☐ Fiscal cost to GDP
■ Nonperforming loans to GDP
▨ Private sector claims to GDP

Note: Private sector claims include private sector claims to nonfinancial entities of deposit money banks and other financial institutions.
Source: Caprio and Klingebiel (1999); IMF (various years).

Malaysia. In addition, declining inventories played an important role in Korea's GDP reduction.

For most of the crisis countries, exports stagnated in 1998. Although export volumes increased, prices were depressed through much of the year, and in value terms exports started to increase only in 1999. With imports

Table 10.1. *Changes in Real GDP, 1998–99*
(percent)

Variable	Indonesia		Korea, Rep. of		Malaysia		Thailand		Average	
	1998	1999	1998	1999	1998	1999	1998	1999	1998	1999
Change in GDP	-13.7	0.2	-5.8	6.6	-6.7	3.7	-8.0	2.5	-8.6	3.1
Contribution to change in GDP										
Domestic final sales	-16.1	-0.8	-12.4	3.3	-27.1	3.3	-12.0	0.9	-16.9	1.5
Private consumption	-1.8	0.8	-5.2	3.2	-5.5	1.6	-3.0	1.0	-3.9	1.5
Public consumption	-1.0	0.1	0.0	-0.2	-0.5	1.6	0.4	0.3	-0.3	0.4
Gross fixed capital formation	-13.2	-1.7	-7.3	0.3	-21.2	0.1	-9.4	-0.4	-12.8	-0.4
Change in stock	-2.3	-9.4	-5.6	11.0	0.4	0.3	-0.3	4.1	-2.0	1.5
Net exports	4.7	10.4	12.2	-7.6	20.0	0.1	4.3	-2.5	10.3	0.1

Source: World Bank data.

contracting sharply in all countries, higher net exports contributed the most to mitigating the GDP decline—10 percentage points on average. By mid-1998 most countries had achieved macroeconomic stability, with exchange rates stabilizing and interest rates starting to decline. By the end of 1998, interest rates in all countries except Indonesia were below precrisis levels.

Conditions improved considerably in the second quarter of 1999, with all countries returning to GDP growth, ranging from (on an annualized basis) 0.2 percent in Indonesia to 3.7 percent in Malaysia and 6.6 percent in Korea (see table 10.1). While interest rates have declined and stock markets have recovered, lowering the costs of capital for corporations, for most countries the recent recovery has not been led by a rebound in capital investment. Exports have picked up, with a substantial part of the increase in export values due to cyclical price effects. However, because imports have also increased, net trade surpluses are not expected to contribute to growth in any of the crisis countries except Indonesia. Private consumer demand is projected to be the most important determinant of growth, followed by inventory rebuilding and increased public spending.

The lack of recovery in capital formation contrasts with the region's historical reliance on investment as an important determinant of growth. Investment is expected to remain below historical levels in the near future, partly because of constraints on the supply of financing and the absence of creditworthy borrowers. Real growth rates of bank credit to the private sector remain negative in all countries except Korea, with Indonesia the most adversely affected (because banks have lent to the government instead of corporations, and because high inflation has sharply reduced the real value of credit).

Interest rates are at unprecedented lows. July 1999 interest rates were less than half those of 1991–96 in Malaysia and Thailand and one-third in Korea (figure 10.2). Thus the supply of domestic savings has been ample, but the unwillingness of financial intermediaries to lend has constrained investment. This raises concerns about whether supply factors have been sufficiently addressed and whether corporate restructuring has been adequate to foster financially viable corporations.

Recent stock price movements for financial institutions' stocks appear to reflect these concerns about progress in bank restructuring and the durability of the recovery. In the past, stock prices seem to have overestimated prospects in the region, and stock markets anticipated neither the crisis nor the depth of the spring 1998 recessions.

After an upswing in the first half of 1999, a correction may again be under way, as average banking stock prices in some countries remain more

Figure 10.2.   *Interest Rates before and after the Crisis*

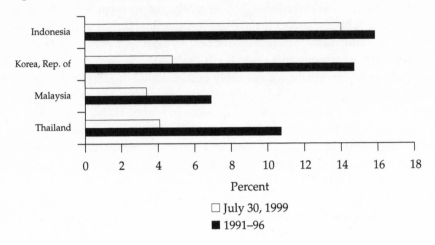

Source: Datastream data.

than 17 percent below their peak in early 1999, and financial institutions' stocks in Thailand are 36 percent below their 1999 highs. This disparity suggests that there can be a prolonged, systematic mismatch between changes in economic growth and restructuring, on the one hand, and equity price movements on the other.

The possibility of a bumpier—that is, W-shaped—recovery should not be surprising. As other countries show, recoveries from a banking crisis often falter (BIS 1998; Caprio and Klingebiel 1997; Kaminsky and Reinhart 1998). In an emerging market economy, it takes an average of three years for GDP growth to return to trend after a banking crisis, and lost GDP is never made up in the average crisis country. Now the countries may be underestimating the risks of a W-shaped recovery.

The parallel often drawn between East Asia's financial crisis and Mexico's 1995 banking and currency crisis is misleading. Mexico experienced a sharp recovery following its balance of payments crisis, but its financial sector was much shallower and corporate distress much less pronounced than in East Asia. Moreover, Mexico had the considerable benefit of a solidly growing neighbor—the United States—which meant that the sharp depreciation of its currency could trigger high export growth. The working capital needs of Mexican corporations were often financed outside the country, mitigating the effect of its weak banking system on the corporate sector.

Given the depth of financial systems and the scale of corporate distress, recovery could take longer in some East Asian crisis countries than in other crisis countries. There might be closer parallels between East Asia's crisis and Japan's protracted bank and corporate restructuring. Both the scale of the problem and the close links between banks and corporations suggest similarities. Japan's banking problems have continued for almost 10 years. Only recently was a comprehensive framework for dealing with banking problems adopted, including public funds to recapitalize the banking system and address banking sector weaknesses, but the reforms were long overdue, and many actions are still needed.

East Asian governments were initially slow to address financial distress. At first they tried to keep insolvent institutions afloat by injecting liquidity (table 10.2), and in doing so, they incurred large fiscal costs. The delayed and sometimes partial response of governments led to financial turbulence and runs on financial institutions. Governments responded to the crisis in public confidence (Indonesia, Malaysia, and Thailand) or foreign currency outflows (Korea) by issuing unlimited guarantees on financial systems' liabilities. These guarantees stemmed the confidence crisis, but weakened governments' need to act comprehensively.

Government responses and progress on financial restructuring vary considerably. Korea moved aggressively to strengthen its banking system through recapitalizations, nationalizations, removal of bad debt, and mergers. However, the government has been less successful in addressing problems in the nonbanking sector (except for closing merchant banks). Indeed, of the 2,069 nonbank financial institutions, only 242, or about one-tenth, had stopped operations as of August 1999.[1] As a result, the top five *chaebol*-affiliated investment trust companies have continued to extend financing to their loss-making affiliates, mainly in the form of bonds with high interest rates. Of the US$34 billion in new capital raised by Korean corporations in 1999, more than half has gone to the top five *chaebols*. Of that capital, 7 percent took the form of new equity, 32 percent consisted of bank loans, and 61 percent was corporate bonds. The Malaysian government has also taken forceful actions, including forcing mergers of financial institutions, injecting public capital, and removing loans from banks' balance sheets.

---

1. Of those, 44 were merged, 144 were liquidated, and 44 had their licenses suspended. Nonbank financial institutions include merchant banks, securities firms, investment companies, mutual saving and finance companies, credit unions, and leasing companies.

Table 10.2. *Financial Distress Resolutions and Bank Recapitalization Strategies*

Category	Indonesia	Korea, Rep. of	Malaysia	Thailand
Initial government response				
Substantial liquidity				
support (US$ billions)	21.7	23.3	9.2	24.1
Percentage of GDP	17.6	5.0	13.0	20.0
Financial distress resolutions				
Number of bank shutdowns	64 of 237	None	None	1 of 15
Number of shutdowns of other financial institutions	n.a.	117	None	57 of 91
Number of mergers of financial institutions	4 of 7 state banks to merge	11 of 26 absorbed by other banks	58 to be merged into 6 groups	3 banks and 12 finance companies
Number of nationalizations	12	4	1 and 3 finance companies	4

(table continues on following page)

Table 10.2 continued

Category	Indonesia	Korea, Rep. of	Malaysia	Thailand
Bank recapitalization strategies				
Public funds for recapitalizations	Plan in place; some bonds issued	Government injected US$8 billion into 9 commercial banks; 5 out of 6 major banks now 90% controlled by the state	Donamodal injected US$1.6 billion into 10 institutions	Plan in place; government injected US$8.9 billion into private banks and US$11.7 billion into public banks
Majority foreign ownership of banks	Allowed, 1 potentially	Allowed, 2 completed and 1 pending	Not allowed	Allowed, 2 completed and 4 pending
Weak financial institutions still in system	Many weak commercial banks	Many weak nonbank financial institutions	Difficult to assess	Some weak and public private banks

n.a. Not applicable.
Source: Ramos (1999); World Bank data.

The Thai authorities have moved aggressively on finance companies and closed down two-thirds of the sector. In contrast, the government allowed banks a transitional period to raise capital through phased-in tighter loan provisioning requirements. At the same time, the government offered to inject tier 1 capital, subject to the condition that any bank accepting public money would have to satisfy certain stringent conditions, including, for instance, meeting strict loan loss provisioning immediately and making management changes. This market-based approach ensures that public funds are only provided when the existing shareholders have most of their capital wiped out. It has the drawback, however, that some banks that need injections of fresh capital may be tempted to delay their application for such assistance, thus prolonging the uncertainty about the health of the banking system. Most nonintervened private banks have resisted public funds—only two domestic banks have accessed public funds. Instead, banks have raised expensive capital on their own. Nonetheless, they remain substantially undercapitalized because of high nonperforming loans.

Of the four East Asian crisis countries, Indonesia has made the least progress in putting its banking sector back on a sound footing. Almost two years after the crisis, most institutions remain severely insolvent or undercapitalized.

The crisis countries have also taken different approaches to asset resolution (table 10.3). Indonesia, Korea, and Malaysia have actively removed bad loans from banks and transferred them to centralized, government-owned, and managed-asset management companies. The Indonesian government has transferred US$28 billion of the assets of closed banks and the worst loans of intervened and state banks—equivalent to 66 percent of the banking system's nonperforming loans—to the Indonesian Bank Restructuring Agency. The Korea Asset Management Corporation purchased about 40 percent of nonperforming loans (worth US$37 billion) at an average of 45 cents to the dollar. Malaysia's Donaharta asset management company has bought 34 percent of nonperforming loans (worth US$11 billion) at discounts of 30–50 percent. In all three countries the transfer of assets has substantially reduced nonperforming loans (figure 10.3). Thailand's government has left the responsibility for loan workout and asset recovery with banks.

Although governments have made significant strides and spent substantial resources to clean up their financial systems, banks remain inadequately capitalized. This judgment is based on an assessment that loan loss provisioning will prove to be inadequate. Due to government injections of capital, bank capital levels appear most solid in Korea and Malaysia, but banks in

Table 10.3. *Asset Resolution Strategies*

Strategy	Indonesia	Korea, Rep. of	Malaysia	Thailand
Set up centralized asset management company to which banking system's nonperforming loans are transferred	Yes. Asset management unit has accumulated US$28 billion of assets.	Yes. Kamco has accumulated US$37 billion assets.	Yes. Donaharta has purchased US$11 billion of assets.	No. The workout of nonperforming loans is decentralized. One large bank has established a private asset management company, and more private asset management companies are being considered
Centralized asset management companies purchase assets at subsidized prices	Yes	Initially assets were purchased above market-clearing prices with recourse. Since February 1998, purchases have been attempted at market prices	Purchased assets are valued by independent outside auditors	n.a.
Nature of agency: restructuring or disposition	Unclear	Not clearly defined; mostly engaged in disposing of assets	Restructuring	n.a.

(table continues on following page)

239

Table 10.3 continued

Strategy	Indonesia	Korea, Rep. of	Malaysia	Thailand
Type of assets transferred	Worst assets	No particular strategy	Loan size (greater than 5 million M$) and mostly business loans secured by property or shares	n.a.
Assets transferred	66% of nonperforming loans, equal to 35% of GDP	40% of nonperforming loans, equal to 11% of GDP	34% of nonperforming loans, equal to 15% of GDP	n.a.
Assets disposed of as percentage of total assets transferred	0.7	4.7	0.1	n.a.

n.a. Not applicable.
Source: Barents Group (1999); Klingebiel (1999); World Bank data.

240

Figure 10.3. *Drop in Nonperforming Loans because of Transfers to the Government*

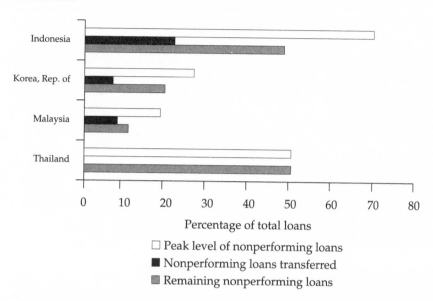

Percentage of total loans

☐ Peak level of nonperforming loans
■ Nonperforming loans transferred
▦ Remaining nonperforming loans

Source: Goldman Sachs and World Bank data.

both countries would be considerably undercapitalized if they were to provision adequately (table 10.4). Banks in Indonesia and Thailand are worse off. Thai banks have raised more than US$11 billion in new capital—about half of it from the government—yet still have a substantial capital shortfall. Indonesia's capital shortfall is the most severe of the four crisis countries, another indication that bank restructuring has just begun.

If banks were to try to recapitalize from earnings, interest rate spreads would have to rise. As banks cannot raise spreads for all borrowers simultaneously (not all can pay), this approach would basically tax profitable borrowers, as they would have to bear the brunt of the increase in lending rates.

Given current levels of capital, loan loss provisioning, and nonperforming loans remaining in banks, spreads in Korea and Malaysia would be relatively close to historical levels. Thus, these banks may be able to cover their capital shortfalls from earnings (see table 10.4). Because their capital shortfalls are so large and solvent borrowers so few, Indonesian and Thai banks are unlikely to be able to recapitalize from earnings. Net interest spreads would have to increase by 2.2 percentage points in Thailand, significantly above historical spreads. Even though two-thirds

Table 10.4.   An Assessment of Banks' Ability to Grow Out of Their Nonperforming Loans
(percentage of banking system assets unless noted otherwise)

Indicator	Indonesia	Korea, Rep. of	Malaysia	Thailand
Current nonperforming loans	34.1	15.9	17.9	27.9
Current loan loss provisions	6.1	2.7	1.9	3.9
Net impaired assets	28.0	13.2	16.0	24.0
Current capital	–15.1	–1.0	1.8	–4.5
Capital shortfall [a]	18.5	4.0	1.7	8.1
Required net interest spread to reach 8% capital adequacy ratio in three years (percentage points)	8.5	2.1	2.0	5.0
Historical net interest spread (percentage points)	4.0	2.0	2.6	2.8
Required net interest spread as share of historical net interest spread (percent)	212.0	105.0	75.0	178.0
Memorandum items				
Capital shortfall (billions of U.S. dollars)[a]	15.0	41.0	4.0	18.0
Capital shortfall as share of 1998 GDP (percent)[a]	12.7	10.7	5.5	15.4

a. Assumes a 40 percent recovery rate on nonperforming loans, a constant loan-to-deposit ratio, and loan growth in line with GDP growth. The capital shortfall is applied to the entire banking system. The calculation on loan loss recovery and growing out of the crisis assumes that the corporate sector will be able to cover the increased interest spread margin.

Source: J.P. Morgan, Goldman Sachs, and Fitch-IBCA data.

of nonperforming loans have been removed from banks' balance sheets, Indonesian banks would have to earn net spreads of 8.5 percentage points—more than twice their historical level—to achieve adequate capital levels within three years.

Governments could let banks fend for themselves, but that strategy entails substantial risks. While Korean and Malaysian banks may be able to recapitalize themselves, the process could have negative repercussions on lending, with capital-constrained banks shifting their asset base from loans to government securities. A shift into government securities would also drive up interest rates for borrowers. Indonesian banks could pursue risky lending in desperate attempts to survive. In addition, capital-constrained banks in all four crisis countries could impede corporate restructuring, because they have limited abilities to absorb losses and so are reluctant to engage in substantial financial restructuring.

While Korean and Malaysian banks may be able to grow out of their problems, albeit with associated risks, whether today's bank management and governance structures would support that strategy is unclear. Korea and Thailand have changed management to some degree; almost no changes have occurred in the other crisis countries. Moreover, the governance framework of banks have not made many improvements, with only Korea bringing its corporate governance framework closer to international practice (table 10.5).

Corporate Restructuring Is Gathering Speed

The state, represented by asset management companies, is an important agent in corporate restructuring in Indonesia, Korea, and Malaysia (see table 10.3). But asset management companies have yet to dispose of many assets and, as global experience suggests, tend to be weak at corporate restructuring in any case (Klingebiel 1999). In Korea, commercial banks were initially designated to be the agents of change. As many of the banks became state-owned, the government has effectively provided leadership. In particular, the Financial Supervisory Commission has issued guidelines on restructuring, instructed banks to establish workout units, and directed large *chaebols* to shed subsidiaries and lower their leverage.

Thailand, by contrast, has adopted a market-based approach, leaving private commercial banks to take the lead on restructuring. In Malaysia corporate restructuring has proceeded with a mix of government (through Donaharta) and private sector involvement. Indonesia has yet to clearly identify agents of change.

All four crisis countries have complemented their frameworks for corporate reorganization and asset resolution with out-of-court, extrajudiciary systems. Indonesia established the Jakarta Initiative, Korea the Corporate Debt Restructuring Committee, Malaysia the Corporate Debt Restructuring Committee, and Thailand the Corporate Debt Restructuring Advisory Committee. These committees and associated restructuring processes generally rely on the so-called London rules—principles for corporate reorganization first enunciated in the United Kingdom in the early 1990s. As the London rules were not designed for systematic corporate distress, countries have attempted to tighten the rules in various ways, and country approaches differ.

Three features are important. First, have all (or most) financial institutions signed on to the accord under regular contract or commercial law? If

Table 10.5. Changes in the Corporate Governance and Management of Banks

| Country | Corporate governance | | Management | |
	Independent outside directors	Changes in top management in majority-owned domestic banks	Performance-based pay	Hiring of foreign experts in domestic banks
Indonesia	None	None	None	None
Korea, Rep. of	Two-thirds of board seats occupied by outside directors	In 6 of the 10 major banks	Being introduced	Frequent
Malaysia	In place	In 1 of 33 bank	Limited	Rare
Thailand	In place, but influence is limited	In 3 of 11 banks	Limited	Frequent

Source: Ramos (1999); World Bank data.

so, agreements reached among the majority of creditors can be enforced on other creditors without going through formal judicial procedures. Second, the approach is affected by whether formal arbitration with specific deadlines is part of the accord. Without such arbitration, an out-of-court system must rely on the formal judicial process to resolve disputes, with associated costs and delays. Third, the approach depends on whether the accord specifies penalties that can be imposed for failure to meet deadlines. Based on these criteria, the framework in Thailand, followed by those in Korea and Malaysia, appears to be conducive to out-of-court restructuring, while the framework in Indonesia is not.

Creditor rights have not significantly changed in any crisis country except Indonesia, but they are well protected relative to other crisis countries. While countries have made bankruptcy procedures more efficient—by, for example, establishing special bankruptcy courts—judicial systems remain weak, especially in Indonesia. In all four countries' lax rules for classifying and provisioning troubled debt are not conducive to encouraging banks to engage in deeper restructuring.

Few of the crisis countries require banks to assess repayment capacity in their lending operations, and all four countries allow upgrades of restructured loans immediately after restructuring. Globally, the more common standard is to upgrade only after several payments have been received and the financial viability of the borrower has been assured. Consequently, banks in the crisis countries have incentives to engage in cosmetic restructuring, including generous reschedulings.

The amount of claims registered and actually restructured in formal out-of-court procedures indicates some progress on corporate restructuring (table 10.6). Indonesia has shown the least success, with debtors and creditors reaching standstill agreements or agreements in principle on only 13 percent of debt.[2] Korea and Malaysia have done the most out-of-court restructuring, with about a third of debt restructured. The depth of restructuring in Korea has been limited, however. About 65 percent of workouts have featured interest rate reductions, capitalization of interest, and deferral of principal, with very little conversion of debt into equity, which would have led to more sustainable restructuring. Malaysia has emphasized subsidized financial support, not operational or financial restructuring.

---

2. The government has also established the Indonesian Debt Restructuring Agency to enable debtors and creditors to protect against exchange risk, but very little debt has been registered under this program.

Table 10.6.   *Corporate Restructuring, August 1999*

Type of restructuring	Indonesia	Korea, Rep. of	Malaysia	Thailand
Out-of-court restructurings				
Number of registered cases	234	92[a]	53	825
Number of cases started	157	83	27	430
Number of restructured cases	22	46	10	167
Restructured debt/total debt (percent)	13	40	32	22
In-court restructurings				
Number of registered cases	88	48	52	30
Number of cases started	78	27	34	22
Number of restructured cases	8	19	12	8
Restructured debt/total debt (percent)	4	8	—	7

— Not available.

a. This number does not take into account restructurings outside the 6th largest to the 64th largest *chaebol*.

Source: World Bank data.

Thailand occupies the middle ground. Although almost a quarter of debt has been restructured, 13 percent of the restructured debt has reverted to nonperforming status in just a few months, suggesting that the restructuring was cosmetic. None of the crisis countries have used many formal bankruptcy procedures, which generally account for less than a fifth of restructured debt. Korea and Thailand have done the most, partly because they have instituted specialized bankruptcy courts.

Countries can expect corporate distress to abate as the economic recovery progresses. Operational performance improved in the first half of 1999 (table 10.7), for example, partly because of operational restructuring and a recovery in exports and domestic demand. Labor reductions and wage compressions are, however, driving the improvements in operational cash flows.

Korea's largest corporations have shed more than a quarter of their workers. Among publicly listed companies, labor shedding is even higher: payrolls were 34 percent lower in mid-1999 than in mid-1997. Labor shedding is less important for publicly traded firms in Malaysia (7 percent) and Thailand (12 percent). Productivity gains are still limited, and should not be expected in such a short time.

Corporate distress—as measured by the share of firms that cannot cover interest expenses from operational cash flows—peaked in most of

Table 10.7. *Operational Performance of Publicly Traded Corporations and Share of Distressed Corporations, 1995–2002*
(percent)

Country	1995	1996	1997	1998	1999 (second quarter)	2000–02[a]	2000–02[b]
Net profit margin							
Indonesia	12.4	13.9	–3.6	–13.3	–8.9	3.3	–2.3
Korea, Rep. of	2.7	0.4	–0.3	–2.6	2.7	3.1	1.1
Malaysia	12.2	12.0	6.9	–2.8	1.3	8.6	6.2
Thailand	7.1	5.1	–3.6	2.2	4.8	6.1	3.7
Firms unable to cover interest expenses from operational cash flows							
Indonesia	12.6	17.9	40.3	58.2	63.8	52.9	57.4
Korea, Rep. of	8.5	11.2	24.3	33.8	26.7	17.2	22.6
Malaysia	3.4	5.6	17.1	34.3	26.3	13.8	15.5
Thailand	6.7	10.4	32.6	30.4	28.3	22.3	27.1

Note: Scenarios for 2000–02 are based on GDP growth recovery as projected by the International Monetary Fund.
a. Projection. Assumes that interest rates stay at current levels throughout the period.
b. Projection. Assumes that interest rates return to historic levels.
Source: World Bank data.

the crisis countries in 1998. Since then, stronger operational cash flows, lower interest rates, and more favorable exchange rates have eased financial distress (except in Indonesia), especially in Korea and Malaysia.

Data for the first half of 1999 indicate that 64 percent of Indonesian firms, 27 percent of Korean firms, 26 percent of Malaysian firms, and 28 percent of Thai firms were unable to cover interest payments from operational cash flows. Moreover, the scope for less corporate distress due to higher economic growth is limited. If interest rates remain at current levels, about a sixth of Korean corporations, a quarter of Thai corporations, and more than half of Indonesian corporations will still not be able to cover interest expenses by the end of 2002 (see table 10.7). The share of distressed firms will be even higher if interest rates return to historic levels. Korean companies have a relatively favorable outlook, because of the strong economic rebound. Yet, they could only survive without deeper financial restructuring if economic growth returns to precrisis levels, an improbable scenario. Malaysian companies appear to have the strongest balance sheets among the four crisis economies and will be able to muddle through without deeper restructuring, because they entered the crisis with the lowest leverage.

East Asia's crisis countries have seen a large increase in foreign direct investment, but it is unlikely to be sufficient to address corporations' needs. Foreign direct investment in Korean companies is estimated to reach US$15 billion in 1999, up from US$2.6 billion in 1996. Foreign direct investment has also risen in Indonesia, from US$4.7 billion in 1997 to US$13.4 billion in 1998, and was projected to reach US$12 billion in 1999. Foreign direct investment in Thailand almost tripled between 1996 and 1998. Only in Malaysia has foreign investment been minimal.

Although lower interest rates have considerably eased the burden of short-term corporate debt service, the operational cash flows of many corporations have seen less improvement. Financial restructuring has often been limited to rescheduling or interest reductions, which does not bode well for sustainable financial positions. Given the high leverage of corporations in East Asia (except in Malaysia), risks are high if interest rates rise. If corporate sectors remain fragile, they will undermine the capital adequacy of financial sectors. As international experience has shown, undercapitalized financial sectors may start lending to financially risky but potentially high-return projects, and they may roll over loans to loss-making corporations, which would make it more difficult for performing borrowers to access credit.

The four East Asian crisis countries maintain high financial-sector restructuring costs, ranging from 15 to 50 percent of GDP, and are swelling public debt (table 10.8). Because Indonesia's public debt was held largely

Table 10.8. *Public Debt, Restructuring Costs, and the Fiscal Impact*
(percentage of 1998 GDP unless noted otherwise)

Indicator	Indonesia	Korea, Rep. of	Malaysia	Thailand
Public debt stock, 1997	48.3	10.5	31.6	6.5
Fiscal recapitalization cost to date	37.3	15.8	10.9	17.4
Expected additional fiscal cost	12.7	10.7	5.5	15.4
Total expected public debt burden	98.3	37.0	48.0	39.3
Annual interest payment on this burden	15.4	2.9	1.5	1.2
Interest payment (percentage of 1998 revenue)	91.8	14.0	6.5	6.5
Memorandum items				
Fiscal deficit (percentage of GDP), 1999	6.5	5.0	5.5	5.0
Interest rate used (percent)	15.7	7.9	3.1	3.0
GDP as a percentage of revenue, 1998	16.8	21.0	23.1	18.4

Source: IMF, J.P. Morgan, and Deutsche Bank data; World Bank staff estimates.

in foreign currency prior to the crisis, the sharp depreciation of its currency caused its debt to jump to 48 percent of GDP at the end of 1997. Financial restructuring costs will sharply raise the ratio of public debt to GDP in all the crisis countries: in Indonesia to over 90 percent and in Korea, Malaysia, and Thailand to 37–48 percent.

These large restructuring costs have caused many observers to question the sustainability of public debt burdens. Fiscal stimulus programs have led to large deficits—more than 5 percent of GDP—and rising public debt in all four countries. If interest rates remain at current levels, interest payments are expected to account for 6–14 percent of fiscal revenues in Korea, Malaysia, and Thailand. In Indonesia almost all fiscal revenues would have to be devoted to interest payments to prevent a larger public debt burden.

In the short run, domestic liquidity and foreign investment (and in Indonesia, large official external financing) have eased funding pressure. East Asian countries have a long history of prudent fiscal management, with several countries in the region reducing their public debt ratios sharply in the mid-1980s following (smaller) financial crises. Nevertheless, future fiscal stability is not assured.

As private investment recovers, public funding will become more difficult because the supply of savings will be more limited. If interest rates rise, the costs of public funding will increase. The rising debt burden will soon require sharp fiscal adjustments to reverse the buildup. The risk entails fiscal adjustments arriving while economies remain frail, bank and corporate restructuring is incomplete, and structural reforms have not fully taken hold.

Containing the rise in public debt will require high receipts from the sale of government assets acquired during the restructuring. Early experiences in the region and from other crisis countries, however, suggest that proceeds from such sales are generally low, especially when management is largely left to public agencies. A further risk is that high interest payments will reduce fiscal flexibility in dealing with adverse shocks, triggering reduced confidence in the solvency of the public sector and leading to higher interest rates. In Indonesia, public sector solvency will need to be addressed directly and rapidly: prolonged uncertainty creates debt overhang, which hampers the willingness of new investors to commit resources.

While East Asian countries have made significant progress during the past two years, the restructuring of East Asia's financial and corporate sectors remains incomplete, in line with cross-country experience. Banks remain inadequately capitalized (if they were to provision for their loan losses at realistic levels), and will find it difficult to grow out their problems, especially in Indonesia and Thailand. By the same token, while corporate restructuring has accelerated over the last year, considerable amounts of corporate debt have not been restructured. Even if corporate restructuring accelerates, the financial viability of many corporations is not assured. Without large debt-equity swaps and debt write-offs, the longer-term financial viability of many corporations is at risk, particularly in Indonesia and Korea.

Governments need to adjust their approach to bank and corporate restructuring, reduce financial systems' capital shortfalls, and enhance the sticks and carrots for corporate restructuring by, for example, requiring financial institutions to adopt more realistic restructuring and to make proper provisions for restructured loans. In Korea this could also mean closer links between bank and corporate restructuring, which can take the form of linking additional fiscal resources for banks to corporate restructuring under a loss-sharing agreement. Thailand needs to move more aggressively in resolving the capital shortfall of large, private institutions, as the banks' current approach prolongs the uncertainty about the health of the financial system. This could entail the government providing longer buyback periods of government shares for existing shareholders while closely monitoring bank performance and demonstrating the ability and willingness to take over institutions in noncompliance. In Indonesia, given the limited capacity in domestic banks and the asset management company, more foreign creditors should be invited to engage in corporate restructuring.

International experience shows that meeting the restructuring costs early will strengthen financial sectors' incentives for loan recovery and proper restructuring and ultimately yield significantly lower costs. In the end, moving the economy to a more sustainable growth path can best reduce the fiscal costs of financial restructuring.

The Risk of an Unsustainable Recovery

Market analysts predict growth rates in the four crisis countries during 2000–10 to be 2 percentage points below those achieved during 1993–96 (Consensus Forecasts 1999). Underlying these growth projections are lower investment rates, because private external capital will be less forthcoming and fiscal deficits will be higher. Achieving even these lower growth rates will require more efficient investment. This, in turn, requires in-depth structural reforms to correct underlying weaknesses and to ensure that current restructuring efforts support medium-term growth.

An assessment of the changes in structural frameworks for financial and corporate sectors suggests that the crisis countries have only partly addressed current weaknesses. Deeper reforms are needed—and early recovery must not inhibit further structural reforms. Ownership changes will also be necessary to avoid a recurrence of past problems. In particular, as governments have played large roles in restructuring real and financial sectors, it will be imperative to divest these assets quickly but fairly.

Although financial regulation and supervision frameworks have improved since the crisis began, reforms have not gone far enough to increase the sectors' overall robustness. A key prerequisite for enforcement and providing greater (but not complete) insulation from short-term political pressures is central bank independence. Korea transferred most—but not all—regulatory and supervisory responsibilities from the Bank of Korea and the Ministry of Finance and Economy to the new Financial Supervisory Service. In Indonesia and Thailand, the central bank remains the banking system's regulatory and supervisory body. But because neither central bank is particularly independent relative to central banks in other countries (Cukierman, Neyapti, and Webb 1992), the strength of enforcement and the ability to keep political pressures at bay are in doubt. Thailand has yet to pass a new central bank law, and political consensus for a more independent central bank seems tenuous. Indonesia's new central bank law establishes the central bank as an independent state institution, but its institutional powers are limited.

Although a number of weaknesses in financial sector regulation have been addressed, many remain. Loan classification and provisioning guidelines often fall short of international best practice and imply substantial forbearance (table 10.9). Regulatory arbitrage between banks and nonbanks, an important cause of the East Asian crisis, has not been entirely eliminated. While finance companies in Thailand are now largely subject to the same regulatory framework as commercial banks, state-owned development banks are still treated differently. In Korea, nonbanks continue to be less regulated and supervised than banks, and regulatory authority over development banks remains with the Ministry of Finance.

The crisis revealed substantial weaknesses in the exit framework for financial institutions, and many of those have still to be corrected. Only Korea has improved its exit framework, putting in place an independent supervisory agency, performing supervision on a consistent and consolidated basis across different types of deposit-taking institutions, phasing out guarantees on banking system liabilities, and adopting a deposit insurance scheme with elements of prompt corrective action. The other crisis countries have yet to establish similar formal frameworks. Weak exit frameworks limit supervisors'

Table 10.9.   *Regulatory and Loan Restructuring Frameworks, Mid-1999*

Country	Loan classification	Loan loss provisioning	Interest accrual	Overall index
Indonesia	2 (2)	2 (1)	2 (1)	2.0 (1.3)
Korea, Rep. of	3 (2)	3 (3)	3 (3)	3.0 (2.7)
Malaysia	2 (2)	1 (1)	3 (3)	2.0 (2.0)
Thailand	3 (1)	3 (1)	2 (1)	2.7 (1.0)
Memorandum items				
Chile	3	2	2	2.3
Japan	4	4	4	4.0
Mexico	2	2	1	1.7
United States	4	4	4	4.0

Note: Countries are scored on a scale from 1 to 4 for each variable, with 4 indicating best practice and 1 indicating furthest away from best practice. Numbers in parentheses are scores before the crises, that is, early 1997. The definitions for each item are as follows. Loan classification: 1 = loans considered past due at more than 360 days; 2 = loans past due at more than 180 days; 3 = loans past due at more than 90 days; 4 = repayment capacity of borrower taken into account. Loan loss provisioning: 1 = 0% substandard, 50% doubtful, 100% loss; 2 = 10–15% substandard, 50% doubtful, 100% loss; 3 = 20% substandard, 75% doubtful, 100% loss; 4 = present value of future cash flow or fair value of collateral. Interest accrual: 1 = up to 6 months, no clawback; 2 = up to 3 months, no clawback; 3 = up to 6 months, with clawback; 4 = up to 3 months, with clawback.

Source: World Bank data.

ability to quickly address financial distress and undermine the threat of exit. A particular concern exists given the guarantees on banking system liabilities that all four countries have provided. Such guarantees reduce incentives for market oversight and place an even larger burden on supervisors.

All four crisis countries have liberalized foreign direct investment (table 10.10). Except in financial services, Malaysia is the most open to such investment. Korea has made the most progress in eliminating barriers to foreign entry, although a number of restrictions remain.

Thailand has not amended its Alien Business Law, however, and a proposal now in Parliament to increase the number of sectors in which foreigners are able to have majority ownership is unlikely to be adopted soon. While ownership restrictions on foreigners can be overcome by setting up indirect holding structures, few foreign investors consider it worthwhile to do so in Thailand. All four crisis countries maintain ownership restrictions and other limits on foreign investment in utilities.

While much debated as one of the main causes of the East Asian crisis, shareholder rights in most countries were not far behind those in other developing countries, and sometimes were even ahead. For example, East Asian countries have an average score of 1 on equity protection, compared with an average score of 0.8 for Latin American countries and an average score of 2.1 for Organisation for Economic Co-operation and Development countries (La Porta, Lopez-de-Silanes, and Shleifer 1998). Creditor rights were on average lower in East Asia than in Latin America and the Organisation for Economic Co-operation and Development, but marginally so. Enforcement of these rights was lacking, however. Minority rights were often violated, and valuations of firms controlled by inside shareholders were far below those of comparable firms, suggesting large-scale expropriation (Claessens, Djankov, and Lang 1999).

Since the crisis, formal minority shareholder rights have improved in Korea and Thailand (table 10.11). Still, many questions remain on the degree to which these rights are being enforced. In Korea, large-scale financial transfers continue among firms within groups, the most recent example being the channeling of SK Telecom profits to loss-making affiliates rather than to shareholders. The key factor is the independence of regulators and the strength of judicial systems. In several countries, securities market regulators are still not fully independent. In Indonesia, courts have not considered any cases involving corporate governance.

Although Indonesia, Korea, and Thailand passed new bankruptcy and collateral laws in 1998, creditor rights have not significantly improved in Korea and Thailand. Although Indonesia is an exception, it remains unclear clear whether its stronger framework will be enforced.

Table 10.10. *Changes in Foreign Direct Investment Restrictions, by Sector*

Country	Finance	Manufacturing	Retail	Utilities
Indonesia	From 49% to 100%; limit on number of branches removed	From 51% to 100% (from 0% to 51% for palm oil plantations)	From 49% to 100%	Still restricted; requires special approval
Korea, Rep. of	From 15% to 100%	From 20% to 100%	From 20% to 100%	From 0% to 49%
Malaysia	Remains at 30% (from 30% to 51% for insurance)	No restrictions	No restrictions	From 30% to 49%
Thailand	Still restricted; requires approval from the Board of Investment	Most sectors do not have restrictions, but must comply with the Alien Business Law	Still restricted; requires approval from the Board of Investments	Still restricted; requires approval from the Board of Investments

Source: World Bank data.

Table 10.11. *Equity Rights, Creditor Rights, and Judicial Efficiency* (as of mid-1999)

Indicator	Indonesia	Korea, Rep. of	Malaysia	Thailand
Equity rights				
One-share one-vote	0	1	1	0
Proxy by mail	0	0	0	0
Shares not blocked	0	+1	0	+1
Cumulative voting	0	0	0	1
Equity rights (sum)	0	2	1	2
Improvement over 1996	None	+1	None	+1
Creditor rights				
Restrictions on reorganizations	1	1	1	1
No automatic stay on assets	+1	0	0	1
Secured creditors first paid	0	1	1	0
Management does not stay on in reorganizations	+1	1	1	1
Creditor rights (sum)	3	3	3	3
Improvement over 1996	+2	None	None	None
Judicial efficiency				
Timetable to render judgment	+1	+1	0	+1
Existence of a specialized bankruptcy code	+1	1	0	0
Efficiency score (sum)	2	1	0	0
Improvement over 1996	+2	+1	None	+1

Note: One denotes that equity and creditor rights are in the law, time limits to render judgement and specialized bankruptcy courts exists. A plus sign indicates an improvement over the law in existence before the crisis, that is, 1996.

Source: Claessens, Djankov, and Klapper (1999); La Porta, Lopez-de-Silanes, and Shleifer (1998).

The banking landscape in the four East Asian countries has changed as a result of the crisis—fewer financial institutions are operating in a more concentrated system. Increased state ownership as a result of government capital injections has accompanied these structural changes. Twenty-one commercial banks have been nationalized, and only four foreign banks have entered (in Korea and Thailand), although new banking technology and increased innovative capacity are badly needed.

In most countries—especially Thailand—family-controlled banks and conglomerates seem set to survive. Similarly, in Korea links between non-bank financial institutions and the corporate sector have not been severed. Indeed, since 1997 nonbank financial institutions have become much more important in Korea, with investment trust companies expanding considerably.

One reason for limited institutional reforms may be the continued concentration of corporate control in the hands of a few families, and the strong political connections that these families possess. In countries in which control is most concentrated, the judicial system is less efficient, the rule of law is weaker, and corruption is more pervasive (Claessens, Djankov, and Lang 1999). This implies that institutional reform may be more limited in East Asian countries with the highest concentration of wealth.

The restructuring since mid-1997 has required active state involvement in the financial and corporate sectors—much greater than in the past and more than governments envisage in the medium term. In the financial sector this includes the state acquiring ownership of many commercial banks and other financial institutions. In turn, this has meant a large role for the state in the corporate sector, either because government-owned banks were involved in corporate restructuring or because they acquired direct ownership stakes in corporations through, for example, debt-equity swaps.

In the corporate sector governments have acquired many claims through purchases by asset management companies. Governments have also been involved more generally in corporate restructuring by designing frameworks and overseeing the restructuring of the corporate sector—including, in some countries, by providing direct guidance on corporate restructuring (as with the restructuring of large business units of Korea's top five *chaebols*). Through asset management companies, state-owned commercial banks, and nationalized financial institutions, governments control an average of 45 percent of financial assets. Korea and Thailand's governments control assets worth more than 100 percent of GDP.

The large role of the state was beneficial in the early stages of the crisis because it allowed for quicker restoration of confidence in the financial sector and stimulated corporate restructuring in some countries. An overly active state, however, complicates the transition to a more efficient economy. In particular, governments need to divest their significant ownership stakes in banks and other financial institutions.

Although there has been interest, governments have made limited progress in selling financial institutions to foreign investors. Korea has attracted foreign investment in two banks, but efforts to sell one large bank have been indefinitely delayed, and another sale might run into trouble because of differences in asset valuation. In Thailand, only two banks have been sold, while three banks have been on offer for more than a year. In Indonesia the sale of a bank becomes mired in controversies. Governments have also had limited success with asset sales by asset management companies. On average, only 8 percent of intervened assets have been sold.[3]

Governments will need to accelerate efforts to increase the involvement of private strategic investors in their financial and corporate sectors. Possible signals of the desire for private involvement would be for governments to share losses on the nonperforming loans of banks and to show a greater willingness to have the private sector acquire defunct assets to work out. Government will also need to move from government-guided corporate restructuring to more market-based restructuring and enhancement of corporate competitiveness. This will require moving to a situation in which many agents—including financial institutions, new investors, managers and owners of corporations, and other stakeholders (including workers)—rather than the government provide the impetus for continuing corporate upgrading and renewal, either directly or under government auspices (as through out-of-court frameworks).

The retrenchment of the state must be carefully phased. Overly rapid privatization of intervened banks may lead to larger ownership by a few families and increased indirect links between banks and corporations. Similarly, growing ownership of corporations by financial institutions could hinder medium-term changes. Close links could reduce incentives for banks to restructure corporations and perpetuate a situation in which banks continue to accommodate the credit needs of corporations without independent monitoring and oversight.

These potential side effects of restructuring need not impede the longer-term changes envisioned in East Asia's crisis countries, but addressing them will require a deliberate strategy to make policy interventions work in the medium term. In all countries, this means that the disposal of assets and divestiture of institutions must be as rapid as possible.

In some countries this may mean a move to more fully funded pension schemes to create institutional investors that can provide independent oversight to the corporate and financial sectors. In other countries, corporate restructuring funds could be created immediately to acquire the ownership stakes now held by banks or the state, allowing them to

---

3. Because governments can hold assets both directly in an asset management company and in intervened financial institutions, sales are taken as a fraction of the sum of asset management company assets and all nonperforming loans of intervened financial institutions.

remain publicly owned but privately managed. Provided that adequate corporate governance is in place, this move could bridge the gap between the need for government involvement in short-term restructuring and the desire for medium-term refocusing of the economy.

References

Barents Group. 1999. "East Asia: Survey of Asset Management Companies." Washington, D.C.

BIS (Bank for International Settlements). 1998. *66ᵗʰ Annual Report*. Geneva.

Caprio, Gerald, and Daniela Klingebiel. 1997. "Bank Insolvency: Bad Luck, Bad Policy, or Bad Banking?" In Michael Bruno and Boris Pleskovic, eds., *Annual World Bank Conference on Development Economics 1996*. Washington, D.C.: World Bank.

_____. 1999. "Episodes of Systemic and Borderline Financial Crises." World Bank, Washington, D.C. Processed.

Caprio, Gerald, and Patrick Honohan. 1999. "Beyond Supervised Capital Requirements: Restoring Bank Stability." *Journal of Economic Perspectives* 13(4): 43–64.

Claessens, Stijn, Simeon Djankov, and Giovanni Ferri. 1999. "Corporate Distress in East Asia: Assessing the Impact of Interest and Exchange Rate Shocks." *Emerging Markets Quarterly* 3(2): 8–14.

Claessens, Stijn, Simeon Djankov, and Leora Klapper. 1999. "Resolution of Corporate Distress: Evidence from East Asia's Financial Crisis." World Bank, Washington, D.C.

Claessens, Stijn, Simeon Djankov, and Larry Lang. 1999. "Who Controls East Asian Corporations?" Policy Research Working Paper no. 2054. World Bank, Washington, D.C.

Consensus Forecasts. 1999. Growth Projections, obtained through Datastream.

Corsetti, Giancarlo, Paolo Pesenti, and Nouriel Roubini. 1998. "What Caused the Asian Currency and Financial Crises? A Macroeconomic Overview." New York University, New York. Processed.

Cukierman, Alex, Bilin Neyapti, and Steven B. Webb. 1992. "Measuring the Independence of Central Banks and its Effect on Policy Outcomes." *World Bank Economic Review* 6(3): 353–98.

Harvey, Campbell, and Andrew Roper. 1999. "The Asian Bet." Duke University, Fuqua School of Business, Durham, North Carolina. Processed.

IMF (International Monetary Fund). Various years. *International Financial Statistics.* Washington, D.C.

Johnson, Simon, Peter Boone, Alasdair Breach, and Eric Friedman. 1998. "Corporate Governance in the Asian Financial Crisis, 1997–98." Massachusetts Institute of Technology, Cambridge, Massachusetts.

Kaminsky, Graciela, and Carmen Reinhart. 1998. "The Twin Crises: The Causes of Banking and Balance of Payments Problems." World Bank, Washington, D.C.

Klingebiel, Daniela. 1999. "The Use of Asset Management Companies in the Resolution of Banking Crises: Cross Country Experience." World Bank, Washington, D.C.

Krugman, Paul. 1999. "Balance Sheets, the Transfer Problem, and Financial Crises." Massachusetts Institute of Technology, Cambridge, Massachusetts.

La Porta, Rafael, Florencio Lopez-de-Silanes, Andrei Shleifer. 1998. "Law and Finance." *Journal of Political Economy* 106(16): 1113–55.

Radelet, Steven, and Jeffrey Sachs. 1998. *The East Asian Financial Crisis: Diagnosis, Remedies, Prospects.* Brookings Papers on Economic Activity 1. Washington, D.C.: The Brookings Institution.

Ramos, Roy. 1999. "Financial Restructuring Scorecard." Goldman Sachs, Hong Kong.

11

The Politics of Corporate and Financial Restructuring: A Comparison of Korea, Thailand, and Indonesia

Stephan Haggard, University of California, San Diego

Systemic financial and corporate distress—the simultaneous insolvency of large numbers of banks and firms—constitutes a distinguishing feature of the Asian financial crisis. Financial and corporate restructuring under such conditions poses a number of unresolved technical problems. However, the issues are not simply technical; they also involve political conflicts over the recognition of losses and their allocation among various parties: shareholders, management, workers, and taxpayers.

Government responses to such crises can be distinguished on several dimensions, but two with particular importance to the success of the adjustment process are the speed and decisiveness of government and its responsiveness to private interests, particularly weak banks and firms. These two dimensions are clearly related. Banks and firms experiencing severe distress possess a strong interest in postponing the recognition of losses. Governments may also have their own political reasons for delay. However, delay can compound losses and increase uncertainty.

Government responsiveness to private interests links to the much-debated problem of moral hazard (Chang 1999), and the extent to which governments effectively guarantee (ex ante) and bail out (ex post) financial institutions and their corporate clients. Of course, bankrupting potentially viable banks and firms has no virtue. In periods of distress, however, all companies have an interest in claiming to be viable. To limit the public costs of such crises, governments require the political as well as administrative capability to distinguish among the competing claims and to impose on banks and firms regulatory conditions that will limit future risks.

Governments cannot avoid shouldering some of the costs of such crises even in the best of circumstances. Consequently, it sometimes becomes difficult to draw a sharp line between rational forbearance toward the private sector and a bailout. Nonetheless, three political factors that influence policy can be identified: the security of government, the cohesiveness of government decisionmaking, and the degree of institutional and political access for private actors. Governments facing electoral or nonelectoral challenges, such as demonstrations and strikes, are more likely to delay and make concessions to stakeholders than those that are politically secure. The formal structure of decisionmaking also matters. Policymaking processes with multiple veto gates are typically less decisive and more open to particular influences than governments in which authority is more concentrated.[1] But choices about financial and corporate restructuring also depend on the nature of government-business relations. Moral hazard, bailouts, favoritism, and limited reform become more likely when top political leaders develop close and nontransparent political relationships with particular firms.

This chapter examines the politics of financial and corporate reform in six administrations in three countries: the Kim Young Sam and Kim Dae Jung administrations in the Republic of Korea, the Chavalit and Chuan governments in Thailand, and the Suharto and Habibie governments in Indonesia. While democratic politics in Korea and Thailand contributed to the initial mismanagement of the financial crisis, they also permitted new reformist governments to come to office. Under Habibie, democratic pressures also provided incentives for reform. In Indonesia under Suharto, more profound political uncertainties over succession made meaningful financial and corporate reform virtually impossible.

Yet all democracies are not created equal. Both the nature of decisionmaking structures and business access to government resulted in

---

1. A veto gate is an institution with the power to veto a policy proposal, thus forcing a reversion to the status quo. The veto gates in modern democracies include the president, legislature, a second chamber of the legislature, a committee within a legislature, the courts, and so on. The preferences of these veto gates may also be more or less closely aligned; thus, the president and legislature may represent distinct veto gates, but may either be of the same party (unified government) or of different parties (divided government).

a more decisive, but also more interventionist, adjustment strategy in Korea than in Thailand. By contrast, close business-government relations weakened the ability of both the Suharto and Habibie governments to make decisions and undermined the credibility of the government when it did. These findings suggest that meaningful financial and corporate reform depend heavily on the broader institutional context, including the independence of regulatory agencies and the transparency of business-government relations.

Financial and Corporate Restructuring: Political Issues and Empirical Patterns

The process of financial and corporate restructuring involves a wide range of policies, from regulation to policies governing foreign investment to tax and competition policy (Claessens, Djankov, and Klingebiel 1999; World Bank 1998; Haggard 2000). However, five issues have proved central to the restructuring process in Asia: the management of illiquid and insolvent banks, bank recapitalization, the disposition of nonperforming loans, the restructuring of corporate debt, and both the reform and operation of bankruptcy procedures (table 11.1). Over the longer run, encouraging foreign entry and reforming rules on corporate governance are also salient.

The first task facing governments was to decide which banks and other nonbank financial institutions were insolvent and nonviable and to stop the flow of public credit to them. For any government to impose the costs of bank failures on depositors is extraordinarily difficult, even if a formal insurance mechanism is not in place. The political challenge, rather, is dealing with shareholders, large creditors, managers, and bank workers. Once a bank is insolvent, managers have few incentives to run it on a commercial basis, and looting can set in. Moreover, insolvent banks pressure the central bank to provide liquidity support and issue blanket guarantees, with adverse implications for monetary and fiscal policy. The Indonesian case shows that failing banks should not necessarily be suspended or closed immediately, but, in contrast, Japan's experience suggests the risk of delay.

The next task is triage—developing a rehabilitation plan for those viable institutions that nonetheless require support and dealing with those that are nonviable and ultimately need to be closed. These decisions, which involve similar conflicts about the allocation of losses, typically crystallize around two related policy issues: recapitalizing the banks and disposing of nonperforming loans. In severe financial crises, the extent of distress and risk to the overall financial system proves so great that injections of

Table 11.1.   *The Politics of Corporate and Financial Restructuring*

Issue areas	Political issues and conflicts
Limiting support to insolvent banks	Decisiveness of government in limiting liquidity support and guarantees to failing banks; allocation of losses among government, shareholders, depositors, bank workers
Bank recapitalization	Decisiveness of government and provision of adequate resources; imposing conditions on banks; limiting costs to government of recapitalization by encouraging private recapitalization
Disposition of nonperforming loans	Decisiveness of government in identifying and financing "carve out" of nonperforming loans; market pricing of asset purchases; timely rehabilitation or disposition of assets; maximizing value
Corporate debt restructuring	Facilitating timely restructuring; imposing conditions on corporates; limiting the cost to government
Reforming and enforcing bankruptcy and foreclosure procedures	Inducing private workouts and acceptance of losses; avoiding bank-corporate collusion at government expense; overcoming resistance to bankruptcy reform and expedited procedures
Encouraging foreign entry	Overcoming nationalist and protectionist pressures
Reform of corporate governance	Overcoming resistance from insiders to greater transparency, corporate accountability, and external monitoring

Source: Author.

public capital to recapitalize the banks become unavoidable. The key political question revolves around the nature and extent of the conditions attached to any support, whether direct or in the form of regulatory forbearance. The government can also use its support to induce the restructuring of both the banks and their corporate clients.

The disposition of nonperforming loans constitutes a third policy area in which there are potential conflicts of interest between the government and banks and debtors. Governments have typically sought to solve this problem either through liquidation or through more ambitious rehabilitation agencies that seek to restructure the assets prior to sale (Klingebiel 2000), both of which present political challenges. A liquidation agency must have a clear mandate to dispose of assets, including to foreigners. If the assets are simply "warehoused," bank balance sheets are cleaned up, but neither banks nor borrowers have incentives to see that obligations are actually serviced. The government can also manage acquired assets aggressively to maximize value, but that too requires not only substantial administrative ability but also a clear mandate to maximize returns to the government.

The indicators in table 11.2 and the cases that follow suggest some interesting patterns across the countries and governments examined here. The Kim Young Sam administration lacked a coherent strategy toward the financial sector. Following Kim Dae Jung's election, the new government quickly established a powerful regulatory agency to manage the crisis and set aside funds to carve out nonperforming loans and recapitalize the banking system. All banks were subject to thorough review, after which five were shut down and merged with others under government direction.[2] Korea's record in disposing of acquired assets seems weak, but it has moved more aggressively than Indonesia. One result of the nationalizations and capital infusions, however, was that the government came to occupy a commanding position in the financial sector.

As in Korea under Kim Young Sam, the Chavalit government initially supported weak institutions. The Chuan government moved quickly to close a number of finance companies and dispose of their core assets over the next 18 months, but moved cautiously to induce banks to recapitalize on their own. This strategy failed, but the conditions of a government recapitalization scheme in August 1998 provided inadequate incentives to participate. The government was forced to manage the crisis through regulatory forbearance and acceptance of a continuing and high level of nonperforming loans.

Indonesia responded decisively to its banking crisis, but the initial closing of 16 banks was badly handled and the government continued to support a number of politically connected banks with disastrous consequences. Deepening political uncertainty increasingly undermined reform efforts. The Habibie government initiated a strategy for recapitalizing the banking sector, but implementation was subject to delay and charges of political interference. By November 1999, when the new Wahid government took office, Indonesia had clearly made the least progress of the three countries in addressing the problems in its banking sector.

---

2. A large number of nonbank financial institutions were also shut down, although many weak ones remained open.

Table 11.2. *Managing Bank Failure and Recapitalization*

Category	Korea	Thailand	Indonesia
Managing bank insolvency Institutional framework	Financial Supervisory Authority, April 1998; Korea Deposit Insurance Corporation	Financial Restructuring Agency, October 1997 (finance companies only); Financial Restructuring Advisory Committee	Indonesian Bank Restructuring Authority, January 1998; authority expanded February 1999
Banks closed and/or merged (percentage of financial sector assets)	5 closed and merged	1 of 15 closed (2 percent)	64 of 237 closed (18 percent); 4 of 7 state banks to be merged into one bank (54 percent)
Other financial institutions closed or merged (percentage of financial sector assets)	17 merchant banks and over 100 nonbank financial institutions (with bank closures, 15 percent)	57 of 91 finance companies closed (11 percent)	—
Nationalizations (percentage of financial sector assets)	4 commercial banks (25 percent)	7 commercial banks (13–15 percent) and 12 finance companies (2.2 percent)	12 commercial banks (20 percent)
Bank recapitalization strategy Initial plan and timing	US$8 billion injected into 9 commercial banks, January 1998.	US$8.9 billion for private banks and US$11.7 billion for state banks, plan announced August 1998	US$41 billion plan announced March 1999 for 9 private banks; all state banks to be recapitalized

(table continues on following page)

266

Table 11.2 *continued*

Category	Korea	Thailand	Indonesia
Total amount disbursed for recapitalization, October 1999, plus estimated remaining fiscal costs (as share of GDP)	13 percent + 4 percent	16 percent + 8 percent	11 percent + 48 percent
Share of financial assets held by state-owned and nationalized banks, August 1999	58 percent	45 percent	78 percent
Financial assets held by state owned and nationalized banks/GDP, August 1999	124 percent	127 percent	79 percent
Asset resolution			
Asset management company and assets, August 1999	Korean Asset Management Company, US$37 billion.	No asset management unit for banks; Financial Restructuring Agency for finance companies	Indonesian Bank Restructuring Authority; US$28 billion.
Assets transferred, mid-1999	26 percent of nonperforming loans, 10 percent of GDP	All assets of closed finance company assets, 2 percent of GDP	66 percent of nonperforming loans, 35 percent of GDP
Assets sold as share of those transferred, mid-1999	4.7 percent	100 percent of core assets of finance companies, but some to government Asset Management Unit	0.7 percent

— Not Available.
Source: Claessans, Djankov, and Klingebiel (1999); World Bank (2000); author's calculations and assessments.

A fourth issue is the corporate restructuring process. As with the banks, corporations might delay financial and operational restructuring and collude with banks at public expense. The government can solve this problem in one of two ways, each of which requires some political capacity. First, it can rigorously enforce capital adequacy and loan loss provisions while providing incentives for banks to engage in out-of-court settlements; this is the so-called London rules approach. This approach depends on the government's ability to credibly commit to its regulatory stance. An alternative strategy is for the government to play a more active role in the corporate restructuring process, from coordinating intracreditor and creditor-debtor relations and monitoring and enforcing agreements, to using various instruments to enforce various financial and operational restructuring objectives. Again, government success will hinge on political as well as administrative capacity.

Foreclosure and bankruptcy laws powerfully affect incentives to corporate restructuring. These laws constitute a final area of potential conflict among the government, banks, and corporations. If foreclosure and bankruptcy laws or their implementation are weak, firms have incentives to delay debt and operational restructuring, and even repayment. Reform of the bankruptcy process and clear enforcement of bankruptcy and foreclosure laws are not only important for managing actual firm failures, but for providing incentives to creditors and debtors to reach out-of-court settlements.

Table 11.3 outlines some indicators on the corporate restructuring process in the three countries. Bankruptcy procedures were stronger in Korea when the crisis hit. Bankruptcy reform was delayed in Thailand and, despite reforms, Indonesia's bankruptcy processes remain weak. In all cases, out-of-court settlement dominated. However, major differences separate Korea from the other two cases. Despite the nominal embrace of the London rules, the Financial Supervisory Commission (FSC) has played a strong role in pushing corporate debt restructuring, resulting in the restructuring of more debt. Moreover, the very concept of corporate restructuring included wide-ranging reforms of corporate governance, ultimately enforced through the government's control of the banking system. In Thailand and Indonesia, debt restructuring has been much slower with much weaker links, if any, to the reform of corporate governance.

Financial and Corporate Restructuring: Political Determinants

A central tenet of political economy, beginning with the literature on political business cycles, is that government actions depend heavily on the

Table 11.3. *Corporate Restructuring*

Category	Korea	Thailand	Indonesia
Corporate restructuring			
Agency and mandate	Corporate Restructuring Coordinating Committee (under FSC, July 1998); nominal London rules, but restructuring linked to reforms of corporate governance	Corporate Debt Restructuring Advisory Committee, June 1998; initially strict London rules, some increase in coordinating function in 1999; no link to corporate governance	Jakarta Initiative Task Force (September 1998), supported by Indonesian Debt Restructuring Agency (April 1998); no link to corporate governance
Out-of-court debt restructured/total debt, August 1999	40 percent	22 percent	13 percent
Bankruptcy			
Bankruptcy law	In place at time of crisis, reformed, April 1998	Reformed April 1998 and April 1999	Reformed April 1998
Efficiency of judicial system index (from 1 = worst to 10 = best)	5.3	5.2	2.2
Foreclosure	Possible	Difficult, reformed April 1998	Difficult
In-court debt restructured/total debt, approx. mid-1999	8 percent	7 percent	4 percent

Source: Claessans, Djankov, and Klingebiel (1999); World Bank (2000); author's calculations and assessments.

government's security of tenure: its time horizons and corresponding discount rates (see, for example, Alesina, Cohen, and Roubini 1997). Incumbent governments facing immediate political challenges are likely to delay policy actions that impose costs in the short run. These challenges may be electoral (impending elections) or extra-parliamentary (demonstrations, riots, and strikes). Electoral challenges are almost by definition less in new governments, although new parliamentary governments may in principle face problems of coalition maintenance. New governments are capable of behaving more decisively than incumbents are because they typically enjoy a honeymoon period and have greater opportunity to reap the benefits of reform (Haggard and Webb 1994).

A second source of indecisiveness lies in the cohesiveness of the decisionmaking process, particularly the number of veto gates through which policy must pass (Haggard and McCubbins forthcoming; Tsebelis 1995; on the financial crisis, see MacIntyre 1999). A decisionmaking system with multiple veto gates will be slow and indecisive, particularly when occupants of the veto gates have divergent preferences. Such an outcome may be desirable if the policy status quo is favorable, but can be costly when there is demand for policy change (see MacIntyre 1999).

The security of government and the cohesiveness of decisionmaking are important for understanding the propensity of governments to delay. However, understanding how governments respond to demands from the private sector requires information on business-government relations, including their transparency. Close relationships can develop between politicians and the private sector in democratic systems in which the nature of the party system and electoral rules provide strong incentives for individual politicians to court business support and in which the policymaking and implementation processes allow politicians to be responsive to business interests. However, reasons also exist to believe that democracies can limit the extent of rent seeking. First, political competition provides oppositions to ferret out the malfeasance of incumbents; political competition itself is a device for monitoring business-government relations. Second, changes of government permit the exercise of power of new coalitions who may not share the same commitments as their predecessors. Crony relationships are likely to be most egregious under authoritarian systems where executive discretion is high and transparency low, and the absence of political competition provides fewer checks on government action. Finally, democracies can mitigate problems of rent seeking through the creation of independent agencies with clear and broad mandates; such agencies are much less likely to enjoy independence under authoritarian rule.

Table 11.4 provides a brief description of the six governments under consideration: the Kim Young Sam and Kim Dae Jung governments in Korea, the Chavalit and Chuan governments in Thailand, and the Suharto and Habibie governments in Indonesia. None were free of risk, but the opportunities for restructuring the financial and corporate sectors were greater in Korea under Kim Dae Jung, particularly in the early part of his administration, than in Thailand or Indonesia, or in Korea under his predecessor.

Korea

The politics of financial and corporate restructuring in Korea began well before the onset of the external crisis in November 1997, and can be traced to the Hanbo scandal that broke in January. The core of the scandal centered on efforts by members of the Kim Young Sam administration and legislators to pressure banks to continue lending to the troubled steelmaker, a classic example of politically generated moral hazard. The exposure of the scandal by the opposition severely weakened the president, who was a lame duck due to a rule prohibiting his reelection, and divided the ruling party. Despite the constitution's allowance for a powerful president, political conditions were highly inauspicious for decisive management of the crisis.

The disposition of the Hanbo case sent mixed signals about the government's intentions with respect to failing enterprises and exacerbated uncertainty about the health of the banking system. The government made no effort to save Hanbo's management, and the firm was effectively nationalized. However, new money was also injected, and when two more of the top-30 *chaebols* folded—Sammi in March and Jinro in April—35 commercial and state banks announced an antibankruptcy pact under which they would extend credit to ailing but viable *chaebols*. As the antibankruptcy pact necessarily called the position of the banks into serious question, the government supplemented the concerted lending and rescheduling effort with initiatives to inject liquidity into the financial system.

Beginning in July, Korean financial and foreign exchange markets entered a period of uncertainty as a result of the Kia crisis, a large conglomerate concentrated primarily in the automotive sector. The Kia crisis broke on June 23 when the chairman of the group exploited the government's weakness and impending elections to appeal for assistance. A highly politicized battle over the future of Kia ensued, in which Kia's management mobilized political support from nongovernmental organizations, unions, and suppliers. As Kia management exploited loopholes in the bankruptcy law, the government vacillated on what to do with the company, and did not finally

Table 11.4. *Political Determinants of Public Policy*

Category	Consequences	Korea	Thailand	Indonesia
Political challenges Electoral challenges	Reduce decisiveness of government; increase propensity to delay and defer to private interests	National presidential elections in December 1997 constitute a major constraint for Kim Young Sam government; Kim Dae Jung faces subational elections (June 1998) and legislative elections (April 2000)	Coalition government poses threat of defections under Chavalit; Chuan initially more secure	Controlled presidential election under Suharto (March 1998); parliamentary elections (June 1999) and indirect presidential elections (November 1999) under Habibie
Extraparliamentary challenges	Depending on intensity, can reduce decisiveness of government; increase propensity to make concessions	Some strikes under both Kim Young Sam and Kim Dae Jung	Antigovernment demonstrations during late Chavalit government; some strikes and demonstrations under Chuan	Widespread antigovernment protests and social violence under Suharto after February 1998; antigovernment demonstrations and continuing ethnic and religious conflict under Habibie
Veto gates	Numerous formal veto gates, and particularly differences of preference among them, slows the decisionmaking process and creates possibility for stalemate	Nominally unified government under Kim Young Sam, but splits between executive and legislature; prior to inauguration Kim Dae Jung enjoys legislative supermajority, but thereafter faces divided government until September 1998	Multiparty coalitions under both Chavalit and Chuan complicate decisionmaking; senate can also slow legislation	Highly concentrated decision-making structure under Suharto; legislative bodies gain in importance under Habibie, but executive still powerful

(table continues on following page)

Table 11.4 continued

Category	Consequences	Korea	Thailand	Indonesia
Business-government relations	Close and nontransparent business-government relations increase risk of moral hazard	Some evidence of corruption under Kim Young Sam (Hanbo case); Kim Dae Jung has weaker ties to business groups	Close relations between legislators and private business in all parties	Close relations between executive and private and family groups and pervasive corruption under Suharto; strong pressure to break such ties under Habibie, but some evidence of continuity (Bank Bali case)

Source: Author.

intervene to move it toward bankruptcy until October 22, only days before Korea began to feel the effects of the stock market collapse in Hong Kong.

Whether a full-blown crisis could have been averted after the shock from Hong Kong is doubtful, but the country's problems were compounded by the inability to pass crucial financial reform legislation. This legislation had been introduced in August, and at the end of the second week of November, it appeared headed for passage. However, the parties disagreed over where the new regulatory agency would be located within the government and whether the National Assembly would have adequate oversight. The affected ministries also lobbied hard to weaken the independence of the new agency. The bills died in committee, adding to the markets' perception of ineffectual and indecisive government.

The contrast between the pre-election and postelection periods could not be starker. Two days after his electoral victory, the President formed a joint, 12-member emergency economic committee, effectively under the president-elect's control. The ruling coalition and the opposition, which continued to control the legislature, agreed to convene a special session of the National Assembly to deal with a series of reform bills. Two further special sessions followed.

The importance of a legislative majority for the course of Korea's economic reform cannot be exaggerated. Table 11.5 suggests the range of the reforms passed during the special legislative sessions held during the transition. Of particular importance were the financial reforms that had been stalled under the previous government. The newly created FSC consolidated financial supervision across all financial entities and markets. However, the power of the FSC did not arise only from its routine supervisory functions, but also from the central role it would play in restructuring the financial sector in the wake of the crisis. The government quickly set aside W 64 trillion (US$49.2 billion, or roughly 15 percent of gross domestic product) for resolving the financial crisis, allocating half to the Korean Deposit Insurance Company for recapitalization and coverage of losses. The other half went to the Korean Asset Management Corporation, which was assigned the task of purchasing and disposing of nonperforming loans.

Operating through the FSC, the government moved swiftly and in a highly directive fashion to address the problems of the banking sector.[3]

---

3. Although the core of the financial sector's problems centered on the commercial banking system, they were by no means limited to it, and the government applied broadly similar principles to these nonbank financial institutions as well. Particularly hard hit were the merchant banks, of which the government closed 16 of 30, and the insurance companies, many of which were technically insolvent.

Table 11.5. *Reform Legislation Passed during the Transition Period, Korea, December 18, 1997–February 25, 1998*

Session	Legislation approved
186th session (December 22–30, 1997)	Act for Establishing Financial Supervisory Institution
	Bank of Korea Act (r)
	Bank Act (r)
	Act Concerning the Restructuring of Financial Industries (r)
	Security Exchange Act (r)
	Insurance Act (r)
	Mutual Trust Company Act (r)
	Depositor Insurance Act (r)
	Merchant Bank Act (r)
	Forward Business Act (r)
	Act concerning the Abolition of the Interest Rates Limits
	Special Consumption Tax Act (r)
	Act concerning the External Auditing of the Corporation (r)
187th session (January 15–21 1998)	Session called to consider labor legislation, but defers to Tripartite Commission
188th session (February 2–16 1998)	Bankruptcy Act (r)
	Corporate Composition Law (r)
	Corporate Reorganization Law (r)
	Monopoly Regulation and Fair Trade Act (r)
	Foreign Investment and Foreign Capital Investment Act (r)
	Corporate Tax Act (r)
	Tax Reduction Act (r)
	Labor Standard Act (r)
	Employment Adjustment Act (r)
	Government Organization Act (r)

r Revised.
Source: Office of the Secretary of the National Assembly.

At the end of 1997, only 12 out of 26 Korean banks satisfied the international capital adequacy standard of 8 percent. In early December, the Kim Young Sam government nationalized the two banks in the worst condition, Korea First Bank and Seoul Bank. After the election, the plans for these banks were toughened to include the write down of shareholder capital and recapitalization in preparation for sale to international bidders.

The next task was to make decisions about the remaining undercapitalized banks. The FSC acted quickly to order the 12 unsound banks to submit rehabilitation plans by late April 1998. No bank plans were approved
outright; 5 of the 12 plans were disapproved, and immediately following
local elections in June, the FSC shut down these banks and ordered the
transfer of their assets into five healthy banks.[4] The basic approach of the
government to the seven conditionally approved banks was to inject capital and purchase nonperforming loans on a selective basis. However, this
took place only on conditions that included the replacement of management and board members, the disposal of nonperforming loans, the in-
ducement of new equity capital, the streamlining of business operations,
and the encouragement of merger.

The heavy leveraging of Korean corporations and the government's
effective control over the banking system also gave it a powerful instrument in seeking corporate restructuring, but the very meaning of that term
was the subject of substantial controversy. One position, associated with
some economists and the *chaebols* themselves, was that the *chaebol* form per
se was not at fault. What was required in the short run was an orderly
process of debt rescheduling, to be negotiated between the banks and the
corporations, and some reforms of corporate governance to make firms
more transparent and accountable to shareholders.

However, the Kim Dae Jung government brought with it a number of
close political advisors who had a much more hostile attitude toward the
chaebols. Believing that the *chaebols* would never willingly reform themselves, these advisors advocated a more command-and-control style of
corporate restructuring, and even mounted an effort to break up the *chaebol*
groups. In the first two years of Kim Dae Jung's presidency, these two lines
coexisted uneasily.

The program of corporate reform was first outlined when Kim Dae Jung
used ad hoc meetings with top *chaebol* leaders to present an "agreement"
on five principles of corporate restructuring (table 11.6). Some elements of

---

4. To compensate the solvent banks for taking over the insolvent institutions,
the Korean Deposit Insurance Company undertook a series of injections that totaled 8.04 trillion won (US$6.7 billion) by the middle of 1999; that amount was
scheduled to rise to around 10 trillion won by the end of the year. To solve the
problem of the nonperforming loans, the FSC devised a purchase and assumption
method in which the viable assets transferred to the acquiring banks while the
nonperforming loans were purchased by the Korean Asset Management Corporation, to be sold later through auctions.

Table 11.6.   *Five Principles of Corporate Restructuring, Korea*

Objective	Measures	Schedule
Enhanced transparency	Adopt combined financial statements	Fiscal year 1999
	Adopt international accounting principles	October 1998
	Strengthen voting rights of minority shareholders	May 1998
	Make appointment of outside directors compulsory	February 1998
	Establish external auditors committee	February 1998
Resolution of cross-debt guarantees	Resolve existing cross-debt guarantees	March 2000
	Prohibit new cross-debt guarantees between subsidiaries	April 1998
Improvement of financial structure	Agree with banks to improve capital structure	April 1998
	Remove restrictions of capital infusions	February 1998
	Introduce asset-backed securities	August 1998
Streamlining business activities	Adopt corporate-split system	June 1998
	Liberalize foreign ownership of real estate	June 1998
	Introduce full liberalization of mergers and aquisitions	May 1998
	Streamline bankruptcy procedures	February 1998
Strengthening accountability	Strengthen the legal liability of controlling owners	June 1998
	Introduce cumulative voting systems	June 1998
	Allow institutional voters rights	June 1998

Source: Author.

the agreement were amenable to legislation, including the areas of corporate governance and competition policy. For example, to increase transparency, revisions of the External Audit Law required that the financial statements of companies in business groups be prepared on a consolidated basis, and it toughened penalties against both external auditors and corporate accounting officers. Changes in the listing requirements to the Korean Stock Exchange strengthened minority shareholders' rights and required listed firms to have at least one outside director. Revisions of the Securities Investment and Trust Law relieved financial intermediaries of the obligation of voting with management and facilitated the exercise of shareholder rights on the part of institutional investors. Removing barriers to mergers and acquisitions served as a check on management, as did liberalization of rules governing foreign direct investment that paved the way for 100 percent foreign ownership of publicly traded companies, including through hostile takeovers.

The government also had to contend with a more fundamental short-term problem of how to deal with the threat of large-scale corporate failure, as well as the underlying problem of extraordinarily high corporate leverage. The immediacy of the problem invited a more directive approach. Over the course of 1998 and 1999, the government used the FSC, and ultimately its de facto control over the banking system, to achieve objectives not specifically legislated, and even of questionable legality.

A three-tiered approach gradually emerged. The first tier consisted of the Big Five: Samsung, Daewoo, Hyundai, LuckyGoldstar, and Sunkyung. These groups held both economic and political importance, and the government sought to deal with them through the negotiation of informal, "voluntary" agreements. The three most contentious issues with the Big Five were the issue of mutual payment guarantees, the reduction of excessive indebtedness, and the operational restructuring of business portfolios. The first issue addressed the common practice for groups to subsidize loss-making units, contributing to weak overall performance and low productivity growth. A revision of the Fair Trade Law during the transition period prohibited the issue of new guarantees from April 1, 1998, and required all *chaebols* to phase out existing ones by March 2000.

The status of promises to reduce the level of debt were much more controversial. Early in 1998, the FSC urged the top 30 *chaebols* to lower their debt-equity ratios from an average of 519 percent at the end of 1997 to 200 percent by the end of 1999. For the Big Five, this commitment was embodied in capital structure improvement plans, agreements with their banks on a variety of restructuring measures: asset sales, including to foreigners; issuance of new equity; debt-equity swaps; and operational restructuring.

Although the firms themselves formulated these plans, one important element of operational restructuring came directly out of the Blue House: the so-called Big Deals. Under the program, the Big Five would swap major lines of business among themselves to consolidate excessive and duplicative investments while simultaneously achieving greater economies of scale (table 11.7). The Big Deal concept contained a number of dubious premises, including the assumption that the Big Five would necessarily reduce surplus capacity or improve competitiveness. The negotiations over the concepts were plagued by sharp differences over the valuation of assets, a variety of problems about how quite different operations would be integrated, and uncertainty about the final corporate form the new entities

Table 11.7.   *The Big Deal Plan, October 7, 1998*

Sector	Company or divisions proposed for swap or merger
Semiconductors	Hyundai Electronics and LuckyGoldstar Semiconductor
Power-generation equipment	Korea Heavy Industries and Construction Company and Samsung Heavy Industries Company
Petrochemicals	Hyundai Petrochemical Company and Samsung General Chemical Company
Aircraft	Samsung Aerospace, Daewoo Heavy Industries, Hyundai Space and Aircraft
Rolling stock	Daewoo Heavy Industries, Hanjin Heavy Industries
Marine engines	Korea Heavy Industries and Construction Company and Samsung Heavy Industries Company
Oil refining	Hyundai Oil Company and Hanwha Energy Company

Source: Author.

would take. Nonetheless, the Big Deals became a litmus test of corporate commitment to the restructuring process and are indicative of the government's directive approach to restructuring.

Throughout 1998 and the first half of 1999, the government engaged in an ongoing public relations battle with the Big Five. The call for explicit Capital Structural Improvement Plans was the first step in this process, followed by the government decision to halt credit to a number of small Big Five subsidiaries in June, and culminating in the public signing of financial pacts between the Big Five and their banks in December 1998. The pacts included four elements: specific commitments to reduce the number of affiliates by target dates, including through the Big Deal mechanism; specific targets for the reduction of debt-equity ratios; an acceleration of the elimination of cross-guarantees between affiliates; and a reiteration of the commitment to reforms in corporate governance. The groups also submitted to a quarterly review process, under the threat that failure to comply would be met by higher interest payments or even a suspension of credit.

The new agreements differed from the principles of a year earlier in their specificity and the monitoring that went along with them. The reduction of debt/equity ratios by a particular date had the most wide-reaching implications, since it appeared to necessitate dramatic asset sales. Yet by April the president was again publicly chiding the *chaebol* for reneging on their promises to sell assets, raise capital, and cut their debt. Data on 1998 performance released in April showed that much of the improvement in the financial position of the Big Five was achieved through asset revaluations and new rights issues. Moreover, both Hyundai and Daewoo had taken on more debt in 1998.

During the spring, it became increasingly clear that the government was headed toward a show-down with one or both of the two firms. Daewoo Motors proved the test case (Jung and Mako 2000). In mid-July 1999, Daewoo Motors admitted to liquidity problems. On July 17, the chairman was forced to pledge personal properties, in the form of shares in an untraded life insurance affiliate and other group collateral to secure rollovers of short-term debt. In a purportedly final effort to secure support, the firm offered a restructuring plan on July 20 that would sell off all but nine affiliated firms, and even those would be largely divested to foreign partners to focus the core of the new group on Daewoo Corporation and Daewoo Motors.

The creditor group, and behind them the FSC, responded by rolling over W 10 trillion in short-term debts and extending W 4 trillion more in new credits. However, the market reaction to both the restructuring plan and the government's decision to support Daewoo was strongly negative, and gradually pushed the FSC toward the position of dismantling Daewoo. The final reorganization plan agreed to with creditors in mid-August allowed for six units to be kept under the condition of selling a number of profitable ones.

The fall of Daewoo will undoubtedly be seen as an important event in Korea's postwar economic history. The government did not altogether avoid support for the firm, since debt was rolled over and some core firms were not liquidated. Moreover, in September and October, the government was forced to establish massive funds to support the investment trust companies, which were big purchasers of Daewoo bonds. However, the conditions were tough, and in his Liberation Day speech on August 15, Kim Dae Jung even signaled an interest in breaking up the *chaebols* into independent units. Although the president retreated from this position, the Daewoo action and the Liberation Day speech sent a strong signal to other groups that brinkmanship would have a high cost.

The second tier of the corporate restructuring effort centered on the so-called 6-64 *chaebols*, and gained momentum after the June 1998 elections. On June 18, 1998, the FSC declared that 55 companies would no longer have access to bank credit. On June 24, 236 financial institutions signed and entered into the Corporate Restructuring Accord that defined the informal workout procedure for troubled firms. A small number of lead banks would take responsibility for negotiating workouts of problem debts with the 6-64 corporate groups, ostensibly under so-called London rules, but the process was closely overseen by the FSC through its Corporate Debt Restructuring Committee.[5]

Although the speed of the process is noteworthy when compared with other countries, some concerns remain, including the fact that contributions from shareholders and operational restructuring have played a less central role than concessionary restructuring of debt: rate reductions, deferrals of principal and interest, and conversion of debt into equity or convertible bonds. This could imply that, as with the larger *chaebol*, another round of restructuring might be required in the future.

The restructuring of small and medium enterprises plays into politics in Korea in a very different way than the *chaebol*. Because of the administration's concern about the employment and equity consequences of small and medium-sized enterprise failure, and Kim Dae Jung's long-standing belief that small and medium enterprises have been slighted by government policy, the approach to this sector has taken a somewhat different form, resembling a kind of corrective industrial policy. Initially, small and medium enterprise debts to the banks were rolled over for six months and for a subsequent six months, and in 1999 the banks began to restructure their debts. However, the government has also shown a concern to restore liquidity to the sector, and has done so through a variety of means, including credit insurance funds, a central bank credit line, and funding for trade finance and four SME restructuring funds. To date, Korea is the only crisis country to aggressively address small business restructuring.

In summary, the politics of financial and corporate restructuring clearly differed between the Kim Young Sam and Kim Dae Jung governments. The Kim Young Sam government began its last year amidst a serious corporate corruption scandal, delays in managing several important bankruptcies, and failures to pass important financial reform legislation, even under pressure from the International Monetary Fund (IMF). The Kim Dae Jung government initiated a broader reform process that included a number of the legal and institutional reforms sought by the IMF and foreign creditors. These were legislated quickly because of the unique political

---

5. The Corporate Dept Restructuring Committee is empowered to act as an arbitration committee if the banks cannot agree among themselves on a workout strategy, or the lead bank and the debtor fail to come to an agreement. If a signatory fails to comply with an approved workout agreement or arbitration decision, the committee can impose penalties (Lieberman 1999).

position enjoyed by the president in the period immediately following the election. Implementation was also expedited by the creation of a new statutory body with a clear mandate for reform.

However, the Korean approach also had a number of more directive elements in the setting of quantitative targets and deadlines for achieving arbitrary debt-equity ratios, a number of organizational reforms of the firm (such as eliminating the chairman's office), the efforts to force firms to readjust their business portfolios (Big Deals) and to concentrate on core lines of business, and in the suggestion that *chaebols* should even be broken up into individual business units. The speed with which the Korean government moved was thus bought about by an exercise of directive powers that rested on a dubious legal foundation. Moreover, these measures carried an important irony in that they involved the Korean government more deeply in the micromanagement of the corporate restructuring process. To some extent this was the result of the dramatic expansion of the government's ownership of the banking system; however, it also reflected Kim Dae Jung's unusual political position as an outsider with fewer connections to the private sector and pressures from the progressive or populist wing of his coalition.

Thailand

As in Korea, the crisis in Thailand struck a government facing substantial political challenges, but unlike Korea those weaknesses were of a more profound constitutional nature (Hicken 1999). All the democratically elected governments prior to the crisis—Chaitichai, Chuan, Banharn, and Chavalit—rested upon shaky multiparty coalitions composed of internally weak and fragmented parties. Parliamentary majorities were constructed from a pool of approximately a dozen parties, and cabinet instability was a chronic problem. The political parties, in turn, were heavily reliant on national and, increasingly, provincial business people with strong personal as well as political interests in financial market and other economic policies.

As in Korea, democratic rule provided the basis for a change in policies. After a long period of policy delay and indecision following the flotation of the baht in July 1997, a new government came to office in November headed by the Democrat Party. The Democrats are a broadly based party with a longer history and more distinct reputation than other Thai parties. They attracted support from a diverse constituency in the south of the country and among the Bangkok elite, and sought to differentiate themselves from the more patronage-based parties that dominated the Banharn and

Chavalit governments and relied heavily on rural political machines for support. Corruption was a recurrent political problem under the Banharn and Chavalit governments, and the Democrats sought to avoid any appearance that the government was supporting failing banks and enterprises.

However, the Democrats were not political outsiders in the sense of Kim Dae Jung, and they confronted a highly concentrated, privately owned banking sector. The party maintained close relations with prominent Bangkok business interests and of necessity relied on other parties as coalition partners; a number of the parties in the Chuan coalition had also been members of the Banharn and Chavalit governments. This sensitivity to business interests, the fractious nature of coalition politics, and the role of the legislature in policymaking all made for a more gradual, remote reform process that was somewhat less dramatic in its accomplishments.

The Politics of Financial Reform under Chavalit

As in Korea, the political constraints on policymaking were visible well before the crisis struck (MacIntyre 1999). Indications of the problems facing the country's financial institutions came as early as 1991 when the Bank of Thailand detected irregularities in the Bangkok Bank of Commerce (BBC). The Financial Institutions Development Fund (FIDF), established in 1985, had a wide range of powers at its disposal to assist and rehabilitate financial institutions whose collapse might have systemic effects, including write-down of capital and replacement of management. However after a 1994 examination, the government agreed to purchase a substantial stake in the bank through the FIDF, but without any write-down of shareholder capital or reduction of management prerogatives (Nukul Commission 1998, paras. 300, 306).

As the extent of mismanagement at the BBC became public in mid-1996 following disclosure by the opposition, there was a run on the bank. The central bank finally took formal control of the BBC and ultimately spent a total of US$7 billion to keep the BBC afloat. This bailout set a dangerous regulatory precedent and severely damaged the reputation of the Bank of Thailand, the FIDF, and the regulatory process generally. The Nukul Commission of inquiry on the crisis sidestepped the issue of outright corruption (Nukul Commission 1998, para. 317), but several politicians within Prime Minister Banharn's Chart Thai Party were known beneficiaries of large loans from the BBC (Baker and Pasuk 1998, pp. 105–110, 259).

In September 1996 Banharn's government collapsed after key coalition partners deserted him, and a close election brought Chavalit's New

Aspiration Party to power as the largest party in the Parliament. Chavalit proceeded to construct a six-party coalition compromising most of the parties from the previous government. He also signaled that he would appoint a cabinet built around an "economic dream team" of highly respected technocrats, notably Amnuay Veerawan as finance minister, to address the country's mounting economic difficulties.

The biggest area of concern in the financial sector was not initially the banks themselves but the finance companies.[6] The end of a prolonged property boom in late 1996, mounting nervousness about unhedged foreign liabilities, and the central bank's misguided effort to support the currency through higher interest rates all conspired to weaken the finance companies. An increasing number turned to the FIDF for support. On March 3, the government suspended trading of financial sector shares on the stock exchange, required all banks and finance companies to make much stronger provision for bad loans, and announced that 10 of the weakest financial companies would have to raise their capital base within 60 days.

However, several senior members of the Chart Pattana Party, the second largest party in the coalition, held controlling interests in some of the 10 targeted institutions and vetoed both the plan and action against the 10 companies. The very fact that they were permitted to remain open meant that—as with the BBC—the central bank had to provide liquidity to keep them afloat in the face of runs by creditors and depositors.

Not only was the government unable to allow the firms to fail or permit foreign takeover, but they were even unable to impose minimal regulatory controls such as raising capital adequacy ratios or stopping the flows of funding through the FIDF. Frustrated by his inability to persuade the coalition's leaders in the cabinet to move on more extensive financial sector reforms, Veerawan resigned from the government on June 19 and within two weeks, on July 2, the baht was cut loose.

The onset of the crisis did not in itself guarantee effective action. Upon taking office, Veerawan's successor, Thanong Badaya announced the suspension of 16 finance companies (including 7 of the original 10), giving them 30 days to implement merger plans. At the same time, however, the Prime Minister announced that no further finance companies would be closed, and that the government would guarantee the closed finance companies loans and deposits. However, Chart Pattana leaders succeeded in

---

6. By the end of 1996, Thailand's 91 finance companies accounted for nearly 25 percent of total credit.

preventing the closure or merger of the 16 finance companies and persuaded the central bank to continue injecting liquidity into the institutions.

In conjunction with the IMF program, Badaya announced that a further 42 finance companies would be suspended, bringing the total to 58.[7] However, charges of corruption and conflict of interest surfaced with respect to the committee given the responsibility of reviewing the finance companies' rehabilitation efforts, the Committee to Supervise Mergers and Acquisitions of Financial Institutions, and the Association of Finance Companies successfully lobbied the government to extend the deadline for restructuring. Under strong pressure from the IMF, the government set up the Financial Restructuring Authority. By this stage, however, the crisis was forcing broader political realignments and effective policymaking ceased. On October 19, Finance Minister Badaya resigned over the reversal of a gasoline tax a mere three days after it had been announced as part of the government's IMF-backed program. On November 3, 1997, a politically crippled Prime Minister Chavalit resigned.

The Politics of Financial and Corporate Restructuring under the Chuan Government

When Chuan assembled his cabinet in November 1997 he enjoyed greater freedom of maneuver than his predecessor. Even though he still required six parties to form a coalition, he was able to insist that the Democrats occupy all the top economic positions as a precondition for forming a government, and moved quickly to strengthen the independence of the Financial Restructuring Agency (FRA). However, from the beginning, Chuan faced a more complex set of political constraints than in Korea. In addition to the problems of maintaining the coalition intact, the government also faced social protest, business opposition to the government's (and IMF's) macroeconomic policy stance, and divisions within the technocratic team itself. These factors contributed to a more gradual reform strategy than that seen in Korea, and one that relied to a greater extent on arm's length and voluntary mechanisms.

The initial financial sector strategy of the government was two-pronged. The FRA would evaluate the rehabilitation plans of the suspended finance

---

7. Like the earlier 16, this batch was given a short period in which to meet tough new capital adequacy rules, merge with stronger institutions, or go out of business.

companies and make judgments about whether they should be left open while simultaneously devising a strategy for liquidating failed ones built around the good bank-bad bank model.[8]

For the 15 banks and the 33 finance companies that initially remained open, the government's strategy was to limit access to the FIDF while substantially tightening loan classification and provisioning rules and capital adequacy requirements. These regulatory measures would force recapitalization and serve the additional purpose of diluting the control exercised by a small number of families who effectively controlled the Thai banking system. At the same time, rules governing foreign ownership were relaxed to allow greater foreign participation, thus sending the message that domestic banks should consider taking on foreign partners.[9]

A number of banks responded to these new incentives. The Thai Farmers Bank and Bangkok raised new equity through share issues, and Thai Danu Bank, Thai Farmers Bank, and the Bank of Asia took on foreign partners. However, a number of banks stood little chance of meeting the recapitalization requirements and were effectively insolvent. The BBC came under public control in December, and the capital of the bank had been dramatically written down. In February, the government took over three more ailing banks: the Siam City Bank, the First Bangkok City Bank, and the Bangkok Metropolitan Bank. In the case of the last two banks, capital was written down to practically nothing, again sending a strong signal to shareholders. However, the size of these banks—which collectively accounted for 20 percent of banking sector assets—made them difficult to close outright, and the difficulty of negotiating sales in a timely fashion, as well as the absence of buyers, seemed to foreclose the option of selling them quickly. Through its recapitalization efforts, the FIDF became the effective owner of all four, although without clear plans for their disposition. With the combination of its equity injections, recapitalization, and earlier

---

8. In early December, the FRA recommended closing permanently all but 2 of the 58 finance companies, quickly resolving a problem that had been lingering for months. In June five additional finance companies were shut down, bringing the total to 63.

9. The government also agreed to a tight timetable for the passage of other legislation that would facilitate the financial and corporate reform process, including new standards for disclosure and auditing, a revision of the bankruptcy and foreclosure laws, liberalization of rules governing foreign direct investment, and the privatization of a number of state-owned enterprises, which was designed in part to help finance the costs of bank restructuring.

liquidity support, the losses of the FIDF in the early part of the year reached 20 percent of GDP.

In summary, the initial stance of the new government toward the resolution of the financial sector's difficulties appeared decisive. The government closed down a number of ailing finance companies. In a series of 11 auctions ending in August 1999, the FRA sold off their assets, although some ended up in the hands of the government's Asset Management Company. The government faced substantial political criticism from interested parties over the low sales prices, but, in the end, the government rode out resistance to the asset sales and realized nearly US$4 billion on them, equal to 25 percent of face value. With respect to insolvent banks, the government took a tough stance with their shareholders, although it backed away from closing the banks outright and absorbed large losses as a result. This pattern is not untypical in crises of this magnitude. With respect to viable banks, the government's strategy sought to limit public expense by forcing private recapitalization and, thus, implicitly breaking the hold that a small number of banks and families had on the financial system.

However, the government's restructuring plans quickly faced both economic and political obstacles. The economic problems centered on the gradual deepening of the crisis, which cast further doubt on the balance sheets of the banks and their ability to recapitalize on their own. Moreover, the government's initial strategy did not directly address the underlying question of corporate debt restructuring. When the government did finally address the issue in June 1998, through the creation of the Corporate Debt Restructuring Advisory Committee, the approach was modeled on the London framework. However, because the reform of bankruptcy and foreclosure laws and laws governing foreign direct investment were delayed, banks and corporations had only weak incentives to engage in serious restructuring efforts. To the contrary, the regulatory forbearance extended in May and the absence of strong foreclosure law encouraged "shallow" restructurings that later proved of questionable merit.

The political difficulties facing the government were of three sorts. The opposition sought as early as January to fault the government for its slow response to the crisis, and mobilized demonstrations of social groups and nongovernmental organizations against the government. More difficult for the government was the growing chorus of complaints from the private sector and the sharp division over the strategy within the cabinet itself. The core complaint of the business lobby and the probusiness wing of the cabinet centered on the question of interest rates and the priority given to stabilizing the baht and reforming the financial sector as opposed to addressing problems in the real economy. Throughout the spring, the government faced ongoing complaints over its high interest rate polices and pressure to relax them or devise other mechanisms to ensure an increased flow of credit. The government responded by making a number of concessions to private sector demands, partly by using the state-owned banks as vehicles to increase lending to adversely affected sectors.

The fourth letter of intent of May 1998 formulated a new reform timetable to speed up the pace of reform of the financial and corporate sectors. Among its key elements, the new timetable stipulated that the banks and finance companies sign memoranda of understanding outlining their plans to meet the new provisioning and loan loss standards. As the mid-August deadline for these MOUs approached, the failure of the government to handle the banking crisis by relaxing liquidity and inducing private recapitalization became apparent. Large banks that were unwilling or unable to recapitalize early, including Krung Thai and Siam Commercial, faced severe distress.

On August 14, 1998, the government unveiled a new initiative for the banking sector. The first element of the new plan dealt with problem institutions more forcefully. The government intervened in two more banks and five finance companies and effectively nationalized pending resolution strategies while also clarifying its strategy to deal with the previously nationalized banks.[10] The second element of the program entailed regulatory forbearance to reduce tier 1 capital requirements from 6 percent to 4.5 percent.

The new strategy's centerpiece entailed a complex, and voluntary, recapitalization scheme, backed by only implicit threats if recapitalization targets were not met.[11] However, the conditions for the money were onerous. Not only would the government have to approve the banks' restructuring plans, but banks would have to adopt end-2000 provisioning requirements immediately; given nonperforming loans of 30 to 40 percent of total portfolios, this would imply an immediate write-off of shareholder capital. Moreover, the government retained its right to displace existing management.

---

10. The BBC was slated for closing, the First Bangkok City Bank for merger with the Krung Thai Bank, and Siam City and the Bangkok Metropolitan for privatization, with the government guaranteeing buyers' potential losses.

11. For tier 1 capital, the government would recapitalize up to 2.5 percent by swapping tradable bonds for preferred shares, and match any private capital up to 4.25 percent on a one-to-one basis, also granting the banks buy-back options.

Not surprisingly, banks showed little interest in the program, turning instead to a number of innovative, but high-cost, short-term instruments to meet capitalization targets: stapled limited issuance preferred stocks and capital augmented preferred shares. By relying on these instruments, bank owners effectively sidestepped the need to raise "real" capital and bought time. Although the government set aside B 300 billion for the program, it had to be modified in June, and by September only 13 percent of the funds set aside for the program had been used (World Bank 1999, p. 15).

The second component of the scheme was to support tier 2 capital and provide incentives for the banks to begin debt restructuring. The government would exchange nontradable bonds for debentures to partly offset write-offs and support new lending. The problem with this second pillar of the program was that while it was attractive to banks, the scheme was not necessarily attractive to debtors who continued to delay payment. This in turn had to do with delays in establishing a legal framework that would support the corporate workout process under the Corporate Debt Restricting Advisory Committee.

In late 1998, the politics of reform focused on a group of 11 reform bills that were conditions of the fifth letter of intent with the IMF: bankruptcy, bankruptcy court, and foreclosure; state enterprise capital; real estate property leasing, land, and condominiums; civil justice procedures; and foreign investment. Failure to pass these laws, and particularly those governing the bankruptcy and foreclosure process, adversely affected the financial and corporate restructuring process. But the existence of multiple veto gates and the influence of interested parties served to further delay the reform process.

Reform of the bankruptcy process had been an IMF condition of the second letter of intent in November 1997, but legislation proposed by the government immediately ran into strong objections from senators who would be adversely affected by the legislation, particularly the heads of two heavily indebted groups, Thai Petrochemical and NTS Steel.[12] When bankruptcy reform was first vetted in early 1998, the central objections centered on the relative powers granted to creditors and debtors in the new process, including the ability to appoint administrators and, thus, influence over the

---

12. The Senate authorizes review and amendment of legislation. If the House objects to the Senate's changes, they are mediated through a joint committee. If the joint committee fails to reach agreement, the House can nonetheless pass its version, but the review process and the publicity surrounding it provided an opportunity for senators opposed to the bill to seek concessions.

restructuring plan, and the absence of provisions that would allow debtors to remain in possession. Opponents feared that the lack of Thai insolvency experts would lead foreign creditors to appoint foreign insolvency professionals who would show less of an interest in reviving the company. The changes introduced by the Senate contributed to a bill that discouraged the bill's use. Moreover, critical accompanying legislation governing foreclosure failed to pass. Between May, when the bill was passed, and August, only five business rehabilitation plans were filed with the courts.

When the amended bills were reintroduced in the fall, the criticism in the Senate now included a range of new issues and changes that would have once again dramatically weakened the legislation.[13] The Senate also sought similar dilutions of the Bankruptcy Court law, such as reducing the power of the court to declare a firm bankrupt if the rehabilitation plan were not approved, stripping the new courts of their power to handle criminal aspects of bankruptcy, and retaining a cumbersome appeals process that had been a major factor in slowing the bankruptcy process.

In the end, the changes brought forward in the vetting process were mostly pushed aside, and the bankruptcy and foreclosure laws passed with procedural concessions to the Senate. However, the process had taken the Chuan government more than 15 months to complete, and even then concerns remained that the procedural concessions with respect to the appeals process made the bankruptcy process unwieldy (Mako 2000). Rather, private innovations through the Corporate Debt Restricting Advisory Committee provided the basis for an increase in the number of debt restructuring agreements, particularly the development of debtor creditor agreements and intercreditor agreements that defined an expedited process; allowed for information sharing, negotiations, 75 percent majority voting approval; and a mechanism of enforcement, including a thorough and expanded role for the Bank of Thailand in the process.

Politics in Thailand, therefore, exerted a powerful influence over policymaking with respect to the financial sector and corporate restructuring. Under Chavalit, there are clear signs of moral hazard related to the way the FIDF interpreted its mandate (Nukul Commission, paras. 329–40),

---

13. The proposed changes included raising the minimum debt limits, prohibiting filing bankruptcy against holders of personal guarantees—a common way to "secure" lending—and even a provision prohibiting bankruptcy suits in cases where the value of the collateral matched the amount of debt outstanding on the day the loan was made.

but the problems ran deeper. Politicians with direct interests in regulated financial institutions influenced the government's decisionmaking, delaying an effective response to the problem. Both intracoalitional and intraparty conflict frustrated the efforts of reformers. These political failings contributed directly to the onset of the crisis by weakening confidence in the Thai financial sector, and deepened it once the devaluation occurred by further delaying adjustment until the change of government.

As with the Kim Dae Jung government in Korea, the Chuan government demonstrates how a new democratic government can exploit a crisis to extend the policy reach of the technocrats. The decisiveness of the government was particularly visible in the handling of the finance companies, the establishment of the FRA, the disposition of assets, and the intervention of the four insolvent banks.

However, the government's action toward the finance companies proved the exception rather than the rule, and the government ended up being much less decisive in other areas. In recapitalizing the banks, the government made a large sum of money available and devised a scheme that would have imposed strong conditions on the banks. But the scheme was voluntary, not used extensively, and ultimately rested on substantial forbearance toward bank owners. The government was slow to move on the issue of corporate debt restructuring and in passing bankruptcy and foreclosure laws, and it was left to the private sector to devise a more coherent strategy. A number of other reforms, including laws liberalizing foreign direct investment, were also slow in coming.

Why does the Thai recovery strategy look less decisive and more prone to forbearance toward the private sector than Korea's experience? The answers can be found in a number of the political constraints outlined earlier. While Kim Dae Jung faced no serious electoral constraint until the legislative elections of April 2000, the combination of parliamentary rule and the dependence on coalition partners meant continual compromise. As the case of the bankruptcy reform shows, when compared with the early days of the Kim Dae Jung administration, Thailand had legislative processes that substantially slowed decisionmaking. While such deliberation is a legitimate function, many of the objections to the reform process clearly reflected the interests of large debtors.

Finally, the political circumstances fed into a third factor: the government's political relationship with the private sector. From the outset, the Chuan cabinet and the party were divided over a range of policies between those around Tarrin, who defended the IMF line and sought to limit government commitments to private actors, and those around Supachai and in the Senate who sought a macroeconomic stimulus, greater government intervention in support of business, and a cautious approach to reform. The very existence of this split increased the power of business, helping to explain the government's forbearance toward the private sector.

Indonesia

Of the three countries discussed here, Indonesia clearly faces the most daunting challenges of financial and corporate restructuring. However, the extent of the country's collapse seems puzzling when viewed solely from an economic vantage. Although there were clearly weaknesses in Indonesia's financial sector, the external crisis seems unlikely to have emanated from it, as was partly the case in Thailand and Korea. As late as the third quarter of 1997, financial reform was not seen as a pivotal issue for investor confidence, yet by the fourth quarter of 1997, the Indonesian banking system was in deep distress.

Any analysis of the rapid collapse of the Indonesian financial sector must begin by noting a series of misguided, if well-intentioned, government policy actions that served to dramatically increase the banking sector's problems. However, the difficulty of formulating an effective response was also influenced by politics. The highly concentrated political structure and the absence of formal checks and balances allowed Suharto to take policy initiatives quickly. Indeed, in the early days of the crisis the regime was initially praised for its decisive response to the crisis.

Over time, however, a variety of political constraints directly undermined confidence in the banking system and limited the capacity of the government to implement reform. These included political challenges that called the very survival of the regime into question, as well as the longer standing problems of close business-government relations and cronyism. Cronyism was important not only as a cause of the financial sector's difficulties, but also because it directly affected the government's efforts to manage the crisis.

The fall of Suharto and the increasingly competitive political environment provided incentives for the Habibie government to restructure the financial and corporate sectors. However, the uncertainty of the transition process also placed new pressures on the government, including populists who wanted to use the Indonesian Bank Restructuring Agency (IBRA) for redistributionist purposes. Debtors and cronies exploited the general political uncertainty and administrative weakness of the government to maintain control of their assets, and in August 1999 a major scandal demonstrated that important continuities existed with the old order.

The Political Economy of Financial Collapse under Suharto

The background to Indonesia's financial difficulties includes the combination of domestic financial liberalization and weak prudential regulation visible in Korea and Thailand, but with several important differences. First, the financial deregulation in 1983 and 1988 allowed industrial groups to acquire banking operations, with corresponding problems of intragroup lending. A second difference is the extent to which foreign borrowing was intermediated through the financial sector. Because Indonesia has long had a fairly open capital account, corporations were able to borrow offshore directly. When the rupiah fell, the debt servicing costs of unhedged foreign liabilities created profound problems for Indonesian corporations, with important implications for the domestic banking sector.

As the rupiah fell, the central bank adopted—quite independently of the IMF—a contractionary monetary and fiscal stance in an effort to support the currency. Lending to the property and construction sectors dried up, and with assets in the property sector sharply devalued, the banking sector was soon in serious difficulty. After turning to the IMF in October, the government devised a strategy for the banking system that included regulatory reform and the rehabilitation of state-owned banks on the assumption it would stop uncertainty, restore confidence in the banking system as a whole, and stimulate the flow of deposits and interbank lending.

On November 1, the government closed 16 smaller banks with 450 branches accounting for about 3 percent of total banking system assets. Several of the banks were controlled by relatives or cronies, which had the advantage of showing the government's evenhandedness and resolve. Notwithstanding the logic behind this strategy, it failed dramatically (see, for example, McLeod 1998). Part of the problem centered on the mishandling of the question of guarantees. However, the problem with the bank closings was also political. The decision to close the 16 banks was challenged by Suharto's second son, Bambang Trihatmodjo, and his half-brother, Probosutedjo, who even went so far as to file lawsuits against the minister of finance and governor of the central bank.

The government's program for the rehabilitation of the banking sector was formally unveiled on January 27. While it contained a number of important reform initiatives, their implementation was affected by the full range of political constraints outlined earlier: a brief reelection campaign, mounting demonstrations against the government strikes, and the formation of a cabinet that included close business associates and members of the Suharto family.

The most important institutional innovation in the new package was the establishment of the IBRA. The IBRA and the Bank Indonesia (BI) ordered full reviews of assets and contingent liabilities to assess the extent of the losses in the banking system, which were to be borne by shareholders and subordinated debt holders and only then by the government under the guarantee scheme. As in Thailand, the government sought to force a consolidation of the banking sector by announcing ambitious new capitalization requirements. In early March, the BI also toughened regulations on the use of BI rediscount facilities, on banks breaching the minimum reserve requirements, and on loan loss provisions (Johnson 1998, pp. 50–51).

Finally, the question arose of how to manage the private sector's quite substantial offshore debt. In contrast to Korea and Thailand, banks accounted for only US$8.6 billion of the US$66.3 billion offshore debt. At the time of the bank reform in January, the government made it clear that it had no intention of using public finances to solve the offshore debt problem. Rather, it would help organize a voluntary framework based on committees of creditors (the steering committee) and debtors (the contact committee). At the same time, however, the head of the government task force said that borrowers unable to meet their obligations should temporarily cease doing so. With no apparent government support for the process, and even encouragement to cease payment, borrowers had little incentive to service their obligations, stalling negotiations.

Shortly after the January initiatives, a period of deterioration set in between Indonesia, the IMF, and creditor countries, centered primarily on the controversial proposal to launch a currency board. An electoral constraint also operated in anticipation of Suharto's indirect election on March 10, and Suharto's public positions on a number of issues hardened. In early March, the IMF, the World Bank, and the Asian Development Bank all suspended disbursements, citing doubts about the government's commitment to the program. Suharto denounced the IMF and suggested that some of the reforms might be unconstitutional. In early March, the head of the IBRA was replaced, casting doubt on its independence, and on March 14 Suharto announced a new cabinet that generally diminished the role of the technocrats.

After the election and installation of the new cabinet, the government sought a rapprochement with the IMF. Corporate and financial restructuring played a central role in the new program announced in April. The most important departure from the IMF's previous approach was its willingness to consider government involvement and assistance in solving the private sector's foreign debt problem, although negotiations with creditors would not be completed until after the change of government. The new program also contained a series of important legal reforms that would undergird the restructuring effort, all to be completed under tight deadlines: revision of the bankruptcy law, establishment of a new commercial court, the introduction of regulations governing mergers and acquisitions, and a new antimonopoly law.

The IBRA and the BI also announced how banks with outstanding credits to the government would be managed, ranging from IBRA supervision to replacement of management to outright closure. Using these criteria, and responding to yet another series of bank runs in early April, the IBRA suspended and nationalized seven small banks. It also assumed management of seven others (six private and one public). These seven banks were substantially more important and included two of the largest private Indonesian banks, Danamon and Bank Dagang Nasional Indonesia, which together made up 20 percent of the banking system's assets and 75 percent of the total liquidity support. Crony banks were also included: Bob Hasan's Bank Umum Nasional and two banks controlled by Suharto's cousin Sudwikatmono and one by Hasjim Djojohadikusumo, the brother of General Prabowo. The credibility of these efforts was further enhanced when the government issued Rp 155 trillion in bonds to IBRA for restructuring purposes in mid-April.

In anticipation of the next IMF review, the government announced a number of agreed-upon policy measures on April 22, including revision of the bankruptcy law and establishment of the commercial court. At this point, demonstrations against the government increased dramatically, triggered by dramatic price increases on a number of consumer goods on May 1. The severity of the challenge to the regime not only derailed the reform process, but it also had a more direct effect on the banking system. In the riots of May 13–14 in Jakarta, the Bank Central Asia, the largest private Indonesian bank, experienced looting at 122 of its branches; the bank was 70 percent owned by Salim, one of Suharto's closest cronies, and 30 percent by two of Suharto's children. Bank runs followed the looting, and the BI was once again forced to intervene to back up the banking system with large liquidity supports.

The Struggle over Assets under Habibie

The new Habibie administration operated under a number of political constraints. First, the government and ruling party faced strong electoral challenges from a variety of new parties leading up to the general elections of June 1999. Habibie also confronted a variety of nonelectoral challenges, any number of which threatened his tenure, including splits with the military, serious ethnic and community violence, and continuing prodemocracy and student protests. Institutional arrangements also became more complex as the cabinet and legislature sought to assert their prerogatives with respect to financial and corporate restructuring.

In addition, while the political position of the cronies was devalued by the fall of Suharto, the general political uncertainty and sheer extent of the country's banking and corporate sector problems provided ample opportunities for continuing corruption and for banks and debtors to resist government initiatives. Moreover, Habibie had his own connections to the private sector, and the ruling party's dependence on business for the funding of its political activities even increased in importance.

At the same time, the government had to contend with a conflicting set of populist pressures. These pressures arose from a variety of political forces that saw advantages in exploiting the crisis to squeeze Chinese asset holders and to use the financial and corporate restructuring process to advance ethnic redistribution (Schwartz 1999, pp. 414–19). At the People's Consultative Assembly in November, the government succeeded in deflecting language that would have instituted a Malaysian-style redistributive program, but such ideas received support from indigenous business groups who stood to profit directly from preferential distribution of IBRA's assets.

Against this array of constraints, Habibie faced strong pressure from the IMF and had his own political incentives to differentiate himself from his predecessor. In particular, political competition increased public pressure on the government to investigate Suharto's wealth and pursue firms and individuals who had profited from close ties to the Suharto government. The result of these conflicting political pressures was a highly politicized reform process that gradually increased pressure on bad debtors before the parliamentary elections, but was also characterized by delays, irregularities, and limited success in recovering assets.

In his August 16 Independence Day speech, Habibie announced his four economic priorities: cleaning up the banking sector, resolving the debt problem, eliminating monopolies, and increasing transparency. Given the further deterioration that occurred as a direct result of the political crisis, addressing the problems in the banking sector was clearly the government's top priority, and in August the government outlined a major package of banking legislation.

The package included a number of measures, but its central feature was a program that combined recapitalization with more aggressive action against weak banks and their clients. The BI-ordered audits—to be completed by October—were to be used to divide the banks into three categories. Category A banks had a capital adequacy ratio greater than 4 percent (62 banks). Category B banks had ratios lower than 4 percent and greater than –25 percent (66 banks). Category C had capital adequacy ratios greater than –25 percent (38 banks). Banks in category A were deemed temporarily sound, but called upon to raise capital to 8 percent in three years. Category B banks were eligible to participate in the recapitalization program. The government would inject up to 80 percent of the capital required to reach the stipulated capital adequacy requirement of 4 percent in the form of government bonds, but only under strict conditions.[14] The presumption was that some of the category B banks and most of the category C banks faced closure if they failed to raise adequate capital.[15]

The big exception to the rule was the government's continuing commitment to six state and 15 provincial banks. Although all fell into category C, all were to be recapitalized. The key political issue with respect to the state banks was not only whether they would be retained or privatized, but whether the government and the IBRA could collect on nonperforming loans or seize assets in compensation for them. The state banks became a central conduit for resources for politically favored parties and projects under Suharto, and the rate of nonperforming loans in state banks was extraordinarily high.

With losses mounting, the negotiation of a new letter of intent with the IMF in November sought to commit the government to announce the result of the audits on the banks and to move forward with the recapitalization

---

14. Banks seeking recapitalization were required to submit a business plan showing that the owners were capable of meeting their share of the initial recapitalization and a schedule for higher capital-adequacy ratios. The plan also required that the banks' owners fully absorb the losses arising from loans extended to affiliated parties, and that all bank obligations obtained from the BI's liquidity support be transferred to IBRA, which would convert them into equity or subordinated loans.

15. Category C banks were required to raise their capital adequacy ratio above –25 percent within a month of completion of due diligence and would be required to produce a business plan bringing their share of intergroup lending to less than 20 percent and their capital adequacy ratios to 8 percent by the end of 1999. These banks clearly had strong interests in seeing the implementation of the program delayed.

program by the end of January. However, the program immediately ran into a series of delays, reversals, and irregularities centering on the question of whether the marginal category B and C banks would gain access to government money. The IMF even threatened disbursement to guarantee that a number of weak banks would indeed close.

On March 13, the government finally announced it intended to close 38 domestic private commercial banks (21 category B and 17 category C), nationalizing 7 and recapitalizing 9 subject to their ability to raise adequate capital by April 21. Eight of the nine made the deadline. Although the plan was hailed as a breakthrough, questions were raised not only about those banks that the government chose to recapitalize, but about the closed and nationalized banks as well. Some cronies and Suharto family members lost their banks, and the government initiated a process of investigation into whether the bank failures were the result of irregularities. However, the government had not proved effective in resolving the banks that it had previously closed.

The fate of the seven larger banks that came under IBRA management proved even more complex. Of the seven, three were suspended (Bank Dayang Nasional Indonesia, Bank Umum Nasional, and Bank Modern), while the other four (Bank Danamon, Bank PDFCI, Bank Tiara, and Bank Central Asia) were to be retained by the government with the intention of restructuring their capital. However, the owners of four of the larger banks accounting for the overwhelming share of all liquidity assistance—Bank Central Asia, Danamon, BDNI, and Bank Umum Nasional—expressed a willingness to strike deals with the government by providing funds and other assets and stretching out the deadline for repayment of liquidity credits. Given that much of the banks' bad lending was to affiliated companies, the government set a condition that the funds and assets provided must cover both the BI's liquidity support and all credits extended to their groups. But given the limited administrative resources of IBRA, the deals held out the possibility that owners might not only continue to control their banks but also their nominally pledged assets.

The nationalization list was also controversial. Nationalization was justified on the grounds that closure of the banks would have adverse effects on the payments system. Nationalization implied that owners would lose control over their assets, and the boards of a number of the banks were purged. However, liquidation would have arguably led to a faster unraveling of the troubled banks' loans and seizure of collateral. Among those nationalized were Bakrie Group's Bank Kusa Nasional, owned by Aburizal Bakrie, head of the Indonesian Chamber of Commerce and a member of

Habibie's board of advisors, and Bank Duta, whose majority was held by one of Suharto's foundations. Both had heavily exceeded related-party credit limits, and both were expected to have negative returns on equity and capital adequacy ratios by the end of 2001.

However, the biggest test for the IBRA was whether it could recover on the accumulating portfolio of assets it held. These assets included those pledged as a result of negotiations with seven major groups over repayment of liquidity credits as well as the bad debts the government held from state banks, and those private banks either closed, nationalized, or recapitalized. In February, Habibie signaled his commitment to recover assets by extending the life of the IBRA for four years and placing it on a more firm legal footing. The agency was also granted quite substantial and controversial quasi-judicial powers to seize assets and to cancel commercial contracts that were thought to impose losses on the IBRA.

In the period before and after the June elections, the government came under increasing pressure from the opposition to aggressively pursue bad debtors. The process began with an effort to identify the largest 20 debtors to the state-owned banks, which accounted for more than half of those banks' nonperforming loans, and to initiate a debt restructuring program with them. These debtors included well-connected business people and some of Suharto's children. IBRA and the banks also began releasing lists of the largest debtors from the nonstate banks and held a high-level meeting with the largest debtors to exploit their political vulnerability—including their identity as Chinese—and to pressure them to sign "letters of commitment" by June 22. These letters would include an agreement for transparency, allowance of IBRA audits, a proposition for a restructuring plan, and agreement to divestments when debtors lacked cash to make repayments. If such agreements were not reached by August 30, the government threatened to take "unpopular steps." By June 22, 173 of the 200 had signed the letters and the government was threatening litigation against the rest.

However, the signed letters of commitment were only the first step in the recovery process. An even more challenging task was how to move from the restructuring of the banks to the task of corporate restructuring. One positive effect of the change of government was the establishment of a framework for the workout of corporate foreign debt. Following the successful conclusion of negotiations with foreign creditors, the government established the Indonesian Debt Restructuring Agency on July 2, which allows debtors to convert their foreign-denominated obligations into rupiah ones—thus removing exchange risk—and shifting the burden of foreign exchange payments to the Indonesian Debt Restructuring Agency.

The framework to facilitate and encourage voluntary corporate debt restructurings was announced on September 9, 1998. The so-called Jakarta initiative was designed to provide a framework for out-of-court negotiations, overseen by the Jakarta Initiative Task Force.[16] The government tried to jump-start the process by making the Indonesian government's investment banking arm, PT Persero Danareksa, a test case by restructuring US$438 million, but by late 1999 only three other major cases were moving through the process.

As in Thailand, the progress of the private restructuring exercise was partly influenced by the bankruptcy process. Unlike Thailand, the problems in the process did not arise in the legislation of the reform. The new law was passed quickly under the Suharto government and contained all of the features that the IMF had sought when making it a condition of the third letter of intent. The problem, rather, was in the weakness of the courts. In the first six months, the bankruptcy court consistently ruled in favor of insolvent business groups in a series of decisions highly confusing to lawyers. In the first six months, fewer than one-third of the 50 petitions filed with the Jakarta Commercial Court actually led to bankruptcies. In a number of cases, the results appeared to rest on a weak understanding of the law, but others appeared to reflect political judgements about the undesirability of liquidation and foreign acquisitions, if not outright bribery.

Despite the importance of these informal mechanisms, it is clear that the major vehicle for corporate restructuring will perforce be the government itself, because it had come to control 78 percent of the banking sector's total assets. To manage these assets, the IBRA set up 5 holding companies managing 200 companies. Although these assets are pledged to IBRA and IBRA exercises shareholders' rights until debts are repaid, owners continue to manage the companies. Approximately US$14.3 billion or Rp 96 trillion are in 216 companies with another Rp 22 trillion in bank loans, half backed by nonproperty assets. However, by August 1999, less than 1 percent of all of the assets IBRA had acquired had been sold.

When compared with the other countries under IMF programs, Indonesia clearly lags in bank restructuring and recapitalization, corporate debt

---

16. The Jakarta Initiative Task Force had the ability to obtain and develop information on companies to be restructured, help design restructuring action plans, facilitate negotiations and encourage participation of creditors and debtors, and speed regulatory approvals for restructurings in progress. The task force could also recommend that the public prosecutor file bankruptcy proceedings against particular debtors if they were deemed to be stripping assets or showed a lack of good faith.

restructuring, and restructuring or disposing of acquired assets. This is, in part, a result of the fact that Indonesia's problems have been much more severe than in the other countries, but the depth of the country's difficulties can also be traced in part to politics. Difficulties in passing and implementing reforms have been affected by elections and nonelectoral challenges, and particularly by the ability of private sector actors to exploit generalized political uncertainty to evade reform.

Conclusion

This chapter attempts to identify some of the main tasks associated with the management of systemic distress and to explain some of the differences that have emerged across the three countries that have fallen under IMF programs.

The first set of points has to do with how democracies and dictatorships fare. Delays caused by electoral and nonelectoral pressures, decisionmaking structures with multiple veto gates, and rent seeking are certainly not absent from democracies, but democracies have the capacity to correct at least some of these weaknesses by monitoring corrupt business-government relations and bringing new reformist governments to office. New democratic governments can be decisive, particularly if they enjoy broad popular and legislative support. These differences can be seen between the Kim Young Sam and Kim Dae Jung governments in Korea and between the Chavalit and Chuan governments in Thailand.

As the case of Indonesia suggests, authoritarian governments may be decisive, but are hardly immune from destabilizing political challenges nor from rent seeking and close business-government relations. Indeed, because of the high level of discretion and low level of transparency, they may be particularly prone to weaknesses in financial regulation and corporate governance. This suggests that some important, but poorly understood, parallels and linkages exist between an accountable and transparent political system and accountable and transparent systems of financial regulation and corporate governance. One important link is that government commitments to private sector actors have strong implications for how firms behave. Without the capacity to monitor those business-government relations, the public is likely to pay the cost of rent seeking, weak regulation, moral hazard, and forbearance.

The cases also shed some light on the role that independent agencies can play in the reform process. In the short run, they can serve to reduce the problems caused by multiple veto gates and private sector resistance.

However, it is important not to confuse cause and effect. The power of the FSC in Korea was ultimately grounded in some base of political, legislative, and party support. The means for providing such support have been lacking in Indonesia; the relative weakness of IBRA is not just administrative but political as well.

Finally, the cases suggest an important trade-off. This study has emphasized on the values of decisiveness during crises: the need to take wide-ranging actions that alter the policy status quo, even in the face of resistance from particular interests. Democracies are perfectly capable of undertaking such tasks, but may be tempted by crisis to achieve their objectives by means not fully grounded in the law or existing property rights. These risks clearly exist in Korea, where a number of government edicts, such as the Big Deals, lacked any clear legal foundation. The reform process thus underlines perennial tradeoffs in democratic governance between the advantages of institutional arrangements that favor decisiveness over deliberation. These tradeoffs must be continually addressed through the democratic process.

References

Alesina, Alberto, Gerald D. Cohen, and Nouriel Roubini. 1997. *Political Cycles and the Macroeconomy.* Cambridge: Massachusetts Institute of Technology Press.

Baker, Chris, and Phongpaichit Pasuk. 1998. *Thailand's Boom and Bust.* Bangkok: Silkworm Books.

Claessens, Stijn, Simeon Djankov, and Daniela Klingebiel. 1999. "Financial Restructuring in East Asia: Halfway There?" Financial Sector Discussion Paper No. 3. World Bank, Washington D.C.

Chang, Ha-Joon. 1999. "The Hazard of Moral Hazard: Untangling the Asian Crisis." Paper presented at the American Economic Association Annual Meeting, January 3–6, New York.

Haggard, Stephan. 2000. *The Politics of the Asian Financial Crisis.* Washington D.C.: Institute for International Economics.

Haggard, Stephan, and Mathew McCubbins. Forthcoming. *Presidents, Parliaments, and Policy.* New York: Cambridge University Press.

Haggard, Stephan, and Steven B. Webb, eds. 1994. *Voting for Reform.* New York: Oxford University Press.

Hicken, Allen. 1999. "Parties, Politics, and Patronage: Governance and Growth in Thailand." University of California, San Diego. Processed.

Johnson, Colin. 1998. "Survey of Recent Developments," *Bulletin of Indonesian Economic Studies* 34(2): 50–51.

Jung, Young Seok, and William P. Mako. 2000. "Korea: Financial Stabilization and Initial Corporate Restructuring." World Bank, Washington, D.C. Processed.

Klingebiel, Daniela. 2000. "The Use of Asset Management Companies in the Resolution of Banking Crises: Cross-Country Experiences." Policy Research Working Paper no. 2284, World Bank, Washington, D.C.

Lieberman, Ira. 1999. "Korea: Corporate Restructuring." Paper presented to the Korea Economic Institute, Korean Economic Working Group, June 8, Washington D.C.

MacIntyre, Andrew. 1999. "Political Institutions and the Economic Crisis in Thailand and Indonesia." In T. J. Pempel, ed., *The Politics of the Asian Economic Crisis*. Ithaca, New York: Cornell University Press.

Mako, William P. 2000. "The Thai Case." World Bank, Washington, D.C. Processed.

McLeod, Ross. 1998. "Indonesia," In R. McLeod and R. Garnaut, eds., *East Asia in Crisis: From Being A Miracle to Needing One,* London: Routledge.

Ministry of Finance and Economy. 1998. The Korea Forum.

Nukul Commission Report. 1998. *Analysis and Evaluation on Facts behind Thailand's Economic Crisis* (English language edition). Bangkok: Nation Publishers.

Schwartz, Adam. 1999. *A Nation in Waiting: Indonesia's Search for Stability,* 2nd ed. St. Leonards, Australia: Allen and Unwin.

Tsebelis, George. 1995. "Decision Making in Political Systems: Veto Players in Presidentialism, Parliamentarism, Multicameralism, and Multipartyism," *British Journal of Political Science* 25(3): 289–325.

World Bank. 1998. *East Asia: Road to Recovery*. Washington, D.C.

_____. 1999. *Thailand Economic Monitor*. Washington, D.C.

12

The Role of Cross-Border Mergers and Acquisitions in Asian Restructuring

Ashoka Mody and Shoko Negishi, World Bank

Cross-border merger and acquisition (M&A) activity has been on the rise worldwide, driving the upsurge in foreign direct investment (FDI) over the past decade, and especially over the past few years. While industrialized countries account for a dominant 90 percent share of the value of world cross-border M&As, in developing countries in East Asia and Latin America, the value of cross-border M&As has been rising significantly. The benefits of such M&A activity remain controversial. However, by enhancing the competition for corporate control, mergers can improve efficiency. Some studies show that acquisitions can be especially useful for restructuring underperforming firms.

Before-and-after comparisons of the cash-flow returns of acquired firms indicate that acquisitions bring higher wealth gains for insolvent firms than for firms under independent workout and that those gains are higher in cross-border transactions than in domestic M&As. At the same time, mergers can destroy value where projected synergies do not materialize or corporate cultures clash (see *The Economist* 2000; Ghemawat and Ghadar 2000).

We are grateful to Richard Newfarmer and others at the Foreign Investment Advisory Service/Poverty Reduction and Economic Management (PREM) Network seminar series. The research was partially funded by the Growth Thematic Group of the PREM network. The views expressed here are those of the authors and not necessarily those of the World Bank.

In this context, cross-border mergers in the East Asian crisis countries are of special interest.[1] Though financial reengineering of corporate debt, including government-sponsored voluntary workout schemes, has made progress, severely distressed firms, particularly in the nontradable sectors, have been compelled to seek buyers for their assets. The governments of the Republic of Korea and Thailand, in particular, have introduced a series of policy reforms to create a better environment for foreign investment and domestic and cross-border M&As to enhance asset reallocation.

In this paper, we will examine empirical evidence of the sectoral patterns of cross-border M&A activity and their relationship to recovery in East Asia. The main findings show that cross-border M&A activity has occurred primarily in the most distressed sectors. Insufficient evidence exists to suggest "fire sales" of distressed assets. We do not find evidence of immediate contributions of cross-border M&As to the restructuring of the troubled economies. The most significant role for cross-border M&As, therefore, lies ahead in longer-term processes, such as operational restructuring and reallocation of assets.

Cross-Border M&A: Trends, Motives, and Impacts

This section reports on cross-border M&A trends and, in particular, compares them with trends in FDI. Before doing so, however, it is important to note that cross-border M&A is a form of FDI. The balance of payment data do not distinguish between M&A and "greenfield" FDI (new projects). As a result, the comparison must be made based on reported values of cross-border M&As; these reported values, unfortunately, include amounts that are not components of the balance of payment reporting of FDI data. As such, the two series cannot be directly compared. The amount recorded as FDI refers to funds channeled through the capital account of a country in relation to both M&A and new projects; these transferred amounts can be equity, reinvested earnings, or intercompany debt (that is, debt issued by the parent to the subsidiary company). In contrast, cross-border M&A data refer to transaction values. If, for example, the foreign acquiring company raises debt within the domestic market to purchase the target company, that amount is also included in the reported values. In practice, such amounts are not likely to be large. Additionally, and perhaps more

---

1. All statistical references to cross-border mergers and acquisitions in this paper involve acquisitions of greater than 50 percent equity stakes from foreign investors unless otherwise noted.

importantly, the acquiring company may borrow internationally to finance the purchase of the target company. Unlike domestic debt, such international debt financing does represent a transfer of resources to the recipient country. However, the comparison with FDI flows breaks down because, as noted, those flows include only intercompany debt. In practice, judging the importance of even this difference is difficult. With respect to FDI, the possibility also exists that the international firm may borrow internationally and then on-lend to its foreign subsidiary.

Cross-border M&As have increased significantly in industrialized and developing countries over the past decade. Although developing countries' share of cross-border M&As is still small relative to that of industrialized countries, transactions in East Asia, such as postcrisis asset sales, and in Latin America, primarily through privatization, have led an upsurge among developing countries. Korea and Thailand in particular have attracted large quantities of M&A activity since 1997. In analyzing these flows, distinguishing between two different motives for M&A activity is helpful; these motives are creating opportunities for the future (strategic partnering) and resolving past problems (corporate restructuring). Most M&A activity occurring in developed countries takes place in industries under competitive pressure as a result of deregulation, technological renovation, or large research and development expenditures, and is thus intended for strategic repositioning. In developing countries, cross-border M&As can immediately provide liquidity and prevent asset losses and enhance resource allocation. In the long term, M&As potentially introduce new management and operation systems, thereby improving efficiency and competitiveness.

Trends and Principal Sectoral Characteristics

According to data assembled by the United Nations Conference on Trade and Development, global cross-border acquisitions (in which foreign purchasers acquire greater than 10 percent stakes) reached US$720 billion in 1999, up 35 percent from US$532 billion in 1998, whereas the majority cross-border M&A value was US$411 billion.[2] Despite the rise in dollar values, developing country M&A declined from US$81 billion (15 percent of total

---

2. The United Nations Conference on Trade and Development introduced new statistics for acquisitions with greater than 10 percent stakes, which are more comparable with FDI statistics. We do not have information for 1999 according to this definition and hence no comparison is made with those statistics that are based on majority acquisitions involving greater than 50 percent stakes.

M&A) in 1998 to US$63 billion (9 percent) in 1999. Cross-border M&As in developing countries grew at an annual average rate of 81 percent during the 1991–99 period, compared with 26 percent annual average growth of FDI flows in developing countries. These decade averages, however, mask the sharp jumps in recent years, such as the 132 percent increase recorded in 1996–97.

Within developing countries, Latin America has been the largest target region of cross-border M&As, most of which have taken place through privatization programs (figure 12.1). Though smaller in M&A size, East Asia has had the fastest M&A growth, at an annual average rate of 106 percent (table 12.1). Unlike in Latin America, cross-border M&A activity in East Asia has occurred largely through sales of private firms.

The recent cross-border M&As in industrialized countries, and to a lesser extent in developing countries, are characterized by large-scale transactions (Ghemawat and Ghadar 2000). Some enormous deals in industrialized economies in 1999 included acquisitions of AirTouch Communications of the United States by Vodafone Group PLC in the United Kingdom for US$65.9 billion and Atlantic Richfield Company of the United States by British Petroleum Amoco PLC in the United Kingdom for US$33.7 billion. Large transactions in developing countries, notably in Latin America, have been closely related to privatization projects, such as the sale of Brazil's national

Figure 12.1.   *World Cross-Border Mergers and Acquisitions, 1991–99*[a]

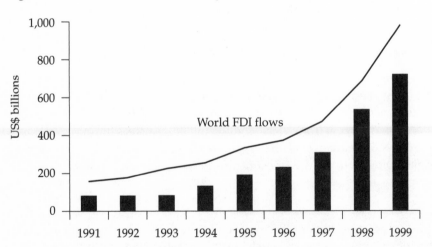

a. Involves acquisitions of a more than 10 percent equity.
Source: World Bank (2000); UNCTAD (2000).

Table 12.1. *Cross-Border Mergers and Acquisitions in Developing Countries*
(US$ billions)

Region	1991	1992	1993	1994	1995	1996	1997	1998
East Asia and the Pacific								
FDI	14.3	22.0	39.1	45.1	52.0	59.9	64.1	64.2
M&A	0.2	0.3	1.2	2.1	1.3	2.0	6.7	10.1
Europe and Central Asia								
FDI	3.4	4.6	6.3	7.0	16.9	15.8	22.8	24.4
M&A	1.1	3.9	2.4	2.4	4.3	2.1	7.8	1.9
Latin America and the Caribbean								
FDI	12.8	15.0	13.7	28.4	29.8	43.6	64.7	69.3
M&A	1.0	6.1	3.8	3.1	6.0	11.2	25.6	31.2
Middle East and North Africa								
FDI	2.8	3.6	3.8	3.4	−0.2	3.3	5.9	5.1
M&A	0.0	0.3	0.2	0.4	0.03	0.2	1.1	1.2
South Asia								
FDI	0.4	0.8	1.1	1.6	3.0	3.5	4.9	3.7
M&A	0.05	0.01	0.1	0.4	0.2	0.2	0.3	0.8
Sub-Saharan Africa								
FDI	1.6	1.6	1.9	3.4	4.2	4.7	7.7	4.4
M&A	0.08	0.07	0.5	0.1	0.3	3.0	1.6	1.5
Developing countries total								
FDI	35.3	47.5	66.0	88.9	105.6	130.8	170.3	170.9
M&A	2.4	10.8	8.2	8.5	12.1	18.6	43.2	46.8

Note: Involves acquisitions of a more than 50 percent equity.
Source: World Bank (2000); UNCTAD (2000).

telecommunications service company Telebras for US$19 billion in 1998 and Argentina's petroleum company YPF SA for US$19 billion in 1999.

What Drives M&A?

M&A activity creates competition for corporate control, which is motivated by both private and regulatory incentives. Private incentives include imperfections and asymmetries in domestic product and capital markets (Caves 1971; Froot and Stein 1991; Hymer 1976; Kindleberger 1969), competitive environment of the market, and differences in tax systems (Scholes and Wolfson 1990). Imperfections and costs motivate firms to pursue M&As to capitalize on monopoly rents or internalize operations. Regulatory incentives include variations in corporate governance (Jensen 1986) and policy frameworks geared toward foreign investment (a comprehensive summary of the literature is provided in Kang 1993). Management that acts in its own interest may cause financial losses to shareholders, which provides a potential for other firms to intervene. Liberalization of foreign entry and ownership opens up more opportunities for cross-border M&A activity.

Although the distinction is not always clearcut, M&A activity can be broadly classified into two categories. In the first category, M&As are mainly motivated by past problems, and attempts are made to create value through restructuring. The second form of M&A is characterized by looking forward and seeking to create value through creative partnerships. Negative features of M&A arise if the first type is driven by distressed firms engaging in fire sales, and the second type of M&A is triggered by firms seeking market monopoly. In both cases, mismanagement may destroy shareholder value.

The upsurge of M&As in the United States in the 1980s reflected the need to revitalize domestic firms and expose them to a new reality of increased global competition. Acquisitions by foreign firms took place in significant numbers. During the 1985–89 period, the value of foreign acquisitions of U.S. firms amounted to more than US$170 billion, 17 percent of total U.S. takeover activity (Harris and Ravenscraft 1991). Japan was one of the major investors, with a US$13 billion outlay in 1988 for acquisitions of 132 U.S. firms (Kang 1993). Motivated largely by the value of restructuring acquired firms, these early U.S. M&As were similar to the M&As in postcrisis East Asia. In U.S. M&As of the 1980s, the firms were under competitive pressure to rationalize and raise profitability, whereas East Asian firms have been struggling to recover from severe financial distress and improve their long-term competitiveness.

In contrast, incentives for strategic partnerships to share costs of the innovation process and extend product variety have largely driven recent megamergers. Strategic partnering through M&As can lead to new forms of oligopolistic competition based on knowledge networks. Strategic M&A activity can increase the operational flexibility of firms to meet new demands that are constantly generated under the continuous process of innovation (UNCTAD 1999). The sectoral examples of M&A demonstrate the pressures for consolidation and rationalization of assets. The telecommunication and banking industries, having gone through a series of deregulatory measures, are dealing with a complex mix of greater competition arising from technological change and the need to supply a worldwide market. Similarly, the oil and chemical industries are facing the challenge of technological renovation. Firms in the pharmaceutical industry, a major target of M&As in industrialized countries, rely heavily on research and development, which makes strategic mergers advantageous. As these examples show, globalization heightens competition, which forces firms to rationalize internal resources, increase access to wider markets, and achieve economies of scale through M&As. Meanwhile, internationalization of operation, management, and financial assets can make firms more resistant to external shocks and volatility as a result of rapid globalization in developing countries.

In developing countries also, deregulation and liberalization of trade and services has opened up more opportunities to foreign investors. However, this first stage of M&A is being driven either by the need to significantly upgrade state-owned enterprises through privatization, or by M&As of troubled private firms.

Exchange rate depreciations and lower domestic asset prices, providing foreign investors with greater scope for acquiring assets, have driven increased M&A activity in economies afflicted with crises. Meanwhile, policy frameworks geared toward foreign entry have been liberalized in those economies. However, domestic firms are faced with large debt repayments and rising interest rates and are thereby forced to restructure. This has particularly been the case for firms in the nontradable sectors that do not benefit much from the export growth resulting from currency depreciation. For some financially troubled firms the only alternative to bankruptcy has been to sell assets. This has led to a concern in East Asia that the current wave of cross-border M&As represents fire sales of domestic assets, which will result in substantial transfer of domestic wealth to foreigners and few prospects for restructuring the troubled sectors.

Benefits of M&A

We focus here on two questions. First, are cross-border M&As different from domestic M&As? Second, do M&As play a special role in restructuring?

CROSS-BORDER M&A. Whether cross-border M&As bring benefits to host countries has not yet been empirically proven. Consolidation and rationalization of resources as a result of M&As—domestic or cross-border—can resolve overcapacity and improve efficiency. However, the immediate impact of M&A activity may be negative because consolidation and rationalization result in reduced employment and possibly reduced competition.

Cross-border M&A activity can be beneficial to a host country when it prevents potentially profitable assets from being wiped out, which is specifically true of M&As involving either privatization of state-owned enterprises in transition economies or sales of financially distressed firms in developing countries. Highly indebted, loss-making companies—state-owned or private—often have no option but to become insolvent unless external resources can sufficiently finance them; given domestic financial constraints, most of these resources probably come from foreign investors. Various examples from the transition economies in Central and Eastern Europe suggest that privatization-related cross-border M&As have played a key role in restructuring domestic firms. A study of the Czech Republic, Hungary, and Poland done in 1992–95 indicates that foreign investment enterprises were more likely to invest, were more export-oriented, and were also faster in restructuring than domestic firms (Hunya 1997).

Other evidence suggests that in Hungary's banking sector, where a major privatization program has been completed, foreign investors have provided technical expertise and financial support and have demonstrated greater independence from domestic political influence than domestic firms. Moreover, the new entry of foreign investors into the retail market of the banking sector has increased competition, thereby promoting the development of innovative services and improving personnel training and marketing (World Bank 1999a).

However, empirical analyses of mergers and acquisitions and corporate restructuring are limited because of the lack of financial information for acquired firms. Financial information of firms whose majority stake is acquired by other operating firms is usually replaced with the consolidated information the acquirers produce shortly after the transactions are completed. Therefore few studies examine the long-term impact of M&A activity on restructuring. Before-and-after comparisons of short-term stock returns of acquired U.S. firms suggest that cross-border M&As bring greater wealth gains than domestic transactions. A comparative study of 1,273 U.S. firms acquired by foreign and domestic firms during the 1970–87 period shows that wealth gains for target firms one to four days after the announcement of mergers (approximated by cumulative abnormal stock returns) are about 10 percentage points higher in cross-border transactions than in domestic acquisitions (Harris and Ravenscraft 1991). Similarly, a study of Japanese M&A activity in the United States during the 1975–88 period concluded that the sale of a majority stake to Japanese firms leads to significantly higher returns than the sale of a majority interest to U.S. firms (Kang 1993).

ROLE IN RESTRUCTURING. Some evidence suggests that M&As can facilitate efficient redeployment of insolvent firms' assets in the longer term. Hotchkiss and Mooradian (1998) focused on the postmerger performance of 55 insolvent firms that were acquired by other operating firms and compared them with nonbankruptcy transactions. The study found that postmerger cash-flow returns of acquired insolvent firms improved in the first and second years by about 6 percent per year, whereas postmerger cash-flow returns of nonbankrupt firms showed no statistically significant improvements. The authors also suggested that potential sources of operating gains for acquired insolvent firms were reductions in operating expenses.[3]

In the long term, however, not only can M&As induce new investment, domestic and foreign, by acquirers and their suppliers, but they can also introduce new managerial, production, and marketing resources to target firms, thereby improving efficiency and productivity (UNCTAD 1999). Eventual integration with the corporate networks of the acquirers can further

---

3. Blumberg and Owers (1996) produced a study of 344 cross-border and domestic M&A transactions of U.S. firms that took place during the 1980–90 period. The study showed that significantly high cumulative abnormal returns in cross-border acquisitions were also observed in domestic transactions.

expand opportunities. Moreover, cross-border M&As bring foreign exchange and help the developing host countries fill gaps in their current accounts.

East Asian Financial Distress and Recovery

In the more than two years since the onset of the East Asian crisis, strong cyclical recovery has started to take place. However, large parts of the corporate and financial sectors in the crisis economies remain in distress. Although lower than historical peaks in some countries, in late 1999, nonperforming loans in these banking systems were still at considerably high levels. In Indonesia, Korea, Malaysia, and Thailand nonperforming loans were respectively 25 percent, 18 percent, 45 percent, and 41 percent of gross domestic product (GDP) and an estimated 50 percent, 15 percent, 21 percent, and 39 percent of total loans.[4] Recovery has been strongest in Korea, which, along with Malaysia, has benefited especially from the strong international demand for electronic products. While such a recovery is likely to continue, the aftereffects of the financial shock will persist, and continued restructuring is essential both to reinforce that recovery and to reduce future vulnerabilities.

Summary of Events

The East Asian crisis has exposed financially weak firms in the corporate sector that have operated on thin margins, and their inability to pay interest following the crisis has aggravated their debt burden. Because their ability and incentives to invest are limited and because such firms constitute a significant portion of the crisis economies, they will continue to act as a drag on investment and growth until the financial claims are resolved, and either their operations return to adequate profitability, or their assets are redeployed. Meanwhile, the distressed banking sector itself requires further recapitalization or consolidation to avoid continued systemic risks and growing fiscal liabilities for governments.

The East Asian crisis has driven many marginal firms into illiquidity and resulted in high levels of accumulated debt and associated interest payments. Consequently, many firms that recently emerged from the worst effects of

---

4. These numbers include nonperforming loans purchased by asset management companies.

the crisis are still in a precarious situation and are vulnerable to further shocks. Furthermore, nonperforming loans by banks and nonbank financial companies have remained exceptionally high. Investment rates have fallen sharply since the onset of the crisis (figure 12.2). Relative to the average of 1992–97, the investment rates in the second quarter of 1999 were down by about 57 percent in Indonesia, 30 percent in Korea, 42 percent for Malaysia, and 40 percent in Thailand. Governments have borne the brunt of bank restructuring. Bank recapitalization costs are significantly large in relation to existing public debt; these costs are estimated at 48 percent, 4 percent, 8 percent, and 8 percent of GDP in Indonesia, Korea, Malaysia, and Thailand respectively (World Bank 1999b). Without the ability to collect on nonperforming loans, debt levels will show a greater than reported increase. In contrast, the proper role for governments to play in corporate restructuring is to facilitate resolution of financial claims and foster the reallocation and mobility of assets.

In the absence of effective bankruptcy regimes, governments in all the crisis countries have instituted out-of-court mechanisms to speed up financial settlements. At the same time, bankruptcy procedures, where needed, have been reformed, which may also help resolution of financial

Figure 12.2.   *Total Investment in East Asia*

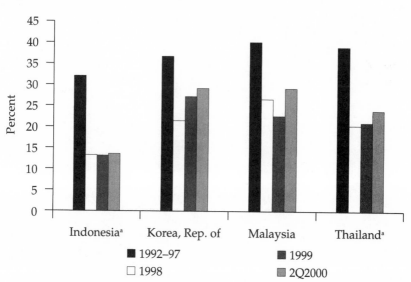

a. Quarter one 2000 data used.
Source: IMF data.

claims in the short run and may provide a sounder basis for improved corporate governance in the long run. Once financial property rights have been clarified, the market system and the private sector should be in a position to undertake the required reallocations of productive assets, but governments can also play an important role in permitting greater asset mobility. Additional reforms following the crisis included short-term tax regime changes to facilitate asset transactions and, more importantly from a long-term perspective, better accounting standards, which should contribute to improved corporate governance through better evaluation of financial assets and liabilities (table 12.2).

Table 12.2. Illustrative Post-Crisis Policy Reforms in Crisis Countries

Country	Loss allocation and transfer	Resource mobility	Corporate governance
Indonesia	Tax exemptions for loan-loss reserves held by banks (March 1998)	Relaxation of foreign ownership restrictions (September 1997); tax exemptions of up to 8 years for new investments in 22 industries (January 1999)	Presence of a corporate secretary to improve disclosure; Bankruptcy Law updated (August 1998); code of best practice for corporate governance (in progress)
Korea	Revaluation and adjustment of capital and foreign exchange losses (August 1999)	Introduction of Foreign Investment Promotion Act (November 1998)	Restrictions on cross-debt guarantees (April 1998); enhancing institutional voter rights (June 1998); introduction of international accounting standards (August 1999); lowering the minimum equity holding requirement to exercise shareholder's rights (1999)
Malaysia	Reduction of corporate tax rate from 30 percent to 28 percent (October 1997); tax exemption on interest from nonperforming loans (effective for 1999 and 2000)	Reduction of real property gains tax rate from 30 percent to 5 percent for nonresidents on the sale of a property held for a minimum of five years (October 1997); exemption of real property gains tax on mergers of financial institutions (October 1998)	Creation of high-level finance committee on corporate governance; code on takeovers and mergers with stricter disclosure standards (January 1999)

(table continues on following page)

Table 12.2 continued

Country	Loss allocation and transfer	Resource mobility	Corporate governance
Thailand	Elimination or deferral of income tax and taxes on asset transfer and unpaid interest (January 1999); introduction of new asset depreciation method (March 1999)	Alien Business Law (August 1998, revised in October 1999); tax-free mergers and acquisitions in cases of 100 percent mergers (January 1999); introduction of Equity Fund, Thailand Recovery Fund for large- and medium-scale companies, and Venture Capital Fund for small and medium-size enterprises (March 1999); reduction of real estate transfer fee from 2 to 0.01 percent of the appraised value (March 1999)	Financial statements of public companies and financial institutions to be in accord with international best practices (1999); requirement of board audit committees (1999); bankruptcy and foreclosure laws amended (March 1999)

Source: Authors.

Sectoral Distress and Recovery

The crisis had a disproportionate impact on firms with existing structural weaknesses, and this has also consequently resulted in uneven recovery. Signs of distress and recovery become apparent after examination of various indicators. Industrial production in manufacturing has shown significant recovery in Korea and, to a lesser extent, also in Malaysia (figure 12.3). This faster recovery reflects in part their greater strengths in sectors such as electronics, computers, and telecommunications equipment. Korean firms have also shown resilience in the transport equipment sector (figure 12.4). Similarly, Thai firms in the transport equipment sector have made a strong bounce back after a sharp decline in output, whereas Malaysian firms are still returning to the precrisis level (figures 12.5 and 12.6). In Korea, Malaysia, and Thailand traditional manufacturing sectors such as chemical products, cement products, metals, and machinery have only shown a limited recovery, but in some cases decline significantly predated the crisis.

More importantly, the most distressed sectors appear to be the nontradable or service sectors where production remains below precrisis levels (figure 12.7). In particular, GDP in the wholesale and retail trade and the finance and real estate sectors show signs of severe distress, with sharp

Figure 12.3. *Industrial Production before and after the Crisis*
(index = 100 at the start of the crisis)

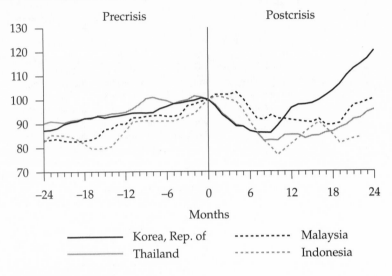

Note: Three-month moving averages.
Source: Datastream data.

Figure 12.4. *Production Index before and after the Crisis in Korea by Industry*
(index = 100 at the start of the crisis)

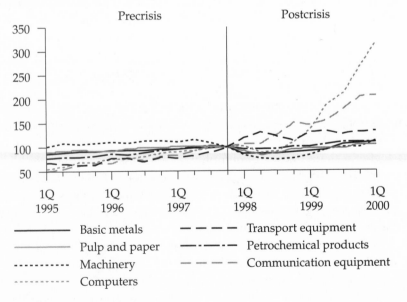

Note: Three-quarter moving averages.
Source: Datastream data.

Figure 12.5.   *Production Index before and after the Crisis in Malaysia by Industry*
(index = 100 at the start of the crisis)

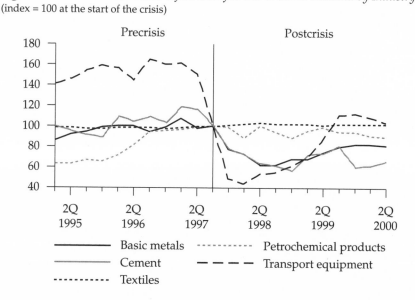

Note: Three-quarter moving averages.
Source: Datastream data.

Figure 12.6.   *Production Index before and after the Crisis in Thailand by Industry*
(index = 100 at the start of the crisis)

Note: Three-quarter moving averages.
Source: Bank of Thailand data.

Figure 12.7.   *Nontradable Production before and after the Crisis*
(index = 100 at the start of crisis)

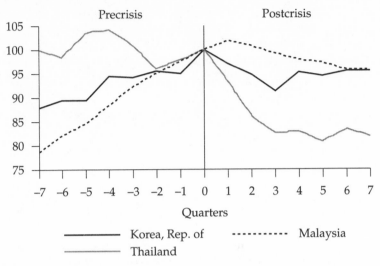

Note: Three-quarter moving averages.
Source: Datastream data.

declines or slow recovery (figures 12.8, 12.9, 12.10). Currency depreciations, which favor traded goods, have reduced the incentive to invest in the nontradable sectors. The share of insolvent firms is significantly higher in the nontradable sectors than in the tradable sectors. For instance, in Malaysia about three-quarters of nonperforming loans were made to enterprises in the nontradable sectors. The high level of distress reflects problems prevalent in the nontradable sectors, which had been characterized by overcapacity and low productivity even before the crisis, reflecting local monopolies in sectors such as retail trade and distribution (Crafts 1999). Low productivity in the real estate sector also reflects excess capacity. The Japanese experience shows that deregulation of domestic trade is an important spur to competition and to increasing productivity (Alexander 1999).

The share of firms unable to pay their debts is significantly higher in the nontradable sectors than in the tradable sectors. Estimates show that distress was especially high in the nontradable sectors of services and real estate in the second quarter of 1999, as could be expected from the trends in nontradable production (table 12.3). For Malaysia, where data describing the sectoral distribution of nonperforming loans is available, the problems have evidently worsened, especially for the nontradable sectors (table

Figure 12.8. *Nontradable Production before and after the Crisis in Korea by Industry*
(index = 100 at the start of crisis)

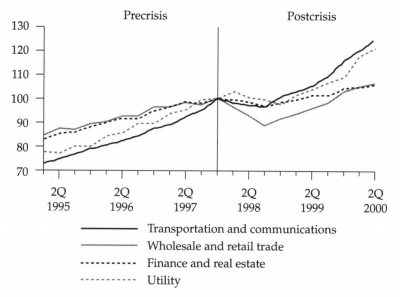

Note: Three-quarter moving averages.
Source: Bank of Korea data.

12.4). Nonperforming loans as a share of GDP by sector rose more rapidly in the nontradable sectors than for manufacturing overall during the period beginning March 1998 and ending September 1999.

Cross-Border M&As in East Asian Restructuring

As noted, cross-border M&As can be useful—and, unlike most other initiatives, private-sector driven—restructuring tools for host economies when distressed firms have limited alternatives for their survival. However, a concern with respect to the possibility of fire sales has been prominent in policy discussions. Fire sales of domestic assets can result in substantial transfer of domestic wealth to foreigners. Whether they do so depends on how fire sales are defined (Krugman 1998). If precrisis asset values were inflated by implicit guarantees that ultimately fail, and the crisis returned these values to their appropriate levels, purchases by foreigners may reflect greater liquidity or superior management skills,

Figure 12.9. *Nontradable Production before and after the Crisis in Malaysia by Industry*
(index = 100 at the start of crisis)

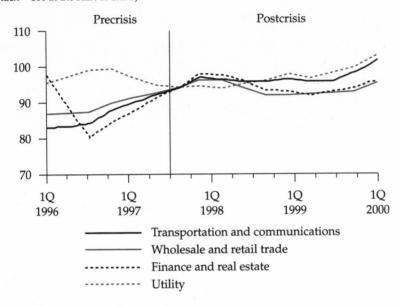

Note: Three-quarter moving averages.
Source: Datastream data.

but properties are sold at equilibrium prices, and no transfer of wealth takes place. Alternatively, if an excessive exchange rate depreciation forces domestic firms to liquidate to pay off short-term debt, foreign firms that are not liquidity-constrained can purchase these domestic firms or projects, which will generate a stream of profit greater than the liquidation value once the exchange rate recovers. The domestic economy loses because of the wealth transfer, more so if foreigners are less efficient at running domestic investment projects than local firms (see Krugman 1998). Though the evidence is not clear-cut, we do not find fire sales to be a significant phenomenon. However, neither do we find obvious evidence for the positive effects of restructuring.

FDI and Cross-Border M&As

Majority-owned cross-border M&A sales in the crisis countries reached US$7.3 billion in 1998, compared with US$3.6 billion in 1997, largely due to

Figure 12.10. *Nontradable Production before and after the Crisis in Thailand by Industry*
(index = 100 at the start of crisis)

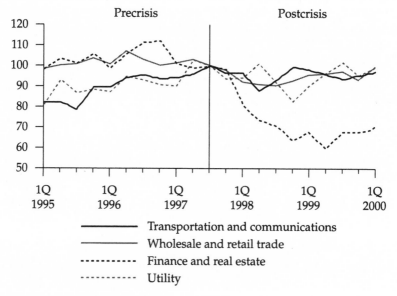

Note: Three-quarter moving averages.
Source: Bank of Thailand data.

Table 12.3. *Financial Distress, 2nd Quarter 1999*
(percentage of firms unable to make debt repayments)

Country	Sector			
	All	Manufacturing	Services	Real estate
Indonesia	63.8	41.8	66.8	86.9
Korea	26.7	19.6	28.1	43.9
Malaysia[a]	26.3	39.3	33.3	52.8
Thailand	28.3	21.8	29.4	46.9

a. Firms in agriculture and utilities bring down the average for all firms in 1999.
Source: Claessens, Djankov, and Klingebiel (1999a).

significant increases in M&A activity in Korea and Thailand. In 1999, the cross-border M&A value (including both majority and minority acquisitions) in East Asia's four crisis countries was US$20 billion, up from US$17 billion in 1998, with US$12 billion in Korea and US$3 billion in Thailand (compared with US$9 billion and US$5 billion in 1998 respectively) (figure

Table 12.4.   *Nonperforming Loans as Share of GDP in Malaysia by Sector*
(percent)

Sector	March 1998	December 1998	September 1999	Change, March 1998– September 1999
Agriculture, forestry and fishing	6.4	11.7	15.0	58.3
Mining	1.9	9.0	6.6	32.5
Manufacturing	24.3	59.1	56.8	32.7
Utility	7.3	13.1	21.2	63.2
Wholesale and retail trade	21.8	46.0	57.2	58.1
Construction	131.8	328.1	342.2	47.1
Transportation and communications	23.4	63.3	52.5	23.5
Financial services	50.5	136.7	210.5	124.2

Source: Bank Negara data.

12.11). Malaysia received a high level of cross-border M&A deals prior to the crisis, but levels did not rise after the crisis. M&As in Indonesia, historically small transactions, doubled in 1999 to US$2.7 billion from 1998.

Figure 12.12 shows the sectoral distribution of cross-border M&As in the crisis countries during the 1997–99 period. Half of the transactions in Indonesia are in light manufacturing (mainly food products) and petrochemicals (mainly oil refining). In Korea and Malaysia, the wholesale and retail trade sector had the largest number of transactions, 24 percent and 30 percent of their respective totals. Korea also had a large share of sales in the petrochemical industry. Other sectors that sold a large number of assets in Malaysia are the finance and real estate and the light manufacturing sectors (comprised of the paper and pulp, textile, and cement industries). In Thailand, the transactions have taken place mostly in the finance and real estate and the wholesale and retail trade sectors, accounting for more than 50 percent of total sales.

Cross-Border M&As and Financial Distress

Though judging the impact of M&As in East Asia is premature, certain conclusions can be drawn. The existing literature on U.S. firms, as noted earlier, compares premerger cash flow performance of target firms with postmerger performance of acquirer firms. However, in cross-border M&A transactions

Figure 12.11.   *Cross-Border Mergers and Acquisitions in Crisis Countries,*
1997–99[a]

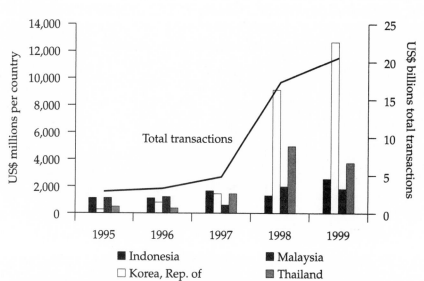

a. Includes both majority and minority ownership.
Source: Thomson Financial Securities data.

in East Asian countries, relative to foreign firms, the size of the acquired
firms is not significant enough to affect the performance of acquirer firms
after the mergers. This means that the postmerger performance of acquired
firms will not be measured by the performance of surviving entities, unlike
the case of the U.S. studies. We focus, therefore, on industry aggregates, recognizing that this reduces the confidence in the findings because aggregate
data masks information on individual firm performance.

We compare the average recovery rate in production since the crisis with
the number of cross-border M&A sales by sector. Cross-border M&A sales
tend to take place more frequently in the sectors showing deeper distress and
slow recovery. In Thailand, 30 percent of mergers and acquisitions occurred
in finance and real estate, where GDP has declined most sharply and recovery has been slowest, followed by the wholesale and retail trade sector. The
petrochemical industry has also stagnated, whereas foreign investors have
shown considerable interest in acquiring assets in the manufacturing sectors.
However, due to a strong upturn, the transport equipment sector did not
need to sell off as many assets (figure 12.6). In Malaysia, foreign investors
have bought majority stakes largely in the wholesale and retail trade and the

Figure 12.12.   *Cross-Border Mergers and Acquisitions in Crisis Countries by Sector, 1997–99*

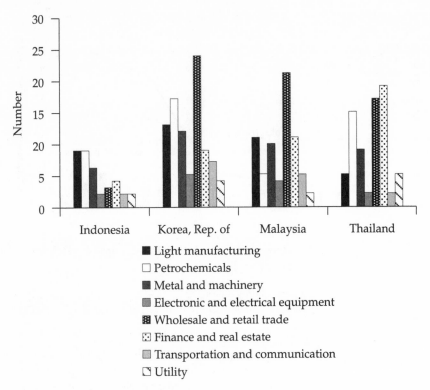

Source: Thomson Financial Securities data.

finance and real estate sectors; these are the sectors that have suffered most from fallen production and sluggish recovery . The average rate of growth in production in the finance and real estate sector remains negative. A relatively small number of cross-border M&A sales has taken place in the utility (electricity, gas, and water) sector, which has shown the fastest recovery among the nontradables. The ratio of the average postcrisis growth rate of production (where positive growth has occurred) to the precrisis rate is 0.09 for the wholesale and retail trade sector, whereas for the utility, food, and basic metal sectors, the ratios are 1.53, 2.21, and 2.31, respectively.

In comparison, Korea's picture is somewhat ambiguous partly because production has not only declined by a smaller magnitude, but it has also recovered more rapidly than in the other crisis economies. Nevertheless, the wholesale and retail trade sector, with the severest fall in production in the economy, has had by far the largest number of asset sales. As was also observed in Thailand, the transport equipment sector, which shows resilience and recovery, has had a relatively small number of asset sales. In 10 out of the 17 sales that took place in Korea's petrochemical industry, assets were sold off to major chemical and allied products companies in Europe, which appears to have been part of increased global oligopolistic competition in the industry since 1998. Meanwhile, overall demand growth prospects for petroleum products in the region augment the high volume of asset acquisitions by foreign investors.

Where appropriate data are available, we can make some tentative inferences on inventory trends in Korea. The patterns in inventory appear to be positively associated with cross-border M&A activity. Industries with low inventory levels, for example the textile, metal, and transport equipment sectors, show the least M&A activity, whereas the machinery and petrochemical industries have the largest numbers of M&A in the tradable sector.

Table 12.5 shows selected companies in the wholesale and retail trade and the finance and real estate sectors, whose majority stakes were sold to foreign acquirers in 1998–99. The return on equity (a ratio of net income to shareholder's equity) in acquired companies had sharply deteriorated prior to the transactions in all cases. Out of the wholesale and retail trade sector in Thailand, the hotel industry is thought to have strong potential for recovery through the involvement of foreign capital. Investors from Asia's newly industrializing economies, European countries, and the United States have been attracted to long-term growth prospects in the industry and to assets that are available in the market at lower prices as the new bankruptcy law forces highly indebted owners to sell them off.

Besides distressed firms' urgent need for liquidity and overall policy measures to encourage cross-border M&As, recent efforts of East Asian countries to recover assets of the nationalized banking institutions have partly driven the large number of asset sales in the finance and real estate sector. Because governments of the crisis countries have become substantial owners of the banking systems as a result of direct takeovers and recapitalization initiatives, the reprivatization of these institutions has remained a priority that will influence the long-term structure and performance of the financial sectors. So far, efforts at privatization have been partially successful, particularly in Korea and Thailand, albeit with problems resulting partly from the continued growth of nonperforming loans that new acquirers have difficulty valuing.

The sale of a 51 percent stake in Korea First Bank, one of the Korea's largest commercial banks, to a U.S. investment fund, Newbridge Capital,

Table 12.5. *Return on Equity of Acquired Companies*

Company	Country	Sector	Sale value (US$ millions)	Return on equity (percent) 2 years	Return on equity (percent) 1 year
Korea First Bank	Korea	Finance and real estate	415.0	–1.8	–162.0
Shangri-La Hotels	Malaysia	Wholesale and retail trade	94.6	7.1	3.5
Bank of Asia	Thailand	Finance and real estate	181.5	15.9	–4.6
Nakornthon Bank	Thailand	Finance and real estate	319.3	–4.0	–341.9
Radanasin Bank	Thailand	Finance and real estate	382.5	–29.0	–283.0
Shangri-La Hotels	Thailand	Wholesale and retail trade	34.7	0.5	–13.9
Golden Land Property Development	Thailand	Finance and real estate	76.3	–1.6	–62.0

Source: Thomson Financial Securities data.

was finally settled in September 1999 after nine months of negotiations. The protracted negotiations centered on the valuation of nonperforming loans that had not been carved out or revealed and on the extent of continued government obligations to assume nonperforming loans following privatization. These issues were particularly serious because Korea First Bank was a principal creditor to the second largest business group, Daewoo, where a creditor-led restructuring continues as a result of increases in debt. The final terms of the agreement require the government to be responsible for any nonperforming loans over the next two years. A number of smaller-scale acquisitions of Korean banks by foreign investors have taken place, including a 17 percent stake in Kookmin Bank by an investment fund led by Goldman Sachs, and a 31 percent stake in Korea Exchange Bank by Commerzbank of Germany (EIU 1999).

In Thailand, continued concerns over the scale of the nonperforming loans and the quality of assets has delayed sales of nationalized banks to foreign investors, although slow but steady progress in the asset resolution process appears to be regaining some foreign investor confidence. ABN-Amro Bank of the Netherlands acquired a 75 percent stake in Bank of Asia, while the Development Bank of Singapore bought 51 percent of Thai Danu Bank in 1998. The United Kingdom's Standard Chartered bought a 75 percent stake of Nakornthon Bank for US$319 million in September 1999 after two years of negotiations. Thailand's government is expected to reimburse Standard Chartered for any loss of interest revenue resulting from the bank's nonperforming loans. One of many minority acquisitions is a 15 percent stake in Thai Farmers Bank to the Government of Singapore Investment Corporation for US$258 million.

As discussed previously, some argue that postcrisis asset acquisitions in East Asia by foreign investors are often based on fire-sale pricing, although evidence has been insufficient to support this argument. Limited information for cross-border M&A transactions in Thailand based on the transaction value of the acquisitions of Carpets International, the Shangri-La Hotel, and United Motor Works suggests that prices acquirers pay per share have been around 70 percent of book value per share. In contrast, nonperforming assets in Thailand have been auctioned at values that are considerably lower than the acquisition values of local firms. The average auction price of nonperforming assets in Thailand has been 28 percent of the book value (table 12.6). The case of Korea also indicates that foreign acquisitions of assets have not been fire sales. Although Korea has suffered the least from domestic liquidity constraints out of the crisis-afflicted economies, total cross-border M&A transactions shot up to US$9 billion in 1999,

Table 12.6. Auction Results of Nonperforming Assets, end of 1999

Bid date	Items	Book value	Auction value as percentage of book value
Financial Sector Restructuring Authority, Thailand[a]			
June 25, 1998	Auto hire purchase contracts	52.0	48
August 13, 1998	Residential mortgage loans	24.6	47
December 15, 1998	Business loans	155.7	25
March 19, 1999	Business loans	221.5	18
July 6, 1999	Construction loans	1.3	8
August 11, 1999	Business loans	129.0	24
November 10, 1999	Business loans	17.8	30
Korea Asset Management Corporation			
September 1, 1998	Business loans	207.5	12
October 30, 1998	Real estate assets	6.0	49
December 9, 1998	Loans secured by real estate assets	564.6	36
May 27, 1999	Business loans	772.4	17
June 22, 1999	Loans secured by real estate assets	1,040.0	51
November 11, 1999	Business loans	811.1	21
December 8, 1999	Loans secured by real estate assets	1,020.0	62
Danaharta			
July 1, 1999	Foreign loans	94.95	55

Note: Book values for:
Financial Sector Restructuring Authority, Thailand in billions of baht
Korea Asset Management Corporation in billions of won
Danaharta in millions of US$.
a. Excludes sales of noncore assets.
Source: Danaharta data; Financial Sector Restructuring Authority data; Korea Asset Management Corporation data.

five times higher than the level in 1998. M&A activity in Korea rose by 32 percent in 1999 despite the considerable appreciation of the won, up 15 percent from 1998. This suggests that foreign acquisitions of assets have been driven not only by greater liquidity from foreign exchange depreciation, but also by new opportunities resulting from an improved policy environment with respect to M&As.

In summary, financial and corporate restructuring is not a short process, and clear outcomes have yet to materialize. East Asia's financially distressed firms have so far made major progress in the rescheduling of debt as a short-term restructuring item. Once the troubled firms stabilize their liquidity position, further steps would be needed toward longer-term restructuring measures—reorganization, changes in management, and reductions in excess capacity—that often require new investments.[5] Successful firms in market economies restructure continually to reposition their businesses and thus remain competitive and survive in the long term. Restructuring occurs when a firm shifts its product mix and cost structure to respond to changes in technology and public policies. Alongside measures of so-called operational restructuring, the firms' assets need also to be rationalized. Reallocation of assets requires effective methods for asset pricing, which in turn requires credible bankruptcy procedures and a market for M&As, including liberal foreign investment rules.

Policy Implications

Cross-border M&A activity can bring most benefit to the host country when facilitated by certain policy frameworks. After a crisis, once the first step of loss allocation and transfer is complete, liberalization of foreign investment and ownership and tax incentives can amplify resource mobility. Introduction of institutional bankruptcy laws and accounting standards, alongside reinforcement of shareholders' rights, will improve corporate governance. Meanwhile, the potential downside of M&A activity, such as higher market concentration and immediate unemployment effects, can be avoided by removing bureaucratic barriers to competition and increasing the flexibility of the labor market.

Loss Allocation and Transfer

East Asian governments have taken several steps to achieve the outlined agenda, as summarized in table 12.2. To facilitate debt restructuring, corporate tax rates have been reduced and tax exempted on interest from

---

5. Claessens, Djankov, and Klingebiel (1999b) indicate that both concentration of ownership and extensive links between financial institutions and corporations are likely to delay restructuring in East Asian crisis economies.

nonperforming assets in Indonesia and Malaysia. Korea and Thailand adopted new methods of capital valuation and asset depreciation that are geared toward the same goal.

Resource Mobilization

The second step of resource mobilization includes measures that are directly related to M&A activity, both international and domestic, such as liberalization of foreign investment and ownership and tax reduction and exemption on real estate transfer. Success of M&A depends heavily on procedural simplicity and clarity.

Since their crises in 1997, both Korea and Thailand have introduced various measures to encourage business consolidation involving M&As, which have led to the rapid rise in cross-border M&As in these two countries. Korea has been providing tax exemption and deferral on capital gains from so-called big deals, that is, exchange of businesses through the transfer of shares. The Korean government also released a new legislative framework in July 1999 to reduce transaction-related taxes incurred in corporate mergers, acquisitions, and divisions. Thailand approved a set of new measures in January 1999, including provisions for tax-free mergers and non-cash acquisition of assets in cases of 100 percent mergers and for the elimination of all taxes on asset transfers from debtors to creditors. Moreover new bankruptcy procedures introduced in March 1999 allow creditors to force business restructuring on insolvent firms. As a result, firms with high liabilities have no other choice but to sell their assets as banks push them to repay their debts.

In addition to these measures, Korea and Thailand have also taken effective steps to deregulate and liberalize their foreign investment policies since late 1997. Korea has opened several sectors to foreign investors since April 1998, including various property businesses, securities dealings, and other financing businesses. The ceiling on foreign stock investment was abolished in May 1998, granting foreign investors the right to purchase all the shares of a domestic firm. Meanwhile, the Foreign Investment Promotion Act of November 1998 offers protection for FDI through national treatment, the reduction and exemption of certain corporate taxes, the provision of financial support for local governments to attract foreign direct investment, and the establishment of foreign investment zones. In Thailand, the Board of Investment has eased its regulations to promote foreign participation in the economy. The twenty-year old Alien Business Law was replaced in August 1998, and revised again in October 1999, to incorporate sectoral liberalization measures. Under the August 1998 provisions, foreign firms are allowed to hold up to 100 percent equity in banks and in finance companies for up to ten years. In addition, 39 sectors have been opened up to increased foreign participation; these sectors include transportation and pharmaceuticals production. Policy liberalization included a temporary measure introduced in November 1998, which expired in December 1999, that allowed foreign firms to own a majority stake in joint ventures that received favorable policy treatment and that authorized them to distribute their products domestically. At present, the proposed cutback of import tariffs is expected to help reduce production costs for both domestic and foreign firms dependent on imported raw materials and intermediate products.

Unlike in Korea and Thailand where the number of cross-border mergers has risen, in Malaysia cross-border M&As have been few compared with its historical performance. Malaysia has, however, had high levels of domestic M&As.[6] Malaysia's 1986 Promotion of Investment Act and other measures provide various tax incentives, including investment tax allowances in the services sector. The high level of domestic M&As activity in Malaysia suggests that the regime is basically a friendly one. However, cross-border activity could remain low, on account of restrictions on the repatriation of earnings. More recently, Malaysia has endorsed an extensive merger program of the banking system, in which all the banking institutions submitted their merger proposals at the end of January 2000.

In contrast, the Indonesian system appears not to favor M&As. Gains from transfers of assets in corporate reorganizations are taxable, and companies cannot transfer tax losses in a liquidation process, merger, or acquisition (Asia Law 1998). Certain exceptions apply to banks, financial institutions, and companies that are going public. The sales of banking institutions have been deterred, due to difficulties in valuation of nonperforming loans as in the other crisis countries. Overall, M&A activity has remained at extremely low levels.

Corporate Governance

Finally, the third step of enhancing corporate governance can also be highly effective in encouraging market-driven M&As. Some studies of ownership structures in East Asian firms suggest heavy family control, which puts

---

6. In total, domestic M&As numbered about 50 to 70 per quarter in Malaysia in 1997–99, while domestic M&As remained low (in the range of 4 to 10) in the other countries.

shareholders at a disadvantage (Claessens, Djankov, and Lang 1999; Claessens and others 1999). Good corporate governance can improve distribution of control. Improvement of enterprise monitoring, disclosure of information, accounting practices, and equity issuance processes are essential for strengthening corporate governance frameworks. Korea and Thailand have taken steps to enhance institutional voter rights and encourage more shareholders to exercise their rights.

The amendment to the bankruptcy code in Thailand, which went into effect in March 1999, is an example of an effective measure to encourage M&As through market forces. In Thailand, financially distressed sectors such as the hotel industry have been attracting a high level of foreign interest for their long-term growth prospects since the bankruptcy laws were amended. The new codes allow creditors to enforce resolution of assets on debtors for repayments.

Meanwhile, Korea's movement toward international accounting standards has been welcomed by foreign investors whose concerns with respect to the acquisition of Korean assets centered on the valuation of nonperforming loans. Korea also introduced new requirements for domestic companies to increase the involvement of noninsiders on their boards.

Overall, governments in all the crisis economies are making efforts to improve corporate governance. These measures have been important for increasing transparency and accountability, though further progress has yet to be made.

Competition Policy and Labor Mobility

Certain policy measures should be taken to avoid any potential downsides and induce the greatest amount of benefit of cross-border M&As. Consolidation and rationalization through M&As may lead to a higher degree of concentration and employment reduction in the host market, which particularly will apply to sectors with excess capacity. Maintaining the right balance between competition and cooperation has been an important concern for East Asian policymakers (Mody 1999; Stiglitz 1996). While ensuring this balance, market-oriented measures need to be taken by reducing bureaucratic restraints to competition and monitoring market shares. Moreover, domestic firms could be provided with incentives to invest in research and development and to form strategic alliances with advanced companies, which will increase competitiveness through continual technological renovation. Meanwhile social security systems could be improved, for example, by tentatively extending the coverage of unemployment insurance to support workers laid off as a result of M&A activity and by providing vocational training to enhance flexibility of the labor market.

Lessons from M&A Activity in Japan

The Japanese case is a good example of where improved regulations governing M&As have contributed to the restructuring process. According to Alexander (1999) and UNCTAD (1999), M&As are occurring in numbers unprecedented in Japan, though their importance to the economy is still small compared with that of the United Kingdom or the United States. The value of foreign takeovers in Japan rose from US$1.1 billion in 1997 to US$6.9 billion in 1998, and then shot up to US$24.2 billion in 1999, accounting for 32 percent of the country's total M&A activity. Major transactions include sales of a majority stake in Yamaichi Securities to the United States' Merrill Lynch in 1998 and in Japan Leasing to General Electric for US$6.6 billion. In addition, a 37 percent stake of Nissan Motors was sold to Renault of France for US$5.4 billion. Similarly, the number of domestic M&As has also risen as M&As are becoming acceptable business transactions among Japanese firms, a fundamental change from the previously held view that M&As are predatory actions.

The elimination of cross-shareholding partly explains the rise in Japanese M&A activity, as the returns on these equity holdings have been persistently low or negative. At the same time, many regulatory constraints on business activities are being removed, and specific measures to facilitate M&As are being instituted. For instance, in 1997 the Japanese Diet amended the Commercial Code to reduce the number of shareholder meetings required to approve mergers. The Holding Company Law of 1997 removes constraints on carving out subsidiaries for sale and allows buyers more freedom in structuring their acquisitions. The securities transaction tax formerly required when an acquisition involved share purchases was discarded in April 1999. In addition, moves to implement international accounting principles and, in particular, consolidated reporting, are bringing more transparency to the operation of subsidiaries.

Conclusion

Foreign investors who see opportunities in corporate distress, lower asset prices, and more liberal policies toward M&As and FDI in general have been attracted to postcrisis East Asia. Cross-border M&A activity in the crisis countries has largely concentrated in the most troubled sectors. Some nontradable sectors and traditional manufacturing sectors suffer from excess capacity as a consequence of overinvestment since the early 1990s, and thereby from lower capacity utilization and reduced production. Moreover, a large number of firms carry large debt repayments due to rising interest rates, whereas other domestic companies are also financially constrained. East Asian governments have taken several steps to encourage M&As and have, to varying degrees, liberalized foreign investment.

However, cross-border M&A activity is still in its early phase in East Asia's financially distressed economies and remains small relative to the stage of development and the size of their economies.[7] The recent upsurge in M&A activity in East Asia, particularly in Korea, is largely attributed to changes in policy environment that used to work against foreign acquisitions of local assets. Liberalization of foreign entry and ownership restrictions alongside introduction of international accounting standards and shareholding systems has exponentially increased access for foreign investors to the local market and enabled them to acquire assets.

The immediate role of cross-border M&As has been to provide funds and to preserve the existing assets that would otherwise have been wiped out. In the long term, M&As can bring in more FDI from the acquirers and their suppliers and new resources in management and production to host countries. Eventual integration with the corporate networks of the acquirers will expand their opportunities for increased industry diversification. Though M&A activity has been most prominent in distressed sectors, at this stage there is little evidence to suggest that cross-border M&A activity has made immediate contributions to restructuring the troubled sectors. We should, however, highlight that the sectoral aggregates may not reflect the full effect of M&As on recovery in the distressed sectors. We will require some firm-level analysis to draw more robust conclusions.

Given the gravity of problems in some sectors, for example in the nontradable sector, the restructuring effects of cross-border M&As may not materialize in such a short timespan. The most significant role for cross-border M&As lies in longer-term restructuring processes such as operational restructuring and reallocation of assets. Foreign participation through M&As could also be more effective in achieving improved efficiency and competitiveness and better corporate governance. Under the circumstances, FDI, in the form of cross-border M&As, has a significant role to play in restructuring and developing financially distressed economies.

---

7. Cross-border M&As account for 0.6 percent of GDP in East Asia in 1998, significantly lower than Latin America's 1.5 percent of GDP.

Fire sales are also not evident. For the few transactions for which we can compare sale prices with book values, the receipts have been surprisingly high. Moreover, Korea has had the highest level of M&A despite having the fewest liquidity constraints. Also, the levels of M&A activity have remained high despite appreciation of exchange rates from their lower levels, especially, but not only, in Korea.

References

Alexander, Arthur. 1999. "Japan Confronts Corporate Restructuring." Background paper for *Global Economic Prospects and the Developing Countries 2000.* World Bank, Washington, D.C.

Asia Law. 1998. *Cross-Border M&A: A Guide to Global Strategic Direct Investment for Asian Companies.* London: Euromoney Publications.

Blumberg, Aryeh, and James E. Owers. 1996. "The Convergence of Foreign Direct Investment and Restructuring: Evidence from Cross-Border Divestitures." *Global Finance Journal* 7(1): 67–87.

Caves, Richard E. 1971. "International Corporations: The Industrial Economics of Foreign Investment." *Economica* 38(2): 1–27.

Claessens, Stijn, Simeon Djankov, and Daniela Klingebiel. 1999a. "Bank and Corporate Restructuring in East Asia: Opportunities for Further Reform." Financial Sector Discussion Paper no. 3. World Bank, Washington, D.C.

———. 1999b. "How to Accelerate Corporate and Financial Sector Restructuring in East Asia." Viewpoint no. 200. World Bank, Washington, D.C.

Claessens, Stijn, Simeon Djankov, and Larry H. P. Lang. 1999. "Who Controls East Asian Corporations?" Policy Research Working Paper no. 2054. World Bank, Washington, D.C.

Claessens, Stijn, Simeon Djankov, Joseph P. H. Fan, and Larry H. P. Lang. 1999. "Expropriation of Minority Shareholders: Evidence from East Asia." Policy Research Working Paper no. 2088. World Bank, Washington, D.C.

Crafts, Nicholas. 1999. "East Asian Growth Before and After the Crisis." *IMF Staff Papers* 46(2): 139–66.

The Economist. 2000. "Merger Brief: The Digital Dilemma." July 22.

EIU (Economist Intelligence Unit). 1999. *Business Asia.* September. London and Hong Kong.

Froot, Kenneth R., and Jeremy C. Stein. 1991. "Exchange Rates and Foreign Direct Investment: An Imperfect Capital Market Approach." *Quarterly Journal of Economics* 106(4): 1191–217.

Ghemawat, Pankaj, and Fariborz Ghadar. 2000. "The Dubious Logic of Global Megamergers." *Harvard Business Review* 78(4): 64–74.

Harris, Robert S., and David Ravenscraft. 1991. "The Role of Acquisitions in Foreign Direct Investment: Evidence from the U.S. Stock Market." *Journal of Finance* 46(3): 825–44.

Hotchkiss, Edith S., and Robert M. Mooradian. 1998. "Acquisitions as a Means of Restructuring Firms in Chapter 11." *Journal of Financial Intermediation* 7(3): 240–62.

Hunya, Gabor. 1997. "Foreign Direct Investment and its Effects in the Czech Republic, Hungary, and Poland." Working Paper No. 186. The Vienna Institute for Comparative Economic Studies.

Hymer, Stephen H. 1976. *The International Operations of National Firms: A Study of Direct Foreign Investment*. Cambridge, Massachusetts: MIT Press.

Jensen, Michael C. 1986. "Agency Costs of Free Cash Flows, Corporate Finance, and Takeovers." *American Economic Review* 76(2): 323–29.

Kang, Jun-Koo. 1993. "The International Market for Corporate Control: Mergers and Acquisitions of U.S. Firms by Japanese Firms." *Journal of Financial Economics* 34(3): 345–71.

Kindleberger, Charles P. 1969. *American Business Abroad: Six Lectures on Direct Investment*. New Haven, Connecticut: Yale University Press.

Krugman, Paul R. 1998. "Fire-Sale FDI." Available at http://web.mit.edu/krugman/www/FIRESALE.htm.

Mody, Ashoka. 1999. "Industrial Policy after the East Asian Crisis: From 'Outward Orientation' to New Internal Capabilities?" Policy Research Working Paper no. 2112. World Bank, Washington, D.C.

Scholes, Myron S., and Mark A. Wolfson. 1990. "The Effects of Changes in Tax Laws on Corporate Reorganization Activity." *Journal of Business* 63(1): 141–64.

Stiglitz, Joseph. 1996. "Some Lessons from the East Asian Miracle." *The World Bank Economic Observer* 11(2): 151–77.

UNCTAD (United Nations Conference on Trade and Development). 1999. *World Investment Report 1999: Foreign Direct Investment and the Challenge of Development*. Geneva.

_____. 2000. *World Investment Report, 1991-2000*. Geneva.

World Bank. 1999a. *Global Development Finance*. Washington, D.C.

_____. 1999b. *Global Economic Prospects and the Developing Countries*. Washington, D.C.

_____. 2000. *Global Development Finance*. Washington, D.C.

13

Asset Management Companies

Daniela Klingebiel, World Bank

In recent decades, many countries have experienced financial crises requiring major overhauls of their banking systems. By one count, 112 episodes of systemic banking crises have occurred in 93 countries since the late 1970s (Caprio and Klingebiel 1999). Bank restructuring often has to be accompanied by corporate debt restructuring as most of the nonperforming loans in the banking system are loans to nonfinancial enterprises. Countries can adopt either flow or stock approaches to resolving distress.

Cross-country evidence indicates that stock solutions are necessary when financial distress is systemic. This type of solution includes the liquidation of banks that are not viable, the disposal and management of impaired assets, and the restructuring of viable banks. For the management and disposal of bad debt, governments have made extensive use of publicly-owned asset management companies (AMCs) that either dispose of assets hived off bank balance sheets or restructure corporate debt. While establishing AMCs is now a resolution strategy that is frequently recommended, little is known about their effectiveness. This chapter analyzes the advantages and disadvantages of AMCs in managing and disposing of impaired assets and

This paper draws on Klingebiel (2000). The reader is referred to that paper for a detailed description of data sources. Joumana Cobein provided valuable input for the U.S. case study; Marinela Dado for the case studies of Ghana, Mexico, the Philippines, and Spain; and Gabriela M. Gonzalez for the Finnish and Swedish case studies. The author thanks Gerard Caprio, Stijn Claessens, Stephan Haggard, James Hanson, Patrick Honohan, Jose de Luna Martinez, Richard Roulier, and Esen Ulgenerk for comments.

measures the effectiveness of such institutions. It does not discuss the advantages and disadvantages of different bank recapitalization strategies, including the use of AMCs as part of these strategies.

Two main types of AMCs can be distinguished: AMCs set up to help and expedite corporate restructuring, and AMCs established to dispose of assets acquired or transferred to the government during the crisis, such as rapid asset disposition vehicles. According to a survey of 26 banking crises (Caprio and Klingebiel 1996), centralized AMC structures were set up in nine countries. In this paper we study seven cases, where data were publicly available. In three countries, Finland, Ghana, and Sweden, governments set up restructuring vehicles. In the four cases in Mexico, the Philippines, Spain, and the United States governments set up rapid asset disposition agencies.

The results of these cases can be summarized as follows. Two of the three corporate restructuring AMCs did not achieve their narrow goals of expediting corporate restructuring, which suggests that AMCs are not necessarily effective tools for accelerating corporate restructuring. Only the Swedish AMC successfully managed its portfolio, acting in some instances as lead agent in the restructuring process. Special circumstances helped the Swedish AMC; the assets acquired were a small fraction of the banking system and were mostly in real estate.

Rapid asset disposition vehicles fared somewhat better with two, the Spanish and U.S. agencies, out of the four agencies achieving their objectives. These successful experiences suggest that AMCs can be effectively used, but only for asset disposition, including resolving insolvent and nonviable financial institutions. Achieving these objectives requires many ingredients, including a type of asset that is easily liquifiable (for example real estate), political independence, a skilled resource base, appropriate funding, adequate bankruptcy and foreclosure laws, good information and management systems, and transparency in operations and processes. In Mexico and the Philippines, the AMCs were doomed to fail from the start because governments transferred a large amount of loans or fraudulent assets to the AMCs creating a situation that is difficult to resolve. Neither of these agencies succeeded at rapid asset disposition, thus the realignment of asset prices was delayed.

The Centralized Versus the Decentralized Approach

While a growing literature details the do's and don'ts of banking crisis management literature (for example, Delargy and Goodhard 1999; Dziobeck and Pazarbasioglu 1997; Sheng 1996; and chapters 7 and 10 in this volume), empirical studies in this area remain sparse. Bank restructuring seeks to achieve many—often conflicting—goals that include preventing bank runs, avoiding a credit crunch, improving the efficiency of the financial intermediation process, and attracting new equity to the banking industry to economize on claims on public finances. As Dziobeck (1998) notes, the style of response has also changed over time. The lack of a unique or optimal blueprint on how to manage systemic financial distress is therefore not surprising.

 Countries can use either flow or stock approaches to resolving banking distress and the overhang of bad debt in the financial system. Whether a country should adopt a flow or a stock solution depends, among other things, on the degree of distress in the system and the extent of the official safety net. Flow solutions usually allow banks to strengthen their capital base over time through increased profits, thus recapitalizing on a flow basis.[1] Cross-country evidence suggests that flow solutions are only successful when banking distress is nonsystemic, and either the official safety net is limited or the supervisory authority is willing to intervene in those institutions whose capital base has further deteriorated. For example, in the early 1990s, U.S. money center banks enjoyed substantial forbearance and successfully recapitalized on a flow basis.[2] Stock solutions are aimed at restoring viable but insolvent institutions to solvency and liquidating nonviable institutions. Stock solutions are necessary in cases where financial distress is systemic.

 The proper management and disposition of impaired assets is one of the most critical and complex tasks of successful and speedy bank restructuring. Successful asset management policies can facilitate bank restructuring by accelerating the resolution of nonperforming assets and can promote corporate restructuring by providing the right incentives for voluntary debt restructuring. Debate continues over what the best model for asset management and recovery is. Should banks restructure debt and accomplish workout themselves —as in the decentralized model—or should bad debt be transferred to a centralized, publicly-owned asset management company charged with resolving the overhang of impaired assets (Claessens 1998; Garcia 1997; Lindgren and others 2000; see also box 13.1)? Empirical

---

 1. Flow solutions also end up taxing either depositors or performing borrowers as banks try to recapitalize from earnings, thus interest rate spreads have to rise. Flow solutions are inherently risky because decapitalized banks have incentives to gamble.

 2. Forbearance proved to be less successful in the cases of the U.S. savings and loan crisis and Japan's banking problems, which have continued for nearly 10 years.

Box 13.1.   *Advantages and Disadvantages of a Centralized, Public AMC*

Advantages

- Provides economies of scale, that is, consolidation of scarce workout skills and resources within one agency.
- Helps with the securitization as the centralized public AMC has a larger pool of assets.
- Centralizes ownership of collateral, providing more leverage over debtors and better management.
- Breaks links between banks and corporations and improves the collectibility of loans.
- Allows banks to focus on core business.
- Improves prospects for orderly sectoral restructuring of the economy.
- Allows the application of uniform workout practices.
- Expedites loan recovery and bank restructuring when given special powers.

Disadvantages

- Banks have informational advantages over AMCs as they have collected information on their borrowers.
- Leaving loans in banks may provide better incentives for recovery and for avoiding future losses by improving loan approval and monitoring procedures.
- Banks can provide additional financing, which may be necessary in the restructuring process.
- If assets transferred to the AMCs are not actively managed, the existence of an AMC may lead to general deterioration of payment discipline and further deterioration of asset values.
- Insulating a public agency against political pressure may be difficult, especially if the agency carries large portion of banking system assets.

---

studies on the usefulness and success of the decentralized versus the centralized approach in asset management have yet to be performed. In this paper, we will analyze the actual performance of AMCs given their stated goals, thus providing insight into whether or not AMCs may be a useful tool in the management of distressed assets.

In general, banks should be better positioned to resolve nonperforming loans than centralized AMCs are because banks have the loan files and institutional knowledge of the borrower. Leaving the problem assets on banks' balance sheets may also provide better incentives for banks to maximize the recovery value of bad debt and avoid future losses by improving loan approval and monitoring procedures. This approach also has the advantage that banks can provide new loans within the context of debt restructuring. Successful decentralized debt workouts require, however, limited or no ownership links between banks and corporations, adequately capitalized banks, and proper incentives for banks and borrowers. For example, the slow speed of restructuring in Japan is in part due to the extensive ownership links among banks, other financial intermediaries, and corporations (IMF 1999). Moreover, for debt workout by banks to be successful financial institutions must have sufficient skills and resources to deal with problem loans.

A decentralized bad debt workout can be accomplished by establishing an internal workout unit that is separately capitalized and is often a bank subsidiary. The sole objective of these units or bad banks is to focus attention on the workout of assets and maximize the recovery rate through active restructuring. A clean break can also help rebuild confidence in troubled banks. However, considerable risks are also associated with private AMCs that are spun off from individual banks. They can be used for window dressing if assets are transferred at book value or above market value, or in other words, when not all losses are taken at the bank level.[3] Even if regulations that require financial institutions to transfer their assets at market valué are in place, the supervisory authority needs to have the powers and the incentives to enforce such rules. Banks that establish separately capitalized workout units, or bad banks, need to be supported by a well-functioning regulatory framework, appropriate disclosure and accounting regulations, and strong monitoring and enforcement by the supervisory agency.

The centralized asset recovery approach permits a consolidation of skills and resources in debt restructuring within one agency, thus centralizing workout skills and information technology, which may be a more efficient way to recover maximum possible value. Centralization can help with the securitization of assets because it concentrates a larger pool of assets. In addition, it focuses the ownership of collateral, thus providing potentially more leverage over debtors and more effective management. Moreover, distressed loans are removed clearly, quickly, and completely from banks, which allows them to focus on their day-to-day activities.[4]

---

3. For example, if the bank is not subject to consolidated supervision, it can transfer problem assets at book value and hide the losses because the ACM's balance sheet is not reconciled with that of the bank. Even if the accounts are consolidated, they may be obscured if the bank takes a minority position (to avoid consolidation at the bank level) and asks connected companies to put up the rest of the equity.

4. Nevertheless, some economists argue that a reasonable amount of small-sized problem loans should remain within the bank's ordinary organization, even if the bulk of bad assets are transferred to a separate AMC. Apart from maintaining a level playing field among the remaining banks, leaving some nonperforming assets in the banks will preserve their capability to work out loans that do not require special expertise. In addition, the transaction cost incurred by transferring small assets may outweigh any potential gains. For more detail, see Ingves and Lind (1997).

Centralized agencies may also have the advantage of being able to break links between banks and corporations and thus being better able to collect on connected loans. Other elements that favor single entities include improved prospects for orderly sectoral restructuring in the real economy, application of uniform workout practices, and easier government monitoring and supervision of workout practices. Finally, another benefit of a centralized agency is that it can be given special legal powers to expedite loan recovery and bank restructuring. Special powers, however, may not compensate for a weak judicial system and may prove less useful if they must be enforced by the judicial system.

A centralized workout unit may, however, also face problems related to its size and ownership structure. If the agency carries a large portion of banking system assets, it may be difficult for the government to insulate such an entity from political pressure. This is true especially in cases where the government is also charged with the restructuring of assets and where a large portion of banking system assets has been transferred. Moreover, a transfer of loans can break the links between banks and corporations, links that may have positive value given banks' privileged access to corporate information, although the value of such information depends on the viability of the corporations in question. If AMC assets are not actively managed, the existence of a public AMC could lead to a general weakening of credit discipline in the financial system and further deterioration of asset values.

Countries have employed variants of these techniques to deal with asset and debt recovery. For either solution, centralized or decentralized asset management, a legal framework that facilitates the workout will be a key element influencing the final costs of bank restructuring (Waxman 1998). A good bargaining position for the holder of the asset and power to act are essential factors for the management of nonperforming loans. Well-functioning legal procedures and good access to courts are therefore crucial. Equally important are laws that facilitate actions by the banks or AMCs to exercise claims on assets and to recover the proceeds of sales of such assets if debt is not serviced. Moreover, for asset management companies to maximize returns, having access to a clean title and not requiring the borrower's consent to the sale of the assets are particularly important.

The Different Types of Asset Management Companies

Two main types of centralized asset management companies exist. These are asset disposition vehicles, which also cover liquidation, and longer-term restructuring vehicles. Whereas the typical objective of asset disposition and liquidation agencies is to sell the assets promptly through bulk sales, securitizations, or purchase and assumption transactions, restructuring agencies have other objectives.

Centralized asset sale agencies are set up to dispose of particular classes of assets that by nature tend to be more easily liquifiable—real estate assets, commercial real estate loans, secured loans that can be either easily sold off or securitized in case of a deep capital market—that were transferred to the AMC during a bank restructuring or recapitalization exercise. To maintain value, assets need to be managed. Even good loans tend to lose value when they are taken from the originating bank unless the AMC monitors them actively. Either the AMC or the originating bank, if it is still in operation, can manage the assets, or management can be outsourced to the private sector. In the case of the bank managing the assets, a loss-sharing arrangement with the AMC could provide incentives for the bank to monitor or manage the assets properly.[5] Liquidation agencies are set up to resolve failed financial institutions by selling assets through purchases and acquisitions, insured deposit transfers, and deposit payoff and sale of the performing or nonperforming assets.

Restructuring agencies are usually set up to operate on a longer-term basis and are aimed at restructuring and liquidating nonperforming loans of nonviable borrowers prior to their sale. Typically, as a first step in the restructuring process, the assets transferred to the AMC are grouped either into viable claims that need to be restructured or into nonviable claims the borrowers of which will be forced into bankruptcy.[6] The overall objective of the AMC, if pursuing a commercial objective, is to make the assets attractive to buyers. The restructuring of viable assets can include—in the case of an industrial company—selling off noncore assets and improving the overall efficiency of operations by reorganizing and reducing staff, cutting other costs, restructuring product lines, and so on. In the case of commercial real estate and residential homes, measures to increase the attractiveness of the properties can include renovation of the properties to adapt

---

5. In Mexico, the management of the assets was left to the originating banks. Despite loss-sharing agreements aimed at providing incentives for the originating bank to continue to manage the assets properly, assets transferred to the AMCs were managed inadequately, which resulted in further deterioration of asset values. This suggests that developing incentive-compatible contracts to prevent asset value deterioration from happening may not be an easy undertaking.

6. To increase transparency and depoliticize the process, third parties should assess the viability of the assets being transferred to the AMC.

them to current market demand or reducing the vacancy ratio, which is a crucial factor in improving cash flow. Because restructuring often requires new lending, the AMC needs to have the capacity to lend.

Private, centralized AMCs are rare. If a substantial amount of bad loans and assets is transferred to an AMC, finding private investors willing to assume ownership without requiring far-reaching state guarantees covering the future value of the asset portfolio is usually difficult. In that case, the government may be in a more favorable position if it owns the AMC rather than provides such guarantees because it might then benefit from any upward price movement of AMC assets. Moreover, in such a scenario, structuring a guarantee in a way that preserves the private owners' incentives to sell the assets at best prices may be difficult. Public ownership is also warranted if the value of impaired assets could be destroyed through fire sale liquidations. In that instance, the gradual sale by a specialized public agency is preferable.

The warehousing of assets in the hopes of obtaining higher prices later may not prevent prices from tumbling because the future supply of assets will be discounted in current prices (Lang, Poulsen, and Stulz 1995; Shleifer and Vishny 1992). This is especially the case for real estate assets, where fire sale losses need not imply an economic loss of value. At the same time, selling assets rapidly establishes floor prices that promote speedier recovery from the economic crisis. This may especially be true for public AMCs, which typically have limited market insights.

The success of centralized AMCs can be assessed on the basis of two dimensions: whether the AMCs achieved their narrow objectives, and whether the banking system returned to sustained solvency.[7] The speed of asset disposition measures the success of rapid asset disposition and liquidation agencies. In this case, an AMC is judged to be successful if assets, including banks, are disposed of within five years. In the case of restructuring agencies gauging whether they have achieved their narrow objectives of accelerating corporate restructuring is more difficult because of little data and the lack of the counterfactual. Thus, they will be considered successful if they sold off 50 percent of their assets within five years, indicating that the existence of a public AMC did not delay corporate restructuring. To assess whether AMCs accomplished their broader objectives of

---

7. Some facilities also pursued the explicit objective of minimizing fiscal costs. However, as we do not have information concerning the counterfactual, we cannot evaluate whether AMCs have achieved that objective.

restoring the banking system to health, two criteria are used. First, we must ask if the banking system experienced repeated financial distress, and second, has real credit to the private sector resumed and aggregate credit growth been positive in real terms.

Evidence

Centralized asset management companies have only recently become a popular component of banking distress resolution strategies; Indonesia, Korea, and Malaysia all set up centralized AMC structures in the late 1990s. According to a survey of 26 banking crises (Caprio and Klingebiel 1996), centralized AMC structures were only set up in nine cases and were particularly popular in Africa.[8] Out of these nine, seven cases with sufficient, publicly available data were selected for more detailed analysis. In four out of the seven cases, the governments of Mexico in 1994, the Philippines in 1981–86, Spain in 1977–85, and the United States in 1984–91 set up rapid asset disposition vehicles. In Finland in 1991–94, Ghana in 1982–89, and Sweden in 1991–94, restructuring agencies were established. The bibliography and reference list provides country sources of the data used in the analysis.

In the analysis, we first lay out the objectives and main characteristics of the AMCs, including the amount of assets transferred relative to banking system assets, the sectoral breakdown of assets, the criteria authorities used for the transfer of assets, and the transfer price. We then study the success of those entities and analyze factors that are key to the success of or are impediments to the success of the AMC structure. Except in the U.S. example, all banking systems in the sample suffered from systemic crises, that is, the aggregate banking system's capital had been exhausted. In all country cases, the authorities adopted financial sector restructuring mechanisms that included the setting up of a centralized AMC structure.

Figure 13.1 provides an overview of the share of banking system assets transferred to AMCs. The figure illustrates that the share of financial system assets managed by AMCs as a result of asset transfers varied widely among the countries. Both as a share of total system assets and as a percentage of gross domestic product (GDP), the Philippine AMC had to deal with the largest share of nonperforming loans as assets transferred amounted to almost 22

---

8. Benin, Côte d'Ivoire, Ghana, and Senegal set up centralized AMCs as part of their bank restructuring mechanisms. Other countries where centralized AMCs were established were Finland, the Philippines, Spain, the United States, and Uruguay.

Figure 13.1.   Assets Transferred to AMCs

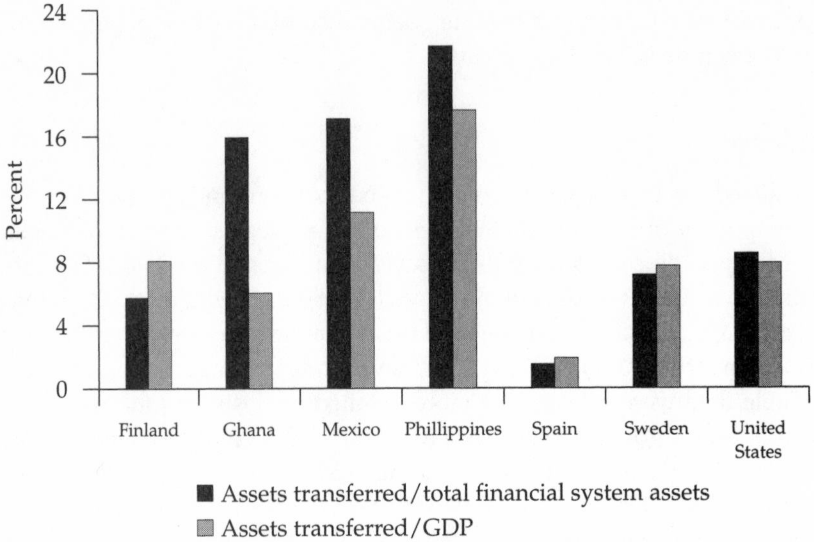

Source: Klingebiel (2000).

percent of financial system assets and 18 percent of GDP. At the other end of the spectrum, Spain's AMCs dealt with only 1.0 percent of financial system assets, or 1.3 percent of GDP. With the exception of the U.S. case, all assets transferred to the AMCs had been previously classified as nonperforming.

Figure 13.2 provides data on the scope of the financial sector crisis, using peak levels of nonperforming loans in the financial system. Because the level of nonperforming loans is a reflection of the real sector's performance, this number can also be used as a rough proxy for the extent of corporate distress. Spain and the United States were the only countries in the sample where the extent of nonperforming loans in the system remained limited, that is lower than ten percent of gross loans. In Finland and the Philippines, official numbers on nonperforming loans reached substantial proportions that account for near or more than 20 percent of financial system assets.[9] In Ghana, more than half of banking system loans were nonperforming. In Mexico,

---

9. Because accounting conventions differ among the countries in the sample, these figures should be treated with caution. Among these countries, Finland, Spain, Sweden, and the United States have stricter classification regulations compared with Ghana, Mexico, and the Philippines.

Figure 13.2.   *Magnitude of Crisis and Resolution Costs*

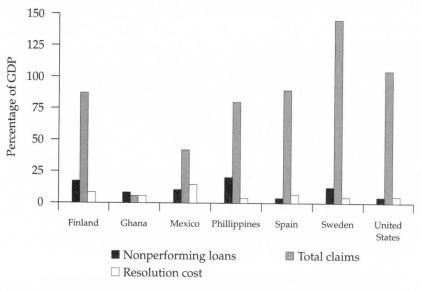

Source: Klingebiel (2000).

nonperforming assets transferred to Fondo Bancario de Protección al Ahorro (FOBAPROA) amounted to 23 percent of financial system loans or 17 percent of financial system assets at the end of 1996.

Rapid Asset Disposition Agencies[10]

Appendix table A.13.1 provides an overview of the main characteristics of the four country examples with rapid asset disposition vehicles. Two of the agencies—the Mexican and the Spanish AMCs—were housed within an existing public agency, the Deposit Guarantee Agency. The Philippine and the U.S. agencies were set up as stand-alone agencies with a limited life span. All four agencies pursued similar objectives. The main goal of Mexico's FOBAPROA, the Philippine's Asset Privatization Trust (APT), the Spanish Deposit Guarantee Fund, and the U.S. Resolution Trust Corporation (RTC) was to dispose of the assets that were transferred to them as fast

---

10. The analysis of the Mexican rapid asset disposition agency, FOBAPROA, reflects information available before the end of 1998.

as possible while maximizing the recovery value of the assets. In contrast, FOBAPROA was also involved in the cleanup and recapitalization of the banks that were still in operation. By the end of 1997, the assets to be disposed of by FOBAPROA amounted to 17 percent of banking system assets compared with the 22 percent on APT's books. APT solely focused on the disposition of nonperforming assets that had been transferred in a one-off transaction. The Spanish Deposit Guarantee Fund and the RTC operated as centralized liquidation agencies, and as such were responsible for resolving financial institutions and the liabilities of which that had been previously taken over or been intervened in. Moreover, the amount of bad debt that was effectively managed and sold by these entities was small relative to financial system assets, 1 percent in the case of the Spanish agency and 8.0 percent in the U.S. case.

FOBAPROA and APT did not achieve their narrow objective of rapid asset disposal. By early 1999, four years after it had been established, FOBAPROA sold only 0.5 percent of its assets, and twelve years after starting its operations APT still has 50 percent of the original assets on its books. In both cases, a variety of reasons hampered the disposal efforts of these agencies (see table A.13.1). The most important of these reasons was the type of assets transferred, that is, whether the assets were politically motivated or fraudulent loans. Having limited independence and great susceptibility to political pressure, neither of the two government agencies was equipped to resolve assets whose initial extension was based more on political connections than on the merits of the projects to be financed. A weak legal framework also hampered asset disposal.

For example, at the time of asset transfer in Mexico, the government had restricted financial institutions, including FOBAPROA, from foreclosing on assets. Moreover, the rapid sale of assets was further hindered by the fact that the agency was insufficiently funded. As assets were transferred from banks at higher than market values, the disposition of these assets would have revealed the true losses of the banking system. Finally, the considerable amount of impaired assets under FOBAPROA impeded effective corporate restructuring in at least three ways. First, the large amount of impaired assets depressed the market values of bank assets generally. Second, continued government control of this large share of total indebtedness encouraged continued politicization of the asset restructuring process. Third, repeated nonperforming asset sales limited banks' incentives to engage in corporate restructuring.

Neither FOBAPROA nor APT was successful in helping to build a more robust banking system. The Mexican banking system remains weak, and one of the two banks that were cleaned up in the Philippine case appears to be in financial distress again. In addition, FOBAPROA's repeated loan purchases at Mexican banks coupled with debt relief for borrowers led to general deterioration of the payment discipline and asset prices. Moreover, loan growth did not recover and remained strongly negative in Mexico.

In contrast, banking sector solvency problems did not reoccur in Spain or the United States. The Spanish and the U.S. agencies met their narrow objectives by disposing of 50 percent of assets within five years. The Spanish Guarantee Fund and the RTC, after some initial problems, were successful in developing fair, credible, and transparent processes and mechanisms for the resolution and sale of financial institutions. These agencies managed to sell those institutions in a relatively short period of time, thus minimizing disruptions for depositors and borrowers (Sheng 1996).

One key factor in the success of the Spanish Deposit Guarantee Fund was that the banks to be resolved were relatively small, which made dealing with them politically easier. Moreover, the largest commercial banks in the system were sound enough to assist substantially in the resolution of the small banks. However, despite success in selling the 26 banks, the Spanish Deposit Guarantee Fund proved less successful at disposing the assets that had been carved out before the sale of the institutions, and a portion of those assets remain with the fund even today.

The RTC's success was helped by the fact that most of the assets to be disposed of were real estate loans or assets or mortgage loans that could relatively easily be bundled and securitized or sold via bulk sales. Moreover, a deep and sophisticated capital market and a recovery in the real estate market also proved advantageous for the RTC, as did an effective organizational and governance structure and skilled personnel.

Restructuring Agencies

In Finland and Sweden, restructuring agencies were tasked with cleaning up banks before their sale to new investors. In Ghana, the government set up a restructuring agency to deal with recapitalized banks. In all three cases, the narrow objective of the restructuring agency was to manage and liquidate nonperforming assets and accelerate corporate restructuring (see appendix table A.13.2).

Arsenal, the Finnish agency, disposed of more than 50 percent of assets after five years in operation and seems to have enhanced corporate restructuring. The following factors worked in Arsenal's favor. First, Arsenal only had to resolve a relatively small amount of banking system assets as assets transferred amounted to 5.2 percent of banking system assets. Second, a large amount of the assets transferred were loans to real estate companies or loans secured by real estate. Third, Arsenal was provided with appropriate funding and had professional management and a skilled human resource base. Finally, a strong economic recovery in which the economy expanded at 4 percent and 5.1 percent in 1994 and 1995 may have helped asset resolution and disposition. However, because Arsenal received nonperforming loans regardless of type and size of asset, using wholesale divestiture techniques may have been more difficult for the agency.

Securum, the Swedish asset management agency, was successful in achieving its narrow objective of restructuring or selling off assets in a relatively brief period of time. In addition, the agency expedited restructuring in the broad real estate sector by acting in some cases as a lead agent enhancing creditor coordination (Bergren 1998). It closed its doors in 1997 five years after being established and having sold off 98 percent of its assets. Several factors contributed to the success of Securum. First, the government transferred mostly commercial real estate assets, which may have been easier to restructure because they did not involve politically sensitive issues, for example, factory worker layoffs. Second, the assets that were transferred to Securum were mostly large, complicated assets that Securum may have had a comparative advantage in resolving. Third, the government only transferred a limited amount of assets, equal to 8 percent of banking system assets. In addition, Securum enjoyed political independence and had appropriate funding. Finally, the economy and the real estate market recovered over that period.

In contrast with the examples of Arsenal and Securum, Ghana's Nonperforming Asset Recovery Trust (NPART) did not achieve its narrow objective of performing a substantial role in the restructuring of the corporate sector and expediting the restructuring process. In the end, the agency engaged mostly in cosmetic financial restructuring by extending maturity, lowering interest rates, and functioning as a collection agency. Factors that contributed to that outcome were the agency's lack of political independence and lack of professional management at the highest level of the institution. In addition, NPART not only had to resolve a large share of outstanding banking system assets, but also more than 50 percent of assets transferred were loans to state-owned enterprises, assets that are typically difficult for government agencies to restructure. Importantly, a weak legal framework hampered the work of NPART. The government attempted to mitigate the implications of a weak legal framework for NPART by granting it special legal powers. Yet this strategy proved largely ineffective because the courts were debtor friendly, and NPART needed the approval of the borrower before it could proceed with the liquidation process.

All three institutions' track records with respect to their broader goals are mixed at best. Sweden and Finland did not record any renewed banking system distress, but real credit to the private sector contracted significantly in both countries in the year following the establishment of the AMCs, indicating that the restructuring of banks was not yet complete (table 13.1). While bank loans to the private sector increased significantly in Ghana, state-owned commercial banks that had been cleaned up through the loan purchase program again appeared to experience problems in the mid-1990s.

Lessons from Cross-Country Experience

Table 13.2 summarizes the main characteristics of the country cases including the size of the banking system, the depth of the capital market, and the quality of the legal framework as measured by the enforcement of creditor rights and the amount of assets transferred to the respective AMCs. As table 13.2 indicates, initial conditions for AMCs were significantly weaker in the developing economies. For example, the legal framework was considerably weaker in developing countries, and capital markets were less developed as the low bond market capitalization indicates. At the same time, AMCs in these countries had to deal with notably larger problems given that the assets transferred to these agencies accounted for a large proportion of banking system assets overall. Governments in Ghana and the Philippines tried to compensate for the weak legal framework by granting superpowers to their respective AMCs. In both cases this strategy proved ineffective. In Ghana, the courts remained debtor friendly, and in the Philippines the overall efficiency of the court system did not improve.

Table 13.3 presents an overview of the main characteristics of the AMCs that were established including the type of assets transferred—real estate assets or politically motivated assets—the independence of the agency, legal superpowers, and funding resources. The table highlights the fact that mainly the following factors hindered the success of the AMCs in developing countries. First, AMCs in developing countries mostly received nonreal estate, state-owned assets, or assets reflecting political connections. Second, many AMCs in developing countries had to resolve large amounts of banking system assets and received assets of all sizes. Third, AMCs in developing countries were not set up as independent institutions and thus were susceptible to political pressure. Finally, they often lacked appropriate funding to dispose of assets quickly. The RTC in the United States was the only agency that outsourced management of the assets to the private sector, which included

Table 13.1. GDP and Real Credit Growth

Country	Year of AMC establishment	GDP growth (percent)				Real credit growth (percent)			
		One year before	Year of set up	One year later	Two years later	One year before	Year of set up	One year later	Two years later
Finland	1993	-3.55	-1.18	4.55	5.06	-8.95	-10.59	-10.63	-3.82
Ghana	1990	5.09	3.32	5.31	3.89	100.44	-16.73	-20.55	41.76
Mexico	1995	4.42	-6.17	5.18	6.71	27.93	-30.70	-36.70	19.56
Philippines	1987	3.42	4.31	6.75	6.21	-21.12	17.04	5.26	11.41
Spain[a]	1980	0.04	1.30	-0.18	1.57	-0.60	2.20	2.00	2.79
Sweden	1992	-1.66	-1.42	-2.22	3.34	-9.21	-2.38	-23.06	-6.23
United States	1989	3.82	3.36	1.23	-0.93	5.63	5.35	0.23	-2.10

a. Year when the Deposit Guarantee Fund was granted legal powers for bank restructuring.
Source: IMF data.

356

Table 13.2. *Characterization of Country Cases*

Country	Enforcement of creditor rights[a]	Initial conditions		Peak level of nonperforming loans (percentage of financial system assets)	Amount of assets transferred (percentage of financial system assets)[d]
		Private sector claims (percentage of GDP)[b]	Bond market capitalization (percentage of GDP)[b]		
Finland	18.0	87	39.7	18.7	5.2
Ghana	1.0	6	n.a.	60.0	50.8
Mexico	6.0	41	1.1	18.9	17.0
Philippines	7.7	79	16.6[c]	23.1	21.7
Spain	8.0	88	43.2[d]	5.7	1.4
Sweden	24.0	145	58.5	10.8	7.4
United States	18.0	103	50.5	4.1	8.0

n.a. Not available.

a. The product of an index of how well the legal framework protects secured creditors and a law and order index. The index ranges from 0 to 24 with 0 as the lowest and 24 as the highest score.

b. Private sector claims and bond market capitalization are shown at the onset of the financial crises in these countries.

c. 1983.

d. 1990.

Source: Author calculations; IMF data; University of Maryland (various editions); La Porta, Lopez-de-Silanes, and Shleifer (1999).

Table 13.3.   Characteristics of Established AMCs

Country	Real estate assets (percentage of transferred assets)	Transfer of politically motivated assets	Agency is independent	Agency has legal super- powers	Agency has appropriate funding
Finland	34	No	Yes	No	Yes
Ghana	Negligible	Yes	No	Yes	No
Mexico	n.a.	Yes	No	No	No
Philippines	Negligible	Yes	No	Yes	No
Spain	8.2	No	Yes	No	Yes
Sweden	80	No	Yes	No	Yes
United States	49	No	Yes	Yes	Yes, after initial problems

n.a. Not available.

Note: Business strategy includes type, size, and amount of assets transferred. Business strategies are judged appropriate if they are in line with agency resources including funding, institutional capacity, and independence from political pressure, and the development of the capital markets.

Source: Author.

foreign investment banks and advisors that may have compensated for the lack of independence and curbed the scope for political interference.

As table 13.4 indicates, two out of three corporate restructuring AMCs did not achieve their narrow goals of expediting corporate restructuring. These experiences suggest that AMCs are not necessarily effective tools for expediting corporate restructuring. Only the Swedish AMC successfully managed its portfolio, acting in some instances as lead agent in the restructuring process. Special circumstances helped in the Swedish case, which made it easier for the AMC to maintain its independence from political pressures and to sell assets back to the private sector. Rapid asset disposition vehicles fared better. Two out of the four agencies that employed this technique, the Spanish and U.S. agencies, achieved their objectives. These successful experiences suggest that AMCs can be effectively used, but only for resolving insolvent and nonviable financial institutions and selling off their assets. Achieving these objectives required many ingredients, including a type of asset that is easily liquifiable, political independence, a skilled resource base, appropriate funding, adequate bankruptcy and foreclosure laws, good information and management systems, and transparency in operations and processes.

Table 13.4. *Evaluating Success*

Country	Objective of AMC	Corporate restructuring and asset disposition			Health of banking system	
		Share of assets disposed (percentage of transferred assets)	Have AMCs achieved their narrow objective	Recurrent problems	Growth of real credit	Have AMCs achieved their broader objectives
Finland	Restructuring	>64	Unclear	No	Negative	Unclear
Ghana	Restructuring	n.a.	No	Yes	Positive	Unclear
Mexico	Rapid asset disposition	0.1	No	Yes	Negative	No
Philippines	Rapid asset disposition	<50	No	Yes	Positive	Unclear
Spain	Liquidation	Majority	Yes	No	Positive	Yes
Sweden	Restructuring	86	Yes	No	Negative	Unclear
United States	Liquidation	98	Yes	No	Negative	Unclear

n.a. Not available.
Source: Author.

Appendix 13.A.   Main Characteristics of Asset Management Companies

Table A.13.1. Rapid Asset Disposition Agencies

Rapid asset disposition	Objectives of rapid asset disposition agency	Asset transfer	Outcome	Key factors
Mexico: FOBAPROA • Set up in 1995; no established duration limit • Public ownership • Centralized entity • FOBAPROA set up as a bank restructuring agency	• Clean up and restructure banks • Sell off or recover assets as quickly as possible, through auction, securitization, or other market mechanisms	• Amounts of assets transferred: Mex\$ 142 billion (Mex\$ 119 billion net of reserves for loan losses) equivalent to 17 percent of banking system assets. • Sectoral breakdown of assets: consumer, mortgage, and corporate loans • Criteria for asset transfer: nontransparent and repeated process (this led to perceptions that some banks received more favorable treatment than others) • Asset price: transfer at book value because assets were not valued prior to transfer	• Transfer of loans did not succeed in restoring the banking system to solvency. Capital deficiency was underestimated, and institutions remained weak after repeated rounds of loan repurchases at greater than market price. Operational restructuring was limited, and bank management was left unchanged. • As weaknesses in the banking sector remained, loan growth did not recover. • By the end of 1998, FOBAPROA had sold only 0.5 percent of transferred assets. The huge overhang of impaired assets impeded effective restructuring in three ways. First, it depressed the market value of bank assets generally. Second, continued government control of such a large share of total indebtedness encouraged politicization of the asset restructuring process. Third, repeated nonperforming asset sales limited banks' incentives to engage in corporate restructuring.	Favorable factors: • Strong economic recovery Unfavorable factors: • Type of asset transferred: politically connected loans assets are difficult for government agencies susceptible to political pressure to handle. • Lack of independence: FOBAPROA was under central bank management, and policy decisions were made by a committee comprised of the minister of finance, the central bank governor, and the president of the financial supervisory body. • Substantial deficiencies in bankruptcy and foreclosure code: when assets were transferred to FOBAPROA, the government restricted financial institutions, including FOBAPROA, from foreclosing on assets. • Insufficient funding of FOBAPROA.

(table continues on following page)

Table A.13.1 continued

Rapid asset disposition	Objectives of rapid asset disposition agency	Asset transfer	Outcome	Key factors
Philippines: Asset Privatization Trust (APT) • Set up in 1987; intended to be closed in 1991, but still in operation • Public ownership • Set up as centralized stand-alone entity	• Orderly and fast transfer of nonperforming assets to the private sector • Administration of the assets pending disposal • Divestiture of large government corporations (starting in 1991)	• Amounts of assets transferred: assets of about P 108 billion equivalent to 21.7 percent of banking system assets • Sectoral breakdown of assets: mining ventures, ships, textile plants, and food processing to luxury hotel resorts; 70 percent of value was held in 15 percent of assets; 75 percent of assets constituted financial claims for which foreclosure procedures had not been completed • Criteria for asset transfer: size and nature of accounts (that is, nonperforming); potential for sale; any special expertise required to dispose of the assets • Transfer price: book value	• ATP did not reach its objective of orderly and fast transfer of assets to private sector. Forty to 50 percent of assets remain in APT's portfolio to date, including those of the largest account, National Construction Corporation, despite macroeconomic environment conducive to asset transfer. • One of the recapitalized banks again faced solvency problems in the late 1990s. Nevertheless, credit growth rebounded relatively strongly.	Favorable factors: • Strong economic recovery Unfavorable factors: • Type of asset transferred: politically connected loans or fraudulent assets are difficult for government agencies susceptible to political pressure to handle. • Rapid asset disposition: legal problems severely hampered asset disposition despite the fact that APT had temporary extrajudicial powers • Weak governance and insufficient funding: APT was neither privately managed nor an independent agency, and budgetary pressures, such as avoidance to reveal losses, reduced APT's commitment to rapid sale. • Lack of disclosure of information on its activities and financial situation to the public: while APT had to submit quarterly reports on performance and financial status to the president and congress, and the process of asset sales remained nontransparent.

(table continues on following page)

Table A.13.1 continued

Rapid asset disposition	Objectives of rapid asset disposition agency	Asset transfer	Outcome	Key factors
Spain: Deposit Guarantee Fund • Set up in 1977; still in existence; given legal capacity to assume bank ownership to initiate bank restructuring (1980); no pre-established duration limit • Public ownership • No stand-alone entity, but part of entity set up to resolve failed banks	• Restructuring of banks for prompt resale by carving out bad assets that new investors were unwilling to take on • Prompt sale of carved out assets with the aim of maximum recovery value	• Amounts of assets transferred: fund took over 26 banks with assets amounting to 1 percent of financial system assets. These banks were restructured and then sold off to new investors. In some instances, large amounts of assets were taken off bank balance sheets and remained for rapid asset disposition in the Deposit Guarantee Fund. • Sectoral breakdown of assets: 8.2 percent was real estate; 72.5 percent was other assets; 19.4 percent was shareholdings. • Criteria for asset transfer: assets that acquirers of banks were unwilling to take on	• Successful in selling intervened banks in relatively short period of time upon acquisition. Banks were sold off on average within one year, indicating that the Deposit Guarantee Fund managed to accelerate the bank restructuring process. • Banks resumed lending in 1980, and credit to the private sector by banks grew in real terms. • The fund was less successful in achieving its aim of rapid disposal of bad assets that had been carved out from banks' balance sheets. • The fund was not involved in resolution of 20 small and medium size banks of the Rumasa group. Due to the scope of the problems of the Rumasa group, the government decided to nationalize the banks and the 200 industrial firms belonging to the group. The government adopted a two-pronged strategy. First, take over control of companies. Second, resell the companies as soon as possible.	Favorable factors: • Fund operated as an independent public agency under private law and appropriate funding and powers (could change management immediately, purchase assets, offer guarantees or counter-guarantees on behalf of restructured banks, grant long-term loans at subsidized rates, or permit temporary regulatory forbearance) for resolving institutions. • Banks to be resolved were small banks, which made them politically easier to resolve, and the fund was not involved in resolution of the politically sensitive Rumasa group. • The largest commercial banks in the system were sound enough to assist substantially in resolving the small banks, albeit under considerable state pressure. Also, competition in the home market from foreign banks provided incentive for Spain's private banks to acquire recapitalized banks while sometimes even assuming losses.

(table continues on following page)

364

Table A.13.1 continued

Rapid asset disposition	Objectives of rapid asset disposition agency	Asset transfer	Outcome	Key factors
				• In terms of disposal of nonperforming assets, the amount of those assets was small (1 percent of banking system assets). • Overall, the fund operated in a benign macroenvironment. Unfavorable factors: • The framework for foreclosures and seizures of collateral was deficient and impeded rapid sale of assets. • The Deposit Guarantee Fund encountered problems with transfer of titles. • The fund experienced lackluster demand for real estate assets.
United States: Resolution Trust Corporation (RTC) • Set up in 1989, designed to operate until 1996; ended operations in 1995	• Social and commercial: RTC was to maximize the net value proceeds from savings and loan crisis resolution, but	• Amounts of assets transferred: RTC resolved 747 thrifts with total assets of US$465 billion. These assets accounted for roughly 23.2 percent of savings and loans assets or 8 percent of total bank and thrift assets in 1989. Of these, RTC sold US$153 billion through asset disposition that was not connected to the sale of the	• RTC was successful in resolving 747 thrifts and disposing of assets that were carved out prior to bank sale. • RTC recovered 87 cents to the dollar.	Favorable factors: • The amount of assets transferred were relatively small (8 percent of financial system assets), and a large part of those assets were performing. Moreover, also notable is that the savings and loans problem affected only a fraction of the U.S. financial system, leaving sound institutions in

(table continues on following page)

Table A.13.1 continued

Rapid asset disposition	Objectives of rapid asset disposition agency	Asset transfer	Outcome	Key factors
• Public ownership • No stand-alone entity; part of entity set up to resolve failed banks	also had a broader mandate of minimizing the impact on local real estate and financial markets. Another part of this mandate involved maximizing available and affordable housing for low to moderate income individuals.	financial institution. • Sectoral breakdown of assets: RTC acquired performing and nonperforming assets. The sectoral breakdown of assets transferred was as follows: 42 percent mortgage loans, 7 percent real estate, 8 percent other loans, 35 percent cash and securities, and 8 percent other assets. • Criteria for asset transfer: insolvency of the financial institution as determined by the Central Bank.		the market as potential buyers of the assets. • The type of assets—mostly performing real estate–related assets and consumer loan assets were transferred—could be sold off through wholesale disposal mechanisms (bulk sales, securitization, and auctions). • The RTC was in an environment marked by deep and sophisticated capital markets. • Adequate governance structures, professional management, and extensive use of private sector contractors were available for asset disposition. The RTC relied on a detailed set of directives and guidelines for its staff and contractors that covered a wide range of operations, including asset management and disposition, contract policies, bidding procedures and marketing. While this reduced RTC's flexibility in handling individual cases, these factors

(table continues on following page)

Table A.13.1 continued

Rapid asset disposition	Objectives of rapid asset disposition agency	Asset transfer	Outcome	Key factors
				minimized the possibility of fraud, made policy and cost evaluation more transparent, and expedited resolution process. • An effective organizational structure including information management systems that can handle large amount of information and management of assets allowed RTC to collect 31 percent of the total assets transferred and reduced the amount of assets needed to be sold by one third. Unfavorable factors: • Sporadic funding of RTC (several pieces of legislation were required to approve funding) hampered speedy resolution of failed savings and loans and increased resolution costs. • Rapid asset disposition was hampered by inconsistencies in the agency's objectives. In addition to its cost minimization and expeditious disposition objective, the RTC was also supposed to structure and time its asset sales to minimize any impact on local real estate and financial markets.

Source: Author.

Table A.13.2. *Restructuring Agencies*

Restructuring	Objectives of restructuring agency	Asset transfer	Outcome	Key factors
Finland: Arsenal • Began activities in 1993, still in operation; expected to close in the year 2000; set up to absorb nonperforming assets • Public ownership • Stand-alone entity	• Established as a clean-up mechanism for the Savings Bank and Skopbank • Manage, restructure, and liquidate nonperforming loans and other holdings, in an orderly manner and at minimum cost	• Amounts of assets transferred: assets transferred had a book value of Fimr 42.9 billion • Sectoral breakdown of assets: only nonperforming loans transferred; real estate assets amounted to 34 percent; client receivables 41 percent; assets under management and other assets 25.3 percent • Criteria for asset transfer: All nonperforming assets transferred to Arsenal regardless of type and size of loans • Transfer price: book value	• At the end of 1997, Arsenal still managed 46.5 percent of the assets that were transferred to it. • By the end of 1997, Arsenal had disposed of 78 percent of the real estate assets it had taken over. • The extent to which Arsenal accelerated corporate restructuring and how active Arsenal was in corporate restructuring remains unclear. • Real lending to the private sector remained strongly negative in real terms in the years after the establishment of Arsenal.	Favorable factors: • A large amount of real assets were transferred, including client receivables, which made loans easier to restructure or dispose as less politically sensitive issues are involved (real estate is considered to be a more cyclical industry). • Appropriate funding allowed Arsenal to mark assets at market value after transfer. • Arsenal had professional management and adequate skilled resources. • A benign macroenvironment, in which real GDP rebounded strongly, and the economy expanded at 4–5 percent in 1994–95. Unfavorable factors: • Transfer of all types of nonperforming loans regardless of type and size of assets may have made it more difficult to use wholesale divestiture techniques and also required Arsenal to build up expertise in different areas.

(table continues on following page)

Table A.13.2 continued

Restructuring	Objectives of restructuring agency	Asset transfer	Outcome	Key factors
Ghana: NPART • Initiated operations in 1990; closed in 1997, 2 years later than stipulated • Wholly owned government agency • Set up as centralized stand-alone agency	• Restructure and recapitalize publicly owned government banks • Restructure companies and expedite corporate restructuring • Maximize recovery value to reduce fiscal burden on the government	• Amounts of assets transferred: about 13,000 accounts were transferred to NPART • Sectoral breakdown of assets: corporate loans from state and private sector companies across industrial and service sectors; most loans collateralized by plant, equipment, and machinery • Criteria for asset transfer: nonperforming assets, otherwise process of asset transfer nontransparent • Transfer price: book value of assets excluding accrued interest	• NPART failed to play a substantial role in expediting or enabling corporate restructuring. • NPART functioned effectively as a collection agency, restructuring its loan portfolio via extension of maturities or modifications to terms and conditions. • While government-owned banks were cleaned up through transfer of assets, and banks were operationally restructured, state-owned commercial banks in Ghana appeared to be in financial difficulties again in the late 1990s. At the end of 1997, state-owned commercial banks had nonperforming loans exceeding 15 percent. • Lending to the private sector did nonetheless recover and turned strongly positive in 1992.	Favorable factors: • While inadequate legal framework hampered the restructuring and sale of assets, an extra-judicial tribunal was set up to mitigate the problem. However, NPART was slow to make use of the tribunal, which often sided with the debtor. • NPART received substantial foreign aid in the form of money and technical support. A team of expatriate experts, out of which two were former U.S. RTC officials, managed the operations of NPART. Unfavorable factors: • A large amount of banking system loans were transferred, amounting to 51 percent of banking system assets, and no clear eligibility criteria for the type of assets to be transferred were established. As a result NPART ended up with disparate set of assets. • More than 50 percent of assets transferred were loans to state-owned enterprises. This type of asset is typically difficult for a government agency that lacks independence to restructure.

(table continues on following page)

Table A.13.2 continued

Restructuring	Objectives of restructuring agency	Asset transfer	Outcome	Key factors
				• Initial funding problems slowed down the establishment of NPART and the development of professional expertise. • Senior management consisted of political appointees. • The agency lacked political independence. • Corporate restructuring efforts being undertaken by various government agencies and NPART were not coordinated. • A weak legal framework caused, for example, asset sales to be impeded by the fact that debtors had to agree with sale of assets.
Sweden: Securum • Set up in 1992; expected to operate between 10 and 15 years; closed operations successfully in 1997 • Public ownership	Securum/Retriva: • Function as clean-up agencies or bad banks for Nordbanken (Securum) and Gotha Bank (Retriva), two banks that	• Amounts of assets transferred: gross value: SKr 67 billion, 4.4 percent of total banking assets (Securum); gross value SKr 45 billion or 3 percent of SKr banking assets (Retriva) • Sectoral breakdown of assets: 80 percent of assets were related to the real estate market; Securum: loans 91.1 percent, share portfolio 6.2	• Securum/Retriva succeeded in managing and selling assets in relatively short period of time. • Most of Securum's and Retriva's assets were real estate assets. Shareholdings were mostly concentrated in construction companies. Thus, while Securum may have helped to expedite restructuring	Favorable factors: • The type of assets—mostly commercial real estate—were easier to restructure as the assets were less politically sensitive (layoffs); high concentration of the economy may have made industrial restructuring easier. Also, transferred assets that were of particular type, size, and

(table continues on following page)

Table A.13.2 continued

Restructuring	Objectives of restructuring agency	Asset transfer	Outcome	Key factors
• Set up as a stand-alone agency Retriva: • Set up in 1993; absorbed by Securum in 1995; public ownership • Set up as a stand-alone agency	government had taken over • Recover maximum values of nonperforming loans transferred to it • Establish best practice in corporate restructuring for private banks	percent, real estate 2.7 percent; Retriva: Loans 86.2 percent, real share portfolio 1.6 percent, real estate 12.3 percent • Criteria for asset transfer: mainly size and complexity of loan: only loans greater than Skr 15 million were transferred, typically consisting of corporation with operations in different countries or complicated structures in terms of subsidiaries; no takeover of assets that could be securitized • Transfer price: assets transferred at book value	in the real estate and construction industry by enhancing coordination among debtors, its impact on the restructuring efforts in other sectors of the economy appears to have been limited. • In terms of restructuring Nordbanken and Gotha Bank, management was changed, and the banks were operationally restructured and successfully sold to private investors. • Real lending to private sector by banks did not recover. In 1993 and 1994, real credit to the private sector contracted significantly.	structure limited the amount of assets Securum had to deal with, making restructuring a more manageable exercise. • Private management and strong governance mechanisms ensured the agency's independence. • The agencies had prompt structured appraisal of assets and a transparent process of asset management, restructuring, and sale. • The agencies had adequate legal frameworks. • The agencies had adequate funding and adequate skilled resources. • A limited amount of assets were transferred (7.7 percent of banking sector assets). • The real estate market recovered. • Economic growth recovered. In 1994, real GDP growth turned positive. Unfavorable factors: • The agencies experienced sporadic bouts of scandal due to the incentive-compensation scheme for employees.

Source: Author compilation.

371

Bibliography and Reference List

Country Sources for Finland

Abrams, Richard K. 1988. "The Financial Reform in Finland." Working Paper. European Department, International Monetary Fund, Washington, D.C.

Aranko, Jorma. 1994. "Reorganization of Financial Market Supervision in Finland." *Bulletin* no. 2/94. Bank of Finland, Helsinki.

Asset Management Company Arsenal Limited. 1995. *Annual Report and Accounts 1994.* Helsinki.

_____. 1996. *Annual Report 1995.* Helsinki.

_____. 1997. *Annual Report 1996.* Helsinki.

_____. 1998. *Annual Report 1997.* Helsinki.

Brunila, Anne, and Kari Takala. 1993. "Private Indebtedness and the Banking Crisis in Finland." Discussion Papers. Bank of Finland, Helsinki.

Financial Market Trends. 1995. "National Financial Markets: Finland." February.

Government Guarantee Fund. 1993. *Annual Report 1992.* Helsinki.

_____. 1994. *Annual Report 1993.* Helsinki.

_____. 1995. *Annual Report 1994.* Helsinki.

_____. 1996. *Annual Report 1995.* Helsinki.

Hemberg, Kjell, and Heikki Soltilla. 1995. "The Financial Performance, Balance Sheet Structure, and Solvency of Finnish Deposit Banks in 1994." Bulletin no. 4/95. Bank of Finland, Helsinki.

Kiander, Jaakko, and Pentti Vartia. 1996. "The Crisis of the Hard Currency Regime in Finland in 1991-92." Discussion Paper no. 205. The Research Institute of the Finnish Economy (ETLA), Helsinki.

Koskenkylae, Heikki. 1998. "The Present State of the Finnish Banking Sector and the Outlook for the Next Few Years." Bulletin nos. 6–7/98. Bank of Finland, Helsinki.

Koskenkylae, Heikki, and Jukka Vesala. 1994. "Finnish Deposit Banks 1980-1993: Years of Rapid Growth and Crisis." Discussion Paper no. 16/94. Bank of Finland, Helsinki.

Laakso, Jyrki. 1995. "Finnish Credit Institutions in a Changing Environment." Bulletin no. 5/95. Bank of Finland, Helsinki.

Nyberg, Peter. 1994. "Decision on Restructuring of the Savings Bank Sector." Bulletin no. 1/94. Bank of Finland, Helsinki.

_____. 1997. "Macroeconomic Aspects of Systemic Bank Restructuring." Discussion Paper no. 1/97. Bank of Finland, Helsinki.

Nyberg, Peter, and Vesa Vihriaelae. 1993. "The Finnish Banking Crisis and Its Handling." Discussion Paper no. 8/93. Bank of Finland, Helsinki.

_____. 1994. "The Finnish Banking Crisis and Its Handling (An Update of Developments through 1993)." Discussion Paper no. 7/94. Bank of Finland, Helsinki.

Pensala, Johanna, and Heikki Solttila. 1993 "Banks' Nonperforming Assets and Write-Offs in 1992." Discussion Paper no. 10/93. Bank of Finland, Helsinki.

Skopbank. 1992. *Annual Report 1991*. Helsinki.

_____. 1993. *Annual Report 1992*. Helsinki.

_____. 1994. *Annual Report 1993*. Helsinki.

_____. 1995. *Annual Report 1994*. Helsinki.

_____. 1996. *Annual Report 1995*. Helsinki.

_____. 1997. *Annual Report 1996*. Helsinki.

_____. 1998. *Annual Report 1997*. Helsinki.

Solttila, Heikki, and Vesa Vihriaelae. 1994. "Finnish Banks' Problem Assets: Result of Unfortunate Asset Structure or Too Rapid Growth?" Discussion Paper no. 23/94. Bank of Finland, Helsinki.

Vihriaelae, Vesa. 1997. "Causes of the Credit Bubble." Bulletin no. 3/97. Bank of Finland, Helsinki.

Country Sources for Ghana

Republic of Ghana. 1986. "Proclaiming and Launching a Program for the Expeditious Disposition and Privatization of Certain Government Corporations and/or the Assets Thereof and Creating the Committee on Privatization and the Asset Privatization Trust." Presidential Proclamation 50. Accra.

_____. 1989. Non-Performing Assets Recovery Law. Accra.

NPART (Non-Performing Asset Resolution Trust). 1990. Operating Policies.

Sheng, Andrew, and Archibald Tannor, eds. 1996. "Ghana's Financial Restructuring, 1983-91." *Bank Restructuring: Lessons from the 1980s.* Washington, D.C.: World Bank.

World Bank. 1984. "Ghana: Managing the Transition." Report no. 5289-GH. Western Africa Region, Washington, D.C.

_____. 1988. "Financial Sector Adjustment Credit (FINSACI)." President's Report: Ghana. Washington, D.C.

_____. 1991. "Second Financial Sector Adjustment Credit (FINSACII)." President's Report: Ghana. Washington, D.C.

_____. 1994. "Ghana: Structural Adjustment Institutional Support Project." Performance Audit Report no. 13262. Washington, D.C.

_____. 1995. "Memorandum of the President of the International Development Association to the Executive Directors on a Country Assistance Strategy of the World Bank Group for the Republic of Ghana." Washington, D.C.

_____. 1995. "Ghana: Financial Sector Adjustment Credit." Project Completion Report no. 14158. Industry and Energy Operations Division. Washington, D.C.

_____. 1997a. "Memorandum of the President of the International Development Association to the Executive Directors on a Country Assistance Strategy of the World Bank Group for the Republic of Ghana." Washington, D.C.

_____. 1997b. "Ghana: Second Financial Sector Adjustment Credit." Implementation Completion Report no. 17249. Private Sector and Finance, Africa Region, Washington, D.C.

_____. 1997c. Performance Audit Report. "Ghana: First and Second Financial Sector Adjustment Credit." Performance Audit Report no. 16789. Operations Evaluation Department, Washington, D.C.

_____. 1998. "Ghana: Financial Sector Assessment Report." Private Sector and Finance Unit, Economic Management and Social Policy Department, Africa Region. Washington D.C. Processed.

Country Sources for Mexico

Aiyer, Sri-Ram. 1996. "Anatomy of Mexico's Banking System During the Peso Crisis." LAC: Technical Department Regional Studies Program no. 45. The World Bank, Washington, D.C.

Alvarez, Rendueles, and Jose Ramon. 1983. "El Tratamiento de las Crisis Bancarias en Espana." In *Crisis Bancarias, Soluciones Comparadas: Seminario Desarrollado en la Universidad Internacional Menendez Pelayo.* Santander: Asociacion Espanola de Banca Privada.

Barnes, Guillermo. 1992. "Lessons from Bank Privatization in Mexico." Policy Research Working Paper no. 1027. World Bank, Washington, D.C.

Lubrano, Mike. 1997. "Update on Status of Disposition of FOBAPROA's Assets." World Bank, Washington, D.C. Processed.

Meigs, A. James. 1998. "Lessons for Asia from Mexico." *The Cato Journal* 17(3): 315–22.

Moody's Investors Service. 1998. "The FOBAPROA Debate: Fiddling while Investors Burn." Special Comment. New York.

Secretaria de Hacienda y Credito Publico. 1998. *Fobaproa: La Verdadera Historia.* Mexico City.

World Bank. 1994. "Fostering Private Sector Development in the 1990s." In *Mexico: Country Economic Memorandum.* Washington, D.C.

_____. 1995. "Financial Sector Restructuring Loan." President's Report: Mexico. Washington, D.C.

_____. 1997. "Mexico: Mobilizing Savings for Growth." In *Mexico: Country Economic Memorandum.* Washington, D.C.

_____. 1998. "Mexico: Financial Sector Restructuring Loan." Implementation Completion Report no. 18012. Finance, Private Sector, and Infrastructure SMU. Washington, D.C.

Country Sources for Philippines

Nascimiento, Jean-Claude. 1990. "The Crisis in the Financial Sector and the Authorities' Reaction: the Case of the Philippines." Working Paper no. 90/26. International Monetary Foundation, Washington, D.C.

World Bank. 1987. "Philippines: Economic Recovery Project." President's Report, February. Washington, D.C.

_____. 1988. "Philippines: Financial Sector Review." Washington, D.C. Processed.

_____. 1992. "Philippines: Economic Recovery Project." Project Performance Audit Report no. 10866. Washington, D.C.

Country Sources for Spain

Casas, Juan Carlos, ed. 1989. *Saneamiento de Bancos: Estudios de Crisis Financieras en la Argentina, Colombia, Chile, Espana, E.E.U.U., Italia, y Uruguay.* Buenos Aires: Ediciones El Cronista Comercial.

Cuervo, Alvaro. 1988. *La Crisis Bancaria en Espana: 1977-85: Causas, Sistemas de Tratamiento, y Costes.* Barcelona: Editorial Ariel.

De Juan, Aristobulo. 1985. "Dealing with Problem Banks: The Case of Spain." Madrid, Spain. Processed.

Fondo de Garantia de Depositos en Establecimientos Bancarios. Various years. *Memoria Correspondiente al Ejercicio 1983 (-1997).* Madrid.

Country Sources for Sweden

Bank Support Authority. 1994. *Annual Report 1993.* Stockholm.

_____. 1995. *Annual Report 1994.* Stockholm.

Berg, Sigbjorn A. 1997. "Bank Failures in Four Scandinavian Countries." Norges Bank, Stockholm. Processed.

Biljer, Marianne. "Finance Companies - Structural Changes." *Bank of Sweden Quarterly Review* 91(3): 5–13. Stockholm.

Blavarg, Martin, and Stefan Ingves. 1996. "Government's Altered Role in Financial Markets." *Bank of Sweden Quarterly Review* 96(3): 36–49. Stockholm.

Dalheim, Bo, Goran Lind, and Anna-Karin Nedersjo. 1993. "The Banking Sector in 1992." *Bank of Sweden Quarterly Review* 93(2): 24–36. Stockholm.

Marterbauer, Markus, Hannes Schweighofer, and Ewald Walterskirchen. 1992. "Von der Deregulierung zur Banken—und Wirtschaftskrise in Schweden." *Wirtschaft and Gesellschaft* 18(4): 515–37.

Securum AB. 1997. Securum AB Summary Report 1992–1996. Stockholm.

Country Sources for USA

Congressional Budget Office. 1991. "Statement of Robert D. Reischauer, Director, Congressional Budget Office, before the Committee on Banking, Housing, and Urban Affairs, United States Senate." CBO Testimony, January 29. Washington, D.C.

_____. 1992. "Evaluating the Resolution Trust Corporation." Washington, D.C. Processed.

FDIC (Federal Deposit Insurance Corporation). 1995. "Final Report on the FDIC/RTC Transition." Submitted to the Committee on Banking and Financial Services, U.S. House of Representatives and the Committee on Banking, Housing, and Urban Affairs, U.S. Senate. December 29th. Washington, D.C.

_____. 1997. "Resolution Handbook: Methods for Resolving Troubled Financial Institutions in the United States." Division of Resolutions and Receiverships, Washington, D.C.

White, Lawrence C. 1992. "The U.S. Savings and Loan Debacle: Some Lessons for the Regulation of Financial Institutions." In Dimitri Vittas, ed., *Financial Regulation: Changing the Rules of the Game*. Washington, D.C.: EDI.

RTC (Resolution Trust Corporation). 1996. "Statistical Abstract August 1989/ September 1995." Office of Planning, Research, and Statistics, Washington, D.C.

Silverberg, Stanley. 1990. "The Savings and Loan Problem in the United States." Working Paper no. 351. World Bank, Washington, D.C.

GAO (United States General Accounting Office). 1986. "Thrift Industry Problems: Potential Demands on the FSLIC Insurance Fund." Briefing Report to the Honorable Stan Parris, House of Representatives: GAO/GGD-86-48BR. Washington, D.C.

_____. 1986. "Thrift Industry: Cost to FSLIC of Delaying Action on Insolvent Savings Institutions." Briefing report to the Chairman, Subcommittee on Commerce, Consumer, and Monetary Affairs; Committee on Government Operations; and House of Representatives: GAO/GGD-86-122BR. Washington, D.C.

_____. 1986. "Thrift Industry: Net Worth and Income Capital Certificates." Fact Sheet for the Honorable Chalmers P. Wylie, Ranking Minority Member, House Committee on Banking, Finance, and Urban Affairs: GAO/GGD-86-100FS. Washington, D.C.

_____. 1987. "Thrift Industry: The Treasury/Federal Home Loan Bank Board Plan for FSLIC Recapitalization." Briefing Report to Selected Members of Congress: GAO/GGD-87-46BR. Washington, D.C.

Reference List

Bergren, Arne. 1998. "Managing Systemic Banking Crisis in Practice: The Swedish Bank Support Process." World Bank, Washington, D.C. Processed.

Caprio, Gerard, and Daniela Klingebiel. 1996. "Bank Insolvencies, Cross-Country Experiences." Policy Research Working Paper no. 1620, World Bank, Washington, D.C.

_____. 1999. "Scope and Fiscal Costs of Banking Crises: Compilation of Information on Systemic and Non Systemic Banking Crises from 1970s Onwards." World Bank, Washington, D.C.

Claessens, Stijn. 1998. "Experiences of Revolution of Banking Crises." Policy Paper no. 7. Bank for International Settlement, Basle, Switzerland.

Delargy, P. J. R., and C. Goodhard. 1999. "Financial Crises: Plus ça Change plus c'est la Même Chose." Special Paper no. 108. Financial Market Group, ESRC Research Center, London School of Economics, London.

Dziobeck, Claudia. 1998. "Market Bared Instruments for Systemic Bank Restructuring." Working Paper no. 98/113. International Monetary Fund, Washington, D.C.

Dziobeck, Claudia, and Ceyla Pazarbasioglu. 1997. "Lessons from Systemic Bank Restructuring: A Survey of 24 Countries." Working Paper no. 161. International Monetary Fund, Washington, D.C.

Garcia, Gillian. 1997. "A Framework for Analysis and Assessment." In William E. Alexander, Jeffrey M. Davis, Liam P. Ebrill, and Carl Johannes Lindgren, eds., *Systemic Bank Restructuring and Macroeconomic Policy*. Washington, D.C.: International Monetary Fund.

IMF (International Monetary Fund). 1999. *International Financial Statistics*, various editions. Washington, D.C.

Ingves, Stefan, and Goran Lind. 1997. "Loan Loss Recoveries and Debt Resolution Agencies: The Swedish Experience." In Enoch Green, ed., *Banking Soundness and Monetary Policy: Issues and Experiences in the Global Economy*. Washington, D.C.: International Monetary Fund.

Klingebiel, Daniela. 2000. "The Use of Asset Management Companies in the Resolution of Banking Crises: Cross-Country Experience." Policy Research Working Paper no. 2284. World Bank, Washington D.C.

Lang, Larry, Annette Poulsen, and Rene Stulz. 1995. "Asset Sales, Firm Performance, and the Agency Costs of Managerial Discretion." *Journal of Financial Economics* 37(1): 3–37.

Lindgren, Carl-Johan, Tom Jose Balino, Charles Enoch, Anne-Marie Gulde-Wolf, Marc Quintyn, and Leslie Teo. 2000. "Financial Sector Crisis and Restructuring: Lessons from East Asia." Occasional Paper no. 188. International Monetary Fund: Washington, D.C.

La Porta, Rafael, Florencio Lopez-de-Silanes, and Adrei Shleifer. 1999. "Investor Protection: Origins, Consequences, Reform." Harvard University, Cambridge, Massachusetts. Processed.

Sheng, Andrew, ed. 1996. "Bank Restructuring in Spain, 1977-85." In *Bank Restructuring: Lessons from the 1980s*. Washington, D.C.: World Bank.

Shleifer, Adrei, and Robert W. Vishny. 1992. "Liquidation Values and Debt Capacity: A Market Equilibrium Approach." *The Journal of Finance* 47(4): 1343–66.

University of Maryland. Various editions. *International Country Risk Guide*. College Park, Maryland.

Waxman, Margery. 1998. "A Legal Framework for Systemic Bank Restructuring." World Bank, Washington D.C. Processed.

Index

(Page numbers in italics indicate material in boxes, tables, or figures.)